RUGBY LEAGUE HISTORY

Western and Southern NSW 1920-1976

GREG RIACH

DEDICATION

This book is dedicated to my brother-in-law Dennis Finn who played rugby league as a five eighth in Group XI during the mid sixties through to the mid seventies. He played for Parkes, Canowindra and represented Group XI and Western Division. A gifted footballer who remained in the bush despite offers from Sydney Rugby League Clubs.

ACKNOWLEDGEMENTS

The majority of my research has come from various newspaper articles. I would like to acknowledge the following ACM newspapers: Dubbo Daily Liberal, The Western Magazine, Parkes Champion Post, Canowindra Star, Forbes Advocate, Gundagai Independent, Narromine News, Oberon Review & Trangie Advocate, Newcastle Herald, Wellington Times and Temora Advertiser.

I would also like to thank the staff at the Canowindra Historical Society & Museum Inc, Wellington Historical Society as well as Macquarie Regional, Narromine, Parkes Shire and Wellington libraries.

Special thanks to Geoff Mann, Kel Brown, Neil Pollock, Brian Hughes (Temora Advertiser), John Collins, Pat Jarvis, Terry Williams, Ian Breen, Mark Zheng, and Barry Ross for allowing the use of their knowledge, support and providing the right to use their published material.

My thanks also to The NSW Rugby League News, Family of League, Australian Football History Society and Dubbo CYMS Old Boys.

Many thanks to my sister Roseanne Finn who provided many hours of her time and energy in researching newspaper clips and photos from the Parkes Champion Post and Shire Library.

Thanks also to Michael Greenwood who was also generous with his time in providing documentation of the Parkes Rugby League history.

A special thank you to my wife Wendy and sister Roseanne Finn for editing written text within the book.

I would also like to thank Tarny Burton, Graphic/Web Designer for her continual help throughout the book and especially the design of the front and back book cover pages.

I could not have completed this document without the help and support of many people who gave generously of their time and were willing to share newspaper articles, photos and their memories. In particular Kel Brown (Dubbo CYMS Old Boys) who started the ball rolling by offering his knowledge of the game and researching past newspaper articles from the Macquarie region. Kel provided me with valuable contacts which enabled access to information about players, competitions, grand-finals and representative games.

Kel put me in contact with Central West's best-known sports journalist, Geoff Mann from Dubbo. From my first contact, Geoff was only too willing to help and was very supportive. Geoff provided me with his own research material which was considerable and included photos and newspaper articles. Without his help and support I would not have been able to complete this book.

Geoff Mann has a love for sport which includes cricket and in particular, rugby league. He has been synonymous with Central West broadcasting and journalism for many years as an ABC sporting correspondent, sports commentator on 2DU and writing a sporting column for the Dubbo Photo News.

Finally, I would like to devote this book to country footballers, teams and administrators who gave small and larger country towns during the decades 80 minutes of fierce and competitive football for the spectators who would travel long distances to watch and support their team.

FOREWORD

When you combine love of rugby league with a passion for local history you feel like you can "reach" for the stars.

In Greg Riach's case he's dived into libraries and trawled through trove and other primary sources to create a wonderful montage of the sport that has embraced western and southern NSW country communities for over a hundred years.

Indeed, many towns and villages are only just discovering their "centenary of football" years and this bountiful tome will become an excellent reference.

I have a feeling there are many tales left "unwrit" so this volume might spark researchers to dig deeper and build from this fabulous foundation.

The early years were all about inter town challenge matches with some local competitions introduced between village teams and larger centres. As we moved into the late 1920s and '30s more formalised Cup competitions came into being and Greg has captured some historic and colourful battles for the likes of the Maher Cup, Jack Hore Gold Cup and Johnnie Walker Cup.

History is always subjective so the recording of stories are always skewed. You will laugh at how different perspectives of the same game or incident are portrayed depending on which team or town you were representing!

There are tales of teams and in some instances, communities that no longer exist. These portray a changing demographic and capture the social impacts of farming, mining and other booms and busts, droughts and floods.

This coffee table collectors item should find a shelf in libraries, local history Collections, in Christmas stockings, on birthdays, Father's Day and sports lovers lists for years.

Superb labour of love Greg. Thank you for pulling so much information and so many colourful aspects of the great game of rugby league into a momentous book.

Geoff Mann Sports Lover

CONTENTS

	Page
Dedication	iii
Acknowledgements	iv
Foreword	v
Introduction	1
1892-1896 The Birth of Rugby League	2
Section 1: Central West and Southern NSW Rugby League History: 1920-1976	3
The Twenties	4
The Thirties	17
The Forties	27
The Fifties	40
The Sixties	76
The Seventies	134
Eugowra Mighty All-Blacks Record Premiership Run 1963-1967	201
Group XI Premiership Team Results 1946-1976 and Club Records	202
Group X Oberon Conquers the Central West 1960-1969	203
Section 2: Representative Teams, International Games and Amco Cup	207
Select Table of Contents for Section 2	208
Representative Games, Teams and Players	209
Amco Cup	295
Section 3: Maher, Jack Hore, Johnnie Walker and Clayton Cups	301
Maher Cup	302
Jack Hore Memorial Gold Cup	319
The Mystery of the Stathis Cup	332
Johnnie Walker Cup / Inaugural Football Challenge Cup Match	335
Challenge Cups Come to an End as Group Premiership Competitions Take Over	339
Clayton Cup	340
About the Author, A Yarn with Pat Jarvis and Author Reflection	346
Bibilography and Further Reading	347

INTRODUCTION

The following book takes the reader on a journey through the history of football in the Far West and Southern NSW commencing from the 1920s through to 1976. Football, as it was called and now rugby league, was one of the main sporting activities during the years in small and larger towns. The town's people would travel long distances to watch their team either by train or motor vehicle in large numbers. The towns formed various competitions such as the Johnnie Walker Cup, Jack Hore Memorial Gold Cup, Maher Cup and ultimately, Group Premierships.

Country towns flourished with employment as farming became well established in the export of wheat and wool and Australia was riding on the sheep's back. Farms were producing wool and the industry gave Australia one of the highest living standards in the world. The economy gave the farmers and community wealth from the primary exports. By the 1950s, wool was synonymous with the Australian way of life.

With the increase in country town economies and thus football clubs, city players and coaches were recruited to guide and improve the players' and clubs' football skills and as a result country players became competitive with city players.

Players aspired to represent their regions against competing regions: South West and Western were predominant and produced a number of representative players. This book highlights the years and successes of the teams and players. Regions selected would play against visiting touring teams: English, New Zealand and French which made the game attractive to the country fans who would travel to witness their local players in action.

NSW country teams were selected to play the best city players at the Sydney Cricket Ground (SCG) and they were tough and fierce matches in which the country boys showed what they were made of. Many country players went on to represent NSW and some Australia.

By the 1990s, the gap between country and city people was widening as the price and demand for wool was falling. The country towns' economies fell and as a result, young people started to migrate to the cities for better employment opportunities.

Exciting, talented country players were enticed to city clubs by the lure of large contracts which country clubs could not match. There were more sports to play in country regions and this gave younger people more choice thus reducing the town's main focus of rugby league.

Rugby league football is more than just a thrilling spectacle of 26 players demonstrating their skills on the ground. The principle strength of rugby league is that it gives ordinary people the opportunity to show their talents and skills. It brings communities and team supporters together to watch their local team in action and return to the local hotels for a postmortem.

The contents of this book were designed to bring back memories of football (rugby league) in Western and Southern NSW. It brings together an era and players who were not only team mates but fierce competitors who all had a mutual respect for each other. It encompasses premiership winning teams, representative teams and the history surrounding them and their players during an extraordinary football period where records were set and in some instances still exist.

1892-1896 The Birth of Rugby League

William Webb-Ellis carries the ball during a school football match played in 1823. According to legend, this action created the rugby style of play and eventually rugby union and rugby league.

Rugby union was widely seen as the sport of upper-class men wealthy enough not to worry about its amateurism.

In 1892 players from Bradford and Leeds received game payments for taking time off work in order to play.

The working-class players could not afford any loss of income.

The Northern clubs worked hard to have the rules changed, however they lost by 281 to 136 votes.

In August 1895 the Northern rugby union clubs held a meeting at the George Hotel in Haddersfield and separated from the Rugby Football Union to form the Northern Football Union, which later became known as Rugby League.

Rugby league was on its way to Australia

By the time England's new "Northern Union" game arrived in Australia it was fundamentally different from that of the "Southern Rugby Union" with lineouts, rucks and two players from each team having already been removed and the play the ball introduced to improve the game's flow.

Rugby league commenced in Australia as a professional sport in 1908 after splitting from the rugby union competition. It was based in Sydney NSW before spreading into country regions

The game started to spread like wild fire in country NSW. Western and Southern Districts of NSW.

With the introduction of challenge cups and group competitions by the early 1920s.

Above: Cartoon lampooning the divide in rugby. The Caricatures are of Rev. Frank Marshall, an arch-opponent of the game payments and James Miller, a long-time opponent of Marshall.

Source: History of Rugby League, Wikipedia. From Wikimedia Commons.

1895-96 First Rugby League Champions in the World

Manningham Football Club

The Manningham Football Club team that won the 1895-96 championship left with the awarded shield. The club was the first rugby league champion of the Northern Rugby Football Union and the first in the world.

T. Bamfort, H. Tolson, J. Thomas, A. Procter, W. Robson, H. Jowett, T. Wilkinson, F. Glegg, H. Whiteoak
A. Wilson, A. Leach, J. Brown, G. E. Lorimer, J. Newton, W. Atkinson, A. Barraclough, A. Padgett, W. Needham,
J. Williamson, R. Sunderland, H. Pickles.

Source: History of Rugby League, Wikipedia. Photo by F. Robinson.

SECTION 1:
Central West and Southern NSW Rugby League History 1920-1976

Clarinda Street Parkes 1920. Source: Parkes In Photos of Years Gone Past

Rugby League Captured by the Reels of History

Source: Kodak Camera History. Com

THE TWENTIES

Football (rugby league) kicks off during the 1920's with the introduction of challenge cups. Intertown rivalry started the ball rolling, games were fierce and competitive, spectators were vocal and in some cases would come to tears if their team lost. The game rapidly spread throughout western and southern districts of NSW, players' skills and knowledge of the game improved with the introduction of paid coaches and players from Sydney who were paid big salaries.

It became almost a religion. Played on Sundays, special trains would be organised for spectators to follow their teams.

This chapter journeys through the 1920s and includes the history behind the game, news articles and images of teams from: Canowindra, Coonamble, Cootamundra, Brewarrina, Dubbo, Eugowra, Forbes, Gunnedah, Junee, Parkes, Narromine and Wellington.

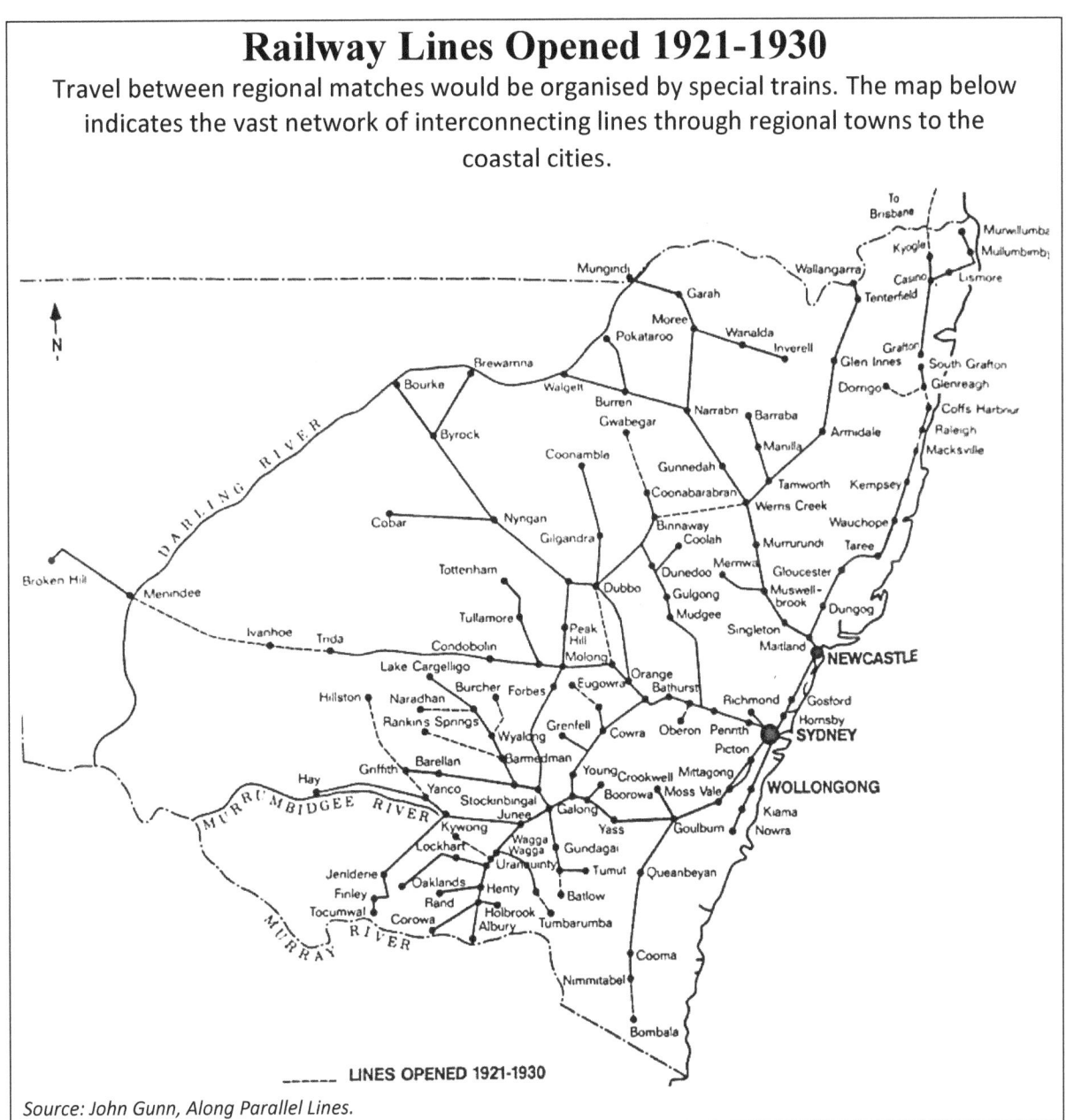

Source: John Gunn, Along Parallel Lines.

Parkes Rugby League History

In 1892 a start was made to clear around 1,500 tree stumps and begin development of The People's Park, a reserve of 81 acres in the general Pioneer Oval / Spicer Park area of Parkes today. The area was slowly developed during the great depression years and beyond to level out the playing surface and included three levels of tiered parking to further improve spectator viewing from cars parked around the ground.

Rugby League was first played in 1920 when the local rugby union club converted to the 13 a side game. The town has been prominent in Country Rugby League's Group XI since 1936 and this venue has hosted local grand finals and representative matches, including:

Western Division Vs Great Britain 1928, 1936
Western Division Vs New Zealand 1963
Western Division Vs France 1955
Western Division Vs Great Britain 1966 and Australia Vs France test match in 1990.

Courtesy of: History parkes.org

Above: left Pioneer Oval and right Spicer Park

One of the fields in the complex was named in memory of Jock Colley, who died suddenly in 2014.

Wayne Thomas (Jock) Colley OAM, pictured right, gave a lifetime commitment to Country Rugby League and was held in high regard as a player and administrator of the game.
Courtesy of: Beverly Colley.

Rugby League in the West

Each time a touring English team visits this country memories of bygone days are revived and wherever the tourists play old followers and those not so old, reminisce on the history of the code, with the players and officials of decades past being mentioned and eulogised for the part they played in popularising the League game.

When was League football first played in the West? It was probably at Orange, in the year following the foundation of the code in Sydney.

It was Orange League which introduced the game further West by sending teams to Wellington, Dubbo and other centres and assisting in the formation of local leagues. Trusting to memory, that was in 1909 or 1910 and from hence on the League game held sway wherever it was introduced.

Within a couple of years Dubbo was able to conduct a competition with half a dozen teams competing. It was fortunate in being able to interest two highly efficient referees in W. ("Billy") Rea and a young Church of England curate, Rev. C. W. Leavers - the latter recently retiring from the charge of his church at that centre.

With the players reaping financial gain in the city, so it followed in the country. First came the professional coach and then the straight-out paid player. Ben Grownow, who toured Australia with an English team later accepted an engagement with Grenfell Club.

"Tedda" Taplin and Dick Vest are names of coaches who quickly flash to mind. Although he was not the first professionally engaged country tutor, Taplin was responsible for the advancement of Rugby League standards in many country centres over a long period of years. Vest was engaged by Forbes League in 1926, after having toured England with the Australian team.

Cup challenge football began to boom and in their keenness to retain or win the most sought-after money-spinners (holders retained from 75 to 100 per cent of gate money), clubs packed their teams with paid players. With Police Sergeant Ferris (later president of the Country Rugby League) as president, Parkes led the way with a wholesale signing up of paid players and was quickly followed by Forbes, which rose to the top, holding the coveted Group XI Championship Shield and Jack Hore Gold Cup, while the game nearly perished in surrounding centres.

It is appropriate to mention that the handsome Group XI Shield was donated by the NSW Rugby League before the formation of the Country Rugby League, when Orange was group headquarters. It is now the prize trophy for the Group XI inter-town competition.

Cup challenge football is now almost a relic of the past, being replaced by Group controlled inter-town competitions. Under this system Leagues are flourishing and the code advancing in public favour.

L. F. MARTIN
19th May 1954

Courtesy of: Geoff Mann, Sports Journalist, Dubbo.

Parkes Rugby League had among its founders Charles Dwyer, Jack Sheahan and Frank Spicer. Opposition to Sunday sport prevented matches in the early days taking place on Council-owned grounds and the venue was at the Welcome, which was outside Council's jurisdiction. There, the club charged spectators for admission and this led to legal action, but no case ever came to court.

When the sports grounds in Parkes became available, teams were rapidly formed including Blues, Ramblers, Magpies, Railway and Old Boys. A group shield competition was introduced and inter-town rivalry became intense. Travel to and from matches was by special train and Sunday night became the top night of the week. The town band often met the victorious local side at the railway station and escorted the players into town where league followers strolled up and down the middle of the main street until late into the night.

Charles Dwyer

Teams which took part in the Rugby League first grade competition back in 1924 were: Blues, Railway, Eugowra, Waratahs, Canowindra and Gooloogong. The League met at Freebains Hotel where under the Chairman, Mr. Tom Hourigan.

Frank Spicer

Courtesy of: Parkes Shire Library Parkes One Hundred Years of Local Government.

The New Grandstand in People's Park

The new grandstand (left) was erected on the People's Park (Spicer Park) for the convenience of the sporting bodies by the Municipal Council and was officially opened for the commencement of the big match yesterday afternoon. The Mayor, in the opening proceedings, said that the work that had been carried into effect on the People's Park made provision for watering the playing area, and also lighting it to permit training at night. On the expenditure the local Rugby League was paying 8 per cent. The grandstand, which was officially opened by the Hon. Fred Flowers, President of the Legislative Council in 1928, had cost 1250 Pounds.

The Hon. Fred Flowers congratulated the Mayor and Aldermen on their efforts to make such splendid provision for sport and the people of the town on their progressiveness. He hoped they would go on improving their playing grounds, which would add to the pleasure of thousands. There was no better preventative against disease than places of recreation such as they had here. He had much pleasure in declaring the grandstand open (Applause).

The official opening was on the 18th July, 1928, the day before the big match between England and the Far West Rugby League team.

Regretably the grandstand has since been demolished to make way for a new multi-purpose sporting complex.

Officially Opened by Hon. Fred Flowers, M.L.C. before West v England Match on Wednesday.

Hon. Fred Flowers, M.L.C.
Patron N.S.W. Rugby League.

Photos Courtesy of: Les Finn.

Article from: Western Champion (Parkes, NSW 1898-1934), p.9.

The Game is Underway

Halves to Centre, Centres to the Wing. League is the game and "The Game is the thing"
Courtesy of: NSW Rugby League, The Rugby League News, July 1926.

1920 Canowindra Football Team

Jack Hore
Member Canowindra Rugby
League Team 1920

Back Row: G. Hickery (Referee), D. Grant, A. Grant, G. McDonald, D. Finn, E Grant, J. Hore, T. Finn.
Middle Row: K. Grant, B. Rice, S. Kirkland, V. Newland.
Front Row: T. Hough, B. McAlister, J. Rice.
Courtesy of: Canowindra Historical Society & Museum Inc.

1920 Forbes Federals Football Team

Top Row: Fred Willis, Ernie Sams.
Back Row: Norman Hudson, Roy Gunn, Percy Rath, Knox Nived, Charger Myledcharane, Dick Hodges.
Front Row: Billy Ryan, Ted Evans, J. Wighton, Reg Fraser, Charlie Rath, Arthur Willis, Sonny Gunn.
Sitting: Billy Phillips, Oliver Twist, Len Rymer.

Courtesy of: Forbes Historical Museum.

1920 South Dubbo Football Team Premiers

Picture, taken 50 years ago, brings back memories for 69 year old Ossie Walkom on the day of the Group grand-final.

The picture shows the South Dubbo Rugby League team who were premiers in 1920.

Mr. Walkom, then 19 years-old, is pictured in the middle of the back row.

On Sunday Mr. Walkom's grandson, Peter, will be playing in the CYMS Juniors side to meet Macquarie.

Ossie Walkom started his football career in Trangie and in 1919 moved to Dubbo.

He joined the South Dubbo team and helped them win the 1920 Premiership, playing at either five-eighth or in the forwards.

Back Row: S. Hutchins, D. Murdock, M. Cameron, A. Gordon, L. Jacobs, O. Walkom, R. Rean, N. McAullife, H. Marks, E. Blatchford, B. Stubbs.

Front Row: D. Angus, J. Ostler, C. Lees, M. Morrison, H. Tighe, H. Corbett.

Sitting: S. Murdock, P. Lees.

Article from: The Dubbo Daily Liberal, September 25, 1970. Republished courtesy of ACM/Dubbo Daily Liberal.

FOOTBALL—JERSEYS
BEST QUALITY ENGLISH COTTON
with White turn down Collars

Available colours and quantities

Sky: 12 dozen   Royal: 9 dozen   Maroon: 8 dozen

Black: 12 dozen   Black & White: 9 dozen   Black & Red: 9 dozen

Black & Gold: 1 dozen   Navy & Gold: 3 dozen

Courtesy of: NSW Rugby League, The Rugby League News, May, 1920.

1922 Gunnedah Football Team

Back Row: Harry Mullane, Romany (Baker) Baker, Charlie Herman, Cecil Pritchard, Hubie Hinton, Andy Neader, Cec (Blue) Hyland, Sid Smith (President),

Middle Row: Vic Gilmore (Secretary), Mick Stevens, Snowy Pitt, Keith Mitchell (Captain), Doug Childs, Fred Martin, Wick McDonald, George Dowell.

Front Row: Jack Pryor, Hec Reading, Billy Parnell.

Winning the Spicer Cup in July 1922

Source: Gunnedah Times, 15 October 1922.

1920 Forbes History

Forbes' first rugby league club formed at a meeting on the 16th April, 1920 and as a consequence a football competition began in 1921 between Forbes Federals, Eugowra, Our Boys and Calarie.

The major competitions in those days were the Jack Hore Cup and the Johnnie Walker Cup and in 1935 the Forbes Federals held both of them.

In 1936 Archie Crippin a Forbes player, was just two years out of school and on the verge of a brilliant playing career when he was chosen to play on the wing for Australia. His time at the top was too brief with a shoulder injury forcing retirement in 1938. He played three tests against Great Britain.

The Forbes Magpies Established 1930

Article from: The Forbes Advocate. Republished courtesy of ACM/Forbes Advocate.

1921 Forbes Football Team

Back Row W. Dempsey, B. Nivin, J. Shepherd, J. Wighton, A. Gunn.

Middle Row: G. Parker, Ned Hayes, N. Coles, W. Varcoe, C. Mylecharane, P. Rath, Ted Evans, G. Jones, N. Flannery, Sonny Gunn.

Front Row: J. Sams, R. Fraser, A. Willis, M. Mckay, C. Rath, J. Baker, D. Cowell, W. Phillips, Stan Gale.

Sitting: Digger Evans, Oliver Twist, Len Rymer.

Courtesy of: Forbes Historical Museum.

1921 Parkes Football Team

Back Row: Broderick, Faull, Toms, Thwaite, Ryan, Jarrett, Dean.

Middle Row: Ted Hunter, Len Hunter, Cecil Pepper, Smith, Dwyer.

Front Row: Field, Fred Pepper, Ryan.

NSWRL.

Courtesy of: Parkes Shire Library. One Hundred Years of Local Government.

Johnnie Walker Cup Rules: June 1922

A meeting of the Dubbo League was held on Tuesday evening at the Fire Station under the presidency of Mr. J. Worthington. There was a fair attendance of delegates. A code of rules for the governing of the Johnnie Walker Challenge Cup competition was submitted to the meeting and approved. The secretary was instructed to send copies of the rules to the following leagues; Wellington, Coonamble, Parkes and Forbes. In this competition Dubbo will have to accept challenges from leagues affiliated with the Central Western League Football Association and will have to defend the title of the cup.

The cup is a handsome piece of jewellery presented by Johnnie Walker Whisky Company.

Article from: The Dubbo Daily Liberal Friday, June 30, 1922. Republished courtesy of ACM/Dubbo Daily Liberal.

1922 Eugowra Blues Competition Winners

Eugowra defeated Forbes 20-11

Back Row: Bob Sutton, Ken Douglas, George Crampton, Albert Pengilly, Murray Wolstenholme, George fox.

Middle Row: Thomas Toohey, Roy Thorncroft, Wilfred Herbert, Jack Little.

Front Row: Clarence Toohey, Dave Greehalgh (Captain), Athur Lowe.

Courtesy of: Rugby League Collection, Central Hotel, Eugowra

1920s Central West Blast From-The Past

Federal Hotel Wellinton

Central Hotel Eugowra

Railway Station Wellington.
Wellington, NSW The Second Oldest Settlement West of The Blue Mountains.

Source: Archives, Australian National University.

1923 Narromine Football Team B Grade Premiers

Back Row: Chris Woolfe Snr (President), Bob Johnston, Cecil Cole, Jack Oates, Bill Collins, Bill (Ted) Sutherland, Jack Madden, Alf Folks, Darby Burge.

Front Row: Jack Clancy, Frank Arnaudon, Dave Murphy, Roy Astil, Leo Tancred.

Team members surrounded by a crowd. The team won the premiership and two trophies.

Courtesy of: The Macquarie Regional Library, Narromine Local History Group.

1923 Narromine Football Team B Grade Premiers

Back Row: Chris Woolfe Snr (President), Bob Johnston, Cecil Cole, Jack Oates, Bill Collins, Bill (Ted) Sutherland, Jack Madden, Alf Folks, Darby Burge.

Front Row: Jack Clancy, Frank Arnaudon, Dave Murphy, Roy Astil, Leo Tancred.

Team members surrounded by a crowd. The team won the premiership and two trophies.

Courtesy of: The Macquarie Regional Library, Narromine Local History Group.

1925 Narromine Hotel

Source: Archives, Australian National University.

1925 Narromine Football Team

Back Row: J. Clancy, W. Smith, Mick Dundas, L.H. Tyson Kierath, C. Dowton, C. Maybury, H. Leadibetter, C. Murphy, C. Cale, F. Arnaudon, F. Draper.

Front Row: J. Millgate, A. Fiddes, C. McKinnon, D. Burge, J. Sibraa, W. Collins.

NSWRL.

Courtesy of: The Macquarie Regional Library, Narromine Local History Group.

1926 Wellington Football Team

WELLINGTON RUGBY LEAGUE CLUB CHAMPIONS OF THE FAR WEST

Back Row: R. Dowton, W. Cook, S. Seach, J. Cowan, C. Rotton, H. Hughes, J. Bullan.

Front Row: J. Kennedy, F. Naveau, D. Davidson, D. McConnell (Captain), B. Naveau, R. White, E. Jones.

Trophies: Coolma Cup, Crawford Cup, Western Stores Cup, Johnnie Walker Cup, Koscusko Cup, Wilkins Trophy, McCormack Cup, Black and White Shield.

Article from: Wellington Times Wednesday October 13, 1926, republished by courtesy of ACM/The Wellington Times.

1926 Junee Representative Football Team

Junee played Temora for the CONDON SHIELD. on 22nd August, 1926. Won by Junee 16 to 8.

Back Row: Officials, G. Schiffman (First Aid), R. Phair (Trainer), S. Rowe (Trainer), J. Parkes (Vice-President), D. Robinson (Trainer), J. Shaw (Manager), E. Wearing (Referee).

Middle Row: T. Humphries, J. Beasley, W. Bellow, G. Clemson, A. Beasley, V. Kane.

Front Row: W. Parkinson, G. Carlaw, C. Turner (Captain), A. Douglas, D. Dealey.

Front Sitting: D. Armour, E. Turner.

Courtesy of: Brian Hughes.

1928 Brewarrina Football Team

Back Row: Jack Biles (Coach), Fidgie White, Moonie Arnold, Jack Schofield, Ted McKenzie, Not Known, Cliff Bradley.

Front Row: Jack Gale, Snowie Dennis, Leo Gale, Splinter Grant, Ted Martin, Bally Hutchinson, Teddy Stephens.

Courtesy of: John Collins, Crowing of the Roosters. Photo: Kay Schofield.

Football Boots History

AD 1526 The earliest recorded "football" boots were listed in the wardrobe of **King Henry VIII.**

They were made by his shoemaker Cornelius Johnson at a cost of 4 shillings. The rugby boot has through the years been developed in tandem with its soccer counterpart (rugby and rugby league).

Original boots were heavy and high ankle, however lighter boots were designed for greater comfort and speed as the game progressed.

Source World Rugby Museum Home. Development of the boot.

Courtesy of: Dubbo Regional Council, Football Boots, Childs, 1930, laced black leather boots.

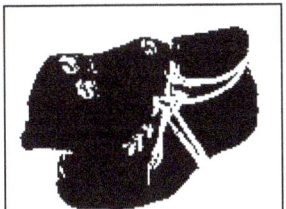
Courtesy of: Canowindra Historical Museum Inc. (Boots worn by Tom Clyburn).

Courtesy of: Yarra Rangers Regional Museum.

Courtesy of: Yarra Rangers Regional Museum (Boots worn by Emerson Woods).

Rugby Ball

William Gilbert (1799-1877) was one of the earliest manufacturers of rugby balls. Gilbert was a shoe and boot maker in the English town of Rugby where, according to legend, the game has its origins. Gilbert made rugby balls using animal bladders for use in matches at the beginning of the 19th century.

The original ball was plum in shape and was changed to a more egg-shape that had four panels to hold it together giving its shape. It made the rugby and rugby league ball more unique from other games such as football (soccer).

The original rugby (rugby league) balls were made of brown leather which became very heavy in the wet weather. A new generation of synthetic balls were manufactured to resist water and came in a variety of colours and patterns.

Source: Rugby ball-Wikipedia, The Free Encyclopedia.

Courtesy of: Rugby Wikipedia.

Courtesy of: Gary Nicolls Sports.

Courtesy: of: Paul Lawson.

Courtesy of: Gary Nicolls Sports.

1928 Maher Cup Game That Changed The Game

Roddy Gilmore, farmer of Canowindra, was a pretty useful second rower. He worked a six-hundred-acre soldier settler's block, carved from the North Bangaroo Estate in 1924. It was said that he, "Cut off the legs of his working trousers to make his football shorts for his first game."

On Wednesday 29 August 1928 he played for Canowindra in the Maher Cup match against the champions of the south, Cootamundra.

The farm was a little closer to the village of Gooloogong than Canowindra, but the latter was where most business was done and Canowindra had a very good football team. Backed by the wealthy Grant families, it had developed into the best side in the Central West. It was here that he learnt the game, from coach and former international Rex "Rocker" Norman.
The team was off to Cootamundra and many pundits thought they would win.

1928 was to be the greatest year for the Canowindra team, which held the Jack Hore Cup for eleven challenges. It was interesting to note that on many occasions, the games were controlled by top Sydney referees.

Wednesday, 29 August 1928 was declared a holiday in Canowindra. An estimated one thousand supporters travelled by special train and motor vehicles from Group 11 and Jack Hore Country, into the heart of Group 9, to the centre of Maher Cup country, some 95 miles away, through Cowra, through Young and Wallendbeen to Fisher Park, Cootamundra. This was only Canowindra's second Maher Cup challenge. Canowindra won the Maher Cup 24-8. However, they lost the match in a protest as Rod Gilmore was ruled outside the ten-mile radius of Canowindra.

Article from: Canowindra Star, September 17, 1928, p.3 Republished courtesy of ACM/Canowindra Star.

Transport to the Maher Cup in the early years

Courtesy of: Brian Hughes & Temora Independent.

1928 Big Salaries
RUGBY LEAGUE STARS AS COACHES
CAPLES, £ 19 A Week

April 1928

Football is a very serious business in the Southern Districts judging by the employment of coaches this season. Big money is being paid by clubs with the object of winning matches, the principal attraction being the famous Maher Cup, at present held by Gundagai.

Wagga has headed the list as far as high salaries are concerned, having contracted with Harry Caples, it was reported at £ 19 a week.

Cootamundra has engaged "Lachem" Robinson at £ 12. Gundagai will have the assistance of "Chook" Fraser, who last year led the team to victory in Maher Cup matches, his services being secured at £ 10 a week.

Teddy Taplin, who coached Young last year, will lead Yeoval, and will get £ 10 a week.

Tumut intends to make a bold bid to regain the cup, which was originally put into competition at Tumut, and has secured J. Marsh, of Queanbeyan for £ 7 a week.

Rex Norman intends remaining at Canowindra for £ 8 a week. Rex started at Canowindra in 1926.

Dick Vest, the ex-international centre three quarter, and W. Lesberg, the crack goal-kicker, from Cootamundra, will strip for Tumut.

Griffith, who have not previously had a coach, have engaged Sheridan of Glebe, at a salary of £ 8.

All these amounts are exclusive of free board and lodging.

"Bill" Brogan, who has to be "tried" by Group 9 for his behaviour in connection with an incident that occurred when Temora and West Wyalong played last year, is likely to lead the latter town's team as coach.

Junee has £ 100 in hand for a coach and Murrumburrah-Harden intend engaging a coach this season.

Temora still has Eric Weissel as captain and coach. His salary, it is unofficially stated, as £ 100 for the season.

NSWRL

Article from: The Boorowa News, Friday, April 6, 1928 Republished courtesy of ACM/Boorowa News.

1929 Cootamundra Football Team

Left-Right: Sid Harris (Captain), Jack James, Jack Walkom, Fred Hayward, Alf Tasker, Jack Dempsey, Gordan Hiton, Algie Faunce, Les Harris, Leo Sheedy, George Purcell, Jack Watson, Bill 'Chips' Phillips, A. Trinder.

Note this may not be a Maher Cup team as stated because Bill Lesberg played in all Cup matches in 1929.

Courtesy of: Neil Pollock, Maher Cup author.

THE THIRTIES

During the 1930s football started to spread in the Far West and Southern regions. Teams played in Shield Cup Competitions, Johnnie Walker, Maher and the Jack Hore Gold Cups. Football was played in small and larger country towns:

Albert, Baradine, Binnaway, Bogan Gate, Bombala, Coonamble, Eugowra, Fifield, Canowindra, Cobar, Condobolin, Cootamundra, Forbes, Parkes, Dubbo, Narromine, Nymagee, Temora, Tullamore, Tumut, Trundle, Warren and Wellington.

This section details some of the events which reflect on the teams, players and its popularity. Balmain played Parkes and representative games started to become a regular event. Football (Rugby League) started to spread in country NSW like wild fire.

PARKES DISTRICT NEWS
From Our Own Correspondents
July 1930

FOOTBALL
MATCH with FIFIELD
BOGAN GATE WIN

BOGAN GATE Wednesday.

The local football team lived up to their great reputation on Sunday by scoring a win against Fifield in their first match of the season.

The ground was practically under water, and as a result the game suffered as an exhibition of football. But was cleanly contested and proved very exciting at times.

Bogan Gate dominated the game from start to finish, despite their lack of condition and won comfortably by two tries (6 points) to one try (3 points).

J Walsh and L Peters scored for the Gate, McKeowen failing to convert either tries and W Summers scored for Fifield but failed to convert also.

Two more sure tries at least were missed by the home team through faulty handling, due to the greasy condition of the ground and ball.

The visitors were entertained at dinner at the Bogan Gate Hotel by the local team. A return match is being played at Fifield next Sunday.

FOOTBALL
Won and Lost
MATCH FOR SHIELD

Trundle Wednesday.

Trundle footballers defeated Forbes Our Boys by 13 to 8 on Sunday last, on Trundle ground. Condobolin will play Trundle for the Group 11 Shield on Sunday next at Trundle.

History tells us that Condobolin won the following week to win the Group 11 Shield.

Condobolin was coached by Jack Cootes.

FOOTBALL
Tullamore Games
COMPETITION FINAL

Tullamore Thursday.

In the recent Knockout Football competition Peak Hill and Tullamore played a draw and it was agreed that the teams should meet again and replay the match. It has now been arranged that the teams will meet on the Tullamore ground on Saturday 12th.

ALBERT FOOTBALL TEAM

Albert footballers took a team to Tullamore on Sunday week and landed a very nice win 19-5.

Football was alive and well in the small regional towns with intertown matches, Knockout and Shield Competitions.

Article from: The Western Champion, July 10, 1930. Republished courtesy of ACM/Parkes Champion Post.

1930 Bogan Gate Hotel

Mr. W. Schofield was the Licensee of the Bogan Gate Hotel, 14/06/1929.

Source: Archives, Australian National University.

1930 Warren Football Team

Left to Right: B. Miller, H. Green, R. Jordan, D. Kennedy, J. Deakin, J. New, T. New, R. White, W. Pearce, P. Cook, A. Verey, B. Azar, J. Pearson, A. Azar.

Courtesy of: John Collins, The Crowing of The Roosters.

Riding on the Sheep's Back

The Phrase "riding on the Sheep's back" is used to allude to wool as a source of Australia's national prosperity. It was used in the golden years of the wool industry when woolgrowers earned a pound (in currency) for a pound (in weight) of wool grown.

Source: Shearing the Rams – Wikipedia. Tom Roberts.   *Source: Donald Alfred Collection.*

1931 Condobolin Premiership Winners

Captain Coach Jack Coote: far right father of Australian Rugby League Hall of Famer, Ron Coote.
Courtesy of: Keith Willis.

Despite winning the Group Premiership work continued in the Condobolin district.

School Days in The Bush

1930s Tichborne Public School.
Courtesy of: Ian & Judy Chambers.

Off to School.

1933 Cobar Rugby League Team

**Wanted Playing Coach
Cobar Rugby League
Football Club**
1st June to 31st August 1933,
Back Position five-eighth.
Terms £2/10/- per week.
Apply Sporting Editor, "Truth"
Newspaper.
Applications close 24th May
1933
J. Ward, Secretary.

Back Row: Bill Prisk, Jack Jones, George Stamp, Charlie O'Donnell, Rusty Holmes.
Middle Row: Val Holmes, Stan Edwards, Bert Hale (Grand Hotel Sponsor), Blue Fox, Harry Bannister.
Front Row: Ron Heap, Arthur Court (Coach), Mac Heap, Bert Bateman.
Courtesy of: John Collins, The Crowing of The Roosters.

1933 DUBBO CHAMPIONS LEAGUE OF THE WEST

As a result of Sunday's Victory
Forbes Well and Truly Beaten in a Hard Game
In Football that was Far from First-class
Dubbo 26 defeated Forbes 10

September 1933

The big-league match, labelled for the "Championship of the West" was played on Sunday afternoon, in the presence of an attendance of nearly record dimensions. The presence of a star League player from neighbouring Group was only possible by Wellington's weak withdrawal from the Johnnie Walker Cup round.

League football is no place for weaklings; as they drop out, the gaps have been filled, in Group 11. Forbes stepped in. Some paid players came, quite good fellows, others were left behind, being booked for a Group fixture at Parkes.

The thirteen that played hard fast football, solid if not showy, but were not classy enough for the local lads, who ran out winners 26-10.

For a front-rank match, as the title at stake betokened, it was the least spectacular of the season and the football, at times, was below expectations. From first to last, it was hard. Both teams were rugged and trained to the hour, both were confident, both played to win. As a team can only play as well as its opponent will permit, the energy and enterprise of the players collectively proved far too strong for any individualistic efforts. Apart from Lane's tries and the usual share of fine flashes by Mason, sparkles were few and far between. With Lane it was pure pace, Mason having to work harder for his tries. Boyle was not once in the picture as an attacking force. He was badly fed and rarely had a chance. In defence he held his own, his pace saving Dubbo on two occasions when a miss might easily have meant a try.

The better team, on the day, undoubtably won. Dubbo dominated the play. Most of its men sparkled, five aided in the aggregate, while Forbes depended upon the trusty toe of Billy Cowderoy to kick its five penalties.

The Teams:

Dubbo: C. Woods, M. Boyle, D. Lane, N. Matterson, J. Mason, J. Larcombe, M. Wheeler, P. Matterson (Captain), C. Friend, S. Rich, W. Moore, M. Douglas, S. Maker.

Forbes: W. Cowderoy, E. Parslow, C. Williard, S. Bartlett, J. Kelly, L. Winterbottom, J. Flynn, B. Clifton (Captain), J. Huxley, B. Gavin, S. McKean, H. McGuire.

Article from: The Dubbo Daily Liberal, Tuesday, September 5, 1933. Republished courtesy of ACM/Dubbo Daily Liberal.

1933 Condobolin Aboriginal Rugby League Team

Aboriginal Team Spicer Park Parkes

Courtesy of: Parkes Shire Library.

Condobolin Railway Station

Courtesy of: Argus News Condobolin.

1933 Wellington Rugby League Team

Back Row: Blue Masterson, Tiger Riley, Nugget Seach, Ron Leamonth, Tom Burrell, Harry Lovett, Bob Haynes, Bullsey Poole (Referee).

Front Row: Harold Smith (Committee), Don McConnell, Joe Deehan, Ron McLaughlin (Captain Coach), Arthur Kitch, Charlie Hoy, Sid Dowton, Harvey Truman (Committee).

Centre: Bruce Smith (Mascot) with the trophies won by the team.

Courtesy of: Wellington Historical Society.

Jim Davis Australian Rugby League Representative

Jim Davis made his debut Test appearance in 1908 against New Zealand, appearing in both matches of the first rugby league international series played by an Australian representative side. At the end of that season, he was selected in the 35-man squad to make the first-ever Kangaroo Tour.

He played for South Sydney, North Sydney and Glebe before moving to Parkes. Davis became depressed when unable to find work during the Depression and on 9th February 1934 he took his life at age of 47.

His body was found in the People's Park in Parkes

1908-1909 Australian Rugby League Team

A suicide note was left. Jim is pictured second row left to right 7th player.

Source: Wikipedia.org/wiki/1908-1909 Kangaroo tour of Great Britain

The Great History of the Coonamble Bears

Coonamble Rugby League Football Club was a foundation club of Group 14 which was formed in 1950 with the juniors starting mid 1950's. Prior to that, the club played in various Cup competitions. Some were the Marigold Cup and the Boronia Cup competitions.

Coonamble were known as the Ramblers back in the 1920's and 30's.

During the 1930's the club regularly employed ex-Sydney 1st graders in the role as Captain/Coach. They were:
1934 Jack Dempsey (St. George 1929)
1935 Frank "Dutchy" Matterson (Western Suburbs)
1937 Jack (Buster) Craigie (Eastern Suburbs 1933-1936).
In 1947 and 1948, the great Dave Brown International and Eastern suburbs player was the non-playing coach.

Coonamble colours were originally black and white and were known as the Magpies until 1962.

During those early years, Coonamble became and still is regarded as the leading club within the Group 14 Competition and now the Castlereagh League.

Throughout the years there has been many winning sides and great players who came to Coonamble to play with the Bears or locals who went onto bigger and greater pastures.

Players such as:
1954-Ian Johnston-Australian Representative.
1955-Keith McDonald-Ex Eastern Suburbs.
1956-Jack McLean-Ex North Sydney and Australian
1957-Frank Fooley-Ex North Sydney.
1960-Ron Boden-Australian Representative and Parramatta.
1960-Earl Harrison-Australian Representative.
1970-Keith "Junior" Hemsworth-St. George.
1988-1991 Steven "Joey" Fulmer-Newcastle.
Ray Hyde, (Ex Eastern Suburbs) who coached the 1957,58,59 premiership sides, which included winning the Clayton Cup in 1958.

Article from: Geoff Mann, Sports Journalist, Dubbo.

Parkes Rugby League Player Who Trialled for South Melbourne VFL Club

1934 Jim Reid:

In 1934 a young Rugby League player from Parkes, New South Wales, took himself to Melbourne with the intention of trying out for the South Melbourne VFL team. An ankle injury put paid to his chances so he returned to play the season out with the Parkes Rugby League Club. His name was Jim Reid and he played either fullback or centre for the previous two years, and his speed on the ground was quite often quoted. He lived in Parkes during the 1930s, and his dad was the licensee of the Royal Hotel.

Jim also said he played on the wing with the South Australian Schoolboys team in the national carnival held in Melbourne in 1924 at the age of eleven.

Why would Jim, as a young man, persist in his attempts to break into VFL ranks when coming from a Rugby League background?

His parents came from Western Australia then South Australia and Jim played Australian Rules in both WA and SA at an extremely competent level and Rugby League was his only option in Parkes. His dream was to become a famous VFL player. Jim played Rugby League for Parkes at the age of 19 against Balmain at Spicer Park Parkes during 1934.

His parents came from Western Australia then South Australia and Jim played Australian Rules in both WA and SA at an extremely competent level and Rugby League was his only option in Parkes. His dream was to become a famous VFL player. Jim played Rugby League for Parkes at the age of 19 against Balmain at Spicer Park Parkes during 1934.

South Melbourne VFL Team, Jim Reid top far right.

Article from: NSW Australian Football History Society. Republished courtesy of NSW Australian Football History Society.

Royal Hotel Parkes

Courtesy of: Parkes in Photos of Years Gone Past.

Court Street Parkes

Courtesy of: Donald Alfred Riach's Collection.

BALMAIN v PARKES
Sunday's Big Match
1st June 1934 Spicer Park

The Big Match:

The officials of Parkes league in arranging for the Balmain first grade team to play here on Sunday, have further evidenced their desire to provide local supporters with first-class football.

The Balmain team, which contains several representative players, contains mostly young men who are making their way into the "big stuff," such as Tommy Grahame, the country lad who plays five-eighth, and whom critics declare is one of the outstanding players of the year.

The Parkes team has been slightly altered to that which visited Forbes last week. Jim Reid, at centre, will be playing his first game since an injured foot at Condobolin. Basil Clifton, the Forbes lock forward, will also strip, and Charlie Smith will be back in the second row, Frank Riles again going to the wing.

Basil Clifton and Forbes football supporters travelled by special train to Parkes for the big match.

So, with the Balmain team out to uphold the honour of the city, and the local men on their toes to atone for last Sunday's defeat, a great game of fast open football should result.

The Teams:

Balmain:

M. Fallon, W. Williams, W. Ballard, M. Pace, H. Slater, W. Johnston, C. Richards, S. Goodwin, G. Simpson, S. Christensen (Captain), H. Mathews, T. Grahame, J. Pidcock; reserves, T. Cox, S. Simpson.

Mr. J. Randall will accompany the visitors as manager and well known ex-representative player, Mr. "Son" Frazer, club selector will also be a member of the party.

Parkes: L. O'Donnell, F. Riles, L. Quinlivan, J. Reid, G. Rees, Bourke, Loughrey, B. Clifton, C. Smith, E. Davis, C. Hodge, R. Wethered, E. Dwyer; reserves, A. Quinlivan, J. Cooper and G. Pugh.

Article from: The Western Champion (Parkes NSW, 1934). Republished courtesy of ACM/Parkes Champion Post.

Forbes Railway

1930s Forbes Railway Station

Courtesy of: Donald Alfred Riach.

Heading for Parkes.

1934 Original Formation of Country Rugby League
When was Country Rugby League Formed?

The group system was introduced in 1922, with neighbouring towns organised into 12 groups.

The Country Rugby League (CRL) was officially formed in 1934, "subject to the NSW Rugby League still being the paramount institution." In 1939 a dispute arose between the CRL and the NSWRL. The CRL wanted a new administration structure and equal partnership in which the NSWRL looked after league in Sydney and the CRL looked after it in the bush.

Courtesy of: Wikipedia, Country Rugby League.

Lachlan Street Forbes On The Move

Source: Forbes Shire Council NSW Heritage Buildings Photo Gallery.

1934 Baradine Rugby League Team

Back Row: Jim Head, Bob Penny, Ted Campbell, Bert Andrews, Reg Webber, Bruce Purdy, C. McCartney (Secretary).

Middle Row: Tiger Louis (Referee), J.Cowan, Sid Evans, Toby Kerr, Bob Thurtle, Frank Thurtle.

Front Row: Bluey Rodgers, Les Ainsworth.

Rugby League football team with seven players standing in the back row with a man on the far right wearing a suit, a coach (on left) and five players seated in the centre row, with the third man a football (with "Dally M" printed on it), and two players sitting on the ground at the front either side of a large trophy cup. "Baradine 1934" and skull and crossbones emblem patch can be seen on the left-hand chest of each player.

Courtesy of: Dubbo Macquarie Regional Library.

1935 Tumut Rugby League Team

Back Row: Alan Miller, Bill McGowan, Cliff Davis, J. Brooks, Col Hargreaves, Bill Hargreaves, Bede Madigan.

Front Row: Gordon McDonnell, Tom Scott, Jim Lyell, Reg Madigan, Bob Dowling (Captain), Lonnie Fields.

Courtesy of: Tumut RSL Club.

THE WESTERN CHAMPION POST FRIDAY, AUGUST 11, 1934

Group Shield

Retained by Parkes

ANOTHER EFFORT BY CANOWINDRA

HOME TEAM WINS BY 12 TO 8

Article from: The Western Champion, August 10, 1934. Republished courtesy of ACM/Parkes Champion Post.

1935 Parkes Rugby League Team

Back Row J. Nash (Manager), J. Hale, E. Vine, S. Josselyn, (President), J. O'Donnell, L. Morrison, J. Heiss (Secretary).

Middle Row: L. Hogan, W. Dakers, V. Flanery, J. Tasker, R. Wethered, R. Hunter.

Front Row: W. Broderick, L. O'Donnell (Captain), P. Dakers.

Courtesy of: Forbes Historical Museum.

1936 Australian Rugby League Representative
Archibald James Crippin originally from Forbes

Archie Crippen played for Forbes in the Jack Hore Gold Challenge Cup match against Tumut in 1935 and was one of their stars being a young lad Crippen, who was later to play for Australia at the age of 18.

Crippin was an Australian rugby league footballer who played in the 1930s. He was a New South Wales interstate and Australian international representative winger.

Only one year out of school and aged 18, Crippin was selected in the Kangaroos side to play Great Britain in 1936. He played in all three Tests on the wing outside captain Dave Brown. He marked his arrival with a brilliant 60m try in the second Test.

Archibald Crippin

Source: Wikipedia, The Free Encyclopedia.

1935 Coonamble Ramblers Rugby League Team

Back Row: E. Sloggett, G. Jordan, P. Hundy, N. Ayoub, N. McKinnon, J. Tracey.

Middle Row: D. Edgell, C. Blackett, J. Sutton, D. Hughes, E. Evans, J. Bassett, A. Adams.

Front Row: J. Birch, T. Scifleet, E. Lees, F. "Dutchy" Matterson (Captain Coach), E. Harris, C. Brookes, B. Doyle.

Courtesy of: Greg Maher.

1938 Eric Budd plays for Canbelego and Parkes

Eric Budd was playing rugby league in Canbelego during the days of the Marcus Clark Cup. He played for Canbelego from 1938 until the outbreak of World War Two.

His best football was after the war, when he left the area and played in the Parkes and Forbes groups.

In 1945 he was selected to the play for Western Division and Country NSW against a Metropolitan team.

Eric, or Eck as he was called played for the Parkes rugby league team (Parkes Blues) as fullback and was an accomplished goal-kicker.

Eric continued to play for Parkes up until the early 1950s and was considered a veteran.

Eric Budd
Courtesy of: John Collins, The Crowing of The Roosters.

1938-1939 Nymagee Rugby League Team

Back Row: R. Davis, G. Russell, A. Ford, F. Carson, A. Luton, W. Hudson, K. McKinnon, E. McLean, R. Darling, W. Ford, J. Mackay.

Front Row: P. Kelly, D. Munro, B. Sullivan.

Ball Boy: T. McLean.

NSWRL

Courtesy of: The Nymagee Notice Board and John Collins.

THE FORTIES

Football (rugby league) was well entrenched in the Western and Southern Districts with numerous competitions: Jack Hore Cup, Maher Cup, Marcus Clark Cup, Johnnie Walker Cup, Group Premierships and the Claytons Cup provided fierce competition. Great players started to emerge and one such was Keith Holman. Teams started to appoint captain coaches from Sydney. The Redfern Aboriginal All Blacks attracted players from country NSW.

FOOTBALL

Dubbo Backs Run Riot In Hore Cup Match
YEOVAL-CUMNOCK DEFEATED 30/2
Bennett Outstanding in Attack

Revealing combination characteristic of the champion team of 1937, Dubbo Rugby League reps, ran riot against Yeoval-Cumnock at the Show Ground on Sunday and retained the Jack Hore Gold Cup by 30/2

July 1940

The challengers held the locals 3-nil at lemons, but the defence wilted in the second half before the persistent attack of the Blue and Whites.

The outstanding backs were Wheeler, Rutherford and Bennett. The latter repeatably straightened the attack and revealed his best form of the season.

Pringle (full-back) moved to centre in the second half and combined nicely with Foxall. Dalton and Patman received more chances than usual and went well. Foxall was safe at fullback.

In the forwards Wand again dominated the scrum and gave the backs a lot of ball. Woods, Frost and Fardell were good supports, but Reilly and Walsh also went well.

The latter converted five tries and scored from a penalty in as many kicks and must monopolise the kicking for the locals in future.

For the challengers Miskell, P. Miller and Housler were the pick of the backs, while Nunn, Sullivan and Day were hard triers in a beaten pack.

Dubbo went to lemons with a three nil lead over Yeoval-Cumnock.

Final Score: Dubbo 30 defeated Yeoval-Cumnock 2.
Dubbo: Rutherford, Reynolds, Patman, Pringle, Dalton and Fardell tries. Walsh kicked 6 goals.
Yeoval-Cumnock: Miskell kicked one penalty goal.

Article from: The Dubbo Liberal and Macquarie Advocate, Tuesday, July 13, 1940. Republished courtesy of ACM/Dubbo Daily Liberal.

RUGBY LEAGUE

Dubbo Beats Western Suburbs in Best Match of Season

Team's Remarkable Recovery

VISITORS RUN OFF FEET WHEN IN LEAD

Rutherford Shines in Fine Forward Display

August 1940

Displaying its best form of the season, in an exhibition of the type for which it was noted about three years ago, Dubbo Rugby League team on Sunday beat Western Suburbs (Sydney) first-grade combination 26-20.

Wests did not score in the second half. Dubbo on the other hand, after being led 20-8 at half time, staged a magnificent recovery and completely over-ran the visitors. Even granting that the latter were weary after a long train trip and a rather active time before the match, it is never the less true that Dubbo's recovery was such as to mark the team's fighting qualities and ability.

If further proof were needed that Dubbo is the champion team of Group 11, its victory over the Sydney side, supplied it.

Article from: The Dubbo Liberal and Macquarie Advocate, Tuesday, August 20, 1940. Republished courtesy of ACM/Dubbo Daily Liberal.

1943 Newtown Jets Rugby League Team Premiers
Two Players Coach Country Teams

Newtown Jets defeated North Sydney in the Grand Final

Back Row: F. Speechley, Tom Kirk, Len Smith, Keith Phillips, Gordon McLennan, Herb Narvo.

Front Row: Paddy Budgen, Norn Jacobson, Charles Cahill, Frank Farrell (Captain), Jimmy Brailey, Tom Nevin, D. Fullerton.

Herb Narvo 1947 *appointed captain coach of Cootamundra Maher Cup side and Group 9 Premiership winning team.*

Norm Jacobson 1950 *appointed captain coach of Condobolin, winning the Group 11 Premiership. In 1951 he went on to captain Western Division against the French touring team at Forbes.*

Courtesy of: The Wikimedia Commons, The Free Media Repository.

1945 Dubbo Railway Rugby League Team

Dubbo Railway Marcus Clark Cup Winners

The old Marcus Clark Cup days brings back memories for many footballers of the early post war period.

The cup faded away when Dubbo entered two teams in the Group 11 rugby league competition:
- Dubbo Macquarie
- Dubbo CYMS.

Back Row: T.See, H. Smith, L. Ravot (President), W. Hann (Secretary), F. Fuller, K. Leary.
Middle Row: E. Enright, N. Howe, N. Priddle, S. Fardell (Captain), J. Hands, B. McMahon, R.Sec.
Front Row: R. Jack, Kelvin Ravot (Mascot), A. Carney.

Article from: The Dubbo Daily Liberal, Wednesday, June 1, 1966. Republished courtesy of ACM/Dubbo Daily Liberal

1946 Wellington Wins Inaugural Group 11 Grand Final

Forbes beaten 11-4. Over 3000 Witness Game.

At Parkes last Sunday, over 3000 people witnessed Wellington defeat Forbes, 11 points to 4, in the grand final of Group 11 inter-town competition. With the victory went the Group 11 Champion Shield and competition prize of £100. It was Forbes first defeat in Group 11 football season.

Although only one try was scored, Wellington backs gave a delightful exhibition of fast football. Their handling was almost faultless and Sutton (five-eighth) revealed himself as perhaps the most brilliant attacking player in Group 11 this season.

Forbes players were glorious in defeat. They strenuously contested every minute of the play and after the game congratulated the visitors and willingly conceded that Wellington was the better team on the day.

Forbes:
A. Fowler, M. Kupkee, K. Quin, K. Galdwell,
I. Clarke, R. Barton, W. Flynn, J. Huggett,
G. Sanderson, J. Stewart, J. Nunn, K. Adams,
D. Edwards.

Wellington:
H. Smith, K. Bridge, F. Lay, W. Powell, E. Parkes,
R. Sutton, B. Drew, L. Lay, R. Montgomery,
T. Dray, W. Skinner, M. Wilson, G. Collins.

Scores: Wellington 11 (T. Dray try, W. Powell 2 goals and M. Wilson field goal).
Forbes 4 (A. Fowler 2 goals).
Mr. Gillard (Wollongong) was appointed by the CRL to referee the game and he gave entire satisfaction.

Article from: The Forbes Advocate, 27 August 1946. Republished courtesy of ACM, Forbes Advocate.

1946 Lithgow Small Arms Factory District Premiers

Top Row: T. Scouler (Vice-Pres), W. Oldfield (Secretary), H. Archer (Gear Steward), H. Jeffery (Vice-Pres), G. Crowe (Masseur).

Back Row: E. Keniff, R. Laycock, J. Deans, F. Eather, G. Harradine, R. Northey, L. Cohen.

Middle Row: C. McAulay (Vice-Pres), J. Doyle, L. Taylor, F. Bell (Captain), C. Hauville, C. Holt, A. Barnes (President).

Front Row: T. Morris, Ian Bell (Mascot), M. Kelly.

The 1946 Lithgow Small Arms Factory team joined the newly formed Group 10 Division in 1947.

Source: 1946 Team photo. Courtesy of: The Lithgow Library.

1946 Aboriginal Footballers the All Blacks
Including players from regional NSW

Aboriginal Footballers

In 1944 aborigines in Sydney formed their own Rugby League football team. In their first season they did not do very well, finishing seventh on the premiership list. In their second season they have improved so much that they have finished in the finals.

The aborigines call themselves the All Blacks. They play in black uniforms and wear the badge (left) in lapels of their coats. Sturdy supporters of the All Blacks also wear the badge which is carved from wood by a member of the team.

All Blacks gain their successes mainly from their great speed and agility, backed up by sound combination. Mr. W. Berryman, vice-president and publicity officer of South Sydney Junior League, in which the aborigines play, is willing to bet the team is the fastest in Australia. "No team in Rugby League or Australian Rules can run man for man with the All Blacks."

Eric Mumbler

The ambition of the All Blacks is to mould into a first-grade side. They have a long way to go but they are keen, well-disciplined, and one of the happiest sides playing. Apart from prowess on the field the team numbers among its players some lively tap dancers, gum leaf musicians, crooners, a guitarist, a violinist and a piano player. The baby of the team is 18.

Officials of the All Blacks as well as players are aborigines. Isaac Bates, is one of the outstanding men in the team. He was considered this season for a cup for the best player under 21 in the district he plays in but unfortunately, he was not residentially qualified.

Some aboriginal players in the All Blacks came from the country. They would find factory work in Sydney during the football season and return to the country for seasonal work. Many lived permanently in Sydney suburbs.

The team was officially formed in 1944 and attracted talented players from all around N.S.W including Eric 'Nugget' Mumbler, Babs Vincent, Merv 'Boomanulla' Williams and Isaac Bates who came from Coonabarabran at the age of 17.

All Blacks Football Team

Isaac Bates

Mervyn Williams

All Blacks are a sturdy bunch. From left to right: Eric Mumbler, Colin Saunders, Laurie Perry, G. "Babs" Vincent, Alan Duren, Cecil Stewart, Isaac Bates, Jackie Sims, Jack McLaren, Roy Williams, C. Jarrett (Vice Captain), Mervyn Williams, Harold Hinton (Captain) and Dick Lord (Ball Boy).

N.S.W State Library, Republished courtesy of: The N.S.W State Library and Pix Magazine p.28/29, October 5, 1946.

All Blacks Aboriginal Football Team Plays Redfern Waratahs
24th August 1946 Semi-Final

Ted Duncan wearing hat and Ernest Duren with the ball talk to the players before the game.

Harold Hinton "Lal" (Captain) and C. Jarrett (Vice-Captain).

Spectacular flying tackle by Laurie Perry.

Cecil Stewart left moves in to assist in a tackle.

All Blacks Isaac Bates scoring a try.

All Black team supporters.

Young boys, Redfern All Blacks supporters at Redfern Oval.

Mervyn "Boomanulla" Williams with Vice-Captain C. Jarrett.

All Blacks defeated Redfern Waratahs 7 points to 6 in front of more than 8,000 spectators. They were defeated the next week by Maroubra Surf Club team, ending the All-Blacks season. Some of our greatest aboriginal footballers moved from country NSW to join city teams.

The team's success had important political, social and symbolic ramifications and an expression of community pride was a significant component in the shift towards self-determination within the aboriginal community.

Courtesy of: The N.S.W. State Library.

1946 Tomingley Rugby League Team

GEOFF MANN

THE following letter came from Bill Hoy of Peak Hill. Bill has some great memories of football in Tomingley in the 1940s, particularly on the modes of transport and showers.

Here is Bill's letter

Dear Geoff

Here's what I remember about Ian Walsh. In the early 50s he was playing for Bogan Gate. They had qualifying boundaries in those days.

Bogan Gate was in 2nd Division then and you couldn't break into rep football from 2nd Division. His dad a retired footballer wanted him to have a chance, so his dad came out of retirement to play for Bogan Gate so they would release Ian to play with Conobolin.

I think from Condo he went to Parkes and then to Forbes. He then went to coach Eugowra; from there to Western District to Country Week, Australia and St. George.

The Tomingley football team, 1946:

Tomingley played against Narromine, Trangie, Warren, Nyngan, Tullamore and Tottenham. I think it was Group 14 or 16.

The photo attached is of the first-grade team. We also had a second-grade side. They called us the "Rugged 13".

Bill Peachey played for Warren. Most players were just out of the armed services then. I believe Bill Peachey is the grandfather of David Peachey.

In 1947 Tomingley played 1st Division in Group 11.

The group was split in two divisions: north and south. The winners of each division played in the final. From memory, the South teams were Peak Hill, Parkes, Forbes, Condobolin, Canowindra and Bogan Gate and the North teams were Tomingley, Narromine, Dubbo, Wellington, Gulgong, Molong and Cumnock-Yeoval, I think. the group should have records of this.

I think it was 1947 that Forbes and Wellington played a draw in the first final. They had a week off and then played again. From memory Wellington won. They were coached by Blue Ley (you could call him a legend). Bill Darney played for Wellington.

Tomingley won their share of games. They had close games against Dubbo; Wellington was too strong. But Tomingley had a fair bit of bad ref calls when we lost, similar to State of Origin today!

The Tomingley team was mostly made up of Ollie Diggers, K. "Bill" Hoy, K. Jones, V. Sheehan, J. Clarke, J. Wilcox, R. Hoy, L. Sheehan, K. Sharkey, G. Cannon, D. Walker and Brian Bolton.

Keith Holman was playing for Dubbo at the time.

Footy flashback: Tomingley's first grade side 1946
J. Clarke, T. Dacey, J. Wilcox, H. Crane, K. Sharkey,
R. Jones, J. Traver, S. O. Leary, N. Cooper, B. Hoy,
H. McNamara, A. Powel.

We had Brian Bolton playing for us. After playing against Dubbo a couple of times they realised how good he was and claimed him back in 1948. He went on to play for Western Division several times.

We travelled on the back of an open truck but as the season progressed we were able to hire a truck with three foot high sides and a green stick up the middle for a ridge pole with a tarpaulin over the top. They were long trips coming home, especially from Gulgong. Players brought their own lunch and tea and mostly had to put in to pay for the truck.

The playing field was marked with a mattock. Goal posts and cross bar were gum saplings, bark on (acted as a cushion). No black dots those days. The field was inside the racetrack at the sports ground.

There was no water, hence no shower after the game in 1946. But in 1947 it improved. They had an old 800 gallon square steel tank with plenty of rust holes; a fire would be lit about lunch time. It had four 44 gallon drums on top of the tank. The drums had the top cut out and they were filled with water carted from a spring the mornng of a home game. These were in an old tin shed down the back pub yard. We had some four gallon buckets with holes punched in the bottom to make a shower which hung from the rafters with wire.

By the time we finished playing the fire would be out but the water was still warm. The players used to give the kids a few bottles of lemonade to stand on the tank and tip water into the shower buckets. After the shower we would go up to the pub for a couple of beers and a post mortem on the game.

On our trip to Gulgong we had to pick up the ref from Dubbo and take him with us. Another time when we played Wellingtion in Wellington we picked up Nippy Ward to ref the game.

The good old days?

Source: KJ "Bill "Hoy, Peak Hill.

Courtesy of: Geoff Mann, Sports Journalist, Dubbo.

1946 Gibsonvale Rugby League Team

Played Maher Cup at Tumut

Back Row: J. Dale, L. Tomlinson, P. Hoskinson, Ted O'Kane, D. Miller, J. Keys, G. Emery.

Front Row: A. Hines, R. Meirs, E. Boal, K. Maybury, Joe Nedrie, Scotty Miller.

The team is in front of Phil Hoskinson's truck, which was their transport. Alice Hodkinson is in front of the truck.

Courtesy of: Brian Hughes & Temora Independent.

1947 Lithgow Arms Factory Rugby League Team
Group 10 Premiers

Back Row: R. Kenniff, J. Leary, M. Simpson, G. Crowe, A. Shawcross, C. Holt, R. Northey.

Middle Row: J. Perry, B. Simpson, M. Ryan, B. Furbank, C. Hauville, S. Simpson, E. Keeley, T. Scouler.

Front Row: E. Green, J. Champion, P. Dawson, F. Bell, C. McAulay, D. Hutchinson, M. Kelly, Ian Bell (Ball Boy).

Lithgow Small Arms Factory won the inaugural Group 10 Premiership by defeating Portland Colts 17/7 in the Grand Final at the Lithgow Showground.

Courtesy of: The Reg Northey Collection.

1947 Former Great Who Played in Dubbo

The great Keith Holman had played a season in Dubbo just after World War 2. It was about 1947 and he was working at the RAAF Base in Dubbo. He came to Dubbo with his friend Eric Bennett from Bennett's Bricks a former Western Suburbs team mate.

Keith, known as "Yappy" Holman played with Waratahs All Blacks in the local competition and fed the scrums for Dubbo in Group 11 and in many Johnnie Walker Cup challenges against teams from Warren, Wellington, Narromine and Coonamble.

Yappy went on to play 32 Tests for Australia, 24 games for NSW and more than 200 matches with the Magpies.

He was a prominent referee, coach and commentator.

He was convinced that his season in Dubbo with strong men improved his ability to take knocks when he returned to the city in 1949.

Courtesy of: Geoff Mann, Sports Journalist, Dubbo.

Keith (Yappy) Holman

1948 Football Grand Final

FOOTBALL

Grand Final of Group Competition

September 1948

Forbes Rugby League appealed against the decision of Group 11 to play the grand-final of the Group competition at Dubbo on Sunday.

The appeal was dismissed and the group executive's decision to hold the match at Dubbo was upheld.

Forbes wanted the match played at Parkes while Wellington favoured the Dubbo venue.

SPECIAL TRAINS

Special trains have been chartered from: Narromine, Forbes and Wellington for Sunday's match.

Mr. L. F. Locke of Wollongong, who is secretary to the Country Rugby League will be in attendance at the fixture which promises to be the most momentous in Western football history.

MAYORAL WELCOME

The Mayor, Ald. E. B. Serisler, will extend a welcome to the teams and officials prior to the game, on the lawn in front of the grandstand.

Article from: The Dubbo Liberal and Macquarie Advocate, Thursday, September 23, 1948. Republished courtesy of ACM/Dubbo Daily Liberal.

1948 Cobar Grand Final Team

Back Row: Bricky Faulkner, Tom Maidens, Val Holmes, Jim Weekes, Dick Martin, Jack Rimmer, Fabien Jermyn, Frank Puckeridge, Tom Budd, Osker Mitchell, Toby Brocker, Ted Sprague.

Front Row: Eric Martin, Bill Neale, Dudley Martin, Toby Wright, Les Warner, Les Brooker (Ball Boy).

Warren defeated Cobar in the 1948 Grand Final 4-0

Courtesy of: John Collins, The Crowing of The Roosters.

1948 Parkes Rugby League Team

Referred to as the Parkes Blues

Back Row: P. Fitzpatrick, N Bernie, A. Turner, E. Budd, K. Wiggins, J. O'Donnell, J. Jones, F. O'Brien, E. Locke.

Middle Row: B. Maguire, R. Daniels, C. Houghton, C. Peam, E. Wakefield, F. Jones, F. Chew.

Front Row: B. Thornton, G. Prior.

Courtesy of: Parkes in Photos of Years Gone Past.

RUGBY LEAGUE
No Football Next Week-end

GROUP SHIELD TO WELLINGTON ON FORFEIT
September 1948

Wellington Rugby League, for the second time in three years' competition play, will hold the converted Group11, Shield.

Molong premiers of Division 2, who were to have met Wellington to decide the holder of the trophy, forfeited early in the week.

It was stated that they did not believe they could beat the Wellington team, as they had several star players out with injuries. The magnificent trophy will arrive in Wellington from Canowindra to-morrow.

The shield will be presented to the Wellington Rugby League by Mr. B. Campbell, NSW Country R.L. President, at the footballers' ball to-morrow week.

There will be no football in Wellington next week-end. The Saturday competition concluded when Souths defeated Shamrocks 12-5 in the grand final last Saturday and efforts by the Rugby League to bring a team here on Sunday proved unsuccessful.

Lithgow and Parkes were contacted with a view to playing here, but both Leagues have disbanded until next season.

CHALLENGE BY FORBES

On Tuesday, a telegram was received by League Secretary E. Poole from Forbes R.L. challenging Wellington for £100 a side, at Forbes on October 10 (Sunday week).

The local league will give the challenge full consideration and will decide at the end of this week whether they will accept the challenge or not.

It is improbable that the challenge will be accepted under the conditions set out in the Forbes telegram.

Forbes would have everything to gain and little to lose if Wellington travelled over there to play. Such a match should draw a gate of a least £200, which would leave Forbes a considerable profit, even though they were beaten.

WELLINGTON'S CLAIMS FOR CLAYTON CUP

It is probable that Wellington League will be this year's holders of the Clayton Cup, a magnificent trophy for Statewide competition presented to the Rugby League team which had scored the greatest number of points during the season.

Wellington with a total of 420 points in 26 matches is almost certain to win the Cup, which was won last year by Temora.

Wellington teams' record is exceptionally good. In 26 matches 20 were won, two drawn and four lost.

Only two defeats were suffered in competition play and 317 points were scored in 16 competition matches against 71 points.

Throughout the entire season, Wellington had only 100 points scored against them.

HIGH INDIVIDUAL SCORES

Highest individual scorer has been the brilliant Stan Mildwater, with 90 points resulting from 14 tries and 24 goals.

Bruce Smith scored 13 tries and kicked 15 goals for a total of 69 points, whilst "Tippy" Dray scored 11 tries and two field goals for his total of 37.

Other high scorers were L. Lay (15 goals, 30 points), Jack Hoffman (9 tries, 27 points).

Every player in the team scored during the season, whilst only one player, front row forward Bill Darney failed to score points in the competition.

TROPHY TO DARNEY

The Rich trophy, presented every year for the most improved player was awarded this year to Bill Darney, whose splendid play over the last three of four matches made him Wellington's best forward.

NSWRL

Article from: The Wellington Times, September 30, 1948. Republished courtesy of ACM/Wellington Times.

1948 Dubbo Rugby League Team Saturday Afternoon Premiers

Back Row: R. Lewis, L. Page, R. Walsh (Coach), M. Ryan, R. Sheridan.

Middle Row: F. Dodd, J. Dodd, D. Wallace, R. Rich, G. Allen.

Front Row: C. Claridge, J. Kennedy, B. Piesley, P. McTiernan (Captain), J. Meredith, V. Sheridan.

Courtesy of: Blast From the Past, Dubbo CYMS Old Boys.

1949 Cobar Rugby League Team Group 15 Premiers

Cobar defeated Bourke in the Grand-Final 8-5 at Davidson Oval Bourke, Cobar's first Group 15 Premiership.

Back Row: Mick Fishpool, Roy Williams, Billy Collins, Eric Martin, Johnny Fowler, Val Holmes, Jack Rimmer, Dick Martin, Oswald Mitchell, Arthur Luton (Referee).

Front Row: Les Harris, Oscar Betts, Bill Neal, Kevin Neale, Jim Weekes.

Courtesy of: John Collins, The Crowing of The Roosters.

Rugby League
Dubbo Now Share Lead in Competition Following Wellington's 8-5 defeat by Narromine

July 1949

Wellington and Dubbo Rugby League teams now share the lead in the Group 11 Rugby League competition as a result of yesterday's matches, Wellington suffered their third defeat in the competition when they were narrowly beaten by Narromine, 8 points to 5, at Narromine, and Dubbo defeated Peak Hill by only 2 points in a very even match at Peak Hill. Final scores there were 10-8.

The Wellington team could not produce their devastating form of the previous Sunday and only spasmodically did the back line show any passing bursts. The match itself was mainly fast and interesting, with tackling particularly hard.

The Narromine team deserved their win. Although sound defensive work by Wellington nullified most of their backline moves, their three-quarters had the edge on Wellington throughout the greater part of the match.

Dubbo went on to defeat Forbes in the 1949 Grand Final 6-4.

Article from: The Wellington Times, Monday, July 4, 1949. Republished courtesy of ACM/Wellington Times.

Western Football Championship

September 1949

LEAGUE STARS TO PLAY BATHURST TEAM

Dubbo Rugby League Representative team winners of Group 11 inter-town competition will clash with Bathurst Railway, winners of Group 10 Championship at Orange on Sunday, September 18 for the Western Districts Championship.

A crowd of more than 4000 people is expected to witness the match. Special trains will run from Dubbo, Forbes and Bathurst. Mr. Bruce Campbell President of Group 11 said that he was sure that at least 1000 supporters from Dubbo and Forbes would accompany the Dubbo team.

Mr. Jack Murray, of Orange will referee the Championship match.

Bathurst Railway have an undefeated record this season. The gate takings on Sunday will be split equally between Groups Ten and Eleven.

The following are the teams:

DUBBO: V. Ryan, J. Butcherine, J. McTiernan, J. Carroll, A. Carney, N. Howe, B. Bolton, N. Crozier, J. Moore, R. Austin, M. Pilon, A. Armstrong, J. Scott and W. McIlwain.

BATHURST: J. Coleman, L. Hadley, P. Burns, G. Patterson, W. Ezzy, M. Kennedy, D. Oates, K. Tonkin, W. Garlick, E. Funnell, P. Harris, T. Copeland and K. Wright.

Bathurst Railway defeated Dubbo 32-11.

Article from: The Dubbo and Macquarie Advocate, Thursday, September 15, 1949 Republished courtesy of ACM/Dubbo and Macquarie Advocate.

1949 Cargo Rugby League Team

Standing (LtoR): John Middleton, Stu Middleton, John Fisher, Doug Fisher, Joe Kelly, Jim Sullivan, Neville Sargent, Jack Middleton, Ned Kelly, Henry Sargent, Max Fields, Max Sargent, Cyrill Mitchell.
Seated: Mick Fisher, Bill Cain, Fisher (Junior), Dan Seal.

Interesting Statistics Cargo Football Team:

Cargo football teams mostly comprised of 4 families. There were 28 Middletons, 22 Fishers, 11 Regans and 11 Thornberrys. The Cargo First Grade Premiership side of 1955 had 9 Middletons in the team.

The Cargo first grade football team were premiers five times in Group Eastern: 1949, 1950, 1954, 1955, 1958. They also played in many Gold Cup matches played on Saturdays in the 1950s, which were as tough as grand finals at times. In 34 games for the famous trophy, Cargo only lost 7 times.

Courtesy of: Canowindra Historical Society & Museum Inc.

Rugby League

1949 CHAMPIONS OF THE WEST
BATHURST RAILWAY BEATS DUBBO DISTRICT
RECORD CROWD £250 "GATE"

September 1949

Playing hard, rugged and at times exhilarating football, Bathurst Railway Club at Wade Park Orange yesterday beat Dubbo District, champions of Group 11, by 32 points to 9, Railway team recently won the championship of Group 10.

It was a game in which all the honours rested with the Bathurst team. At no time did they appear to be in danger.

A Record crowd of approximately 3,500 witnessed the game. A special train brought Dubbo supporters whilst Bathurst supporters rolled up in large numbers to support the local combination. The sum of £250 was taken at the gates.

Article from: The National Advocate Bathurst, Monday, September 19, 1949. Republished courtesy of ACM/National Advocate Bathurst.

Tumut's One Point Win in Group 9-17 Grand Final at Cootamundra

Tumut defeated Griffith by one point in the grand final of the 1949 Group 9-17 Rugby League competition at Cootamundra yesterday Tumut wins by 11 points to 10.

August 1949

The game was played before a crowd which paid £135 at the gate. The match was very hard with most of the play confined in the forwards. Tumut deserved their win. They were the lighter side and had to fight from bell to bell because of Griffith's superiority in the scrums.

- Griffith led 7-4 at half time.
- Tumut scored one try and converted four goals.
- Griffith scored two tries and converted two goals.
- Final score Tumut 11, Griffith 10.

Tumut team:
F. Dowling, D. Cullen, N. Brogan, G. Cook, A. Shelly, P. Roddy, M. Harris, K. Wade, J. Flint, E. Shelly, J. Alston, F. Stanfield, E. Wortes.

Griffith team:
T. Bourke, O'Doughlan, F. McNabb, K. Bridge, R. Mathews, B. Smith, J. Phitzner, P. Galvin, J. Kelly, W. Tilden, C. McNabb, M. Navin, J. Ford.

Article from: The Daily Advertiser Wagga, August 29, 1949. Republished courtesy of ACM/Daily Advertiser Wagga.

COOTAMUNDRA'S GREAT MAHER CUP WIN

At Fisher Park, on Saturday, Cootamundra completely outplayed Tumut to hold the Maher Cup in the final game of the 1949 series. Cootamundra won by 38 points to 5. September 1949

A very large crowd packed Fisher Park, on Saturday, to see the clash between Tumut, the Group 9 competition winners and Cootamundra the Maher Cup holder. Tumut having defeated Harden-Murrumburrah in the Zone 1 semi-final and Griffith in the competition grand-final, could well claim that it was the leading team in Group 9 and 17.

It was realised by local supporters that the boys from the hills would provide stern opposition for "Walsh Warriors". However, Cootamundra was quietly confident that it could stop the light blues' victorious run. How Cootamundra handed out one of the most convincing Maher Cup defeats of all time will be something to talk about whilst ever this town remains the great football team which it is.

Nobody who saw Saturday's game could have any doubt which is the champion football team of the Riverina.

It is doubtful if any country team in N.S.W. could have held Cootamundra on Saturday's form.

The gate was £225.

Cootamundra: 38 (J. Schofield, J. Henniker, R. McDonell, 2, N. McDonell, J. Crowe tries, L. Wheatley try, 5 goals)
Defeated Tumut 5
(P. Roddy try, K. Wade goal).

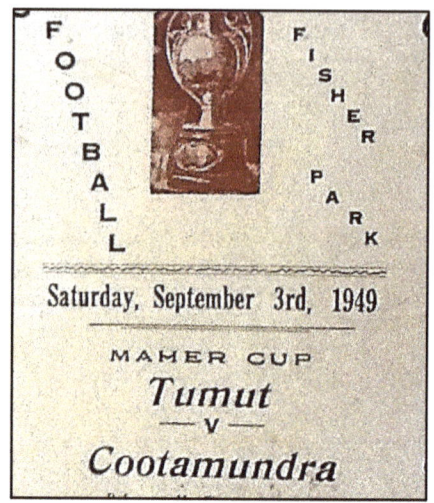

Tumut Team: F. Dowling, G. Cook, J. Roddy, A. Shelley, Y. Lyons, P. Roddy, M. Harris, K. Wade, J. Flint, E. Shelley, J. Alston, F. Stanfield, E. Wortes.

Article from: The Cootamundra Herald, September 5, 1949 Republished courtesy of ACM/Cootamundra Herald.

1949 Cootamundra Rugby League Team

Back Row: Bede McDonnell (referee), Jack "Onion" Bell, Lionel Wheatley, Keith Tull, John Gillette, Roley McDonell, Mick Howse, Phill Michael, Bill Baker, Jack Malone.
Front Row: Harold Fuller, Jim Crowe, Jack Schofield, Jack "Duck" Walsh (Captain Coach), Leslie Fuller (Ball boy), Kevin Wheatley, Jack "Junior" Henniker, Noel Crowe, Ken Mulrooney, Ray Ward, Les Wood.
Keith Tull, was selected in the 1949 Country Firsts Team as a centre and goal-kicker.

Courtesy of: Neil Pollock, Maher Cup author.

THE FIFTIES

Football (rugby league) starts to be played in group competitions and this section includes Group 10, 11, 14 and 15 teams, players and premiership winning teams: Baradine Magpies, Cobar, Condobolin, Coonamble, Lithgow Small Arms Factory, Peak Hill, Narromine, Parkes, Forbes, Dubbo Macquarie, Orange CYMS and Temora.

Macquarie wins three premierships in a row and Parkes wins all three grades creating a record. Cootamundra and Temora win the Group 9 premierships. Baradine Magpies created a Goup 14 record winning five consecutive premierships from 1951-1955.

Newspaper articles describe how the game was played and the players who were prevalent in Group 11 during the fifties including Leo Nosworthy, Ian Walsh, Bob Weir, John George and Don Parish to mention a few.

It was a time of three-point tries, unlimited tackles and the hooker was a major factor in a team's success by winning the scrums and gaining ball possession.

Rugby League
HARD TRAINING FOR PEAK HILL MATCH
July 1950

The Wellington Rugby League first grade team will be out to avenge its first round defeat at the hands of the Peak Hill team when it travels to Peak Hill next Sunday. The Wellington team's stocks are high following the convincing win over Narromine last Sunday. Enthusiasm and keenness at training is the highest since early in the season.

The Wellington selectors have retained the team which played last Sunday, although there is some doubt of the fitness of winger Bruce Smith who injured his shoulder in last Sunday's match.

Coach Les Lay has concentrated on movements from the ruck and scrum base at training this week and the Wellington forwards will on Sunday give greater protection to the little half-back find, Doug Parrish.

The Peak Hill team, led by ex-Sydney player F. "Buster" Harvey, has improved remarkably this season with halves, slippery Brian Barnes and newcomer K. Sharkey, playing particularly fine football.

Ex-Wellington All Blacks player H. Keeds will play centre for Peak Hill. Keeds has developed into a robust, hard-running and sure tackling centre and had proved one of Peak Hill's most consistently good players. His clash with former team mate Herb Smith should be interesting.

THE TEAMS

Wellington:
Fullback: C. Johnson.
Back-Line: P. Brown, H. Smith, B. Cohen, A. Turner, B. Smith (one to be omitted).
Halves: J. George, D. Parrish.
Lock: T. George.
Second row: J. Huggett, J. Cornish.
Props: C. Colllins, W. Darney.
Rake: K. Elgar.

Peak Hill:
Fullback: B. Zeidler.
Wingers: F. Harvey, D. Walker.
Centres: H. Keeds, K. Wright.
Halves: K. Sharkey, B. Barnes.
Lock: K. Jones.
Second row: K. Rodda, H. Graham.
Props: S. Carey, K. Stone.
Rake: L. Rodwell.

The Wellington buses will leave at 9:30 a.m. Limited bookings are available at C.J. Frecklington's and the Club House Hotel.

Article from: The Wellington Times, Thursday, July 6, 1950. Republished courtesy of ACM/Wellington Times.

Condobolin Wins Group 11 Grand Final Defeating Dubbo 16-6
Minor Premiers & Premiers
Gate Record Smashed Receipts Total £340

September 1950

A Western District football record was shattered at Spooner Oval last Sunday, when gate-takings and programme receipts totalled £340 for the Group 11 grand final between Dubbo and Condobolin.

Norm Jacobson

When the teams met in the final the previous week, Dubbo won, 10-8, but Condobilin displayed wonderful team work in the grand final to turn the tables and convincingly win by 16 points to 6.

The exhibition given by the teams was well worthy of the large attendance and the thunderous roars of the rival barrackers.

A magnificent exhibition by captain coach Norm Jacobson, plus the superb physical condition of his team, paved the way for Conobolin's slashing victory.

Final Scores: Condobolin: Tries-K. Hall (2) C. McAlister and J. Walsh (1). Goals-H. Wright (2). **Dubbo:** Goal-E. Bennett (3).

Teams:

Condobolin: Full-back-H. Wright, Three-quarters-N. Holmes, N. Jacobson (Captain-Coach), N. Bell, C. McAlister, Five-eighth-R. Collins, Half-back-K. Hall, Forwards-R. Morris, N. Staines, R. Jefferies, I. Walsh, I. Roberts, N. Bacigalupo.

Dubbo: Full-back-R. See, Three-quarters-N. Howe, L. Whites, R. Dalmazzo, J. Dunn, Five-eighth-E. Bennett (Captain-Coach), Half-back-J. O'Keefe, Forwards-G. Clarke, M. Pilon, G. Armstrong, W. Hill, J. Scott, J. Hands.

Referee: Mr. McAlpine (Parkes).

Article from: The Forbes Advocate, September, 1950. Republished courtesy of ACM/Forbes Advocate.

1950 Condobolin Rugby League Team Group XI Premiers Defeats Dubbo

President's Report:

Mr. Norman Doyle, President, submitted his report for the 1950 season.

LADIES & GENTLEMEN.

I wish to submit the following brief outline of the activities of the Condobolin District Rugby League for season 1950. During the season the Condobolin League reached its goal and achieved its ambition when it became champion of Group 11 and holders of the coveted Group Shield which was last held by Condo in the early years' of 1930s seasons, under the leadership of the popular Jack Coote, when it was the Challenge Trophy.

Condobolin came from the bottom of the competition ladder in 1947 to the top in 1950, an achievement of which any team would be proud. It represents a triumph of perseverance, patience and good management and a real feather in the cap of our Captain Coach, Norm Jacobson and the players who one and all gave him their full measure of support and co-operation.

Jack played five first grade seasons with the Sydney Roosters 1929, 1930, 1935, 1936 and 1937.

During the early 1930s Jack was captain coach of Condobolin, New South Wales and won the premiership shield with them in 1931. He retired at the end of the 1937 NSWRFL season.

Article from: Lachlander and Condobolin Western, February, 1951. Republished courtesy of ACM/Forbes Advocate.

Lindner Oval Home of Rugby League in Peak Hill

Most people would associate Lindner Oval with sport, in particular Rugby League. The local team, Peak Hill Roosters, play their home games at Lindner Oval where the vocal crowd cheer them on, despite the lack of recent success. However, 1951 saw Peak Hill crowned as premiers of Group 11 in the Country Rugby League Competition.

Courtesy of: Parkes Shire Library. A History of Peak Hill and District.

1951 Peak Hill Wins Group Championship

WELLINGTON DEFEATED 12-0 RODDA SCORES TWO TRIES

Before an all-time record crowd for an inter-town match, Peak Hill defeated Wellington 12-0. Peak Hill played like a team inspired, each man rising to the occasion grandly and proving themselves worthy holders of the Group Champions for 1951.

Article from: Peak Hill Express, Friday, September 7, 1951. Republished courtesy of ACM/Peak Hill Express.

Central Hotel Peak Hill

Where the Peak Hill Roosters head after the game.

Courtesy of: Parkes Shire Library. A History of Peak Hill and District.

1951 Peak Hill Rugby League Team Group 11 Premiers

Back Row: "Nobby" Charters, Bruce Zeidler, Kevin Stanford, "Boy" Tipping, Kevin Stone, Harold Keed, Rex Wagstaff.

Middle Row: Kevin Wright, Ray Stone, Ron Wilkinson, Colby Doyle, Henry Rodda, Ray Elliott, Darcy Walker.

Front Row: Brian Barnes, Laurie Rodwell, Jack Lackey Captain/Coach, John Fulmer, Ray Foulkes.

Mascot: Peter Tipping.

Courtesy of: Parkes Shire Library. A History of Peak Hill and District.

1951 Wellington Rugby League Team

Back Row: John "Blue" Huggett, John George, Herb Smith, Leo Chemello, Alf Thomas, Bulley Lee, Pat Rich, Claude Collins.

Front Row: Doug Parrish, Bruce Smith, Rolf Trudgett, Clarrie Johnson, Joe Cohen.

NSWRL.

Courtesy of: Wellington Historical Society.

1950 Cobar Rugby League Team Group 15 Premiers

Back Row: Dick Obray, Bossie Mitchell, Les Harris, Fabian Jermyn, Jack Rimmer, Dick Jackson, Authur Merlow, Bobby Walsh.

Front Row: Doug Bellchambers, Bruce Coath, Kevin Neale, Bill Neale (Coach), Billy Collins, Alan Gillgan.

Cobar defeated Warren at Nyngan Oval 7/2.

Courtesy of: John Collins. The Crowing of the Roosters.

1951 Baradine Magpies Rugby League Team

Baradine Magpies First Grade Rugby League Team, created a Group 14 record with five consecutive winning premierships:
1951, 1952, 1953, 1954 and 1955.

Back Row: Kevin Head, Gordon Head, Jim Birchell, John Deans, Joe Kable, Billy Wilson (Captain Coach), John Davies.

Front Row: Pappy Masman, Peter Sheridan, Ken Meyers, Gordan Taylor, Noel Ashby, Merv Edwards.

Courtesy of: Gregory Maher.

1952 Wellington Rugby League Team

Back Row: Frank Smith, Teddy Donn, Ned Williams, Eddie Donn, Brian Charlton, John Huggett, Keith Miller.

Front Row: Jack Garnish, Eric King, Geoff Chamberlain, Noel Reynolds, Ken Dowton, Les Dowton, Arthur Pont, Kevin Miller (ball boy).

Courtesy of: Geoff Mann, Sports Journalist, Dubbo.

1952 Orange CYMS Rugby League Team Group 10 Premiers

Orange Cyms win three consecutive grand finals in the Group 10 Rugby League Competition.

Grand Final results:
1952 defeated Bathurst Charleston 13-2.
1953 defefeated Lithgow St Patricks 9-4.
1954 defeated Lithgow Small Arms 7-2 and Clayton Cup winners.

Back Row: D. McInerney, T. Thurn, E. Mitchell, R. Mitchell, J. West, W. Fitzpatrick, R. Kerwick, D. Bacigalupo.

Middle Row: W. Carroll (Manager), D. Crump, A. Kelly, J. Cudmore (Captain), Rev. N.F. Grant, T. Kerwick, J. Hennesy, L. Commins, P. Newland (Coach).

Front Row: L. Davidson, T. Ryan (Mascot), T. Hagar, V. Byrne.

Courtesy of: Group 10, Orange CYMS Rugby League Club.

Old rivals meet in league final

A record crowd is expected at Narromine Oval on Sunday next when Wellington will meet traditional rivals, Dubbo, in the final of Group Eleven Rugby League competition.

September 1952

On the following Sunday the winners of the final will meet Narromine in a grand final.

Whether Wellington can defeat Dubbo is a question being hotly debated in the town and district.

Wellington and Dubbo are the traditional "enemies" of the Group and a meeting of these teams would have drawn a record gate.

The teams had the opportunity, but the Dubbo executive wanted the match played at Dubbo and refused to toss a coin to decide whether it would be Wellington or Dubbo grounds.

The stalemate was solved when the Group executive allotted the game to Narromine ground.

During the competition the teams have each had a victory over one another. Wellington won 10-9 at Dubbo in the first round. While at Wellington in the second round Dubbo won 14-7 after Wellington had led 7-0 at half time.

Each side has had a victory over Forbes, but Dubbo had beaten Narromine which feat has so far, been beyond Wellington.

Since the resignation, through injury, of former coach, Tom Lawler, Mr. Les Lay has been coaching the team.

Mr Lay, who coached Wellington in former years and who also coached the Western Division team which met the Frenchmen, has had immediate success with two consecutive wins.

Asked his opinion about Sunday's game, Mr. Lay said, "It's a funny game, football, but I would say Wellington has a good chance."

League President, Mr. O. Schwarzer, commented "Now it is our turn. " No one would have this team, but, believe me, when I say that I really think the boys will win on Sunday and then win the grand final as I predicted several weeks ago.

"They have hit top gear at the right time," Mr. Schwarzer added.

Other staunch league followers, Messrs Jim Bourke, Jack Bliss, Claude Gersbach and Harry Wykes, considered the team has moulded into a formidable combination and could easily win the competition.

NO CHANGES IN TEAM

Narromine:
The selectors have not made any changes in the team, which is:
Fullback: C. Johnson.
Wingers: L. Dowton, C. Williams.
Centres: B. Cohen, K. Bell.
Five-eighth: B. Smith.
Half: W. Gaynon.
Lock: A. Thomas (Captain).
Second Row: J. Cornish, B.Lee.
Props: O. Collins, P. Mcharg.
Hooker: C. Bell.
Reserve: W. Fowler.

Dubbo:
The Dubbo team, as announced is:
Fullback: T. Rutherford.
Wingers: D. Priddis, R. Dobson.
Centres: B. Bolton, A. Howe.
Five-eighth: K. Deacon (Captain).
Half: V. Lance.
Lock: E. Dodd or K. Finn.
Second Row: B. Perry, N. Whitely.
Props: A. Armstrong, N. Wallace.
Hooker: J. Warner.

The referee Mr N Johnson.

Article from: Dubbo Liberal and Macquarie Advocate, Thursday, September 2, 1952. Republished courtesy of ACM/Dubbo Liberal and Macquarie Advocate.

Dubbo Wins Group 11 Football Final-Parkes Defeated 19 to 9

(By "Centre")

September 1952

Dubbo won the Group XI Rugby League championship on Sunday when it defeated Parkes by 19 points to nine.

The win was a triumph for Dubbo forwards who out-rucked and out-hooked their opponents and showed superiority in every department of forward play. The win gave Dubbo a record of no defeats this season on its home ground. About 2300 people saw the match.

Alan Armstrong stood out as the star Dubbo forward. The manner in which he ran from the rucks and set his back line moving was a feature of the game.

George Clarke capped off a grand performance with two tries and a goal.

George has been Dubbo's most consistent player this year and he will go down in the records as one of the most valuable players and staunchest club men the town has had.

Jack Warner, who has had mixed success as a centre forward, rose to the occasion and paved the way to victory by winning the set scrums by 21 to 16.

Jim Moore, as lock forward, did all that was asked of him and the way he looked after the halfback Walsh, was a vital factor in the win.

Ned Dodd and Noel Whiteley worked hard and helped to complete a grand performance by the Dubbo forwards.

Deacon Outstanding

Deacon as usual was outstanding. This young coach has obtained great results and has risen to the occasion when most needed.

His behaviour on and off the field has been exemplary and the congratulations of every lover of Rugby League football goes to him for the excellent job he has done for the code in Dubbo.

John George was a thorn in the side of the Parkes backs.

Ron Dobson's strong runs helped to send George on his way time and time again. His tackling was outstanding and was the cause of quietening Chew and Noakes.

Last and not least in the Dubbo team was fullback Brian Bolton. His handling and positional play was in international class.

If only he could have developed a strong kick with either foot he might easily have been on a tour of England.

Chew won the toss and forced Dubbo to run into the sun.

After ten minutes of play it was evident that Dubbo would be hard to beat. The forwards settled down to their task immediately and gained superiority.

The first thrill of the game came when Chew picked up a dropped pass by Dobson from Deacon and nearly went in. A fine tackle by Bolton stopped the movement.

Dubbo's first points came from a ruck on the Parkes 25-yard line.

Cole running through fast picked up a loose ball and went through untroubled to score wide out. Clarke failed to convert.

Best Movement

Dubbo went to a 6-nil lead with the best movement of the match. Carter sent a fast pass to Deacon who cut four men out and passed to George. George with a tricky run, beat the rest and passed to Clarke, who had come through fast to make the extra man, who scored in the corner.

Chew opened Parkes' score with a nice penalty goal from near the side line but just before half time, Clarke made the score 8-2 when he landed a penalty from 40 yards out.

Dubbo applied the pressure from the commencement of the second half and it was not long before it went further ahead. Armstrong broke from the ruck, ran through some would-be tacklers and passed to George who went in under the posts. Deacon converted and Dubbo had a commanding lead 13-2.

Chew kicked another goal and then Armstrong made another try with a fine run-down field, he could have easily scored himself but passed to Clarke who was in support and Clarke registered his second try.

From a scrummage on the Dubbo 25, McDonald broke through to register Parkes' first try. Chew converted to make the score 16-9.

Parkes fought back at this stage and looked like dominating play when Clarke intercepted a pass from Chew to Noakes. He sped down centre field and passed to Dobson who with a determined run, scored well out.

This was the last score of the match and at the final bell Dubbo had emerged Group Champion by 19 points to 9.

Parkes First Grade Team Training Squad:
J. Jones, F. Chew, H. Tomkins, O. Sykes, R. Daniels, M. Rodgers, T. Noakes, A. Frawley, B. Bailey, N. Kelly, F. Jones, L. Prior, I. Johnstone, A. Willis, W. Davis, P. Ryan, "Saus" Dwyer, Norm Miskell (Coach).

Article from: Dubbo Liberal and Macquarie Advocate, Thursday, September 2, 1952. Republished courtesy of ACM/Dubbo Liberal and Macquarie Advocate.

1952 Western League Championship
Dubbo Wins Western League Championship
Dubbo 8 defeated Orange CYMS 5

Ex-Lithgow footballer Ron Dobson yesterday rocked the powerful Orange-CYMS side with a whirlwind try which put Dubbo on the road to winning the Championship of the West. Dubbo won 8-5 after one of the most hotly-contested League battles ever staged at the City Sportsground.

Scores:
Dubbo: Two tries were scored for Dubbo by Ron Dobson, Howe and Deacon kicked a goal.
Orange CYMS centre three-quarter Cummins touched down a try and Cudmore kicked a goal.

Article from: The Lithgow Mercury, September 15, 1952. Republished courtesy of ACM/Lithgow Mercury.

DUBBO LEAGUE TEAM TO PLAY HERE ON SUNDAY
(By "Centre")

April 1953

Dubbo Rugby League supporters will have their first opportunity next Sunday of assessing the real value of their team, when Dubbo will meet Wellington on the Dubbo oval.

In its two previous matches Dubbo showed that it has the material to regain the Group trophy and that it possesses the leader capable of achieving that goal. However it must be realised that every team in Group 11 is stronger than it was last year because all teams, for the first time in the history of Group 11, are led by State "glamour" players.

Dubbo: has its year's coach Keith Deacon.
Wellington: has Balmain five-eighth Tommy Lawer.
Parkes: Manly Warringah's half back Ken Arthurson.
Condobolin: State hooker Ken Fogarty.
Peak Hill: Renowned State forward "Dutchie" Holland.
Canowindra: The wooden spooners of the group over the last two years, has engaged prolific goal kicker, International centre and Australian Captain Joe Joergenson.
Narromine: has won its three trials against Warren, Dubbo and Peak Hill.
Parkes: has lost to both Forbes and Condobolin and Wellington lost to Dubbo.
Nothing is known here of Canowindra trial matches.

Rough Tactics

Unfortunately some of the trial matches have produced rough and unsavoury football.

At Narromine two reserve grade players were sent from the field for punching in the match against Dubbo.

Peak Hill lost "Dutchie" Holland on the same ground a week later.

Three players were sent off for illegal play in the Condobolin-Parkes trial. They were Ken Fogarty (Condobolin) and V. Frawley and J. Heggie of Parkes.

Ex-country representative player Fred Chew fractured his nose in the same match.

At last Monday's meeting of the Dubbo League the Judiciary Committee for 1953 was appointed. The members comprising this committee are Messrs: Stroud, Musgrove, Brook, Fitzgerald, and Egan. All these men have had considerable experience in this thankless work.

At the next League meeting, the selection committee for the season will be chosen.

Ken Arthurson AM: In a match between Northern and Southern Zones in April 1953, Parkes' First Grade Coach was badly injured. He spent three months in hospital recuperating from a fractured skull and never played Rugby League again. Ken Arthurson went on to be one of Rugby League's greatest administrators, rising to become Chairman of the Australian Rugby League from 1984 to 1997.

Article from: Dubbo Liberal and Macquarie Advocate, Thursday, April 16, 1953. Republished courtesy of ACM/Dubbo Liberal and Macquarie Advocate.

1953 Rugby League Notes

Group 11 First Grade Competition Table

TEAMS:	Play	Win	Loss	Draw	Points F	Points A	Points Table
NARROMINE	14	11	3	0	199	104	22
FORBES	14	10	3	1	230	104	21
DUBBO	14	9	4	1	218	112	19
WELLINGTON	14	6	6	2	145	176	14
PARKES	14	6	7	1	175	174	13
PEAK HILL	14	4	10	0	110	169	8
CANOWINDRA	14	3	9	2	110	278	8
CONDOBOLIN	14	2	9	3	129	192	7

Forbes missed the minor premiership by a single point, but supporters should not lose heart. Under the captaincy of Athol Halpin and good team spirit and co-operation, Forbes came right into the forefront of Group 11 football, with all three teams' firsts, reserves and under 18's qualifying for the inter-town semi-finals. Until the last game by Dubbo, Forbes appeared certain to finish at the top of the first-grade points table.

Dubbo seems to be Forbes' hoodoo team each year. It is the only team to beat Forbes twice this season. Forbes players are not likely to give a thought to the jinx as an extra opponent to be conquered to secure the prize-money. Halpin and his men are still brimful of confidence and determination.

Article from: Forbes Advocate, Friday, August 14, 1953. Republished by courtesy of ACM/Forbes Advocate.

Wellington Beat Dubbo 9-6 in League Group Final

August 1953

Before a record crowd, which completely filled Narromine Sports Oval yesterday, the Wellington Rugby League team won the final of Group Eleven competition by inflicting defeat on favourites Dubbo.

The game was dominated by hard rucking. Wellington forwards who, despite the loss of ball in set scrums, overcame this disadvantage by consistently obtaining possession from the rucks.

Wellington was always in command of the game, which was a thrilling match worthy of a Group final and Wellington fully deserved their win.

A splendid try by Bruce Cohen early in the second half gave Wellington a 7-2 lead.

Article from: Wellington Times, Monday, August 31, 1953. Republished courtesy of ACM/Wellington Times.

Record crowd expected for League Grand Final at Dubbo on Sunday

Wellington Rugby League representative team will play Narromine in the grand final of the Group Eleven competition at Dubbo on Sunday next when a record crowd is expected.

In the early match at 1.30 p.m., Cumnock, winners of the Eastern Division, will play Fifield, winners of the Western Division, in a match that should be a fitting curtain raiser for the big game.

September 1953

The match will bring League football to a close for the season, although the winners will endeavour to win the Bruce Campbell Cup for the premier team in Western NSW.

Holder of the Cup, Dubbo, were eliminated last Sunday.

Wellington and Narromine teams are evenly matched, although Narromine has the more imposing record, being undefeated by Wellington either this year or last.

In the last match of the second round of the 1952 season Wellington were defeated by Narromine 12-10 to eliminate Wellington from the semi-finals.

This year Narromine has defeated Wellington on both occasions, the teams have met 22-12 at Narromine and 5-3 at Wellington.

In the last match Wellington led 12-4 at half time, but were overwhelmed in the second half. In the game at Wellington both sides scored one try and the game was won for Narromine when fullback Powell kicked a field goal near the half way line.

The Narromine team includes several outstanding players in Nosworthy, McCarry and Powell and the team went through the first round of the current competition undefeated.

In the second round of the competition, the team met defeat at the hands of Parkes, Forbes and Dubbo and the latter team also scored in the semi-final last Sunday week.

Mr. F. Ring appointed referee

The appointment of Mr. Fred Ring, of Wellington, as referee for this important match is a distinct compliment to him.

Mr. Ring is regarded by many as the best referee in the country districts.

The action of the Group in appointing a Wellington resident as referee is an indication of the fairness and accurate interpretation of the rules which has marked his career as a referee.

THE TEAMS:
WELLINGTON
Fullback: C. Johnson
Wingers: C. Williams, B. Cohen
Centres: K. Bell, H. Smith
Five-eighth: B. Smith
Scrum-half: W. Gaynon
Lock: A. Thomas (Captain)
Second Row: J. Cornish, B. Lee
Props: C. Collins, P. Meharg
Hooker: C. Bell
Reserve: W. Fowler.

NARROMINE
Fullback: J. Powell
Wingers: D. Gardner, D. Oates
Centres: A. Abbott, E. Robertson
Five-eighth: L. Nosworthy (Captain)
Scrum-half: J. McGarry
Lock: R. Walsh
Second Row: J. Weir, J. Smith
Props: W. Darney, J. Dundas
Hooker: R. Smith.

The train for Dubbo leaves Wellington at approximatley 10.15 a.m. and will leave Dubbo on the return journey at approximately 6 p.m.

Article from: The Dubbo Liberal and Macquarie Advocate, Thursday, September 3, 1953. Republished courtesy of ACM/Dubbo Liberal.

Narromine 1953 Group Premiers Wellington Defeated 25-8 Before Record Crowd

(By the Narromine League Reporter)

In a brilliant display of fast, open football Narromine defeated Wellington 25/8 at Dubbo on Sunday to win the Group XI premiership, the shield and a prize of £250.

Visitors from points as far apart as Condobolin, Bourke and Orange joined with what appeared to be the combined populations of Wellington and Narromine in paying just on £800 to see the grand-final.

September 1953

Winning the toss Wellington's skipper Thomas decided to play into a fairly strong breeze. From the very start Narromine skipper Nosworthy had his team on the attack and soon had Wellington in trouble. Kelvin Oates tried a run on the wing and Jock Weir had an attempt at goal. Shortly afterwards Powell raised the flags with a two pointer.

Wellington advanced into Narromine territory and Gaynon had an unsuccessful shot at goal, but Jack Smith made a good run down the blind side and again was almost in.

McGarry ran from the base of the scrum, Powell came in, passed to Nosworthy, who beat the opposition to score under the posts. Powell converted and Narromine led 7/0.

WELLINGTON SCORES

Gaynon's third attempt at goal gave Wellington their first score, but Powell landed another goal to maintain Narromine's lead.

Dick Smith was winning a good share of the ball, McGarry was constantly varying play and with Nosworthy exploring the blind side. Powell was coming up to join in passing movements and when McGarry beat the defence he was there to take the ball and go over wide out, converting the try to make the score 14/2.

The tackling of Walsh, Nosworthy, Robertson and Abbot was playing havoc with the maroon backs.

Wellington attacked and Gaynon added another two pointer heartening Wellington players and supporters, but half time came with Narromine 10 points in the lead.

SECOND HALF

Wellington came back full of fight for the second half. Aided by the breeze they had Narromine defending and when Gaynon added two goals and brought the score to 14/8 Wellington supporters became vocal.

Then, in a dash down the centre, Nosworthy passed to Kelvin Oates, on to Walsh, who went over but was recalled.

From then on the pace was fast. Narromine players were handling the ball in brilliant passing bursts which had spectators on their feet. It was classical football. Wellington was kicking to relieve pressure but the ball would be brought back putting Wellington on the defence again.

With the result a foregone conclusion Narromine put even more vigor into the game. Dick Smith was playing a whale of a game in the open as well as winning the ball from the scrums.

Getting the ball from a set scrum McGarry ran for the open side, drew the defence and in-passed to Walsh, who went over unopposed.

Article from: Narromine News & Trangie Advocate Tuesday, September 8, 1953. Republished courtesy of ACM/Narromine News & Trangie Advocate.

1953 Narromine Group 11 Rugby League Premiership
Western Divisional Championship Cup Winners

1953 Narromine Group 11 Premiers

Back Row: Max Milgate, Ashly Abbot, Fred Wilkins Jnr, Jock Weir,
Fred Wilkins Snr, Joe Dundas, Doug Oates, Jack Smith.
Front Row: John McGarry, Ron Walsh, Jack Powell,
Leo Nosworthy, Kevin Oates, Unc (Ewen) Roberts.

1953 Orange CYMS Group 10 Premiers

Orange CYMS Rugby League team
Left to Right J. Ryan, J. Kelly, W. Fitzpatrick, J. Thurn, J. Dalton,
V. Byrne, T. Hagar, L. Davidson, L. Cummins, E. Mitchell,
J. Redmond, R. Patten, J. Hennessy.

N.S.W. Country Rugby League Presents

Western Divisional CHAMPIONSHIP

FOR BRUCE CAMPBELL CUP

Narromine, Sept. 20, 1953

ORANGE CYMS
(GROUP X PREMIERS)

v

NARROMINE
(GROUP XI PREMIERS)

Referee: Mr. F. Ring.
Linesmen: Messrs. R. Walsh and V. Ryan.

PRICE 1/-   N° 818

Narromine rounded off a most successful season by defeating Orange CYMS on Sunday to win the title of Western Division champions and presented with the Bruce Campbell Cup for the next twelve months.

Mr. J. Hartcher of Forbes, secretary of Group 11 and secretary of Western Division Rugby League, presented the Bruce Campbell Cup to Leo Nosworthy captain coach of Narromine.

Courtesy of: Macquarie Regional Library (Narromine) and Orange CYMS Rugby League Club.

Transport Between Games Started To Change With Car Ownership

Wikipedia.Org/Wiki/Holden

After the hardship and deprivation of the 1930s and the anxiety and rationing of the 1940s, Australia experienced great optimism, growth and prosperity in the 1950s.

A Holden was the first car many families owned and ended up being a 'must have' possession. It boosted national pride and was an outward symbol of personal prosperity.

The car enabled country rugby league-supporters to follow their teams and in most cases were allowed to park around the football field perimeter.
Pioneer Oval at Parkes is a great example of viewing the game from your car.

The sound of car horns would echo as the teams scored tries.

Parkes' Forwards Dump Narromine In Thrilling Final

(By "Hooker")

1954 Grand Final

The tigerish tackling and play by the Parkes forwards against the favoured Narromine team paved the way for their victory in the 1954 Group XI Rugby League premiership on Sunday.

Forced to play one man short for 70 minutes of the game, Parkes players shadowed key Narromine players and allowed them no room in which to move and played brilliant football to clinch victory. Parkes gained the lead from an early penalty and were never headed, although Narromine which opened its account in the second half, looked likely to score on several occasions and provided the crowd of 2400 at Parkes with many thrills.

September 1954

Two minutes after the start of play Narromine was penalised for a ruck infringement and Macdonald landed a nice goal for Parkes to lead two-nil.

Not to be denied Narromine drove play back to the Parkes' 25 where Darcy, the Narromine left winger, appeared to be in a scoring position but the cover defence dragged him down inches from the line.

Parkes was on the defensive when Goodwin relieved the pressure with a good line kick to get his team out of trouble.

It was now the home team that was on the attack and once again Narromine forwards were caught offside, this time was right under their own goal posts and Macdonald made no mistake with his kick. Parkes 4, Narromine 0.

It was after Macdonald landed his second goal that winger, Chew, of Parkes broke down with an old injury and he was unable to take any further part in the match.

It was tough luck for Parkes and this meant a re-organisation of players with centre Cunco being moved on to the wing and lock Gain was brought out into the centre.

Nosworthy was now switching play back into his forwards, but the Parkes pack was holding its own in the tight play.

A lucky break came for Parkes when a Narromine forward kicked downfield to fullback Cudmore, who caught the ball 30 yards out and with no effort kicked a field goal. Parkes 6, Narromine Nil.

Receiving the ball just over half way Nosworthy broke through and looked dangerous but his pass went astray. Noakes picked up the loose ball and racing 40 yards passed the ball infield to Priestley who passed to Willis then on to Goodwin who dropped the ball with a clear field ahead.

If Goodwin had held the pass, Parkes would have gone further ahead as Bargwanna was out of position and the Narromine defence was beaten.

Just before half time Darcy appeared as though he must go in, but centre Noakes sent him crashing out of touch right in the corner with a full-blooded tackle.

Half time scores were: Parkes 6 Narromine Nil.

Soon after play started in the second half, Narromine registered its first points when Bargwanna kicked a penalty goal from just wide of the posts on the 25. Parkes 6 Narromine 2.

Play was now beginning to become tough and the referee was kept busy handing out cautions mostly to Narromine players and from a penalty Macdonald raised the flags for his third goal. Parkes 8, Narromine 2.

Once again Narromine was on the attack and from a ruck McGarry raced to the blind side, well timed a pass to Nosworthy for the latter to crash his way over in the corner with the defenders on top of him. Bargwanna missed with the kick. Parkes 8, Narromine 5.

Excitement was now running high and once again the referee was kept on his toes watching rough play.

Nosworthy had shifted Wilcox out to the wing position and Darcy was playing five-eighth.

This appeared a bad move as the cover defence of Parkes would not give Darcy any room in which to move in and this player is very dangerous in attack when he has room to get moving.

Continued next page:

Article from: The Dubbo Liberal and Macquarie Advocate, Tuesday, September 7, 1954. Republished courtesy of ACM/Dubbo and Macquarie Advocate.

Parkes' Forwards Dump Narromine In Thrilling Final
(By "Hooker")
1954 Grand Final

Continued from previous page:

The match was put beyond doubt when Priestly scored in the corner to make the final scores Parkes, 11 Narromine 5.

Parkes forwards covered themselves with glory on Sunday. Having to play a man short in the pack, due to the injury of Chew, they out played the experienced Narromine six in all departments, except the set scrums.

Although beaten for the ball in the scrums, Dwyer made amends by helping to retrieve the ball from the rucks.

Best player on the ground was Gain, as against Dubbo last week he gave a classical display. He outplayed Walsh and his tackling of Nosworthy and Wilcox was devastating. His work with Noakes was one of the factors of his team's victory.

Cudmore shaded Bargwanna on the day. He often caught Bargwanna out of position and his line kicking had more direction.

Jock Weir was the best of the forwards and gave a tireless display of hard forward play.

The Referee was Mr. Fred Ring of Wellington.

Article from: The Dubbo Liberal and Macquarie Advocate, Tuesday, September 7, 1954. Republished courtesy of ACM/Dubbo and Macquarie Advocate.

1954 Parkes wins all three grades in the Group 11 Premiership

The first club in Group 11 to complete the trifecta:

Parkes First Grade defeated Narromine: 11-5

Parkes Reserve Grade defeated Wellington: 8-7

Parkes Junior Grade defeated Dubbo: 3-0.

1954 Blazer

Colin Macdonald

Courtesy of: The Parkes Rugby League Club, President, Tony Dwyer.

1954 Parkes First Grade Rugby League Team

Group 11 First Grade Premiers

Back Row: R. Johnson (Secretary), R. Burns, C. Macdonald, A. Willis, T. Crowley, J. Dwyer, B. Russell (Vice President).

Middle Row: A. Petty (Treasurer), F. Chew, J. Cuneo, R. Goodwin, R. Priestly, K. Dymond, K. Keeble (President).

Front Row: V. Mitchell (Ball Boy), M. Philpott, J. Gain, J. Cudmore, R. Ridley, T. Noakes, A. Prior (Ball Boy), J. Parker (Mascot).

Absent: P. Bracken (Captain-Coach).

Courtesy of: The Alan Macdonald Collection.

1954 Parkes Reserve Grade Rugby League Team

Group 11 Reserve Premiers

Back Row: S. Goodwin (Coach), L. Torrens, B. Finley, V. Frewley, H. Ridley.

Middle Row: J. Adams (Committee), J. Bryant, A. Heraghty, R. McGirr, J. Barling, A. Bryans, A. Kelly, M. Rodgers (Committee).

Front Row: V. Mitchell (Ball Boy), M. Philpott, R. Burns, N. Gordon (Captain), N. Hunter, L. Townsend, A. Prior (Ball Boy), J. Parker (Mascot).

Courtesy of: The Alan Macdonald Collection..

1954 Parkes Junior Grade Rugby League Team

Group 11 Junior Grade Premiers

Back Row: F. Chew (Coach), A. Petty (Tresurer), T. Bleechmore, M. Macdonald, K. Venables, N. Godfery, (Committee), J. Cassidy ('Assistant Secretary).

Middle Row: V. Mitchell (Ball Boy), S. Walker, A. Baker, J. Barling, G. Barling, B. Davis, A. Prior (Ball Boy).

Front Row: A. Reardon, B. Chew, T. Brogden, R. McGirr (Captain), J. Connor, R. Barter, J. Parker (Mascot).

Courtesy of: The Alan Macdonald Collection.

1954 Cootamundra Rugby League Team Group 9 Premiers

Cootamundra Bulldogs defeated Temora Dragons 21-7 Fisher Park September 3rd, 1954

Back Row: Lionel Wheatley, Ian Reid, Peter Kirby, Mick Howse, Fred De-Belin.

Middle Row: Darrell Fazio, Merv Ryan, Roley McDonell, Kevin Negus, Jack Slavin.

Front Row: Neil McDonell, John Graves (Captain/Coach), Algie Metcalfe.

Courtesy of: Neil Pollock, Maher Cup author.

1954 Narromine Rugby League Team

Back Row: Jock Weir, Fred Wilkins, Noel Powell, Leo Nosworthy, (Captain Coach), Joe Dundas, Jack Smith, Max Milgate.

Front Row: Ron Walsh, Kevin Wilcoxon, Maurie Wright, John Maurie, Victor Darcy, Absent: Alan Bargwanna. Ball Boy unknown.

NSWRL.

Courtesy of: Macquarie Regional Library Narromine.

1954 Lithgow Small Arms Factory Rugby League Team

Identified names of players only in no particular order:

Bill Young, Ron Case, Jim Patterson, John Hoy, Alby King, Billy Dowler, Jack Green, Laurie Bennett, E.P. Nightingale, Alan Patrick, Jim Knight, Jim Hoy, Ern Matthews, Bertie Simpson, Bill Kelly, Tony Joseph, Donald James Considine, Ray Quinnell.

Lithgow Small Arms Factory were defeated in the 1954 Group 10 Grand Final by Orange CYMS 7/2 at the Bathurst Sports Ground.

Source: 1954 Team photo. Courtesy of: The Lithgow Library.

1954 Nyngan Grand Final Rugby League Team

Cobar defeated Nyngan 14-13 in an historical Grand Final

Nyngan Team:
Back Row: N. Wright, A. Wright, D. Wright, J. Holland, T. Lonergan, K. Wilson, J. Pritchard.

Front Row: D Brigdon, V. Healey, C. Parker, N. Thompson, B. Barringer, R. Walsh.

Captain Coach: "Dutchy" Holland who previously played for Australia.

1954 Cobar Group 15 Premiers:
W. Collins (Captain), T. Collins, D. McGuiness, J. O'Brien, D. Bell-chambers, K. Neale, A. Gilligan, A. Knight, E. Martin, P. Bradley, L. Turner, P. McInerney, D. Martin.

Courtesy of: John Collins, The Crowing of the Roosters. Photo: Nygan Museum.

1954 Cootamundra Defeat Young

On 12 June 1954 more than 4000 enjoyed seeing Cootamundra defeat Young for the Maher Cup.

Players from left: Darrell Fazio, Algie Metcalfe, Kevin Slavin, Kevin Negus, Roley McDonell, Merv Ryan, Ian-- Reid, Lionel Wheatley, Peter Kirkby, Fred de Belin, Mick Howse, Keith Henniker, John Graves (Captain-Coach).

Courtesy of: Neil Pollock, Maher Cup author

DELAY IN START OF GROUP 11 COMP. UNTIL MAY 22
(By "Scrum Half")

The Group XI Rugby League competition has been put back for one week and the first round of matches will now be played on Sunday, May 22.

This decision was reached at a Group meeting at Parkes on Saturday following the application of some towns for an extension of the competition start.

May 1955

Article from: The Dubbo Liberal, Wednesday, May 4, 1955. Republished courtesy of ACM/The Dubbo Liberal.

BLUES MORALE HIGH FOR SEMI-FINAL CLASH WITH FORBES
(By "Hooker")

August 1955

A record crowd is expected to see the Group 11 semi-final between Dubbo and Forbes at Victoria Park oval on Sunday afternoon.

Fireworks are likely in the clash between Australian Test five-eighth Darcy Henry and Dubbo's brilliant Brian Bolton, who will be playing centre.

Last night at training all Dubbo players were full of confidence and trained as hard as though the competition was just starting.

Group XI Semi-Finals On Sunday

The Group 11 Rugby League semi-finals will be played next Sunday at Dubbo and Narromine.

The games are:

First Grade:
- Dubbo v Forbes at Dubbo
- Narromine v Wellington at Narromine.

Reserve Grade:
- Dubbo v Parkes at Dubbo
- Wellington v Peak Hill at Narromine (the winner of this game to play Forbes).

Article from: The Dubbo Liberal, Friday, August 26, 1955. Republished courtesy of ACM/Dubbo Liberal.

Bolton and Rutherford Neutralise Danger from Darcy Henry

EASY VICTORY PUTS DUBBO IN FINAL OF GROUP
(By "Hooker")

August 1955

Dubbo first-grade representative team played its way in the finals of Group 11 competition by soundly defeating Forbes 27-12 on Sunday, in a semi-final game which was marked by almost complete subjugation of the Forbes and Australian star, Darcy Henry.

Brian Bolton and Tommy Rutherford, who shared the responsibility for Henry's eclipse, played all-round superlative football.

In the final next Sunday Dubbo will meet Wellington who went down to Narromine, the minor premiers in the other semi-final. Narromine won 12-5.

Article from: The Dubbo Liberal, Tuesday, August 30, 1955. Republished courtesy of ACM/Dubbo Liberal.

Group Final at Wellington

The Group 11 Rugby League first-grade final between Wellington and Dubbo will be played at Wellington show ground.

The winner will meet Narromine in the grand-final.

The location of the final was decided yesterday on a toss, Wellington winning.

Dubbo and Wellington 1ˢᵗ Grade Teams

Wellington	Position	Dubbo	Position
C. JOHNSON	FULLBACK	C. RUTHERFORD	FULLBACK
B. SMITH	WING	K. CUDDY	WING
K. BELL	CENTRE	K. ANNETT	CENTRE
J. McDONALD	CENTRE	B. BOLTON	CENTRE
B. COHEN	WING	P. PROWSE	WING
L. O'BRIEN	FIVE-EIGHTH	V. HATTON (Captain)	FIVE EIGHTH
C. KELLY (Captain)	HALF	J. GEORGE	HALF
W. DARNEY	FRONT ROW	R. KITSON	FRONT ROW
C. JOHNSON	HOOKER	R. RICH	HOOKER
A. THOMAS	FRONT ROW	E. CLOSE	FRONT ROW
C. BELL	SECOND ROW	A. NILON	SECOND ROW
J. CORNISH	SECOND ROW	C. CAMPLING	SECOND ROW
B. LEE	LOCK	K. FINN	LOCK

Scrum Practice

The Redfern All Blacks

Pictured left All Blacks practice scrummage.

Scrums are the method of restarting play after an accidental knock-on, drop ball or when the ball has gone out of play. The players from both teams pack down closely together with their heads down attempting to gain possession after the halfback from the opposing side feeds the ball into the centre of the scrum.

The two hookers from either side rake at the ball attempting to guide the ball towards the back of the scrum.

Courtesy of: The N.S.W. State Library.

Narromine Plays Wellington 1955 R.L. Group Grand Final

Narromine is to play Wellington on Sunday in the grand final of Group XI Rugby League competition. The game is to take to place at Dubbo. The teams are considered to have equal chances, although Narromine supporters are highly optimistic.

September 1955

Narromine's president, Mr. E. Barber, said to-day: "Originally Wellington had accepted our terms to come to Narromine for the game, but under strong opposition from some quarters they had to withdraw. Then the two clubs agreed to play at Dubbo. The game promises to be a thriller and should draw a record crowd for Group Eleven," Mr. Barber said.

COACH IS CONFIDENT

Narromine's captain-coach, Mr. Leo Nosworthy, said last night that he felt more confident about Sunday's game than any other game in which Narromine has competed.

The junior grade final between Dubbo and Forbes and the reserve grade between Parkes and Forbes will also be played at Dubbo on Sunday.

Wellington defeated Dubbo 7/3 last Sunday to win the right to play Narromine for the Group Premiership.

Article from: The Narromine & Trangie Advocate, Tuesday, September 6, 1955. Republished courtesy of ACM/Narromine & Trangie Advocate.

WEAKNESS IN PACK COSTS DUBBO THIRD FINAL IN ROW

(By "Hooker")

September 1955

Spectacular, but at times rough play, highlighted the surprise defeat of Dubbo in the first grade final of the Group 11 competition on Sunday.

Wellington won 7-3 to make Dubbo's defeats in group finals three in succession.

Wellington won the game in the forward line where they outplayed the lighter and less experienced Dubbo pack at the rate of two scrums to one.

Football Grand Final At Dubbo

- First grade: Narromine plays Wellington.
- Reserve grade: Parkes plays Forbes.
- Junior grade: Dubbo plays Forbes.

Narromine went on to defeated Wellington 27/2 Group X1 1955 Grand Final at Dubbo

Article from: The Daily Liberal, Tuesday, September 26, 1955. Republished courtesy of ACM/Daily Liberal.

1955 Coonamble Rugby League Team

Back Row: K. McDonald (Captain Coach), J. Bremmel, Pal Hemsworth, Tumbler Edwards, Johnny Quilkey, Ron Bowden, Dickie Craig, Ray Campton.

Front Row: Graham Edwards (Ball Boy), Noel Bacigalupo, Tuggy Pennell, Alan Head, Joe Evans, Phil Morrisey.

Courtesy of: Gregory Maher.

1955 Cobar Rugby League Team Group 15 Premiers

Marcus Clark Champions.

Back Row: L. Jermyn, E. Martin, J. Martin, A. Gilligan, L. Turner, D. Martin, I. Rice.

Front Row: J. O'Brien, K. Neale, W. Collins, T. Collins, G. McKeown, D. Bellchambers.

Courtesy of: John Collins, The Crowing of the Roosters.

1956 Lithgow Small Arms Factory Group 10 Premiers

Rugby League Premiership to the Factory Team. CYMS Downed 10-4.

Lithgow Factory won the 1956 Group Ten Rugby League premiership at Bathurst yesterday when they beat Orange CYMS 10-4.

CYMS led 4/2 at half time, but Factory came out in the second half and showed the form that had taken them to many victories during the season.

In greasy conditions the Factory backs threw the ball around in dry weather fashion and their two tries were the result of brilliant backline moves.

Star full-back Barry Russell landed only one goal but notched a great try which really clinched the match. He came into the backs, made the extra man between King and Kirkland and raced brilliantly to the corner out pacing the cover defence.

King had scored an earlier try from another typical Factory move.

Winger Kirkland sealed CYMS fate with a great field goal in the closing stages.

For CYMS Hennessey never stopped trying in the second half.

Referee McIlhatton gave a good display and should have pleased both teams and spectators alike.

Final score:

- Factory 10 (K. King, B. Russell tries; B. Russell goal, K. Kirkland field goal) Defeated:
- CYMS 4 (J. Grannall 2 goals).

Courtesy of: The Central Western Daily, September, 1956. Republished courtesy of ACM/Central Western Daily.

The Condobolin Rugby Football League

PROGRAMME

FOR

SUNDAY, 5th AUGUST, 1956

CONDOBOLIN v. PEAK HILL

A. SCHRADER, President   W. J. ROSTRON, Secretary

NEXT HOME GAME

CONDOBOLIN V. NARROMINE

Sunday, 19th August, 1956

REFEREE: Mr. DUKES

CONDOBOLIN
Colours: Blue and Gold.

G. Kellock (1).

P. Kane (2), R. Wilcox (5).
R. Willis (3), P. Timmins (4).

B. Gaffney (6).

E. Kane (7).

J. Peebles (8), (Captain).

T. Butler (9), M. Maybury (10).

N. Williams (11), K. Pettit (13).

N. Ticehurst (12).

PEAK HILL
Colour: Yellow.

N. Gallagah (1).

R. Wilcox (2), C. Elliott (5).
R. Elliott 3, J. McIntosh 4, (Captain).

B. Barnes (6).

N. Edwards (7).

J. Glasson (8).

T. Hando (9), C. Hackett (10).

K. Stone (11), B. Wright (13).

J. Stove (12).

1956 Condo Now Minor Premiers

In one of the hardest games of football ever played at Parkes, Condobolin narrowly defeated Narromine 8-7 on Sunday to win minor premiers' crown in the 1956 Group XI competition.

Scores of cars made the journey to Parkes to give support to the Condobolin team. Narromine supporters also were present in big numbers and were very voluble.

After being defeated by Narromine on the last two occasions on which these two teams met, Condobolin were determined to atone for their previous defeats and played like a team inspired to beat their experienced and very tough opponents.

Courtesy of: Keith Willis, 1956.

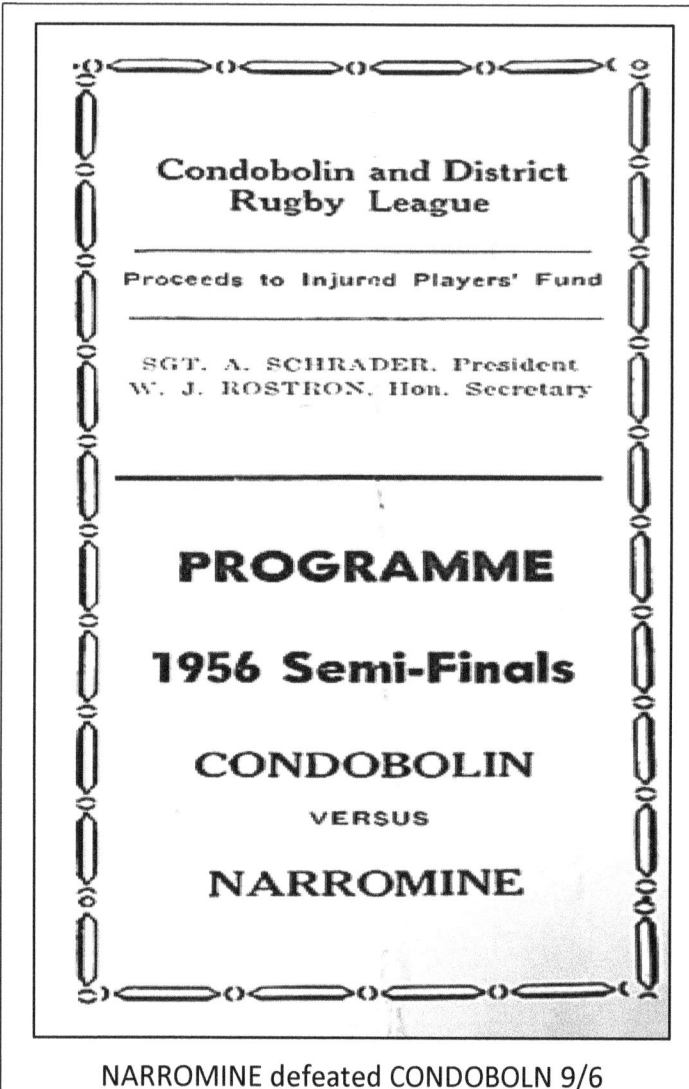

Condobolin and District Rugby League

Proceeds to Injured Players' Fund

SGT. A. SCHRADER, President
W. J. ROSTRON, Hon. Secretary

PROGRAMME

1956 Semi-Finals

CONDOBOLIN
VERSUS
NARROMINE

NARROMINE defeated CONDOBOLN 9/6

CONDOBOLIN
COLOURS: BLUE AND GOLD.

G. KELLOCH (1).

K. WILLIS (2), C. BILLINGTON (5).
P. TIMMINS (3), K. BEARDMORE (4).

B. GAFFNEY (6).

E. KANE (7).

J. PEEBLES (8), (Captain).

H. GELPIUS (9), M. MAYBURY (10).

V. WILLIAMS (11), K. PETTIT (13).

T. BUTLER, (12), N. TICEHURST.
(One to be Omitted).

NARROMINE
COLOURS: RED AND WHITE.

B. SULLIVAN (1).

C. THOMS (2), A. ABBOTT (5).
E. ROBERTSON (3), N. HOWE (4).

L. NOSWORTHY (6), (CAPTAIN).

J. McGARRY (7).

P. NEW (8),

R. WALSH (10), B. WEIR (9).

J. SCOTT (11), P. WILKINS (13).

J. SMITH, (12)

Group XI Rugby League
1956 Competition Finals
Pioneer Oval
Parkes
SUNDAY, SEPTEMBER 9th
FIRST GAME COMMENCES AT 12.15 PM SHARP

First Grade

DUBBO:	CONDOBOLIN:
COLOURS: BLUE & WHITE.	COLOURS: BLUE & GOLD.
1. J. DIGGINS	1. G. KELLOCH
2. B. JAMES	2. H. PAUL
3. K. CULLEN	3. P. TIMMINS
4. R. LIGHT	4. K. BEARDMORE
5. B. PERRY	5. C. BILLINGTON
6. D. STROUD	6. B. GAFFNEY
7. K. MILTON	7. E. KANE
8. B. McMAHON	8. I. PEBBLES
9. B. CASEY	9. H. GELPIUS
10. C. CAMMPLING	10. M. MAYBURY
11. A. CURREY	11. T. BUTLER
12. B. CURREY	12. J. TICEHURST
13. N. DODD.	13. K. PETTIT, K. WILLIS.
(REFEREE: F. RING)	

Dubbo defeated Condobolin at Parkes and moved on to play Narromine in the Grand Final at Victoria Park Dubbo.

Narromine Outclasses Dubbo In Rugby League Grand Final
September 1956

Members of the Narromine Rugby League's first grade team are receiving congratulations on their excellent game at Dubbo on Sunday last when they defeated Dubbo 16/7 to win the premiership for the second time in succession and the third time in all.

The first score of the match was a penalty goal by Ray Light which gave Dubbo a lead of 2-nil, but it was only a temporary advantage.

Narromine captain Bob Weir made a very determined run after eluding several Dubbo defenders, sent the ball to Robertson who went over for an excellent try. Thoms converted, giving Narromine a lead 5 to 2.

Thoms who was kicking magnificently landed two more penalty goals, Narromine 9 Dubbo 2.

Diggins raised the flags from a penalty for Dubbo just on half time. Narromine 9 Dubbo 4.

Second half Dick Smith scored under the posts for Narromine and Thoms converted. Narromine 14 Dubbo 4.

Dodd scored a try in a handy position for Dubbo and Diggins failed to convert. Narromine 14 Dubbo 7.

Thoms kicked his fifth goal from a penalty and when the full-time whistle was blown Narromine was victorious by 16 points to 7.

Leo Nosworthy once again proved himself the master tactician. His superb judgement and split-second thinking has been Narromine's greatest asset right throughout the season.

Bob Weir gave one of his greatest performances and on many occasions his brilliant runs left the opposition standing.

Article from: The Narromine News and Trangie Advocate. Republished courtesy of ACM/Narromine and Trangie Advocate.

1956 Condobolin Rugby League Team

Back Row: E. Gill (Ass Team Manager), K. Pettit, P. Timmins, K. Beardsmore, B. Williams, Peebles (Coach), T. Butler, N. Ticehurst, G. Kelloch, M. Mabury, E. Paul.

Front Row: K. Gordon (Team Manager), B. Gaffney, K. Willis, C. Billington, R. Hazleton, E. Kane, J. Drinkwater, (Vice-President).

John Roberts (Mascot).

Courtesy of: Keith Willis.

The Game Moves On

Source: Okeydokey, Landscapes.

PREMIERSHIP TO CONDOBOLIN BY 20 POINTS TO 8

(By "Hooker")

Pioneer Oval Parkes

September 1957

Condobolin were the minor premiers in the 1956 season only to be beaten by Dubbo in the final at Parkes and not making the grand-final.

However, 1957 was to be their year by defeating Parkes at Pioneer Oval in the grand final by 20-8 and becoming the 1957 Group 11 Premiers.

Spearheaded by a mobile tough pack of forwards, Condobolin yesterday stream rolled its way to victory in the grand-final of the Group 11 first-grade competition.

After leading Parkes 13-2 at half-time, the Lachlanders ran out winners by 20 points to 8.

Captain of Parkes Merv Lees started off well, but after taking a severe battering from the hands of Timmins he dropped out of the limelight.

He went to fullback 15 minutes from the end, with Deland moving up to the three-quarter line.

Condobolin was best served in the backs by Kelloch and rugged centre Pat Timmins and for Parkes Meadows made some nice breaks.

Final score:

Condobolin: 20 (E. Kane and T. Kane Tries. G. Kelloch 7 goals)

Parkes: 8 (D. McDonald 4 goals).

Jim Peebles

Article from: The Dubbo Liberal, Monday, September 16, 1957. Republished courtesy of ACM/Dubbo Liberal

1957 Condobolin and Parkes Grand Final Teams

CONDOBOLIN	PARKES
Colours: Blue and Gold	Colours: White, Red and Blue
FULLBACK	**FULLBACK**
G. KELLOCH 1.	L. DELAND 1.
WINGERS	**WINGERS**
P. KANE 2, R. WILCOX 5.	R. BARTER 2, J. CONNORS 5.
CENTRES	**CENTRES**
R. WILLIS 3, P. TIMMINS 4.	N. MASON 3, D. SEPTO 4.
FIVE-EIGHTH	**FIVE-EIGHTH**
B. BARLOW 6.	M. LEES 6, (Captain).
HALF-BACK	**HALF-BACK**
N. KANE 7	G. MEADOWS 7.
LOCK FORWARD	**LOCK FORWARD**
J. PEEBLES 8, (Captain Coach).	T. CROWLEY 8.
SECOND ROWERS	**SECOND ROWERS**
M. MAYBURY 9, N. McCAULEY 10.	D. McDONALD 9, W. SENSE 10.
FRONT ROW FORWARDS	**FRONT ROW FORWARDS**
P. TICEHURST 11, M. GAVEL 13.	N. GORDON 11, K. HARTIN 13.
HOOKER	**HOOKER**
N. TICEHURST 12.	J. DWYER 12.

1957 Condobolin Rugby League Team

Back Row: Col Hackett, Max Maybury, Pat Timmins, Don Lewis, Gus Kelloch.

Middle Row: Keith Willis, Noel Ticehurst, Mark Gavel, Pat Ticehurst. Jim Pebbles, (Captain Coach).

Front Row: Team Manager Elly Gill, Father Joe Coyte, Rex Wilcox, Ted Kane.

Courtesy of: Keith Willis.

1957 Eugowra Rugby League Team Group 11 Premiers

Group 11 Second Division:
Eugowra 18 Peak Hill 10

Back Row: Theo Wykamp, Phil Townsend, Harry Turner, Howard Dudgeon, Frank Cheney (President), Alan Rawsthorne, Viv Rawsthorne, Jack Shine (Secretary), Brian Medcalf.

Front Row: Barry Turner, Bob Cross, Ian Walsh (Captain Coach), Gary Wykamp, John Haywood, D. Greenhalgh (Ball Boy).

Courtesy of: Rugby League Collection, Central Hotel Eugowra.

1957 Hermidale Rugby League Team Lynch Cup Premiers

Hermidale won 1955 and 1957 Lynch Cup Premierships

Back Row: T. Jeffery, R. Hawley, W. Dewhurst, R. Cooney, B. Gudgeon, C. Marshall, W. Linke.
Front row: K. Jeffery, R. Bourke, T. Piper, R. O'Neil, J. O'Neil, T. O'Neil, Jeff Hawley (Ball boy).

Courtesy of: John Collins. The Crowing of the Roosters.

1957 Coonamble Rugby League Team Group 14 Premiers

Back Row: Phil Martin, Noel Bacigalupo, Roley Green, Brian Byrnes, Phil Morrisey, Alan Head, John Hughes, Elwyn Edwards.

Front Row: Noel Trudgett, Frank Foodey, Ray Hyde, Norm Bryant, Mike Digges.

Courtesy of: Gregory Maher.

1958 Coonamble Rugby League Team Group 14 Premiers

1958 1st Grade Group 14 Premiers & Clayton Cup Winners

Back Row: Brian Byrnes, Alan Head, G (Pudden) Head, Ron Pellett, Tumbler Edwards, Ray Hyde, Geoff Ryan.

Front Row: Noel Trudgett, Roley Green, Cecil Wright, Joey Evans, Colin Head, Jimmy Slack-Smith.

Courtesy of: Paul Wheelhouse and Roley Green.

1958 Temora Rugby League Team Group 9 Premiers
Six Maher Cup Games

Back Row: Brian Matthews, Barry Roberts, Perce Williamson, Barney Roberts, Alan Lynch, Bob Sait (Captain Coach), Tony Gelfius, Peter Shields, Alan Knight, Stan Barrington (Selector), Neville Pittendridge (Treasurer).

Front Row: John Kelly, Fred Meale (Manager), Len Henman, Albert Williams, Ron Allen, Kevin Moye, Laurie McKenzie, Col Fairhall, Bert Howe (Selector), Jack Stephenson (President), Paul Howe (Mascot).

Absent: Ray Kerry, Jim Kerry, Bob Keen.

Courtesy of: Brian Hughes & Temora Independent.

WALLY TOWERS KICKS FORBES TO VICTORY
(By HOOKER)

September 1958

The curtain fell on the first-grade Group 11 Rugby League competition yesterday when 3000 spectators braved the rain and cold to see Forbes defeat Cumnock 16-3.

In a heavy ground the six tough forwards backed up by another good exhibition of goal-kicking by Wally Towers, paved the way for their team to become premiers for 1958.

It wasn't until 1958 that Forbes claimed a Group 11 premiership, but the 1946 grand final loss was controversial. As the Forbes Advocate reported:

Many feel the 1946 side should have been the first to win the Group 11 premiership after being beaten by Wellington in the grand final replay 11-4.

Forbes defeated Cumnock in the 1958 Grand Final to take out their first Group 11 Premiership winning 16-3.

Article from: The Dubbo Liberal, Monday, September 22, 1958. Republished courtesy of ACM/Dubbo Liberal.

1958 Forbes Rugby League Team Group 11 Champions

Back Row: K. Graham, N. McKay, I. Fowler, D. Dwyer, T. Williams, W. Towers.

Middle Row: J. Bradley (Captain-Coach), G. Rossiter, W. Parslow, J. Rolfe, P. Martin.

Front Row: B. Condon, J. Lasker.

The players' names may not be in order.

Courtesy of: Forbes Historical Museum.

1958 Cobar Rugby League Team Marcus Cup Champions

Back Row: W. Sprowl, W. Collins, R. Pike, E. Brown, J. Butler, W. Morelli, A. Merlow, L. Brooker, K. Rogers.

Front Row: J. Edwards, L. Thompson, T. Collins, K. Neale, J. Martin, G. Sedgeman, Ball Boy: Alec Brown.

Courtesy of: John Collins, The Crowing of the Roosters. Photo: Les Brooker.

1958 Orange CYMS Rugby League Team Group 10 Premiers Western Championship Cup Winners

Back Row: E. Hayden, L. Commins, E. Kelly, R. Lindfield (Coach), P. Commins, T. Commins, J. Thurn.
Middle Row: J. Maloney (Selector), J. Hennessy, J. Evans, J. Kelly (Captain), Fr. Grannall, C. Fahy, L Davidson, N. Parker (Manager).
Front Row: P. Farrell, E. Maguire, (Mascot), D. Hyland. Insert: T. Hunt (Vice Captain), L. Kelly.

Match Details:

Orange CYMS won a hard-fought grand-final against Oberon 17–6 after leading 6–2 at half-time.

Oberon chased the ball throughout the 80 minutes as it was usually being held by members of the dominant CYMS backline. In the second half CYMS penetrated Oberon's defence to score three tries, which gave them the match and the grand final win.

Final Score: Orange CYMS 17 defeated Oberon 2.

Courtesy of: The Orange CYMS Rugby League Club.

Orange Emmco Rugby League Team

The way it was:

Players from both teams would in single file, head towards the centre field and the referee would toss a coin. The winning captain would choose the direction of play and receive the ball from the kick off.

Both sides would shake hands and move to their positions ready for the game to start.

Some of the players in this photograph include Dick Clark, Rev Kent, Eddie Peters and Jack Cowden.

Courtesy of: Geoff Mann, Sports Journalist, Dubbo.

Follow up: Neil Dicks and the Tooraweenah Challenge Cup

Geoff Mann

1958 Challenge Cup

LAST week's item requesting more information about the Tooraweenah Challenge Cup blazer grew a life of its own.

The request was discussed, forwarded, researched and returned during the week.

Thanks to all those who were happy to contribute information, in particular to Max Bonnington.

We even managed to track down a photo of the old Tooraweenah team, below. Here's what we discovered.

The Challenge Cup was a "one-off" in 1958. A publican at Quambone wanted to start a competition between the number of smaller towns who were not involved in Group 15, Warren, Tooraweenah and Gular were invited to compete in a four round comp, that is, they played each other four times.

We are not 100% sure but we believe that one Cup was to be held by a team and played for on a weekly basis with the team holding the Cup putting it up for challenge from whichever team they were drawn against that day. The other trophy was for the team that won the over-all competition.

Both trophies are still behind the bar in the Tooraweenah Hotel today.

Neil Dicks (whose name was on a receipt inside the blazer's pocket) was a shearer around Tooraweenah.

He played in that team and for several more years, including when Tooraweenah-Mendooran had a one year stint in Group 14. Apparently he left the district and moved to Victoria many years ago.

His wife gave the blazer to a Salvation Army Store when Neil died around 2003.

I spoke to Neil's sister Lois Raglus a few days ago. She was "stoked" to hear that the blazer had come back to NSW! He always wanted to be back home, she said.

To add to the above, a researcher at the State Library of NSW tracked down an item in the Gilgandra News from July 1958 which mentioned that Neil Dicks had had "the game of his life", scoring a try in the first half.

For the record the paper reported that the Tooraweenah Thirteen defeated the Gular Rovers 22-7.

Tooraweenah Challenge Cup Team

Back Row: Ivan Priddis (coach), Oliver Buckley, Paddy Gale, Gordon Manusu, Ron Buckley, Sam Buckley, Ray Maberly (we think), Kevin Buckley, Johnny Duncon, Cecile Jones, and Keith Broadman (who may have been a sponsor).

Front Row: Neil Dicks (partly hidden), two unknowns, Glen McGrath, Alan (Austin) Levings. The ball boy was Dennis Brew.

Courtesy of: Geoff Mann, Sports Journalist, Dubbo.

SPINNERS' SPORTLIGHT

George Smith led Parkes to shock win over Forbes

Parkes' firsts continued its great bid to reach the Group XI Semi-finals with a sensational 14-13 victory over the highly-fancied Forbes team at Pioneer Oval, Parkes yesterday.

A big crowd paid £243 to see the home team hold off a tense challenge by Forbes in a thrilling finish.

July 1959

Parkes forged to a 12/5 advantage after leading 7/5 at half time, but Forbes rallied grandly to lead 13/12 with about 15 minutes to play.

The final score of the game came five minutes before full time when George Smith landed a splendid penalty goal.

The Parkes victory was a great triumph for captain-coach George Smith, who was once again one of the best players on the field.

Despite lack of interest by players earlier this season, when Parkes appeared as likely "wooden spoon" candidates, Smith never gave up and is now being rewarded for his efforts.

I do believe the Smith's coaching of Oberon last season got the team to the grand-final after a bad patch in the first round.

Our Parkes observer reported that the home team's relentlessness when on the defensive and a great performing pack of forwards carried the day.

Forbes was the more impressive and dangerous in attack, but the "little difference" that meant a win or loss was George Smith.

Following a fine try and two goals in the first term, Smith was also the spearhead of Parkes' offensive in the second.

Several minutes after the resumption of play Smith broke into the clear with a great run before sending winger Hetherington in for a try.

Forbes struck back boldly when 14-stone winger John Bullus raced down the flank, drew the fullback, Stepto and passed in field to Bradley who sent halfback Lasker in for a try which Thompson converted.

Still throwing the ball about well, Forbes went to the lead when centre Jukes snapped up a loose ball to position Thompson for a try.

Both teams threw everything in over the last 15 minutes and the crowd went wild.

With five minutes of play left Parkes was awarded a penalty just near half-way and Smith kicked a beauty into the wind from 45 yards out.

Forbes had a chance almost as the bell was ringing, but Thompson's kick from near half-way went wide.

Forwards, Kevin Hennessey, Jack Dwyer and Tommy Williams, with support from Kyle Fulwood were splendid for Parkes.

Ron Lynch was the best of a somewhat disappointing Forbes pack, but the backs, headed by Lasker, Bullus, Condron and full-back Thompson were always dangerous.

Forbes' loss yesterday has considerably lessened the team's chances of displacing Macquarie as minor premiers.

Scores:
Parkes 14: (G. Smith, R. Hetherington tries and G. Smith, 4 goals) defeated Forbes 13: (D. Forbes L. Lasker, P. Thompson tries and P. Thompson 2 goals).

Article from: The Dubbo Daily Liberal, July 20, 1959. Republished courtesy of ACM/Dubbo Daily Liberal.

MACQUARIE WIN EXPECTED CYMS ARE CONFIDENT

(By "Hooker")

With the minor premiership all "sewn up" Dubbo Macquarie should go on to another win, when it plays Peak Hill in the Group X1 match-of-the-day at No.1 Oval on Sunday and after its success over Narromine CYMS hope for a repeat performance at Eugowra.

August 1959

After the run-away victory over CYMS and a good win against Wellington the Macquarie side was today rated 25 points better than Peak Hill.

It must be remembered however, that Macquarie will be without match-winning winger Don Parish, who will be in Sydney playing for Country against City.

The first-round clash between Macquarie and Peak Hill gave the Dubbo team its first "fright" of the season, when Peak Hill went within an ace of winning.

Swiftness in the three-quarter line and speed among the tough forwards is expected to ensure a Macquarie victory on Sunday.

The reserves and juniors are also expected to register good wins. Both teams played draws against Wellington but should prove far too strong for Peak Hill.

EUGOWRA v CYMS

Hoping to show that last week's win against Narromine was "no splash in the pan," CYMS with an improved side, is quietly confident of accounting for Eugowra, which is in the first four.

CYMS Reserves are now almost certain to make the semi-finals and a win on Sunday will ensure them of a chance of winning the competition.

A re-cast of the CYMS Juniors team against Narromine failed to give them victory and it is now doubtful if the youngsters, after many good showings will make any more.

Tomorrow, in conjunction with the Nyngan-to-Dubbo cycle road race, a challenge match is to be played between the Commercial and Castlereagh hotels.

In past seasons these games have proved a big draw card and tomorrow should be no exception.

This all-important "test" will commence as soon as the big road race is completed, so all players are requested to present themselves to their coaches and trainers no later than 2.30pm.

During the past week I have been watching the teams train at their top and first-class entertainment is assured.

Both combinations include many ex-Sydney and Dubbo 1st grade players and neither of the coaches, Jack Tooth (Commercial) and Jim Toohey (Castlereagh) will hear of defeat.

It was ony right and proper that regardless of expense, a first-class referee should be engaged for this classic.

Proceeds of this game will go to a worthy cause Westhaven School.

GROUP 11 DRAW

Macquarie v Peak Hill
Eugowra v CYMS
Narromine v Wellington
Condobolin v Parkes
Forbes, bye.

Article from: The Dubbo Daily Liberal, August 14, 1959. Republished courtesy of ACM/Dubbo Daily Liberal.

Highlights and Lowdown on Weekend Sport
INCENTIVE FOR PARISH IN CITY COUNTRY GAME

Considerable Dubbo interest will be focussed on the display of young Macquarie R.L. winger Don Parish for Country against City on Sunday.

Parish will be making his final bid for inclusion in the 1959 Kangaroos touring team of 26 which will be announced on August 22.

August 1959

Two NSW-Queensland Inter-State games will be played in Sydney next week and the young Dubbo winger has a good chance of being included in one of the NSW teams at least.

Country Rugby League officials said yesterday that they believe fullback Darryl Chapman, hooker Ian Walsh, centre Col Ratcliff, lock Ron Lynch and winger Don Parish will make claims for Kangaroo selection.

Country team manager Mr. M. Throughgood said: "With so many places in the Kangaroo team wide open our players have a wonderful incentive to do well on Sunday. This is the best country team for a long time. There is not a real weakness in the side."

GROUP GAMES

Apart from who will finish in second place Forbes, Wellington or Eugowra interest has momentarily slipped from the Group 11 first-grade scene since Dubbo Macquarie annexed the minor premiership last week.

Both Wellington and Eugowra must win on Sunday to stay on level points terms with Forbes, who have the bye this week.

Two minor grade teams, CYMS Reserves and Narromine Juniors, are badly in need of wins to stay in the running for semi-final positions.

Wellington centre Pat Miller is almost certain to become the fourth player to score 100 points in the first grade competition on Sunday. He has scored 99 to date and the players in front of him are Don Parish (121), Noel Gavin (106) and George Smith (100).

Don Parish

Article from: The Dubbo Daily Liberal, August 14, 1959. Republished courtesy of ACM/Dubbo Daily Liberal.

1959 Brewarrina Rugby League Team

The Brewarrina Rugby League team played Cobar on their home ground in 1959 and were the first team to defeat Cobar on their home ground in eight years. Brewarrina won 3-2.

Back Row: Ron McKenzie, Jackie Grant, Jackie Evers, Ronnie Hart, Kenny Biles, Nat McCouchey, Bronte Davis, Donny Beetson.

Front Row: Alfie Biles, Jimmy Ryan, Allan Norton, Bobby Caton, Ernie Grange, Rob Ryan (Ball Boy).

Article from: The Dubbo Liberal, Wednesday, September 2, 1987. Republished courtesy of ACM/Dubbo Liberal

Three Country Footballers from Eugowra

IAN WALSH	BARRY BEATH	JOHN HOBBY

Eugowra Captain Coach 1957 – 1961 1957 Winning Group 11 Second Division Premiership. 25 Tests for Australia 1959 – 1966 Australian Captain Coach 1966 94 Games for St George. Won four Premierships with St George: 1962, 63, 64, 65. Undoubtedly one of the greatest country footballers. Born in Parkes and family lived in Bogan Gate.	Eugowra 1962 – 1965 Played in the 1962 – 1965 Group Eugowra 11 Premiership teams. 1 Test for Australia 3 Matches for N.S.W. 1 Match for Country N.S.W. 198 Games for St George. Won one NSW Premiership with St George. One of the many players from the bush who had success in representative teams and in Sydney.	Eugowra Captain Coach 1962 – 1965 Three Group 11 Premierships with Eugowra. Represented: Western Division, Newcastle, Riverina and Country. John Hobby could have furthered his football career, however he wanted to remain in the bush. One of the greatest and most respected players of his time.

Courtesy of: Rugby League Collection, Central Hotel Eugowra.

Ian Walsh

Ian Walsh who is acknowledged as one of the most successful Captain Coaches in history of rugby league has strong links with Parkes and district. Walsh is the son of the late Mr. Jack Walsh and Mrs. Dorrie Walsh. Mr and Mrs Walsh Snr were well known and respected members of the Bogan Gate farming community. Mrs Walsh now resides in San Souci.

Ian was born in Parkes and travelled by bus each day from Bogan Gate to attend Parkes High school. Walsh's first association with football in Parkes was a member of the Webb Street football team. This club, which had the late Mr. Vic Philpott as president played in local junior Saturday morning competitions.

Over a period of 12 years commencing in 1949, Walsh played in group football with such clubs as Bogan Gate, Condobolin, Parkes, Forbes and Eugowra.

Courtesy of: Parkes Shire Library, Parkes One Hundred Years of Local Government.

Above: Ian Walsh

SPINNER'S SPORTLIGHT

NOSWORTHY & COMPANY TRAIN ALL-OUT FOR THE BIG CLASH

Whether or not Dubbo Macquarie Rugby League can overcome a three-weeks lay-off is the vital question in its Group XI first-grade grand final against the match-hardened Wellington side at Kennard Park on Sunday.

Latest reports show that both teams will be at full strength-and confident for a clash which could provide a thrilling climax to the 1959 season.

August 1959

Personally I feel that the Dubbo team has enough strong points in its game to counter any lack of match practice.

Coach Leo Nosworthy intensified training this week with long sessions on Tuesday night and last night and has called a further run tonight. At training last night the Macquarie side kept going hard for a long spell at No. 1 Oval and all players appeared to be in good shape.

Tactics will play an important role on Sunday and in this department Nosworthy would possibly have no peer in the Group.

Macquarie's back division which has been its trump card this season, should lay the foundation for a premiership win.

Experienced halves Johnny George and Leo Nosworthy are expected to pack too many guns for the Wellington combination of Reynolds and McCarroll.

Hard Struggle

The centres Schiemer and Moore, will have a hard struggle with Miller and Musgrave, but in the rest of the back division the "Blues" are definitely stronger.

Custodian Tommy Rutherford, although he has lost some of his former dash, is still the Group's best and he's a great tackler.

Wellington is still without its regular hooker, Jack Costyn and Ross Bartier should therefore win enough of the ball to give his backs ample opportunities.

If this is the case Wellington will certainly have to reproduce its great tackling display against Forbes last Sunday to keep the speedy Macquarie backs in check.

Macquarie possess a more mobile set of forwards but the Wellington pack could gain the ascendancy in tight play.

All points taken into consideration, Macquarie will no doubt favour opening up play, while the home team would fare best if it is tight and close.

Wellington has retained the side which defeated Forbes last Sunday in the final re-play with one exception. Peter Boden has been taken out of the second row and replaced by Jack Cornish.

The teams are:

Macquarie:
Fullback: T. Rutherford
Winger: R. Light
Centres: D. Schiemer, D. Moore
Winger: D. Teale
Five-eighth: L. Nosworthy
Half-back: J. George
Lock forward: B. Ridley
Second row: P. Rawlinson, B. Pilon
Front row: A. Curry, B. Perry
Hooker: R. Bartier.

Wellington:
Fullback: B. Smith
Winger: L. Carlow
Centres: L. Musgrave, P. Miller
Winger: B. Cavanagh
Five-eighth: C. McCarroll
Half-back: J. Reynolds
Lock forward: P. Johnson
Second row: C. Bell, J. Cornish
Front row: A. Thomas, V. Lewis
Hooker: J. Stubberfield.

REFEREE: Mr. E. McAlpine.

Article from: The Dubbo Daily Liberal, August 14, 1959. Republished courtesy of ACM/Dubbo Daily Liberal.

1959 Dubbo Macquarie Rugby League Team Group 11 Premiers

Group 11 Premiers and Clayton Cup Winners

Back Row: T. Rutherford, R. Bartier, D. Teale, R. Light.
Middle Row: C. Rich (Strapper), P. Rawlinson, B. Perry, A. Currey, D. Schiemer, L. Delaney (Treasurer).
Front Row: R. Pack (President), R. Ridley, B. Pilon, L. Nosworthy (Captain), D. Moore, J. George, R. Lane (Secretary), K. Jamieson (Mascot).

Courtesy of: Dubbo Macquarie Rugby League Club.

1959 Orange CYMS Rugby League Team Group 10 Premiers

Back Row: J. Carney (Masseur), J. Thurn, T. Commins, J. Kelly, E. Kelly, P. Commins, R. King, E. Haydon, H. McDonald (Manager).

Middle Row: J. Maloney (Selector), J. Evans, J. Dalton (Secretary), D. Allsopp, L. Davidson (Captain), Rev. J. Grannall, N. Parker (Manager), I. Commins (Vice Captain), T. Tracey (Selector).

Front Row: B. Taylor, T. Hunt, C. Fahy, G. Davidson (Mascot), J. Gersbach, D. Hyland, K. Maguire.

Inserts: D. Croucher, P. Farrell, R. Lindfield (Coach).

Group 10 Premiers and Western Championship Cup Winners

- Orange CYMS defeated Lithgow Workers 5-4 at Bathurst Sports Ground in the Group 10 grand-final.
- Lithgow held a slim 4-2 lead at half time from two goals from G. McMillan.
- The score remained unchanged until 12 minutes to go, when the ball was played brilliantly to CYMS halfback Carl Fahy in shocking conditions, he kicked the ball over the Workers' backs and the ball stopped dead in a pool of water near the Lithgow goal line.
- Tom Commins raced through as the ball floated on the water, kicked the ball, picked it up and splashed over for the only try of the match.

Courtesy of: Michael Downey, (Orange CYMS), Reunion Book.

Fourth Premiership for Nosworthy
VICTORY FOR MACQUARIE FIRSTS AND JUNIORS
September 1959

With such perfect weather conditions, the setting at Kennard Park provided an excellent back ground to climax the 1959 season and with two extra gates the Group's finances must be at an all-time high. Patrons paid £750 at the gate yesterday.

Despite three early casualties Macquarie firsts fought to win in good style and as most keen judges expected, the side's speedy backs paved the way for the win.

In the opening stages of the game Nosworthy came in for some "special" attention and played out the rest of the game with injured ribs which noticeably affected his play.

Young second-rower Peter Rawlinson suffered an ankle injury and Tommy Rutherford played through the first half in a black-out following a heavy knock.

Rutherford could not remember any of the first half of play apart for the first few minutes.

Winning the scrums 18 to 7 Macquarie was always dominant in the backs and its three tries all came from good back-line thrusts and backing up.

Centres Doug Moore and Dave Schiemer were always dangerous especially Schiemer, with best support from winger Light and custodian Rutherford.

Scores:
MACQUARIE: 19 (D. Schiemer, R. Light, R. Ridley tries, T. Rutherford 3 goals) defeated
WELLINGTON: 11 (J. Stubberfield try, B. Smith 4 goals)

Half-time scores: Macquarie led 10-3

REFEREE: Mr. E. McApline.

JUNIOR GAME:
Macquarie Juniors defeat Forbes 12 points to 3 in a tough but entertaining game.

Article from: The Dubbo Liberal, September 15, 1959. Republished courtesy of ACM/Dubbo Liberal.

1959 Coonamble Win its Third Premiership in a Row

1957 Premiers

1958 Premiers

1959 Premiers

The 1959 Premiership winning team included the following players:
Brian Byrnes, Tumbler Edwards, Joe Evans, Ray Hyde (Captain Coach), Jimmy Slack-Smith, Ron Pellet, Roley Green, Alan Head, Cecil Wright, Josh Yeo, Peter Yeo.

Courtesy of: Roley Green, Coonamble.

THE SIXTIES

This section includes news articles on matches, players and premiership winning teams. Dubbo Macquarie 1959 to 1961, ends its three year premiership run. Oberon 1961 premiers Group 10, 1960 Canowindra Group 11 Eastern Zone Premiers, Forbes were Group 11 premiers in 1962, Carcoar Group 10 in 1962 and Nyngan Group 15 in 1966.

Eugowra starts its five year consecutive premiership wins from 1963 through to 1967. Group 11 premiers were Narromine 1968, Dubbo CYMS 1969 and Forbes 1970. Group legendary players of the time, John Hobby and Leo Nosworthy, were instrumental in leading their teams to victory.

In 1969 Parkes were red hot certainties to win the premiership, however Dubbo CYMS had other plans. Two young Parkes junior players (brothers) were destined to represent Group 11 and Western Division.

Decisive R.L. trial win
MACQUARIE ACCENT STILL ON SPEED
March 1960

Group 11 Premiers Dubbo Macquarie displayed pre-competition form with a decisive 26 points to five win over Dubbo CYMS in a trial match at No. 1 Oval Dubbo on Sunday.

In the supporting trials Macquarie reserves who won the premiership last season, beat CYMS by 13 points to two and 1960 junior premiers CYMS defeated Macquarie Juniors by 15 points to two.

A Runaway Win for Macquarie CYMS Go Down Fighting
May 1960

Dubbo Macquarie first-grade continued on its Group 11 rampage with a demoralising 54-nil victory over Parkes in a fourth-round game yesterday.

Other features of the round were Wellington's narrow 13-12 win against Peak Hill and Dubbo CYMS losing by 21 points to 13 at Forbes.

Article from: The Dubbo Liberal, March 28 and May 20, 1960. Republished courtesy of ACM/Dubbo Liberal.

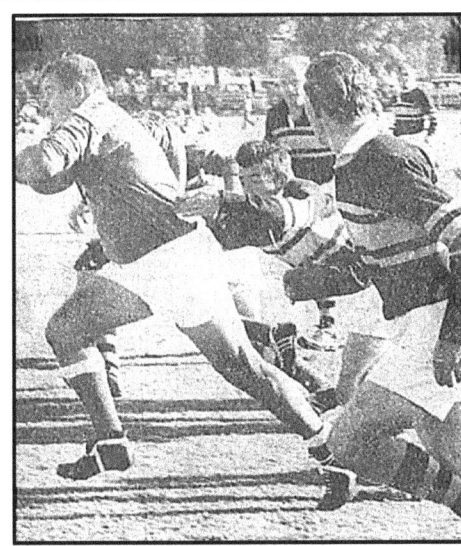 

Dubbo CYMS front rower Mick Wilson crashes through the Canowindra defence as John Kelly and John Traves move across in cover defence and Wilson pictured right one of Group 11 finest forwards.

Courtesy of: Blast From the Past, Dubbo CYMS Old Boys.

Action Shots from 1960 Season

Above Left: A Forbes player is well held by CYMS winger Gary Yeo at yesterday's rugby league match at Dubbo. Also, in the picture are CYMS players Gary Heares and Terry Piesley.

Above Right: Parkes first-grade player Bill Tonkin brushes off one CYMS player and tries to escape from another, Gary Heares, during the CYMS-Parkes match at No. 1. Oval on Sunday. Parkes won 31-15.

Dubbo CYMS first grade rugby league winger Garry Yeo (left) and team coach Doug Moore (right) move in to gather a loose ball spilled by Wellington five eighth Paul Boden (No 6) after a heavy tackle in the main game on Sunday. CYMS won the match 18-4.

Courtesy of: Blast From the Past, Dubbo CYMS Old Boys.

1960 Mudgee Rugby League Team Group 14 Premiers

1960 Mudgee Group 14 Premiers

Mudgee Castlereagh Shield Winners

1960 Mudgee First Grade side with the Castlereagh Shield which the team received after winning the Group 14 Premiership, defeating Coonamble in the Grand Final 11-10.

Back Row: P. Hibbert, K. Gleeson, (R. Gasnier who presented the team blazers), J. Flynn, J. McDonald, A. Golden.

Front Row: B. Harvey, P. Donohue, N. Large, D. Parkin (Captain Coach), K. Condon, P. Condon, B. Stevens.

Mudgee Guardian Reports:

Perhaps never before in the history of Group 14 has such a thrilling finish to a grand final been seen as last Sunday.

Coonamble were on their way to win four Group 14 Rugby League Premierships leading 10-6 when the final bell was about to ring.

A thrilling climax originated on the western side of the ground about halfway, when lock, Donohue, skirted a ruck, ran to Gleeson's, wing and shot him the ball.

Gleeson, with "Scorchy" Condon at his side, headed for the line. He "dummied" and shot one to his teammate, who without the ball bolted down field and drew quite a number of defenders. Gleeson meanwhile streaked over to touch down and the Mudgee supporters went haywire.

Then came the really big moment. As Ken Condon dug out a mound for the conversion, the silence was split by the strident clanging of the full time bell.

If he kicked this, Mudgee would win by a point. If he missed, Coonamble would take out their fourth first grade premiership.

It is history now that the kick was never in doubt. And the prolonged bedlam of congratulatory noise that followed will perhaps never again be equalled here or anywhere else. Final Score: Mudgee 11 defeated Coonamble 10

1960 Coonamble Grand Final Team

Back Row: Peter Yeo, Brian Byrnes, Greg Wilson, Tumbler Edwards, Alan West, Joe Evans, Ron Pellett, Earl Harrison.

Front Row: Roley Green, Josh Yeo, Jimmy Slack-Smith, Barry Cant.

Ball Boy Cecil Wright

Reg Gasniner

Article from: The Mudgee Guardian, August 16, 1985. Republished courtesy of ACM/Mudgee Guardian.

Peak Hill grabs fourth place as Wellington fails
(By "Spinner")

Peak Hill took fourth place in the Group XI first grade semi-finals with its win against Eugowra and with the defeat of Wellington in the final competition round yesterday.

Peak Hill defeated Eugowra by 13 points to 5 and Wellington went down by 32 points to 2 to minor premiers Macquarie in a rough encounter at Kennard Park.

August 1960

Forbes defeated Condobolin by 26 points to 20 and CYMS beat Parkes by 15 points to 12 at Dubbo No. 1 Oval.

Prior to yesterday's play both Wellington and Eugowra had to win to have a chance of getting in the top four.

Macquarie and Forbes will play in the first semi-final at Dubbo and Condobolin will meet Peak Hill at the former's home ground in the other.

RESULTS AT A GLANCE: Macquarie defeated Wellington 32-2, Dubbo CYMS defeated Parkes 15-12, Forbes defeated Condobolin 26-20, Peak Hill defeated Eugowra 13-5.

Article from: The Dubbo Liberal, Monday, August 29, 1960. Republished courtesy of ACM/Dubbo Liberal.

SPINNER'S WEEKEND ROUND-UP

NOSWORTHY INJURED IN FIRST MINUTE
CYMS LOSE DALEY AND RICE

July 1960

Top bracket teams Macquarie, Forbes, Condobolin and Eugowra all scored comfortable wins in round 12 Group 11 first-grade competition games yesterday.

Returning to Macquarie team after a three-matches suspension, coach Leo Nosworthy was taken off with a leg injury less than a minute after the start of the game against Narromine at No. 1 Oval Dubbo.

Article from: The Daily Liberal, Monday, July 18, 1960. Republished courtesy of ACM/Daily Liberal.

SPINNER'S WEEKEND ROUND-UP

Forbes meets Macquarie in grand final at Dubbo

September 1960

Forbes qualified to meet Dubbo Macquarie in the Group XI first grade grand-final with a hard earned 11 points to four victory over Peak Hill in the final at Pioneer Oval, Parkes, yesterday. Immediately after the final officials of Forbes and Macquarie met in the centre of the field and tossed a coin to decide the venue for the grand final next Sunday.

Coach Leo Nosworthy called correctly, so the big game will be played at Dubbo's No.1 Oval.
In the other games at Parkes yesterday Macquarie and CYMS reserves won their semi-finals decisively and Wellington juniors beat Forbes in a close junior semi-final.

Article from: The Dubbo Liberal, Monday, September 12, 1960. Republished courtesy of ACM/Dubbo Liberal.

1960 Dubbo CYMS Junior Grade Group 11 Premiers

Back Row: S. Archer (Coach), R. McPherson, K. McAlister, J. Munday, R.M. McDonald, B. McTiernan, B. O'Conner, R. Hopkins, M. Wilson, D. Kesby, A. Wilson (Trainer).

Middle Seated: Chaplain Father Creed, T. Smith (Captain), P. Ford (President).

Front Row: R. Roff, G. Yeo, G. Day, P. Moore.

Insert: A. McArthy, B. Leary.

The first CYMS team to win a grand-final.
CYMS defeated Forbes 11-9.

Courtesy of: Blast From the Past, Dubbo CYMS Old Boys.

Macquarie sweep through to second season premiership

NOSWORTHY'S TRIUMPH FIVE COACHING WINS SINCE 1946

(By "Spinner")

Dubbo Macquarie won its second successive Group XI premiership with a sweeping 22 points to 7 grand final victory over Forbes in a rough encounter before a big crowd at No. 1 Oval yesterday.

The game developed into a wild brawling affair over the concluding stages, climaxed by the sending off of Macquarie full-back Tommy Rutherford and Forbes forward Noel Parker just before full-time.

Final Score: Dubbo Macquarie 22 defeated Forbes 7.

September 1960

Despite threatening weather, a big crowd paid £536 to watch the three matches yesterday.

Macquarie's first grade victory was a personal triumph for coach Leo Nosworthy, without doubt the greatest coach in Group 11 since the competition commenced in 1946.

In that period Nosworthy has coached five teams to premiership honours.

Macquarie is only the second team to win the premiership two years running. Narromine did it in 1955 and in 1956 under Nosworthy's leadership.

The grand-final yesterday left no doubt that Macquarie was clearly the superior combination and one of the top teams if not the top side in the country districts of N.S.W.

With a good share of the ball, Macquarie hammered Forbes into submission early in the second half after playing patchy football in the first.

The roughness of play over the final stages marred the game as a spectacle. Had referee Leary maintained more control Macquarie would have won by a greater margin.

Once again, the whole Macquarie team turned in a first-class performance.

Outstanding for my money were evergreen half-back Johnny George and forwards Barry Perry and Bob Ridley.

George was always there and did a power of work.

Perry turned in his best game of the season, both in the open and the rucks. He was going just as strongly at the finish.

Above: Leo Nosworthy Captain Coach Narromine 1953/1956.

Article from: The Dubbo Daily Liberal, Monday, September 19, 1960. Republished courtesy of ACM/Dubbo Daily Liberal.

1960 Canowindra Group 11 Eastern Zone Premiers

Canowindra defeated Cumnock in the Grand Final
Back Row: Garry Fisher, Johnny Marsh, Robert Grant, Bob Grimshaw, John Williams (coach), Eugene Marsh, Dick Marsh.
Front Row: John Fitzgerald, Terry Ryan, Kevin Middleton, Bobby Rice, John Kelly, Reg Cassidy.
Courtesy of: Robert Rice Canowindra.

KEN IRVINE WINS DUBBO GIFT
(By "Observer")

March 1961

International rugby league winger Ken Irvine ran brilliantly to win the Dubbo Festival of sport Gift 120 yards footrace from a top-class field before a big crowd at No.1 Oval on Saturday night.

Running off 2 ¾ yards Irvine finished with a great burst of speed to beat Sam Martin of North Sydney off 5 yards and Dennis De Valance of Clontarf, also off 5 yards, and take first prize of £150 on the £400 programme.

A feature of the Gift meeting was that the same six runners qualified for both the Gift and the sprint finals a unique occurrence in professional foot running.

Ken Irvine

Irvine showcased his speed at a specially-arranged event specifically in an attempt to break the professional world record over 100 yards. Irvine won the event and equalled the record of 9.3 seconds. Above: Irvine also won the Dubbo Gift after starting from behind scratch, again displaying his great publicised speed.

Article from: The Dubbo Liberal, Monday, March 27, 1961. Republished courtesy of ACM/Dubbo Liberal.

1961 Oberon Rugby League Team Group 10 Premiers

Back Row: Kevin Hawkin, Peter Glendenning, Rolf Trudgett, John Rush, Vince Everingham, Tony Paskins, Don Elwin, Peter Richards.

Front Row: Brian Harvey, Norm Brown, John Brien, Laurie Evans, Col Elwin.

Oberon defeated Lithgow Workers in the Group 10 Grand Final 23 to 7, the beginning of their seven consecutive Group 10 premiership wins.

Courtesy of: The Oberon Review News. Republished courtesy of ACM/Oberon Review News.

MACQUARIE WINS DRAB CYMS GAME

(By "Observer")

Dubbo Macquarie had a comfortable 23-5 win over Dubbo CYMS at Victoria Park Oval yesterday in a drab and scrappy match.

Throughout the game there were only three moves of any class, and all yielded tries. Spoiling tactics by both teams kept play tight.

May 1961

Tempers frayed during the second half and fighting broke out on several occasions.

In one scuffle towards the closing stages of the match Leo Nosworthy received a broken jaw and was taken to hospital for treatment after the match.

Nosworthy was the "brains" behind all the Macquarie moves and even with a broken jaw played solid football.

Once again, however he spoiled a wonderful performance by consistently roughing up CYMS players in tackles.

The referee had occasion to warn him several times together with CYMS players.

Macquarie is now the only un-beaten team in the Group competition. Eugowra was surprisingly defeated by Peak Hill yesterday.

Next week's match between Macquarie and Peak Hill should be a thriller.

Playing on the wing Tom Rutherford proved how versatile a player he is by adopting the position comfortably and scoring two glorious tries.

Young second-row forward Max Ison was the pick of the Macquarie forwards. His penetrating runs and brilliant cover defence were a pleasure to watch.

Athol Curry was his usual self and made much ground with his long, barging runs.

Reserve-grade hooker Ray Hill, promoted to the firsts, turned in a sterling performance and won Macquarie a great share of the ball.

Peter Rawlinson, playing in the lock position, turned in a good game but, like Nosworthy became punchy on several occasions.

Nosworthy receives broken jaw

Half-back Ron Boden led his backline well and made many moves when in possession.

Centres, Les Wilson and Wally Towers accounted well for themselves. Tower kicked four goals from seven attempts.

Full-back Garry Carter performed well and was sound in defence. Perhaps a good goal-kicker for CYMS would have brought a different outlook to the game.

Goal-kicker Tim Smith had a bad knock, landing only one goal from seven attempts.

Smith also lacked his penetrating power and played a dull game.

On several occasions he was caught out of position and his tackling left much to be desired.

Barry Harris had a quiet day and nothing outstanding. He tackled well but stood off in attack rather than lead it.

CYMS five-eighth Ray McTiernan played a first-class game and on many occasions over shadowed his rival Nosworthy.

McTiernan played constructive football throughout the match and made the sole try scored by CYMS.

He broke through the defence on several occasions and was unlucky not to have scored twice.

His tackling was solid and with Max Ison, was the best player on the field.

Article from: The Dubbo Daily Liberal, May 29, 1961. Republished courtesy of ACM/Dubbo Daily Liberal.

UNDEFEATED RECORD LOST
Brilliant Wellington Win over Macquarie

June 1961

By "Observer"

Wellington R.L. had a brilliant 7/5 victory over the previously undefeated Macquarie team at Kennard Park, Wellington, on Sunday.

The match was one of the hardest seen in Group 11 competitions for many years and it was a good indication that better things are to come from the Wellington team.

Wellington half-back Paul Boden, brother of international Ron Boden, was the star of the match.

His cleaner passing and switching of play from behind the scrums put Wellington on the attack time after time.

Perhaps the best feature of the game was the brilliant cover defence which he displayed.

Super tackling by Boden saved at least three certain tries.

In the forwards Don Feltas was the outstanding player.

He made many fine barging runs and his defence was as solid as a rock at all times.

Macquarie attacked more than Wellington but was unable to finish off the movements.

Time and again the Macquarie players were inches from scoring and bad passing lost possession to Wellington.

Peter Rawlinson was a tower of strength until he received a nasty knock which left him dazed throughout the match.

Rawlinson scored Macquarie's sole try when he broke through the Wellington defence just over half way and outpaced the opposition to score a great try near the posts.

Barry Hope was the destroying factor of the match with his superb goal kicking.

During the first half he landed a terrific goal from over half way to put Wellington in front 5/3.

Then, with only ten minutes to go, he kicked the winning goal from 55 yards out to give Wellington a great 7/5 victory.

Macquarie received an early setback when Barry Perry received a knock on the leg which left him a "cripple" for the remainder of the match.

Ray Hill was ordered from the field after an incident in the scrum from which Wellington hooker Greenwood was taken off with broken ribs.

On the day Wellington was the superior team and the win was a credit to them.

Article from: The Dubbo Liberal, Tuesday, June 13, 1961. Republished courtesy of ACM/Dubbo Liberal.

1961 Brewarrina Rugby League Team Defeats Cobar

1961 Brewarrina Group 15 Premiers

In the first semi-final Brewarrina defeated Cobar for the first time in years 15-13. Cobar failed to make the Group 15 grand-final.

In the other semi-finals, Nyngan defeated Bourke for the right to challenge Brewarrina in the grand-final.

The 1961 grand final was won by Brewarrina defeating Nyngan 26-5. It was to be their first Group 15 Premiership.

Brewarrina Group 15 Premiers:
B. Caton, R. Knight, J. Evers, J. Grant, A. Biles, J. Ryan, A. Norton, P. Stevens, A. McCaughey, N. McKenzie, M. Cobb, E. Grange, R. Hunt.

1961 Cobar Team
Back Row: I. Rice, R. Pike, D. McLean, T. Knight, I. Thompson, B. Harvey, T. Forbes.
Front Row: L. Jermyn, J. Josephson, W. Collins, P. Storey, T. Collins, W. Howett.

Courtesy of: John Collins, The Crowing of The Roosters, Cobar Rugby League.

CYMS will meet tough opposition

Dubbo CYMS will travel on Sunday to Parkes, where the local boys are favoured to defeat the consistent CYMS team.

Bill Tonkin, the Parkes captain-coach, has his team in top form and their co-ordination has improved considerably in recent matches.

June 1961

Tonkin, in particular, is in terrific condition and playing hard throughout the 80 minutes.

A feature of his play is a splendid cover defence, which never faulters.

The main destroying factor in the Parkes team is centre Wally McArthur.

A delight to watch when in possession of the ball, McArthur is a wonderful goal kicker and has won many matches for Parkes with great goals.

There are no holes in his defence and CYMS will have to mark him constantly.

Co-centre B. Lawler, son of international referee Darcy Lawler, has a great deal of potential and combines well with McArthur.

CYMS, will have to use its forwards to full advantage if it is to beat Parkes, as this seems to be the only section of Parkes team with a possible gap in it.

All these forwards have been playing well, especially Carson and Smith, who are fiery front-rowers with a lot of toes when in possession.

The CYMS three-quarter line will have to smarten up. It is being caught flat-footed too often and the fast Parkes team will take advantage of this.

The only backs to show any promise for CYMS are John Fisher and full-back Tim Smith.

Both play constructive football and, if at their best on Sunday, could cause headaches for the Parkes team.

Above Bill Tonkin in action for Parkes

Article from: The Dubbo Liberal, Monday, September 11, 1961. Republished courtesy of ACM/Dubbo Liberal.

Dubbo CYMS History

Dubbo CYMS Rugby League was formed in 1947, playing in the local Saturday competition until they were accepted into the Group 11 competition in 1958.

The club struggled in its infancy and in 1960 won their first Group 11 premiership with the under 18 juniors. It took until 1966 for the club to record its second premiership with the reserve grade winning the Group 11 competition.

In 1968 Ken McMullen was appointed the first-grade coach and things started to improve under his leadership. Details of their successes follow in this and the seventies section.

MACQUARIE'S THIRD GROUP PREMIERSHIP

(By "Observer")

Before one of the biggest crowds ever to watch a Group XI Rugby League grand-final the powerful Dubbo Macquarie team had a convincing 23/11 victory over Forbes to win its third consecutive premiership yesterday.

In the two earlier games Dubbo Macquarie defeated Wellington 13-9 in the Reserve grade and the vastly-improved Forbes Juniors side scored a great 7-3 victory over Condobolin.

September 1961

A superior team combination proved the match-winning factor for Macquarie first-grade and a great deal of credit must go to captain coach Leo Nosworthy.

Nosworthy is a great tactician and he had his "boys" at their peak for yesterday's grand-final.

Nosworthy himself played one of his best games of this season.

Several times he chopped the Forbes defence to pieces with hard, busting runs.

John George played another great game in the half back position.

His service from the base of the scrum played a big part in the "Blues" victory.

Doug Moore and Don Teale were kept busy in the centre positions and acquitted themselves excellently.

Wingers Wally Towers and Paul Sabine had a feast of the ball throughout the match and made many long runs.

Tom Rutherford turned in an outstanding display in fullback position. Always safe in defence, his twisting runs gained much ground when he was in possession. Of the threequarters I thought that Nosworthy and Rutherford possibly just overshadowed the remainder.

Macquarie forwards have laid the foundation of many victories and yesterday's performance was no exception.

Bob Ridley and Athol Currey played the whole 80 minutes tirelessly.

Ridley made many crashing runs to gain tons of valuable ground. He tackled solidly and was never out of position.

Athol Currey shone out like a "lone star" in the close forward play.

His crashing runs continually left a trail of tacklers behind and his own tackling was punishing throughout the match.

However, it takes six men to make a pack of forwards and no one could say Currey and Ridley did the lot.

Max Ison returned to the side to replace Barry Perry and his performance was excellent.

He made several long runs which put Macquarie in a handy position.

Peter Rawlinson and Ron Soden also played well in second-row position.

Soden was every thing throughout and Rawlinson added much valuable support.

Hooker Ross Bartier played well and held his own against the experienced boot of Fred King.

The Forbes performance was disappointing especially during the middle of the game.

Far too much "rough house" tactics spoiled what could have developed into a thrilling grand-final.

Rubagotti played constructive football throughout the match and his quick thinking to exploit the little kick paid off handsomely.

The performance of Eric Gilligan was disappointing. He is a top-class player but did not put his shoulder to the wheel when times were tough.

He was often out of position and was lucky not to be ordered from the field after kicking Peter Rawlinson.

Rawlinson badly injured his nose in the final against Forbes at Dubbo a fortnight ago.

Forbes never really looked like a grand-finalist team, even from the opening of the game.

The superior condition and combination of the Nosworthy-coached, Macquarie team was too strong.

Article from: The Dubbo Liberal, Monday, September 25, 1961. Republished courtesy of ACM/Dubbo Liberal.

1962 Carcoar Mid-West Community Cup Premiers

Back Row: F. Turner (secretary), R. Davis, A. Kind (Captain), J. Connolly, K. Kind, M. Turner.

Middle Row: P. Higgs, T. Van Dartel, R. Patterson, K. Bright, J. Van Dartel.

Front Row: A Bright, J. Cardwell, L. Turner.

Carcoar won the Cup nine times from 1957-1969 with Cullen Bullen taking the cup in 1961, ending their ten-year run.

The Mid-West Community Cup was a Rugby League competition in the Central West area of New south Wales. The premiers are awarded the Blayney Citizens' Cup, the oldest continuously awarded trophy in country Rugby League, with Neville the first recipients in 1913.
Some of the 40 teams who competed for the cup over the years are: Blayney, Browns Creek, Cullen Bullen, Milthorpe, Manildra, Rylstone-Kandos, Rockley and Wallerwang.

Source: Mid-West Cup Wikipedia, The Free Encyclopedia.

Belubula Street and Railway Station Carcoar

Carcoar is a small country town in Mid-West NSW with a population of around 300.

Source: Carcoar Wikipedia, The Free Encyclopedia.

Fred King

Fred King, left, captained the Forbes Rugby League First Grade Team in 1962 and led his team to win the grand-final by defeating Wellington 16-4.

King made a move to Parkes as a paid player where he played under Rex Percy in 1964 before being made captain-coach in 1965, where the club won the minor premiership before a 5-4 loss to Narromine in the preliminary final.

A clever hooker and powerful forward with Forbes and Parkes throughout the 1960s, King went on to become Group 11 and Western Division President. He was also the manager of the Western Division Amco Cup 1974 winning team.

Article from: The Parkes Champion Post. Com. Au/Story/5149644. Republished courtesy of ACM/Parkes Champion Post.

Weekend Sports Preview

(By "Observer")

The semi-finals of Group XI Rugby League competition at Victoria Park Oval, will highlight sporting events in Dubbo this weekend.

Dubbo Macquarie will meet Wellington in the main game of the day and this could be the final chance for league followers to see Macquarie in action on the home ground this season.

September 1962

Macquarie and Wellington are at full strength.

Macquarie's hopes rose last night when Peter Rawlinson proved his fitness and will return to his second-row position.

Merv Rich and John Evans, however, will miss the game.

Wellington's performances of late give a slight edge, but with the match being played on the fast Victoria Oval Macquarie is expected to be hard to beat.

In the reserve-grade final Dubbo CYMS and Wellington have entered extremely strong teams and this should develop into a tough battle.

The junior clash between Macquarie and CYMS has always been an interesting clash and Sunday's semi-final should be a thriller.

The teams for Sunday are as follows:

MACQUARIE First Grade:
T. Rutherford, P. Sabine, R. Pack,
D. Teale, W. Towers, G. Klenthis,
J. George, L. Nosworthy (Captain),
R. Hill, P. Rawlinson, A. Currey,
B. Perry, R. Bartier.
Reserves: P. Shields, P. Harris

WELLINGTON First Grade:
M. Hobbs, E. Coles, R. Cavanagh,
A. Jones (Captain), R. Bullock,
C. Sutton, P. Boden, K. Sutton,
J. Stubberfield, J. Reynolds,
V. Gersbach, B. Hope, J. Dean.

REFEREE: Mr. N. Johnson, Cumnock.

Article from: The Dubbo Liberal, Friday, September 14, 1962. Republished courtesy of ACM/Dubbo Liberal.

WELLINGTON WINS BEFORE RECORD CROWD

Fast pace decides
Wellington 28 defeated Dubbo Macquarie 10
(By "Observer")

September 1962

A record crowd of 2,678 yesterday cheered Wellington from the field following its 28 points to ten, victory over Dubbo Macquarie in the Group 11 Rugby League first grade semi-final.

Features of the match included:
- An outstanding performance by young Wellington centre Ross Bullock.
- Tom Rutherford, Dubbo Macquarie fullback, ordered from the field for alleged punching.
- A faultless display by Dubbo Macquarie captain-coach Leo Nosworthy, appearing in his final match for the team.
- The superior condition and combination of Wellington, especially in the three-quarter line.
- Macquarie, noticeably lacking match practice, was unable to maintain the pace.

Opposing captains Leo Nosworthy (left) and Allan Jones shaking hands prior to yesterday's semi-final. In the foreground are the young mascots from Dubbo Macquarie and Wellington.

Article from: The Dubbo Liberal, Monday, September 17, 1962 Republished courtesy of ACM/Dubbo Liberal.

Great Farewell Game by Nosworthy

Star of the day was young outside centre Ross Bullock, who scored a 70 yard try and featured in many solo bursts during the game.

Bullock, a product of the Wellington juniors, has a bright future ahead of him as a League player.

The only Macquarie player to excel was Leo Nosworthy. He drove the "Blues" continually and led them in all attacking and defensive moves.

Nosworthy gave a polished display as his "farewell" match to the local crowds.

The Macquarie defence was poor. Wellington players continually stepped under head-high tackles to go into the attack.

Two of Wellington's tries came about when the Macquarie backline stood off swallowing a series of dummies.

The Macquarie forwards held their own against the big Wellington pack and although none were out-standing they played as a team and did a lot of work.

Slow ball distribution and standing too deep in defence contributed to Macquarie's defeat.

Barry Perry and Athol Curry, the powerful front-rowers played tirelessly especially in defence.

Ross Bartier also played well but was unable to win the ball for Macquarie from the set scrums.

Ray Hill and Peter Rawlinson turned in solid displays from the second row.

Halves John George and George Kienthis had a quiet day. Centres Wally Towers and Don Teale were kept extremely busy and played poorly.

Their defence was not as solid as it usually is. Teale continually allowed Wellington centres to break through his high tackles and he continually mishandled.

Macquarie wingers Ron Pack and Paul Sabine had a quiet day, seeing the ball on few occasions.

Until ordered from the field early in the second half Tom Rutherford was also having an off day.

Continued next page:

Article from: The Dubbo Liberal, Monday, September 17, 1962. Republished courtesy of ACM/Dubbo Liberal.

Great Farewell Game by Nosworthy

Continued from previous page:

He was continually caught in possession and his usually reliable defence was lacking.

Along with Ross Bullock and Wellington Captain Coach Allan Jones also played a great game.

His powerful breaks through the centres allowed Bullock to swing into attack continuously. Jones' cover defence was also sound.

Winger Barry Cavanagh played well and worried the Macquarie defence with smart runs down the sideline.

Mike Hollis made a pleasant return to the team and continually joined the backline to make the extra man.

Barry Hope again kicked well for Wellington, landing four goals from seven attempts.

Ken Sutton played a tough game from the lock forward position, ably supported by Val Gersbach, John Reynolds and Jim Stubberfield.

Hooker John Dean gave Wellington a feast of the ball and assisted greatly in the team's victory.

Halves Col Sutton and Paul Boden also played well, as did winger Erin Coles.

Article from: The Dubbo Liberal, Monday, September 17, 1962. Republished courtesy of ACM/Dubbo Liberal.

SOLID WIN BY WELLINGTON

(By "Observer")

Wellington Rugby League first-grade team yesterday won the final of the Group XI competition with a convincing 19/8 victory over Eugowra.

September 1962

A large crowd filled Pioneer Oval, Parkes, to see the fast finishing Wellington team qualify for the grand-final with a solid victory over Eugowra.

Wellington will now play Forbes in the grand final at Forbes next Sunday.

Wellington won yesterday in the first half leading 19-0 at half-time.

Brilliant combinational play by the Wellington backline, the captain-coach Allan Jones and Ross Bullock paved the way.

Jones and Bullock have proved a superb combination in the centre and are certain to cause Forbes some headaches next week.

Barry Cavanagh again put up a sterling performance on the wing and fullback Mike Hobbs continually joined the three-quarter line in aggressive moves.

Halves Paul Boden and Colin Sutton played well and fed the backline continually.

In the forwards Barry Hope stood out with powerful running and excellent goal kicking. During the season he has scored 99 points in first-grade.

Val Gersbach and Ken Sutton continually put Wellington on the attack, while John Reynolds, Jim Stubberfield and John Dean all played solid games.

Eugowra never allowed to move freely, gave a poor display, especially during the first half.

Lack of cover defence enabled Wellington to score all its tries in the first half.

The team rallied slightly in the second half to score eight points to Wellington's nil, but was no match for the "Maroons".

Five-eighth Ken Smith tried continually for Eugowra, with best support from Lionel Bloomfield and captain - coach John Hobby.

Article from: The Dubbo Liberal, Monday, September 24, 1962. Republished courtesy of ACM/Dubbo Liberal.

CONVINCING VICTORY BY FORBES

Forbes won the 1962 Group XI premiership on its home ground on Sunday with a convincing 16-4 victory over Wellington.

Fred King Forbes Captain Coach

October 1962

Forbes also won the reserve-grade premiership defeating Dubbo Macquarie 17-2.

Parkes won the junior premiership with a 16-11 victory over Dubbo CYMS.

An all-out effort in the first 20 minutes of the second-half enabled Forbes to win its second Group 11 premiership.

Trailing

Trailing 4-3 at half time, Forbes struck back early in the second half, notching three quick tries and a goal to take a clear 14-4 lead.

In the closing stages of the match fullback Brian Collits landed another penalty goal to make the final score 16-4.

The whole Forbes team played well and bettered the opposition in all departments.

Led by Fred King, Don Dwyer and Cec Cassidy, the Forbes forwards gave the team a feast of the ball from the rucks and set scrums.

John Lasker played his usual wily game at half-back, well supported by Des Shead and Brian Collits.

The Wellington back line had many lapses and was unable to penetrate the Forbes defence to any great degree.

The Pick

Allan Jones, Mike Hobbs and Paul Boden turned in solid performances in the back line while Barry Hope, Val Gersbach and Ken Sutton were the pick of the forwards.

In the closing stages of the match fullback Brian Collits landed another penalty goal to make the final score 16-4.

Allan Jones Wellington Captain Coach

Article from: The Dubbo Liberal, Tuesday, October 2, 1962. Republished courtesy of ACM/Dubbo Liberal.

1962 Forbes Rugby League Team Group 11 Premiers

Back Row: Cec Cassidy, Mick Wilson, Ray Drabsch, George Rossiter, Alan Taylor.

Middle Row: Deacon Dwyer, Noel Parker, Fred King (captain-coach), Don Parslow, Barry Anderson.

Front Row: Kerry Smith, John Lasker, Des Shead and Brian Collits.

Photo from: Celebrating a Century of League Our Grand Final Glory, Republished courtesy of ACM/Forbes Advocate.

1963 Dubbo CYMS Rugby League First Grade Team

Back Row: R. McTiernan, M. Wilson, M. Ensor, N. Healey, R. Carson, B. O'Connor.

Front Row: C. Eastburn, T. Smith, D. Frazer, F. Byrne, R. Hopkins, W. Peckham, J. Kempston.

Courtesy of: Blast From the Past, Dubbo CYMS Old Boys.

1963 Canowindra Group 11 Eastern Zone Premiers

Canowindra defeated Cumnock in the Group 11 Eastern Zone Grand Final
Right: Bobby Rice, a member of the 1963 premiership winning team.

Courtesy of: Robert Rice Canowindra.

Golden years for the mighty Eugowra Blacks

Pictured The Eugowra Blacks

1963 team:
Back Row: Mark Toohey, Ray Pegilly, Ian McClintock, Vince Toohey, Alex Gilmore, John Taylor, Frank Glover, Ted Porch, Barry Beath, Maurie McClintock.

Middle Row: Noel Pengilly, John Porch, Maurie Cummins, John Hobby, (Captain Coach), Billy Haydon, Ken Smith.

Front Row: Kevin Norris, David Greenhalgh, Lionel Bloomfield, Barry Turner.

1967 team:
Back Row: David Greenhalgh, Don Glasson, Mal Morgan, Ted Porch, Col Pritchard (Captain Coach), Mick Beath, Alan Bell, John Porch, Dennis Madden.

Front Row: Basil Toohey, Ian McClintock, David Glasson, Darryl Jones, Brian Turner, Dick McGrath, Mark Toohey.

Courtesy of: Eugowra Historical Society Museum, Judith Smith.

Central Hotel Eugowra

The Central Hotel was the main meeting place after the games where players and supporters would celebrate the mighty Blacks' victories.

Courtesy of: The Central Hotel Eugowra.

John Hobby A Bush Rugby League Legend

John Hobby

For a man who never played Sydney football, John Hobby had an amazing 17 year career.

He toured New Zealand with NSW Country in 1968, as well as representing Country Seconds four times, playing six matches against International touring teams, representing three divisions in a total of 30 plus games, playing for four Groups and winning six premierships as a captain/coach.

Highly respected by his team-mates and opponents alike, John gave back plenty to the game he loved after his playing career had finished.

Born in Coolah on 24 July 1938, John attended the local primary school where he began playing Rugby League in 1946. After leaving primary school, he made the 110 kms south journey each way, five days a week, to study at Mudgee High from 1952 to 1954. In 1952 he was forced to give football away after being kicked in the head by a mule at a circus. This resulted in a fractured skull and for most people, football of any kind would never be considered. But he began again with a local under 15s in 1953 and the under 18s the following season.

He was moved up to Coolah first grade side in 1957, where his father, Marsden, was a long team senior official and played with them until the end of 1959 before joining Bathurst Railways in 1960 and 1961. While with Railways in 1960, he represented Western Division in the Country Championship, as he also did in 1961 and on 1st June 1960 was a member of the Western Division team which defeated France 14-7 at Dubbo. He also gained selection for Country Seconds in 1960. Bathurst Railway made the Group 10 Final in 1960 and the semi-finals in 1960 in 1961 and John played strongly in both games.

In 1962 he began the first four successive seasons as Eugowra captain/coach, winning the minor premiership, but going down in the final to Forbes. As this was his first captain/coaching job, John made himself unavailable for any representative selection. Forbes went on to defeat Wellington in the grand-final.

For the next three seasons, 1963-1965, Eugowra won the Premiership and John represented Western Division each season, as well as playing with Country Seconds in 1963 and 1964. In 1963 he also played for Western Division against New Zealand at Parkes and in 1964 played his second international against France, when Western Division won 17-11 at Orange.

Courtesy of: Barry Ross, March 23, 2017, (Republished article from "Family of League").

1968 Country Rugby League Team Toured New Zealand

John Hobby was also a member of the 1968 NSW Country Rugby League Team to tour New Zealand in 1968.

Back Row: G. Atherton, A. Elford, I. Kennedy, P. Kelly, A. Buman, J. Bonus, L. Hutchings.

Middle Row: T. Pannowitz, P. Inskip, J. Hobby, B. Carlson (Coach), L. Simmons, A. Thomson, A. Powell.

Front Row: J. Hattam (Manager), R. Crowe, D. Grimmond, W. Bischoff (Captain), K. Broad, R. Costello, J. O'Toole (Manager).

Courtesy of: NSW Rugby League, The Rugby League News, 1968 Country Team Toured New Zealand May, 1968.

Two of Group 11's Finest Players: John Hobby and Ken Smith

John Hobby avoiding a would be tackler.

Ken Smith carrying the ball.

1963
Represented Western Division in the Country Championships.
Represented Western Division against New Zealand.
Represented Country Seconds.
Won the Group 11 Grand Final (Eugowra 13 def Forbes 0).
1964
Represented Western Division in Country Championships.
Represented Western Division in the State Cup.
Represented Western Division v France.
Represented Country Seconds.
Won the Group 11 Grand Final (Eugowra def Forbes 8-7).
1965
Represented Western Division.
Represented Western Division in State Cup.
Won the Group 11 Grand Final.
(Eugowra 22 def Canowindra-3).

Ken Smith was born in Ryde and commenced his football career with Burnside Schoolboys. He played Under 18's with Concord West (coached by Harry Wells) and in 1959 he was approached to play First Grade Rugby League in Eugowra. At Eugowra, Ian Walsh was the coach for the 1959 and 1960 seasons without any success and then John Hobby took over in 1962 with immediate success by taking out the Minor Premiership.

1963 was another excellent season and Ken was chosen in the Group 11 team as five-eighth. In 1964 with John Hobby as Captain/Coach and Ken Smith as five-eighth Eugowra won Major titles.

Courtesy of: Barry Ross, March 23, 2017 (Republished article from "Family of League").

1963 Earl Harrison

Earl Harrison

1963 Kangaroos: Earl Harrison front sitting first on the left

A tough tackling farmer from Gulargambone became Australian rugby league player 378 when he played his first Test against New Zealand in 1963. The young five-eighth was playing for Gilgandra at the time and capped a remarkable season where he was outstanding for Western Division, Country, NSW and in New Zealand when his name was read out for the 1963 Kangaroo Tour of Great Britain.

Article from: The Dubbo Photo News, December 27, 2018, by Geoff Mann.

FORBES IN RL GRAND FINAL

Forbes rugby league first-grade team moved into the grand-final of the 1963 Group XI competition yesterday, with an 8-5 win over Condobolin at Pioneer Oval, Parkes.

September 1963

The first-grade fixture between joint minor-premiers Forbes and Condobolin provided tight hard football.

Forbes scored all the points in the first quarter hour of play when Kerry Smith scored a try and converted and Barry Anderson scored.

Condobolin scored its five points towards the middle of the second half when Tack scored a try and Barry Lemon landed a penalty goal.

Apart from these two periods play was scoreless with Forbes and then Condobolin continually turning defence into attack.

Ten minutes before full time, hookers Fred King (Forbes) and Stan Archer received their marching orders for continually putting their feet up in the scrum.

Condobolin will now go into next week's final against Eugowra, the winner of this match will meet Forbes in the grand-final the following week.

Article from: The Dubbo Daily Liberal, Monday, September 16, 1963. Republished courtesy of ACM/Dubbo Daily Liberal.

Help is on its way

George Atchison Parkes Superintendent was one of the many ambulance officers on hand for many league games at Pioneer Oval Parkes.

Courtesy of: NSW Rugby League, The Rugby League News, June, 1928.

Eugowra in Grand Final

(By "Observer")

Eugowra first-grade rugby league team yesterday moved into the grand-final of the Group XI competition by defeating Condobolin 9-2 at Spooner Oval Forbes on Sunday.

September 1963

The Condobolin club missed out on getting its three representative teams into the grand final when the first-grade team performed poorly against Eugowra.

With captain-coach John Hobby out because of injury, Eugowra's win was all the more convincing.

Hobby was injured at work during the week but it is hoped he will be fit for next Sunday's grand-final against Forbes.

Condobolin lost hooker Stan Archer midway through the second half but despite this dominated the scrums 18-10.

Despite its feast of the ball, Condobolin was not dangerous in attack.

Poor handling, especially by centre Tony Packham, contributed much towards Condobolin's defeat.

Packham was heavily tackled early in the game and from then on never handled the ball cleanly.

Eugowra played tight constructive football from the first whistle and after scoring points was never headed.

Morris McClintock scored Eugowra's only try and Frank Glover landed three penalty goals.

Condobolin's two points came from a penalty goal by Barry Lemon.

Eugowra's forwards paved the way for their team's victory by softening up and out playing the Condobolin forwards.

Barry Beath, Noel Pengilly and Ray Pengilly were the pick of the Eugowra forwards with Ken Smith and Lionel Bloomfield heading the backline.

Bob Lemon, Ron Clothier and Barry Lemon were the pick of the Condobolin players in defence while Mick Nairn was always strong in attack.

The highlight of the match was the dynamic leadership of Lionel Bloomfield and the good team spirit displayed by the Eugowra team.

All grand-final matches will almost certainly be played at Parkes.

Article from: The Dubbo Liberal, Monday, September 23, 1963. Republished courtesy of ACM/Dubbo Liberal.

All in the game

Courtesy of: NSW Rugby League, The Rugby League News, August 1926.

EUGOWRA WINS FIRST RUGBY LEAGUE GRAND FINAL

Eugowra First Grade won their first Group XI premiership when they defeated Forbes in a grand-final at Parkes last Sunday. Spectators paid £740 to watch the fixture.

Eugowra 13, Forbes 10

September 1963

Both teams gave a good display of defence for it was not until the final stages that the first try of the match was scored.

Forbes and Eugowra had ample opportunity to put up the points of penalties. Eugowra could call the tune in this department as their goal kicker, Frank Glover, was in real kicking form. Of the fulltime total of 13 points, Glover landed 10 with four goals and a conversion in the second half.

Forbes kicker, Kerry Smith, couldn't impress the linesman with his kicks at goal and was unsuccessful on a number of attempts. Forbes could have matched Eugowra point for point had they a kicker in the same class as Glover.

The Eugowra defence suffered a real battering throughout the match, but held like a stone wall till fulltime. Only a few Forbes players were able to penetrate the Eugowra defence only to be faced with the cover defence which brought them to a sudden halt.

Forbes defence was also functioning well, but Eugowra were getting a lot more penetration. Eugowra forwards Barry Beath, John Hobby and B. Turner continually smashed through Forbes forwards and Beath earned the reputation as the best attacking forward on the field. This Eugowra forward never stopped running all day and was still at it when the final whistle blew.

Forbes had a territorial advantage for the majority of time in the first half but as hard as the Forbes backs tried, they could not penetrate far enough to look dangerous.

SECOND HALF

Eugowra were on top of Forbes early in the second half, but the pattern of "give and take" was soon underway.

Forbes in this half appeared to get a little more penetration and on a number of occasions went close to scoring tries.

On the first of these near misses, Herbert and Anderson broke away on halfway and Anderson was little more than a step from the Eugowra line. On this and similar occasions in this half Forbes lost the scoring chance by going offside and being penalised.

BLOOMFIELD OFF

Eugowra scrum half, Lionel Bloomfield was right in the thick of the defence trying to stop Anderson from scoring. In the play Bloomfield suffered a nasty kick in the eye that forced him to leave the field and left him groggy well after the match finished. While playing he suffered a real battering from the Forbes forwards, but weathered the storm and played on in grand style.

Eugowra centre Maurice McClintock set Eugowra up for their first and only try of the match. Inside the Forbes half, McClintock got away from the Forbes defence and ran for Kerry Smith's wing. McClintock then positioned the goalmouth but kicked too hard and the ball went dead.

Barry Beath, with a number of savage drives through the Forbes forwards, made up the leeway for Eugowra and Ken Smith Eugowra five-eighth found an opening and placed the ball down for a try, Frank Glover converted for the final points of the match.

IN A NUTSHELL

Eugowra were just too good on the day. Many Forbes supporters had to admit that Eugowra were the better team. Their heavy forwards Beath and Pengilly, penetrated for the reason that Forbes let them run too far.

Forbes were over anxious and went offside too close to their line and Glover did the rest for Eugowra.

Forbes had their chance with penalties but Kerry Smith and Kevin Hanns just weren't accurate enough with their kicks.

Scrum half John Lasker and hooker Fred King tried as hard as they could but failed to meet referee Kevin Dwyer's approval. On many occasions Lasker would have been scratching to fit a golf ball into the scrums.

The whole Eugowra team played so well that it would be unfair to mention individual names.

Article from: The Forbes Advocate, September, 1963. Republished courtesy of ACM/Forbes Advocate.

Rugby League Broadcast History 2PK Parkes

Norm Spicer

Parkes and district fans who were unable to travel were able to tune in as Norm called the game.

Norm Spicer was one of the game's characters on radio 2PK football game broadcasts taking over from his father Frank.

He was a very descriptive match caller and Ray Tuxford provided comments in between. Ray was referred to as Ray Rugby League.

Other commentators to follow were: Barton Prior, Bernie, Chris Smith and Tony Wright.

BERNIE WRIGHT and CHRIS SMITH

At 12 noon on Sunday prior to the Big Match we'll Preview the Grand Final and Review the 1984 Season.

CHRIS SMITH will be calling the second half of the Reserve Grade Grand Final.

Article from: The Parkes Champin Post, September 14, 1984.

Proud Family Tradition

Tony Dwyer's appointment to his first Group 11 Grand Final today continues a proud family refereeing tradition.

In so doing Tony becomes the third member of the Dwyer clan to control the Group decider following the path developed by grandfather Charlie and father Kevin.

From 1962 to 1968, Kevin Dwyer was recognized as one of the best whistle men in the country. Dwyer controlled seven consecutive Group 11 Grand Finals from 1962 to 1968 and a host of divisional and international matches. He became the first Country referee to be appointed to the Seconds match on SCG before a crowd of 30,000 when country scored a late try to win 19-18.

Tony and Kevin reflect on Tony's appointment to the 1999 First Grade Grand Final

Tony Dwyer's appointment to his first Group 11 Grand Final today continues a proud family refereeing tradition. In so doing Tony becomes the third member of the Dwyer clan to control the Group decider following the path developed by grandfather Charlie and father Kevin.

From 1962 to 1968, Kevin Dwyer was recognized as one of the best whistle men in the country. Dwyer controlled seven consecutive Group 11 Grand Finals from 1962 to 1968 and a host of divisional and international matches. He became the first Country referee to be appointed to the Sydney v Country First lines and then two years later he controlled the Seconds

Kevin Dwyer's long list of achievements to mention a few: Newcastle v New Zealand match, Newcastle v Illawarra Country Final and Great Britain v Riverina and many others. He retired from refereeing in 1968 after achieving all he had set out to do.

Tony continues to follow in his grand-father's and father's foot-steps as President Parkes Rugby League Club

Article from: Geoff Mann. Republished courtesy of Tony Dwyer Parkes Rugby League President.

Magic Sponge:

Rugby league players during the 1960-1970 era, would have been attended to by their trainer with a bucket of water and the magic sponge.

The "magic sponge" is a name used jokingly for what appears to be a regular yellow sponge which, when applied by a physio to a player's injured body part, seems to have incredible healing powers. A player, who was just seconds earlier rolling around in what looked to be agonizing pain, with just a few "magic sponge" rubs is healed and ready to go back into play like nothing happened. Ambulance officers were on the sidelines to attend to serious injuries.

Sand Boy:
Another memory is when the "sand boy" would run onto the field with a bucket of sand used to mount the football for a shot at goal. The sand bucket was replaced with a plastic mount.

Toe Poking Kicks at Goal:
For several decades of rugby league, "toe-pokers" took kicks at goals. The ball was placed flat on a pile of sand and kicked with the front of their boot. It was not altogether effective.
Right Toe Poking boots.

Around the Corner Kicking:
All changed in 1974 with the game changer John Gray, who introduced us all to around the corner kicking. Standing the ball upright and approaching it from an angle provided immediate results and soon the toe-pokers were relegated to the history reels.

Source: Canowindra Historical Society Inc.

1964 Dubbo CYMS First Grade Rugby League Team

Back Row: Neville Bowe (coach), Terry Carolan, Mick Wilson, Wayne Peckham, Max Ensor, Tim Smith, Barry O'Connor, Ray McTiernan, Tony Linnane.

Front Row: John Kempston, Brian Lake, Elwin Porter, Don Fraser, Ray Hardie.

Courtesy of: Blast From the Past, Dubbo CYMS Old Boys.

1964 CYMS defeated Forbes in Group 11 Reserve Grade Final

Left: Wayne Peckham, of Dubbo CYMS, tackles one of the Forbes players in the reserve-grade final at Parkes yesterday, CYMS won the game 7-6.

The following week Dubbo Macquarie defeated Dubbo CYMS in the 1964 Group 11 Reserve Grade Grand-Final at Pioneer Oval Parkes 7-0.

Courtesy of: Blast From the Past, Dubbo CYMS Old Boys

1964 Macquarie Street Dubbo

Source: John Fullagar Facebook, NSW State Archives Collection.

Group XI round-up
POSITIONAL SWITCHES BY EUGOWRA & FORBES

September 1964

Eugowra and Forbes first-grade teams have each dropped a man and made several positional changes to help strengthen their chances of winning the Group 11 grand-final at Pioneer Oval, Parkes, on Sunday.

Eugowra has dropped front-rower Ray Pengilly to give Barry Beath a run, Beath missed out last week and his place in the second row was taken by Alex Gilmour.

Eugowra v Forbes

Eugowra:	Forbes:
1. D. Greenhalgh	1. G. Gelligan
2. T. Porch	2. R. Drabsch
5. I. McClintock	5. B. Gee
3. J. Porch	3. B. Anderson
4. M. McClintock	4. D. Turner
6. F. Glover	6. D. Shead
7. L. Bloomfield	7. J. Lasker
8. J. Hobby	8. R. Burge
9. N. Pengilly	9. C. Herbert
10. A. Gilmour	10 K. Nicholson
11. B. Beath	11. D. Dwyer
13. D. Glasson	13. R. Fathers
12. V. Toohey.	12. D. Forsythe.

Half Ken Smith who in last week's final suffered a cut on his knee which required 14 stitches is replaced by Ted Porch, who will play on the wing.

Brian Collits has been dropped from the Forbes team, and his place as fullback is taken by George Gelligan, who has proved an excellent player in that position.

Gelligan's place on the wing has been taken by speedy Ray Drabsch who missed the game in which Forbes qualified for the grand final.

These are the only changes made to the Forbes team.

To let Ted Porch into the Eugowra side as winger John Porch will play in Frank Glover's usual position as a centre, and Glover will take Ken Smith's place in the halves.

Coach John Hobby who played a game last week and left his opponents flat-footed, is sure to put everything he has into the important match. He seems to be at his best in important games.

The return of Ted Porch in the backs should do nothing to weaken the fast-moving line and players are confident that this week's changes can only strengthen it.

John Porch at five-eighth and half-back Lionel Bloomfield should play well together although the loss of Smith may have slightly weakened the combination.

John Porch and Morris McClintock have proved themselves in the centres in past matches and should give excellent performances. McClintock was troubled by injuries earlier in the season, but is in top form for the game.

David Greenhalgh is fullback and his attacking method will boost Eugowra's chances. He is also an excellent goal-kicker and if he is called upon, should not "muff" many.

With only two changes in its line, the team will present a formidable foe to the Eugowra men.

Halves John Lasker and Des Shead will lead the back line into battle, and their proven understanding and method of play gives their team a vital edge.

Ray Burge, who formerly played in the centres, must have proved himself the right man to play lock during the last game, because he has been left in that position.

Barry Anderson in the centres has a big task on Sunday, but support from Don Turner should mean that the side could get plenty of ball to the wingers.

Article from: The Dubbo Daily Liberal, Dubbo, September 16, 1964. Republished courtesy of ACM/Dubbo Daily Liberal.

EUGOWRA TAKES SECOND TITLE IN A ROW
One point win over Forbes 1964

A record crowd at Poineer Oval Parkes, saw Eugowra first-grade Rugby League team win its second Group XI grand final in succession.

The side, captained by John Hobby, scored an 8 - 7 victory after 80 minutes of first class football against Forbes.

Eugowra 8 defeated Forbes 7

Article from: The Dubbo Daily Liberal, Monday, September 11, 1964. Republished courtesy of ACM/Dubbo Daily Liberal.

1964 Eugowra Rugby League Team Group 11 Premiers

Back Row: Kevin Dwyer, Mal Mongan, Noel Pengilly, Ray Pengilly, Ian McClintock, John Hobby, Ted Porch, Barry Beath, Barry Turner, Lionel Bloomfield.

Front Row: Bill Hurcum, Jack Hay, Pike Greenhalgh, Charlie Dwyer, Bob Middleton, Bob Phillips, Ken Smith

Courtesy of: Rugby League Collection, Central Hotel Eugowra.

GRAND FINALISTS AT TOP STRENGTH

First grade rugby league grand finalists, Eugowra and Narromine have made one change each for Sunday's clash at Pioneer Oval, Parkes.

- Eugowra centre John Porch is unavailable for Sunday and Morris McClintock returns to the side.
- Vic Judd, the Narromine second rower is injured and his place is taken by Jim Hollman.

September 1965

Eugowra will be out to win its third consecutive premiership and is confident its powerful team can do it.

Narromine, after a decade "on the outer" is equally as determined to bring victory back to its town.

The "new look" Eugowra backline is one which could well trouble Narromine.

Former halfback David Greenhalgh has gone back to fullback and Dennis Madden is playing half.

Ken Smith, the leading Group 11 five-eighth partners Morris McClintock in the centres. Mark Toohey will play five-eighth.

This is the successful combination that defeated Parkes and as yet Narromine has not played against.

Eugowra's brilliant pack of forwards must surely mark it as the likely 1965 premiers.

The Glasson brothers, David and Don are playing great football and could prove too much for Narromine props Arnold Gillespie and Malcolm Dawes.

Eugowra second row pair international Barry Beath and Darrell Jones have too much experience for their Narromine opposites Jim Hollman and Barry Shepherd.

John Hobby, one of the most brilliant tacticians in the Group completes the Eugowra lineup as lock. He is opposed by Mick Manning who is turning in some great displays also.

Once again the backline will hinge around its coach Bob Weir in the centres.

Weir was the dominating figure in his team's 5-4 victory over Parkes in last Sunday's final. He will be marked by Ken Smith and the battle between this pair could be a feature of the match.

Weir will have to soften the Eugowra attack especially in the centres if his team is to do any good.

Weir's partner in the centres, John Griffin, is a capable player, with plenty of speed but he too is well marked by Morris McClintock. There should not be a great deal of difference in wingers.

Each team has a strong pair, dangerous in attack and usually sound in defence.

However in attack Eugowra's David Greenhalgh has an advantage over Don Sullivan.

The functioning of the backlines will depend on the halves' performances.

Rod Swindle and Colin Coffee have developed a strong combination and they could give Narromine a handy advantage.

Mark Toohey and Dennis Madden are together for the second time and under pressure from the opposition they may make some vital mistakes.

Eugowra's forwards will undoubtedly dictate the trend of the match and I expect Eugowra to win the match.

Narromine's main hope of victory lies in its three-quarter line if it can get going.

Its goalkicking winger Des Walsh, if he is in form, may be a vital man in the Narromine team.

Article from: The Dubbo Daily Liberal, Friday, September 24, 1965. Republished courtesy of ACM/Dubbo Daily Liberal.

1965 Eugowra v Narromine

Position:	Eugowra:	Narromine:
Fullback	- D. Greenhalgh	- D. Sullivan
Winger	- I. McClintock	- D. Walsh
Winger	- E. Porch	- N. Newman
Centre	- K. Smith	- R. Weir
Centre	- M. McClintock	- J. Griffin
Five-Eighth	- M. Toohey	- R. Swindle
Half-Back	- D. Madden	- C. Coffee
Lock	- J. Hobby	- M. Manning
Second Row	- D. Jones	- J. Hollman
Second row	- B. Beath	- B. Shepherd
Front Row	- David Glasson	- A. Gillespie
Front row	- Don Glasson	- M. Dawes
Hooker.	- V. Toohey.	- W. Hinkley.

1965 Eugowra Rugby League Team Group 11 Premiers

Back Row: David Glasson, Bill Adams, Ian McClintock, John Hobby (Captain Coach), Vince Toohey, Ted Porch, Barry Beath, Ken Smith.

Front Row: Mark Toohey, Basil Toohey, Darryl Jones, Maurice McClintock, Don Glasson, David Greenhalgh, Dennis Madden.

Courtesy of: Rugby League Collection, Central Hotel Eugowra.

Full speed towards the try line

Source: Okeydokey, Landscapes

1965 Third League Title To Eugowra

Eugowra yesterday won its third successive Group XI rugby league grand final with a crushing 28-2 victory over Narromine. Playing in temperatures well over 90 degrees, Eugowra proved far too fit and fast for Narromine.

The fast, powerful Eugowra backline cut the Narromine defence to ribbons and many times seemed to be in for a try but was pulled down only feet short of the line.

Eugowra opened the scoring about five minutes after the start when David Greenhalgh landed a penalty from halfway and from this point on Narromine was hardly in the game.

For most of the first half Narromine was forced to defend grimly as Eugowra kept up its relentless assault.

For 20 minutes the ball never left the Narromine half. Then Narromine broke away and ran the ball deep into Eugowra territory.

A dropped pass on the edge of the 25 with only one man left to beat cost Narromine the best chance of scoring and Eugowra again took control and forced the play back deep into Narromine ground.

Taking the ball from a play-the-ball half-back Ken Smith weaved through the Narromine defence, stepping out of three tackles and then slipped the ball outside to winger Ted Porch who dived over for the first try of the game.

David Greenhalgh landed the difficult conversion and Eugowra had taken a 7-0 lead.

With half time approaching Narromine kicked off only to be forced back again.

A penalty about 15 yards inside Narromine's half gave David Greenhalgh another two points and the players went to the half time interval with Eugowra leading 9-0.

Play in this half had been fast with Eugowra being by far the better team.

Determined defence and a bit of bad luck prevented it from holding a much bigger lead.

Narromine although outclassed by Eugowra boys at no stage completely folded under the pressure applied to them and their never say-die defence kept them in the game.

Eugowra lost Ian McClintock at half time and he was replaced by Basil Toohey, brother of Mark and Vince already on the field.

Too fit and fast

From the kick-off Narromine forced play to the Eugowra line only to have Ted Porch gain possession and weave his way out through the advancing Narromine players to put his team on attack once again.

With play well inside the Narromine 25, Eugowra players were pulled down only feet short of the line as Narromine held out desperately.

From a play the ball, the ball was swung out to Eugowra's big second rower Barry Beath who crashed over the line with three Narromine defenders hanging on to him, to touch down for his team's second try.

Only a couple of yards to the left of the uprights, Greenhalgh missed an easy kick, but the Eugowra try scoring spree had just started.

Minutes later Narromine made its first and last score of the day when winger Des Walsh landed a long penalty to make the score 12-2.

Eugowra's next try was disallowed but soon afterwards Greenhalgh landed another difficult penalty and Narromine was fighting for a lost cause.

Beath backed up Ken Smith to take a good pass and ran around the defence to score directly under the posts. Greenhalgh converted and Eugowra went to a 19-2 lead.

With the Eugowra backline moving and thinking as one, the Narromine defence never stood a chance and three unconverted tries later the slaughter was brought to an abrupt end.

All three of those tries were the result of splendid backline movements that left Narromine flat-footed.

How Eugowra could keep up this pace was beyond the understanding of the Narromine boys who were obviously feeling the heat.

For Narromine Bob Weir, Colin Coffee, Wal Hinkley and Don Sullivan were the outstanding players.

All worked hard and set the perfect example to the rest of the team.

Bob Weir in particular, although his team was hopelessly beaten from the start, continually rallied his players to make a game of it.

He tackled everything that came his way and a lot more that he had to chase.

Weir, with Smith, Beath and the Glassons of Eugowra would have been the best on the field.

Final score: Eugowra 28 Narromine 2

Article from: The Dubbo Daily Liberal, September 30, 1965. Republished courtesy of ACM/Dubbo Daily Liberal.

Eugowra out of Western Rugby League Challenge

Eugowra Rugby League, the Group XI champion team, has withdrawn its challenge to Oberon, the Group X champions

September 1965

A spokesman for the Eugowra Club advised Group Ten Secretary, Mr. Vic. Byrne of the decision yesterday.

Eugowra originally challenged the winner of the Group 10 competition provided it won the Group 11 competition.

Last week Eugowra scored an easy win over Narromine to take the title and Oberon had a similar win over Workman's Club.

It is believed that the increasing hot weather conditions had something to do with the Eugowra decision.

The final of the Group 11 competition at Parkes last Sunday was played in temperatures of more than 90 degrees and some of the players have still not recovered.

It is also understood that Oberon had decided that they would not have been able to play the match because of injuries.

Mr. Byrne disclosed yesterday that the gates at the four "big" matches, two semi-finals, final and grand final had totalled £2.220/4/-.

This was £326/16/- more than 1963 when the four games returned £1,893/8/-.

Expenses to stage last Sunday's grand final totalled £466.

Of this amount programmes took £108/10/-, referees expenses £85, ground rental £65, ground staff £61 and insurance £58.

Article from: The Dubbo Daily Liberal, September 30, 1965. Republished courtesy of ACM/Dubbo Daily Liberal.

Final Points as Season Ends

Last two points.

Game Over.

Courtesy of: NSW Rugby League, The Rugby League News, September 1966.

Reflection On Two Young Group XI Players

Dennis (Fatty) Finn started playing football at high school and joined local junior teams. He captained the winning under eighteen team to the Group XI premiership in 1966, which started a successful football career. He commenced playing in the weight divisions, for example, six sevens, seven sevens, then under sixteen and eighteen divisions and eventually went on to first grade for Parkes and Canowindra. He also represented both Group XI and Western Division.

Dennis was chosen to play for the Parkes High School senior open team against Cleveland Street Boys. It was an annual event and he was then probably the youngest player to be chosen.

Dennis and his young brother Bruce, referred to as Skinny, played in the weight division together and on a number of occasions were invited to play for Parkes Marist School against Peak Hill and Dubbo teams. They were chosen because of their ability to win matches and as it turned out it was a wise decision.

Bruce also played first grade for Parkes and representative football for Group XI and Western Division. He played for Western Division against England at Bathurst (1970) and went on to play for Balmain.

Group X1

Western Division

Canowindra

Group X1

Western Division

Balmain

1966 Blazer

Bruce and Dennis Finn

Courtesy of Parkes RLC

In their youth Dennis and Bruce lived with their parents at the Commercial Hotel in Parkes and during that time a number of first grade footballers stayed including one of Parkes' Captain Coaches Billy Tonkin. I believe they used to polish his football boots.

They were surrounded by great players, teams and personalities during the sixties and this may have had a big influence on them both as their football careers were ready to take off.

1966 GRAND FINAL TEAMS PIONEER OVAL PARKES

CANOWINDRA 1st Grade Colours: Gold, Black V	**EUGOWRA 1st Grade** Colours: Black
FULLBACK: P. Carroll. (1). **THREE-QUARTERS:** D. Kearns (2), B. Jeffress (5), R. Boden (3), L. Hamilton (4). **FIVE-EIGHTH:** R. Middlelton (6). **HALF-BACK:** I. Rice (7). **FORWARDS:** R. Ryan (8), R. Rice (9), R. Kinsella (10), J. Newcombe (11), J. Kelly (12) T. Tobin (13). **RESERVES:** L. Ryan (Forward), J. Ryan (Back).	**FULLBACK:** D. Greenhalgh (1). **THREE-QUARTERS:** E. Porch (2), I. McClintock (5), F. Glover (3), K. Smith (4). **FIVE-EIGHTH:** M. Toohey (6). **HALF-BACK:** D. Madden (7). **FORWARDS:** B. Turner (8), D. Jones (9), David Glasson (10), J. Porch (11), V. Toohey (12), Don Glasson (13). **RESERVES:** B. Toohey, M. Rawsthorne.
DUBBO MACQUARIE RESERVES Colours: Blue and White Bars	**DUBBO CYMS RESERVES** Colours: Green and White V
FULLBACK: T. Nelson (1). **THREE-QUARTERS:** C. Simpson (2), G. Trudgett (5), T. Williams (3), Pat Williams (4). **FIVE-EIGHTH:** R. Feeney (6). **HALF-BACK:** D. May (7). **FORWARDS:** D. Crowley (8), M. Low (9), Peter Williams (10), W. Stratford (11), J. Wallace (12), R. Soden (13). **RESERVES:** W. Carr, T. Kelly, L. Pearce.	**FULLBACK:** D. Frazer, (1). **THREE-QUARTERS:** C. Carolin (2), K. Piesley (5), A. McPhail (3), R. Leary (4). **FIVE-EIGHTH:** K. Connolly (6). **HALF-BACK:** P. Marks (7). **FORWARDS:** B. O'Sullivan (8) G. Haeres (9), D. McLean (10), P. Sullivan (11), K. Brown (12), R. Puckridge (13). **RESERVES:** B. Knudson, R. Archer, P. Edwards.
PARKES JUNIORS Colours: White and Red and Blue V's.	**FORBES JUNIORS** Colours: Black and White Bands.
FULLBACK: D. Kelly (1). **THREE-QUARTERS:** P. Faukner (2), K. Hackett (5), D. Finn, Captain, (3), R. Houghton (4). **FIVE-EIGHTH:** B. Finn (6). **HALF-BACK:** L. Wakefield (7). **FORWARDS:** R. Neilsen (8), R. Harrison (9), N. Blackett (10), T. White (11), A. Kelly (12), T Helm (13). **RESERVES:** K. Job, R. Grant.	**FULLBACK:** P. Hammond (1). **THREE-QUARTERS:** P. Shannon (2), A. Croft (5), R. Martins, (3), B. Jayet (4). **FIVE-EIGHTH:** M. Walker (6). **HALF-BACK:** M. Grant (7). **FORWARDS:** B. McCullock (8), B. Huggart (9), B. Hicks (10), T. Roberts (11), N. Stonham (12), B. Shine (13). **RESERVES:** M. McLuckie (Back), W. Day (Forward).

1966 JUNIORS TAKE GRAND-FINAL HONOURS 7-4

The Parkes Rugby League junior team took out the Group XI grand-final with a narrow 7-4 win over Forbes at Pioneer Oval yesterday.

Parkes led 5-2 at half time.

The second half was marred by rain which fell throughout the 40 minutes play and made conditions difficult. The field became slippery and the ball greasy and hard to hold.

Parkes scored the only try of the match in the first 15 minutes of play. Parkes always appeared to have an edge but it was starved of possession. Forbes won nearly every scrum in the first half and had the ball for almost the whole 40 minutes. But Parkes was equal to the occasion and held out all Forbes' attacks. Captain Dennis Finn's defence was inspirational to his side. Finn moved up quickly and his solid tackles repeatedly broke up Forbes' moves. A Kelly scored the only try and R Houghton converted two goals. Forbes player P Hamond converted two goals.

This was the fourth time Parkes and Forbes had met during the season and Parkes won on each occasion although the margins were only small.

Parkes players Dennis Finn and Laurie Wakefield were always dangerous.

Forbes captain Mick Walker and Bill McCullough were outstanding.

Dennis Finn led the team to victory and was the most outstanding player on the field and went on to establish himself as one of the Group X1 finest five eighths.

Article from: Parkes Champion Post, 1966. Republished courtesy of ACM/Parkes Champion Post.

Parkes Junior Team after the Grand Final in the dressing shed.
Coach: Jock Gartshore.

Courtesy of: Roseanne Finn.

1966 Parkes Junior Grade Group 11 Premiers

Back Row: D. Kelly, K. Job, T. White, R. Houghton, R. Harrison, R. Grant.
Middle Row: K. Hacket, B. Finn, D. Finn (Captain), R. Neilsen, L. Wakefield, T. Helm.
Front Row: N. Blackett, A. Kelly.

Courtesy of: Roseanne Finn.

1966 Dubbo CYMS Reserve Grade Group 11 Premiers

CYMS Second Group 11 Premiership

In 1960 Dubbo CYMS under 18 junior rugby league team recorded the club's first ever grand final victory and Group 11 premiership.

It took until "1966" for the club to record its second premiership with the reserve grade winning the Group 11 competition.

CYMS defeated Macquarie 14-6 in the Group 11 Grand Final at Pioneer Oval Parkes.

Dubbo CYMS reserve-grade player Col Balfour, tackles Macquarie reserve grade hooker Bill Hutchinson around the legs in the grand-final at Pioneer Oval Parkes.

Courtesy of: Blast From the Past, Dubbo CYMS Old Boys.

Eugowra Set Rugby League Record

Eugowra rugby league team yesterday broke the Dubbo Macquarie record winning its fourth successive Group XI first grade premiership.

Eugowra became the St. George of the bush when they steamrolled a much lighter and younger Canowindra side in the 1966 grand-final at Parkes yesterday.

September 1966

They defeated a gallant Canowindra 13 in a bright but one-sided match by 22 points to 3 yesterday before a near record crowd at Pioneer Oval.

The win gave Eugowra their fourth successive premiership breaking the Macquarie record they equalled last year.

Ron Boden must be praised for the way he brought the young Canowindra team from second last on the competition ladder to fight out the grand final in two seasons.

Canowindra were out-weighted and outplayed by a much more experienced and older Eugowra side yesterday.

Play began at a fast rate and it was not until the 14th minute that a score was put on the board.

Eugowra were awarded a penalty for two of the Canowindra forwards being off side.

Glover did not make any mistakes and put the ball squarely between the posts.

Eugowra 2, Canowindra nil.

Eugowra were quickly on attack and they began to use their weight in the forwards to soften up Canowindra.

It was in this progress that Eugowra muffed a chance to score when McClintock knocked the ball on inside the Canowindra 25.

In the 21st minute Eugowra were awarded another penalty right on Canowindra's 25 but Glover failed with his kick at goal.

David Glasson set up a great try for Ken Smith in the 23rd minute and Smith went as straight as a gun barrel for the line. Glover again failed badly with his attempt at goal.

Eugowra 5, Canowindra nil.

Shortly afterwards Canowindra showed a glimpse of the form that took them into the grand final when Peter Ryan intercepted and flicked a neat pass to Bill Jeffress who outpaced the defence in a 60-yard dash to score in the corner without a hand being placed on him.

Len Hamilton who was not in good kicking form failed with his attempted conversion.

Eugowra 5, Canowindra 3.

In the final minutes of the first half, Eugowra were awarded two penalties and Glover raised the flags on both occasions.

Eugowra 9, Canowindra 3.

Just before half time Jim Newcombe of Canowindra was taken from the field with his index finger broken and his replacement was the versatile Len Ryan.

After the spell Canowindra were the first to receive a penalty and Len Ryan failed with his attempt at goal.

In a very hard five minutes Canowindra were awarded another two penalties but Ryan could not raise the flags.

Eugowra swung into attack in the 15th minute and after superb backing up they went in for a try to give them a handy lead.

Eugowra 12, Canowindra 3.

Ten minutes later Darryl Jones dived over the line to add another three points to Eugowra's tally after Eugowra had stormed the Canowindra line for some minutes. Glover had a change of luck and his kick was a good one.

Eugowra 17, Canowindra 3.

In the 30th minute Toohey for Eugowra, was in again, this time about 15 feet out from the posts. Glover having one of his off days was not successful with his attempt at goal.

Eugowra 20, Canowindra 3.

In the 33rd minute Glover made another attempt at goal and after being awarded a penalty and this time he put the ball straight between the posts.

Eugowra 22, Canowindra 3.

Canowindra won the scrums 10 to 9 and were awarded 10 penalties to 6.

Canowindra's best players were Ian Rice, Bob Rice, Ray Middleton, Len Hamilton and Bill Jeffress.

Eugowra: All the players combined well and were much stronger in defence and attack.

Article from: The Forbes Advocate, September, 1966. Republished courtesy of ACM/Forbes Advocate.

1966 Canowindra Group 11 Grand Final Rugby League Team

Back Row: Peter Ryan, Geoffrey Ryan, Terry Carroll, Brian Eakin, Stephen McNaught, Lenny Hamilton, Len Ryan.

Front Row: Ron Bowden, John Kelly, Daryl Kearns, Bob Rice, Billy Paul, Dickie Middleton.

Left: Canowindra 1966 Grand Final team defeated by Eugowra 22-3.

Ron Bowden Captain Coach.

Courtesy of: Canowindra Historical Society & Museum Inc.

1966 Eugowra Rugby League Team Group 11 Premiers

Back Row: Mark Toohey, G. McGrath, Bill Adams, David Glasson, Basil Toohey, Ted Porch.

Middle Row: Mick Rawsthorne, Don Glasson, Darryl Jones, Ken Smith, Dennis Madden, Vince Toohey, Barry Turner.

Front Row: John Porch, David Greenhalgh, Ian McClintock.

Courtesy of: Rugby League Collection, Eugowra Central Hotel.

1966 Nyngan Rugby League Team Group 15 Premiers

Back Row: K. Munday, F. Smith, P. Barnes, J. Leahey, K. Lovett, J. Griffiths, L. Richardson, K. Pearson.

Middle Row: D. Lee (Coach), C. Hughes, D. Smith, H. O'Connell, K. Markwell, N. Carter, R. Boatswain.

Front Row: I. Burns, R. Taylor, L. Beetson, C. Marchall.

Nyngan defeated Goodooga in the Grand Final 29-2.

Courtesy of: John Collins, The Crowing of the Roosters. Photo: Mark Beetson.

HISTORY WRITERS

September 1966

Eugowra isn't the only country rugby league club to establish a record this season, not by a long shot In fact records have been toppling all over the country. Eugowra, however, have a link with three record breaking performances.

Their fourth successive win in the Group 11 first grade premiership last Sunday set a record fot this Group.

The record previously was three in a row set by Leo Nosworthy's all-conquering Dubbo Macquarie sides 1959, 1960 and 1961.

But perhaps the best achievement of all was John Hobby's success at Newcastle.

Hobby, last year's Eugowra coach, led Newcastle Western Suburbs team to its first premiership win in many years with a 31-9 win over Cessnock in the grand-final.

This also was Hobby's fourth successive premiership. He led Eugowra in their three previous wins.

But Hobby's performance with Newcastle Western Suburbs Club will go down in history. The club took out seven titles this season, Western suburbs won Newcastle minor premiership in all three grades, the grand-finals in the three grades and the club championship.

And Hobby was rated one of the outstanding players of the season in a particularly strong Newcastle competition.

Another Eugowra player, Barry Beath, missed out on sharing in the St. George record run only because of an injury which kept him out of the finals.

Records also were established in Group 10 by Oberon when they won the Western Challenge Cup for the sixth successive season.

Oberon also took out the major and minor premierships in first grade and the reserve grade premiership.

At West Wyalong, where international prop Ron Crowe was the coach, the club became the first to win all three Group Nine grand-finals in one season.

Article from: The Dubbo Daily Liberal, September 28, 1966. Republished courtesy of ACM/Dubbo Daily Liberal.

1967 Coonamble Bears Rugby League Team

Back Row: John Café, Fowlhouse, Welsh, Barry Woods, Ramie Harris, Bill Webb, Mervyn Smith, Bill Gidd, Ian Smith, Cork Nicol, Michael Barlow, Pat Hemsworth, Julio Zappacosta, Jeff Nash.

Front Row: Shane Horan, Ray Cleary, Trevor Cook, Mick Flanagan, Frank Cant, Darby Adams, Steve Browning.

Mervyn Smith was regarded as one of the greatest players to play for Coonamble. He originally played for Moree but wanted to play for Coonamble, however Moree would not release him. To enable him to play for Coonamble, he changed his name from Mervyn Sampson to Mervyn Smith.

Mervyn Smith sixth player from the left top row.

Courtesy of: Greg Maher, Sports Article Coonamble Times, June 2018.

1967 Eugowra and Oberon set the records	
Group 11 **Ist Division Premiers** **Eugowra** 1963, 1964, 1965, 1966, **1967.** Eugowra defeated Parkes 14-3 at Pioneer Oval Parkes to take out their fifth consecutive premiership.	**Group 10** **Ist Division Premiers** **Oberon** 1961, 1962, 1963, 1964, 1965, 1966, **1967.** Oberon defeated Bathurst Charleston 22-2 at the Bathurst Sports Ground to take out their seventh consecutive premiership.
Oberon went on to win in 1968, 1969 and 1970 making it 10 consecutive Group 10 Premierships. The records still remain.	

Parkes Seek Berth Plus Revenge

August 1967

Parkes 'pipped on the post' by Eugowra for the Group 11 Rugby League minor premiership, wlll be seeking revenge as well as a grand final berth in the match at Canowindra on Sunday.

The two teams are at peak strength for Sunday's semi-final which should be one of the best matches of the season.

Eugowra won the minor premiership on a countback. The two teams have shared honours equally through the season.

In the first competition round, Eugowra beat Parkes 14-11 but in the second round the scores were reversed 10-0 in Parkes' favour.

However Eugowra will enter the game slight favourites as they have been most impressive in their last two matches.

At their latest outing they beat Dubbo CYMS 17-2 while Parkes had to struggle to beat Narromine 9-4.

Parkes is not lacking in strength with Jock Gartshore, the Group 11 second rower, right back to his best.

Eugowra will also have Basil Toohey back at his lock position in opposition to Allan Jones, the Parkes captain-coach.

Parkes will find most of their problems will come from the Eugowra back-line which is even bigger than Parkes.

Ted Porch and Colin Pritchard Eugowra's centres who wreaked havoc with the CYMS defence, will again be the two for Parkes to watch.

Dennis Madden will also need close attention with his field goal kicking.

But in the place of goal kicking, the advantage swings back to Parkes.

John Bonham their half is one of the top kickers in the Group.

Eugowra will be stronger on Sunday than when they played CYMS because of the return of forward Don Glasson.

Glasson missed the game against CYMS with an ankle injury but will rejoin brother David in the front row for the final.

The forward clash between the two sides could be the deciding point of the game.

Article from: The Dubbo Daily Liberal, Friday, August 25, 1967. Republished courtesy of ACM/Dubbo Daily Liberal.

PARKES SIDE BEATS EUGOWRA AT THEIR OWN GAME

August 1967

Parkes took Eugowra on at their own game and scored a narrow 7-1 win in the second Group XI first grade rugby league semi-final at Canowindra yesterday.

Parkes went into the game as 5/4 outsiders but finished with most of the crowd of more than 1100 convinced they had seen the 1967 Group XI premiers in action.

John Bonham, Parkes half-back and kicker, proved a key figure in his side's win, kicking two good penalty goals. The only try of the match came when Jones broke clear and flicked the ball to second rower Brian Piercy who dived over 10 yards from the corner. Bonham was unable to convert. Dennis Madden kicked a field gold for Eugowra.

Scores:
Parkes 7 (Brian Piercy try and John Bonham 2 penalty goals).
Eugowra 1 (Dennis Madden field goal).

Article from: The Dubbo Daily Liberal, August 28, 1967. Republished courtesy of ACM/Dubbo Daily Liberal.

Eugowra's Chances Fade With Defeat
FIRST GRAND FINAL BERTH FOR 10 YEARS

August 1967

The writing is on the wall. A magnificent Parkes 13 yesterday established themselves as a team to beat in the battle for the 1967 Group XI Rugby League premiership when they downed the 1966 premiers, Eugowra, in a Rugby League "battle royal" at Canowindra Recreation Ground.

Parkes finished all over Eugowra and for the first time in their five-year domination of Group 11 Rugby League, the minor premiers were beaten at their own game.

The win gives Parkes its first grand final berth since Merv Lees' gallant 1957 side which was defeated by Condobolin.

Article from: The Parkes Champion Post, August 28, 1967. Republished courtesy of ACM/Parkes Champion Post.

The Mode Of Transport Moving Forward

Source: Wikipedia Australia 1930s   *Source: Eugowra Photo. Taken by Greg Riach*

EUGOWRA BOUNCES BACK INTO GRAND FINAL BERTH

September 1967

Eugowra bounced back into the fight for the Group XI first grade premiership with an impressive 17-8 win over Canowindra in the rugby league final yesterday.

They will go on to meet Parkes in the grand-final at Pioneer Oval Parkes.

Canowindra's captain-coach Ron Boden received a knock in the first half and was subdued for most of the game.

Final score: Eugowra 17 defeated Canowindra 8.

Article from: The Dubbo Daily Liberal, Monday, September 4, 1967. Republished courtesy of ACM/Dubbo Daily Liberal.

1967 Grand Final Teams Pioneer Oval Parkes

First grade

PARKES
(White, Red V)
FULLBACK: M. Leary 1.
THREEQUARTERS:
K. Taylor 2, L. Wakefield 5, R. Maxwell 3, A. Hepperlin 4
FIVE-EIGHTH:
D. Finn 6.
HALF:
J. Bonham 7.
FORWARDS:
A. Jones. 8 Captain
B. Piercy 9, D. Kirwin 10.
J. Gartshore 11, T. Williams 12, G. Knowles 13.
RESERVES:
R. Houghton, R. Carter.

EUGOWRA
(Black)
FULLBACK: D. Greehalgh 1.
THREEQUARTERS:
D. Jones, 2, I. McClintock 5, T. Porch 3, C. Pritchard 4
FIVE-EIGHTH:
M. Toohey 6.
HALF:
D. Madden 7.
FORWARDS:
B. Turner 8.
A. Bell 9, J. Porch 10.
David Glasson 11, D. McGrath 12, Don Glasson 13.
RESERVES:
G. Hoswell, B. Toohey.

Referee: K. C. Dwyer, Touch Judges: K. MacRea, B. Kitch

Reserve grade

PARKES
FULLBACK: D. Davidson 1.
THREEQUARTERS:
P. Franks 2, R. Sinderberry 5, P. Littler 3, M. Blackstock 4.
FIVE-EIGHTH:
A. Hawken 6.
HALF:
L. Bloomfield 7, Captain.
FORWARDS:
J. Treweeke 8.
R. Carter 9, N. Blackett 10.
J. Hodge 11, J. McQuillan 12, R. Aitken 13.
RESERVES:
J. Barker, E. Helm.

CANOWINDRA
FULLBACK: G. Fisher 1.
THREEQUARTERS:
J. Traves 2, J. Slattery 5, K. Traves 3, B. Jeffress 4.
FIVE-EIGHTH:
B. Sutton 6.
HALF:
G. Simpson 7.
FORWARDS:
A. Slattery 8.
B. Moon 9, B. Middleton 10,
T. Tobin 11, J. Breen 12, M. Kinsella 13.
RESERVES:
R. Jones, K. Hodge.

Referee: N. Johnson, Touch Judges: K. MacRea, P. Williams

1967 Parkes Reserves Win Thriller After Extra Time

Parkes Rugby League Reserve grade team took out the Group XI Reserve grade premiership with a thrilling 16-10 win over minor premiers Canowindra at Pioneer Oval yesterday.

An extra 10 minutes each way had to be played when Canowindra scored a disputed try just on the full-time bell to draw 10 all.

Parkes scored two great tries in extra time to seal the match.

The match proved a real thriller as not much separated the two sides.

Parkes with the help of a strong following wind in the first half, battled to hold a 5-3 lead at the interval.

Centre Pat Littler scored a try early but a Canowindra forward forced his way over after some scrappy play to even the score at 3 all.

David Davidson kicked his first goal after four attempts for Parkes to lead 5-3 at half time.

Davidson and Canowindra half Gary Simpson each kicked a penalty early in the second half and Parkes led 7-5.

Canowindra was forced into handling errors on its own line and Parkes threw everything into its attack.

Bloomfield held a difficult pass and sent to Peter Franks who crossed for a good try.

Parkes led 10-5 and appeared to have the game in its keeping.

However, Canowindra fought back and hammered the Parkes line in an all-out bid to save the game.

A Canowindra player was tackled across the Parkes line and appeared unable to ground the ball. However, referee Mr. N. Johnson (Cumnock) awarded the try despite protest by Parkes players involved in the tackle.

The try was converted and the full-time bell went with the score 10 all.

Parkes survived a big scare when Canowindra halfback Simpson intercepted a loose Parkes pass on the Canowindra 25. However, Parkes' winger Peter Franks at top speed gathered Simpson in about 15 yards short of the line.

Parkes rallied and winger Peter Franks crossed for a good try engineered by five-eighth Alan Hawkins.

After the change-over for the final 10 minutes front rower John Hodge crashed over for a great try to seal the match.

Captain coach Lionel Bloomfield suffered a badly gashed head early and a damaged shoulder later in the game. Despite his injuries Bloomfield stayed on and directed play well.

Winger Peter Franks was taken off just before the finish with an injured shoulder.

Five-eighth Alan Hawkins played splendidly. His defence and backing up in attack were first class.

Winger Peter Franks had a great match swinging the game with his efforts.

The forwards played well and matched the Canowindra pack. Front rowers Bob Aitken and John Hodge were outstanding.

The remaining forwards Reg Carter, Jack Treweeke, Neville Blackett and John McQuillan all played strongly.

Eugowra Juniors defeated Canowindra 8/5 in a keenly fought grand-final.

Article from: The Parkes Champion Post, September 11, 1967. Republished courtesy of ACM/Parkes Champion Post.

1967 Eugowra Rugby League Team Group 11 Premiers

Back Row: David Geenhalgh, Don Glasson, Malcom Mongan, Ted Porch,
Colin Pritchard (Captain Coach), Michael Beath, Alen Bell, John Porch, Dennis Madden.

Front Row: Basil Toohey, Ian McClintock, David Glasson, Darryl Jones, Barry Turner, Dick McGrath, Mark Toohey.

Courtesy of: Rugby League Collection, Central Hotel Eugowra.

RECORD FOR EUGOWRA GRAND FINAL THRILLER
PARKES CRUSHED IN SHORT BURST OF SCORING

Eugowra with a 20 minutes scoring burst in yesterday's grand final dismissed any hope Parkes entertained of winning the 1967 Group XI rugby league premiership.

Eugowra trailed Parkes 0-3 at half time but after 20 minutes of the second half led 9-3 to clinch the first-grade premiership for a fifth successive year.

The crowd of more than 2,500 which packed

Pioneer Oval at Parkes were treated to one of the best Group XI grand-finals in years, with Eugowra running out winners by 14-3.

September 1967

Yesterday was the grand final and Eugowra were determined to return home with the premiership shield which they had brought to the oval.

But until the second half it looked as though they might go home empty handed.

Parkes matched Eugowra in every department of the game in the first half and thoroughly deserved their lead.

Centre Ray Maxwell, who was one of Parkes best players, had beat four Eugowra players to score a minute from half time.

Their hooker Tom Williams had given them a glut of possession in the first half and their cover defence kept Eugowra at bay.

It was a worried Col Pritchard, Eugowra's captain-coach, who addressed his team at half time in the dressing room.

They came back with a vengeance in the early stages of the second half.

Eugowra half back Dennis Madden's right boot played an important role in the team's fightback.

Parkes had been able to contain Madden well in the first half but early in the second half he constantly put Eugowra on the attack with his long kicks in touch.

Pritchard himself set the pace for his team when only four minutes into the second half he crashed over to level the scores at 3 all.

Ted Porch who had narrowly missed two penalty goal attempts in the first half gave Eugowra the lead when he converted the try. Eugowra 5, Parkes 3.

Eugowra maintained the pressure and were soon attacking the Parkes line again.

Mark Toohey the Eugowra five-eighth, made a good run but after being well tackled shot the ball one handed to Madden from the ground.

Madden hardly seemed to aim the ball but it scored between the posts and took the score to: Eugowra 7, Parkes 3.

The game had changed with Dick McGrath winning most of the ball for Eugowra.

Parkes in their eagerness to get possession were ruled offside by referee Kevin Dwyer only 30 yards out, in front of their own posts.

Porch's kick was right on the line and Parkes trailing 3 to 9 threw themselves into a frenzied finish to retrieve the game.

The Parkes backline began to function smoothly again and captain-coach Allan Jones at lock set off many good moves.

Ray Maxwell and Laurie Wakefield, the winger, almost scored several times and for a ten-minute period Parkes kept Eugowra defending in their own 25 yards area.

But Madden continued to upset Parkes with his kicking with only two minutes to go he brought off another field goal which was over the Parkes crossbar before the Parkes defence realised what he planned. Eugowra 11, Parkes 3.

Then right-on-full-time Madden again kicked through and Darrell Jones regained possession for Eugowra after Wakefield mishandled.

Eight Eugowra players chimed into the movement from the play the ball and Pritchard went in almost untouched as the defence could not decide where the ball would go next.

The full-time hooter sounded as Porch lined up his kick and he hurriedly booted the ball well wide as dozens of spectators ran onto the ground.

Pritchard was chaired from the field by his team mates and it completed a great first season for him.

Final Score: Eugowra 14 (Pritchard 2 tries, Porch 2 goals and Madden 2 field goals) defeated Parkes 3 (Maxwell 1 try).

Article from: The Dubbo Daily Liberal, Monday, September, 11 1967. Republished courtesy of ACM/Dubbo Daily Liberal.

The 1968 season saw Narromine eliminate Parkes from the race to the Grand Final and went on to play Dubbo CYMS at Pioneer Oval Parkes in an extremely tough match in front of a crowd of approximately 4,000. Narromine defeated CYMS 12-4 to take out the 1968 Group 11 Premiership.

Cobar Roosters defeated Brewarrina 7-4 to win the Group 15 Premiership at Nyngan.

NARROMINE SWEEP TO HONOURS IN BIG LEAGUE

Narromine swept to Group XI Rugby League premiership honours at Parkes yesterday with a powerhouse 12-4 win over Dubbo CYMS.
Led by former State centre Bob Weir, Narromine dictated play for most of the game and were always in front.

September 1968

More than 4000 people, the biggest Group 11 grand final crowd for many years, watched Narromine methodically go about the business of winning the biggest game of the season.

Despite losing the scrums 19-9 and the penalties 10-6, Narromine's unyielding defence and orthodox but determined attack proved too great for CYMS captained by former Eastern Suburbs halfback and five-eighth and Rugby Union international Ken McMullen who tried desperately to turn the tide but could never overcome Narromine's general superiority in all departments.

After the game McMullen said: "We played our best but Bob Weir and his boys were just too good on the day".

"Maybe, Narromine's extra game against Parkes meant the difference," he said.

Weir was elated after the game. "We were too good on the day but CYMS tried hard and went well," he said.

Weir said Narromine's game against Parkes last Sunday week had made "the world of difference" to his team.

Yesterday's win gave Narromine its fourth premiership win, having won honours in 1953, 1955, 1956 and 1968.

It was Dubbo CYMS first tilt at the grand final

Narromine virtually won the game in the first 20 minutes of play.

With bustling tactics and sound defence, Narromine forced CYMS into errors and nullified CYMS greater possession of the ball.

CYMS Not Good Enough

Under these tactics CYMS failed to settle down and trailed 7-2 at half time. They never bridged the gap.

Narromine scored two tries and kicked three goals to CYMS two goals.

This clearly indicated Narromine's superiorty on the day.

Narromine lock Bourchier and halfback Charlie Burrows harrassed McMullen constantly with the result that CYMS backline failed to function at full capacity.

Playing in the centres Weir had the best game on the ground.

His crashing runs down field upset the CYMS defence and his cover defence was copy-book.

Narromine's bigger pack of forwards played a vital role in gaining the uper hand.

They dominated the smaller CYMS forwards and made better use of the ball.

Scores:
Narromine 12
(N. Newman, A. Hutchison tries.
D. Walsh three goals) defeated
CYMS 4 (G. Miller two goals).
Referee: Mr. K. Dwyer.

Article from: The Dubbo Daily Liberal, September, 1968. Republished courtesy of ACM/Dubbo Daily Liberal.

HAIL THE VICTORS

Here they are, the Group XI Rugby League premiers, Narromine. They were pictured after beating Dubbo CYMS 12-4 at Pioneer Oval Parkes on Sunday. Tired, but jubilant, the team chaired Captain Coach Bob Weir around the oval as he held the premiership shield aloft.

Courtesy of: Narromine Library and Macquarie Regional Library.

1968 Narromine Rugby League Team Group 11 Premiers

Back Row: Alan Hutchison, Arnold Gillespie, Norm Newman, Malcolm Dawes, Bob Smith, Terry Hunter, Byron Hutchison, Des Walsh, Hayden Bennett.
Front Row: John Griffin, Bob Weir, Charlie Burrowes, Murray Bourchier.

Courtesy of: Narromine Library and Macquarie Regional Library.

1968 Tribute to a leader

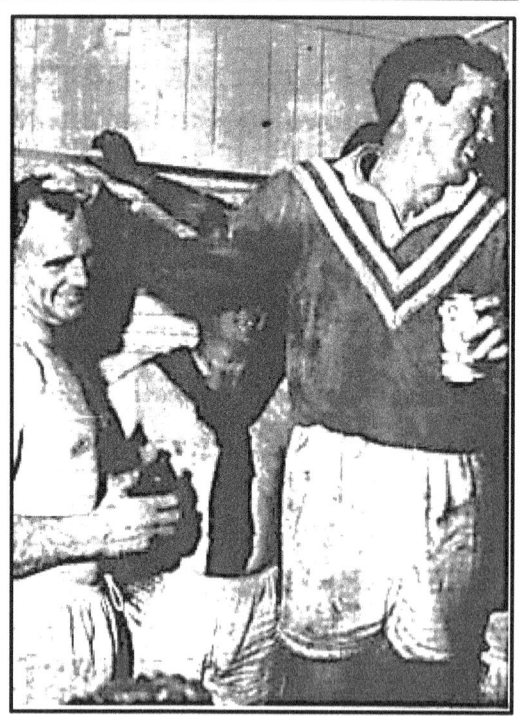

The two most dynamic Rugby League players in Group 11 have a friendly drink after yesterday's Grand Final at Parkes. Dubbo CYMS captain-coach Ken McMullen pats Narromine captain-coach Bob Weir on the head in the dressing room after Weir had led his team to a 12-4 victory over CYMS. Weir a twice State representative played a great match and led his team to victory over CYMS. McMullen an Australian Rugby Union representatve, tried hard, but could not rally his team sufficiently to defeat Narromine in the closing stages. After the game, Weir said it was a hard match and the CYMS team played well. He said he thought everyone of his team members had played well.

Article from: Dubbo Daily Liberal, Monday, September 23, 1968. Republished courtesy of ACM/Dubbo Daily Liberal.

BOBBY WEIR CLINCHES BIG DAILY LIBERAL R.L. AWARD

August 1968

Bob Weir, one of the greatest Rugby League footballers Group 11 has produced in recent years, was today declared the winner of the "Daily Liberal's" bonanza Best and Fairest Player competition.

Weir, the Narromine captain-coach, yesterday was awarded his second straight major three points award which gave him an unassailable five-point lead over the field.

Pictured above: Bob Weir with his wife Judy.

Article from: The Dubbo Daily Liberal, Monday, August 5, 1968. Republished courtesy of ACM/Dubbo Daily Liberal.

1964 Bob Weir Captained Country Seconds Team

Bob Weir one of Western NSW greatest players, represented Western Division, Country Firsts and NSW.

Courtesy of: Phillip King's "A History of Narromine & District".   *Courtesy of: NSW Rugby League News.*

1968 Cobar Rugby League Team Group 15 Premiers

Back Row: J. Stephens, P. Fox, R. Gordon, T. Knight, W. Schofield, G. Greer.

Middle Row: B. Harvey, S. Ralph, M. Francisco, R. Pike.

Front Row: J. Goonrey, J. Josephson, B. Wynd (Captain), J. Ralph.

Ball Boys: Shane Josephson, Bradley Wynd.

Absent: P. Brown, R. Porter.

1968 Grand Final:

The grand-final was held at Nyngan on September 8th and was a fiercely contested match against Brewarrina who had beaten Cobar twice throughout the season and were the Minor Premiers and the favourites. Although Cobar deserved their win, the game was in the balance until the final minutes. In front of a crowd of 2,000, Brewarrina were leading 4-2 when Jim Goonrey scored a try in the final moments of the game.

Cobar's gallant 13 were led by Captain Brad Wynd playing as five-eighth. He was superb in attack and tenacious in defence. His kicking was accurate landing a 50-yard penalty goal. Tom Knight was easily the best forward on the field.

Final Score: Cobar 7 Brewarrina 4.

Courtesy of: John Collins, The Crowing of The Roosters.

Dave Brown

The "Bradman of Rugby League" and a true legend of the game. He was a hero to Cobar Players.

Cobar referred to as the Roosters adopted the colours, red, white and blue in 1936. Apparently, the Cobar players had been inspired by the great Australian player Dave Brown. Brown was born in 1913 and therefore of similar age to the Cobar players of his generation.

He helped Eastern Suburbs to two premierships, 1935-1936 and was acknowledged as the greatest player of his generation.

He was known as the 'Bradman' of rugby league for his freakish point scoring and holds the record for 38 tries the most in one season.

Courtesy of: John Collins, The Crowing of The Roosters.

CYMS BATTLE TO WIN MACQUARIE MATCH

Dubbo CYMS scored a well deserved 9-0 win over Macquarie in the first round of the "Dubbo Derby" played at No. 1 Oval yesterday.

April 1969

Macquarie's lock forward, Brian Gee passes the ball during the CYMS Macquarie match at No. 1 Oval yesterday. Gee is being tackled by CYMS second rower, Ross Packeridge, while Macquarie's hooker John Wallace and CYMS front rower Mick Wilson watch the position of the ball.

Moving in to support Packeridge is second rower Barry O'Connor and winger Ross Patton. CYMS won the match 9-0 to become the first holders of the Ces Martin Memorial Cup.

Article from: The Dubbo Daily Liberal, Monday, April 14, 1969. Republished courtesy of ACM/Dubbo Daily Liberal.

CYMS take one point victory in thriller at Forbes

McMULLEN STEERS HIS TEAM TO FINAL SPOT

August 1969

Dubbo CYMS, brilliantly led by Ken McMullen advanced to the final of the Group 11 Rugby League competition with a thrilling 17-16 win over Forbes at Forbes yesterday.

In a thriller from start to finish, first one then the other team gained the lead and finally CYMS scored the winning try with 10 minutes to go. Pictured right: Ken McMullen passing the ball.

Article from: The Dubbo Daily Liberal, August 18, 1969. Republished courtesy of ACM/Dubbo Daily Liberal.

Parkes Turn on Power Display
Narromine Swamped 35-7 in League Surprise

Parkes emerged as red-hot favourites for the Group XI Rugby League premiership when they thrashed Narromine 35-7 with a superb display of open football in the second semi-final at Narromine yesterday.

August 1969

Right: Parkes second rower, Ray Neilsen who scored a try against Narromine yesterday; narrowly missed scoring again in this action shot.

Far Right: Star Parkes centre, Ken Rodwell is a picture of concentration as he boots one of his four goals during the match.

Scores:
Parkes 35 (J. Bonham 2, T. Scurfield, L. Wakefield, C. Glapiak, R. Neilsen, W. Hetherington tries Bonham 2 goals, field goal, Rodwell 4 goals). Defeated:
Narromine: 7 (T. McNichol try; D. Walsh 2 goals).

Ray Neilsen with the ball

Ken Rodwell

Article from: The Dubbo Daily Liberal, August 25, 1969. Republished courtesy of ACM/Dubbo Daily Liberal.

CYMS Baffle Narromine to Head for Grand Final Again
CYMS 19 defeated Narromine 8

Dubbo CYMS in a great display of wet weather football which completely baffled Narromine, strode towards the Group XI Rugby League first grade grand final with a 19-8 win in the final at No. 1 Oval yesterday.

August 1969

Below left: CYMS front rower, Tony Kelly, is surrounded by Narromine players during the CYMS-Narromine clash on No. 1 Oval. Narromine's five-eighth, Bill Shadlow is moving in to put Kelly on the ground.

Narrromine's front rower, Des Walsh (partly obscured) is running in to make sure Kelly doesn't get away. Kelly was one of CYMS best players in the encounter and he crossed for two tries.

Below right: Three of CYMS stars yesterday celebrate their great win over Narromine. They are (from L to R) winger Mike Pelly, who scored a try, lock Brian O'Sullivan and second rower Terry Hunter. All three had good games with Hunter in particular, having his best game of the season.

SCORES:
CYMS 19
(G. Yeo 3, M. Pelly, K. Murray tries; K. McMullen 2 field goals).
Defeated
Narromine 8
(J. Dodd, M. Boucher tries; J. Edmunds goal).

Article from: The Dubbo Daily Liberal, August 25, 1969. Republished courtesy of ACM/Dubbo Daily Liberal.

1969 Group XI Finals and lead up

Dubbo CYMS RLFC was admitted into the Group 11 competition in 1958 & although they had won Premierships in both Reserve and Junior Grades in the early years, a First Grade Premiership had eluded them.

In 1968 things were to change with CYMS signing the current Sydney Eastern Suburbs Rugby League half back and former Australian Rugby Union half back Ken McMullen as Captain Coach.

Ken introduced a new, fully professional attitude to CYMS, with the results coming in his first year with a First-Grade Grand Final position only to go down narrowly to Narromine 12/4, however a huge improvement in only one year as coach.

On the back of a great year in 1968, CYMS were looking forward with confidence to the 1969 season.

1969:

Parkes was the team to beat, easily winning the minor premiership on 33 points, with only one loss and a draw for the season. Narromine came in second on 26 points. Forbes third on a count back, also on 26 points and CYMS making the semi-final cut on 22 points.

All money is on Parkes to win the 1969 Premiership and hard to disagree, however the season had a way to go and the business end was just starting.

Finals:

The first weekend of the finals saw Parkes beat Narromine to go straight to the Grand-Final.

Dubbo CYMS just got away with Forbes 17/16 at Forbes, with Forbes being eliminated and CYMS moving on to play Narromine in the final the following week.

At the end of a torrid encounter, it was Dubbo CYMS 19 defeating Narromine 8 and in some way making up for their loss to Narromine in the 1968 Grand-Final.

Dubbo CYMS were to meet Parkes in the Grand-Final at Pioneer Oval in Parkes.

Although Parkes had only been beaten once through the season and were considered almost unbeatable by the majority of punters, Dubbo CYMS felt they were just hitting their straps and were confident their momentum had benefited by playing each week of the final series and their game coming together at the right time.

Okeydokey, Landscapes

Parkes has a great team and home ground:

Playing Parkes at home with their great team which included captain coach Allan Jones, big prop Jock Gartshore, hooker Tom Williams & a great backline including Laurie Wakefield, Terry Scurfield, John Bonham, Bruce Finn & Ken Rodwell, was always going to be a hard Grand Final to win.

In addition to the obvious strength of the Parkes team, it was the loss of CYMS champion fullback Geoff Miller who was injured in last week's game that worried them the most. Although his replacement Fred O'Sullivan will do a good job, Nugget will be missed.

Article from: The Dubbo Daily Liberal, September, 1969. Republished courtesy of ACM/Dubbo Daily Liberal.

The Parkes RL Scoring Machine

August 1969

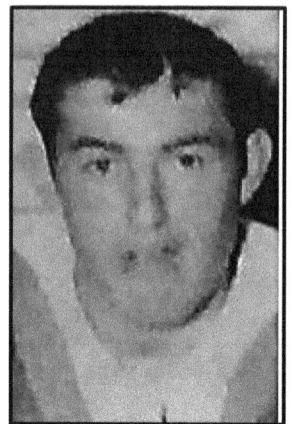   

Above: left to right John Bonham, Terry Scurfield, Ray Neilsen and Laurie Wakefield.

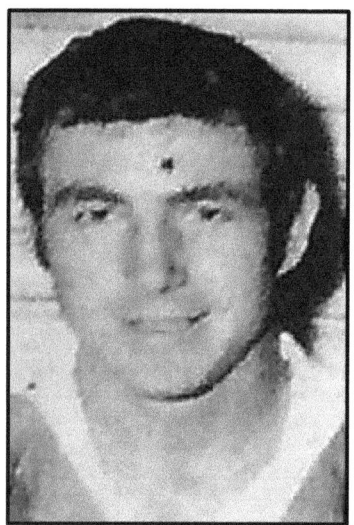  

Above: left to right Charlie Glapiak, Wayne Hetherington and Ken Rodwell.

PARKES IN DEVASTATING FORM WHIPS NARROMINE 35-7

The Parkes Rugby League Team's premiership chances soared sky-high with its 35-7 win over Narromine in a one-sided Group 11 Semi-Final at Narromine yesterday.

Article from: The Parkes Champion Post, August, 24, 1969. Republished courtesy of ACM/Parkes Champion Post.

Grand Final Fever

Parkes, like Dubbo, is a town beset with grand final fever, although not as demonstrative as Dubbo.

September 1969

In Dubbo, where streamers, banners and green and white adornments are the order of the day, football fever is evident.

But in Parkes, the scene is different. They are talking about it, but there is not much evidence of it.

"Although there's not many streamers around town, you only have to walk out the door to hear people talking about the match," Parkes president Fred King said.

"It's in everyone's minds and I can guarantee that most of the town will be at the oval on Sunday," he added.

Parkes this season have their best chance of winning the Group 11 premiership since 1954.

And celebrations are already being planned for the victory by most of Parkes' citizens.

"You can take it from me, if we get up, the Leagues' Club will be so full you won't be able to squeeze a cat into it," said King.

CYMS good win over Narromine last week has shaken the complacency of many Parkes residents.

An aura of complacency was given in a Sunday paper last weekend following a report from Parkes.

The report stated that last week's final between Narromine and CYMS looked like being a waste of time because Parkes were a foregone conclusion for the premiership.

Although Parkes are the hottest Group 11 premiership favourites for years, CYMS showing last week proves they will be no pushover.

"We're confident down here, but not overconfident and I think it will be a close game," King said.

"CYMS proved last week they will be a tough side and they have the advantage of playing in last year's grand final," he added.

Parkes will run onto the field through a large archway erected outside their dressing room and it will be decorated in red, white and blue streamers.

King's Comment

Parkes' president (Fred King) this week gave a message to CYMS players and supporters on the eve of the grand final clash.

"I'd like to congratulate Ken McMullen and the CYMS boys on reaching the grand final for the second year in a row." King said.

"I'm a great admirer of their brand of football. They always play it hard, clean and fast."

"I've also got a lot of time for Dan O'Sullivan CYMS president, whom I admire as one of the fairest, most conscientious and best administrators in the Group."

"As, president of Parkes, I naturally cannot say that I would like to see CYMS win on Sunday."

"Our fellows are in top condition and ready to go and if CYMS win, it will be well deserved."

"This should be a wonderful grand final and all I can say is may the better team win on Sunday. I hope and think it will be Parkes."

Article from: The Dubbo Daily Liberal, Friday, September 5, 1969. Republished courtesy of ACM/Dubbo Daily Liberal.

Copybook Tackle

Ken McMullen

How to tackle

A flashback to Sunday's match when CYMS thrashed Narromine to go into Sunday's grand-final at Pioneer Oval Parkes.

Left: CYMS captain coach Ken McMullen traps a Narromine player with a copybook tackle. McMullen poses perhaps the biggest danger to Parkes on Sunday.

Norm Johnston, from Cumnock is undoubtably the best referee in Group 11 and has been very consistent this season.

Article from: The Dubbo Daily Liberal September 5, 1969. Republished courtesy of ACM/Dubbo Daily Liberal.

THE GRAND FINAL 1969 CYMS OR PARKES

Parkes, say the experts

The 1969 Rugby League season in Group XI reaches a climax on Sunday with the first grade final between CYMS and Parkes at Parkes.

September 1969

For the winners there will be the plaudits of all while the losers will receive a bad luck pat on the back and "better luck next year" wish.

The final whistle on Sunday afternoon will prelude wild rejoicing for the winning team.

For it has been a long time between sips of the victory for Sunday's combatants.

For Parkes a win on Sunday will herald the club its first premiership for 17 years.

For CYMS it will mean a first, first grade premiership ever in the club's short but successful 11-years existence.

Both teams will give their all for the full 80 minutes and the winners will have an even more hectic experience afterwards in celebrating,

So, it would be a good idea if Parkes first graders trotted down the street on Saturday and purchased a bottle or two of hangover pills each, for they will be the ones doing the victory celebrations after next Sunday's match.

Parkes with a great record in 1969 losing only one game will defeat CYMS on Sunday and so become the 1969 Group 11 Rugby League premiers.

And it is only just, for Parkes, having lost only one game (and that by one point) throughout the season, probably have more claim to the premiership honours than CYMS.

It will be a close and exciting game, for CYMS have troubled Parkes greatly in their two encounters for the season.

In the first round they played a seven all draw with CYMS having decided honours in the match.

Parkes turned the tables by winning 8-2 in the second-round encounter, but CYMS had four top players out and several others playing out of position.

A look at the positions shows Parkes have an edge in the backs while the forwards even themselves out.

And this is where Parkes will and must use speed to their advantage for they have speed to burn.

Parkes have a superior backline to CYMS and their, concentrated speed in this department should prove too much.

Parkes fullback, Laurie Wakefield, is a better fullback all round than Fred O'Sullivan, his CYMS counterpart.

Wakefield is just the man to field McMullen's short kicks through and turn defence into attack.

On the wings, Charlie Glapiak, with an edge in speed over Mike Pelly should be given many opportunities while Tony Heperlin and Gary Yeo should be an even match.

Terry Scurfield and Ken Rodwell, Parkes' brilliant centre combination, should prove more than a handful for Kerry Murray and Neil Dodd.

Murray came back to his best last week and Dodd is a solid reliable centre, but both lack the individual brilliance of the Parkes' pair and the speed off the mark.

At half, John Bonham is the best Ken McMullen has come up against this season and he will bear close watching in this his almost certain last appearance in Group 11 before going to Newtown next season.

Article from: The Dubbo Daily Liberal, Friday, September 5, 1969. Republished courtesy of ACM/Dubbo Daily Liberal.

The Men for the Match

The following are profiles of players engaged in the first grade grand final on Sunday.

September 1969

CYMS

Fred O'Sullivan: Unorthodox and ungainly but is a very deceptive and elusive runner, catches a ball beautifully and defends very well.

Mike Pelly: Hard and determined runner with an excellent sidestep. First season in top grade Rugby League and his experience could be a telling factor.

Gary Yeo: Hard runner who scored three tries last week. Aggressive tackler whose ball and all tackles prove very effective on many occasions.

Kerry Murray: Big, strong centre who came right back to his best last Sunday. Fiery and aggressive defender but will play a big role on Sunday.

Neil Dodd: Perfect foil for Murray. Not brilliant but very solid and his containing of Leo Foster last Sunday was a superb lesson in how to handle the man.

Ross Patton: Not a brilliant footballer but is very safe and is the man to have in a grand-final. Uses his head rather than his brawn and defends well.

Ken McMullen: The genius behind CYMS. Not playing as marked a role this season as he was last year but is very, very dangerous and is the best tactical kicker in the group.

Gary Hearns: Rough, tough lock who plays a big role in softening up his opponents. Gets going right from the opening whistle and adds stability to CYMS.

Terry Hunter: Brilliant second rower who came right back to his best last play. Speedy runner and a great cover defender.

Tom Jordan: Key player in Sunday's grand-final. Fierce and determined runner from the rucks and a great crash tackler.

Tony Kelly: The best thinking prop in Group 11. Intelligent play around the rucks has yielded him many tries this season and he is a vital part of CYMS attacking play.

Mick Wilson: Big rough and tough. Running the best, he has done all season and injects much needed fire into the CYMS pack.

Kel Brown: Great hooker who has only been beaten once for the ball this season. Runs hard from dummy half and is a resolute defender.

PARKES

Laurie Wakefield: Top class fullback now recognised as the best in Group 11. Runs well in attack, catches well and defence is faultless.

Charlie Glapiak: Highly promising winger who is a very fast runner. Handles well and his defence is near perfect.

Tony Hepperlin: Not speedy, but very strong and runs determinedly. Very safe player who is a neccessity in a grand-final.

Terry Scurfield: Plays a stone above his weight. Fast, backs up and is capable of making a break. Very strong defender and has improved out of sight this season.

Bruce Finn: Like his opposite, he is a safe player whose defence is the keynote of his game. Distributes very well to his backs.

Ken Rodwell: Fast, good in attack and can change the game. Great defender.

John Bonham: A danger man to CYMS. Very fast to the loose ball and makes many breaks from dropped passes. Exploits a little kick very well and a capable goalkicker.

Allan Jones: Undoubtably the best lock in Group 11. Safe, stable player who gives his all for the full 80 minutes.

Wayne Hetherington: The more brilliant of Parkes' second row twins. Runs very well with the pace and is a beautiful sidestepper into the open.

Ray Neilsen: Not as brilliant as Hetherington but is more rugged. Does a power of work in tight stuff and covers well.

Jock Gartshore: Has come into his own this year with a series of very strong performances. Tackles very well and runs hard.

Peter Barnes: The "find" of the final series. Played a blinder against Narromine with his hard running and excellent defence.

Tom Williams: The most experienced hooker in Group 11. Strikes very fast, runs hard and distributes well from dummy half.

Mind On Job

Allan Jones

Article from: The Dubbo Daily Liberal, Friday, September 5, 1969. Republished courtesy of ACM/Dubbo Daily Liberal.

THE START OF IT ALL

McMULLEN'S BOOT WON THE HONOURS

Dubbo CYMS Rugby League committee should dust Ken McMullen's boots in gold and keep them for posterity.

September 1969

Above: Ken McMullen leads his team onto the field

McMullen and his merry band of 12 cohorts sprang the surprise of the season by downing Parkes 16-12 and win their first ever grade Group 11 Rugby League premiership yesterday.

It was a magnificent win and all 13 CYMS players deserve full credit for the way they won even though the game was marred by an incident a minute from fulltime when CYMS prop Mick Wilson was sent from the field.

Parkes were beaten by a better team on the day but McMullen's golden boots contributed 10 of the team's points and it was a performance no-one is likely to forget for a long time.

Pictured below: big prop, Mick Wilson walks dejectedly from the field after being sent off with a minute to go in the CYMS-Parkes grand final yesterday.

Mick Wilson

Final Scores: CYMS 16 (Gary Yeo 2 tries; K McMullen 5 goals) defeated
Parkes 12 (K. Rodwell, B. Finn tries; J. Bonham 2 goals, K. Rodwell field goal)

Article from: The Dubbo Daily Liberal, Monday, September 8, 1969. Republished courtesy of ACM/Dubbo Daily Liberal.

1969 Final Victoria Park Dubbo and Grand Final Pioneer Oval Parkes

Above Left: Narromine prop Arnold Gillespie (11) brings down an opponent with help from lock Murray Boucher. CYMS second-rower Bryan O'Sullivan looks to lend a hand to his overwhelmed team mate.

Above Right: Tom Jordan passes to lock Gary Heares before being tackled by a Parkes defender leading to a try in the 1969 Grand Final.

Courtesy of: Blast From the Past, Dubbo CYMS Old Boys.

Castlereagh Hotel Dubbo

Dubbo CYMS rugby league players refer to the Castlereagh as the Vatican.

Source: Archives, Australian National University

1969 Dubbo CYMS Rugby League Team Group 11 Premiers

BACK ROW: Ray Brassington (trainer), Mike Pelly, Garry Haires, Kerry Murray, Mick Wilson, Tony Kelly, Allan McPhail (secretary)
CENTRE ROW: Boy Tipping (snr-vice pres), Dick Hasler, Clive Carver, Fred O'Sullivan Dan O'Sullivan (pres), Neil Dodd, Ken Eggleton, Geoff Miller, Hilton Carver (assist. sec)
FRONT ROW: Tom Jordan, Garry Yeo, Kel Brown, Ken McMullen (capt-coach) Ross Patton, Brian O'Sullivan

Courtesy of: Blast From the Past, Dubbo CYMS Old Boys.

1969 Dubbo CYMS Reserve Grade Group 11 Premiers

CYMS Premiers:

Dubbo CYMS won both first and reserve grade Group 11 premierships at Pioneer Oval Parkes.

Left: Doug Madden, Peter Brown and Charlie Cook chair CYMS reserve grade captain Eddie Powter off the field after winning the Group 11 Grand-Final.

Dubbo CYMS defeated Parkes 8-4.

Courtesy of: Blast From the Past, Dubbo CYMS Old Boys.

THE SEVENTIES

Daily Liberal Award Winner: Allan Jones, Group 11 best and fairest player. Premiership winning teams: Forbes 1970, Peak Hill Second Division 1970, CYMS 1971, Coonamble Bears 1971, Cobar Roosters 1971, 1972, Parkes 1972, 1973, Narromine 1974, CYMS 1975 and Narromine 1976. Teams' most common mode of travel was the bus. Newspaper articles tell the story and provide details of the players who stood out during an exciting period of rugby league.

DUBBO LIBERAL AWARD WINNER

September 1970

This year the Daily Liberal approached the Referees' Association who consented to judge the competition but a ruling from the Country Rugby League prevented them from doing so.

The judges appointed were the official time keepers at each match – same judges who officiate in the John Munday official Group 11 juniors award.

Parkes Rugby League captain-coach Allan Jones will take his once in a lifetime trip to Singapore in February.

Jones (30) plans to retire next season at this stage. 'I know I'm like Melba - retires and then comes back but I think at this stage I'll have to give it away.'

Jones has just gone into business in Parkes with former Parkes and Country prop Jock Gartshore. The pair were in partnership in the building trade for a while but recently bought a service station in Parkes.

Elated as Jones was after winning the prize, it was nothing like the elation of his wife.

And so, ends the 1970 Daily Liberal Best and Fairest competition won by one of the most popular footballers to go round for a long time Allan "Ocker" Jones.

"Ocker" Jones Celebrating.

Article from: The Dubbo Daily Liberal, Friday, September 19, 1970. Republished courtesy of ACM/Dubbo Daily Liberal.

Forbes Advocate
Magpies meet CYMS in muddy grand final
August 1970

The season saw Forbes (Magpies) and Dubbo CYMS play in the Group XI Grand Final at Victoria Park Dubbo. It was the weather that made the headlines when Forbes beat CYMS at Victoria Park which "was underwater in most places and was nothing but a mud-heap" in heavy rain.

There were only two tries scored in the match, one to each side. CYMS winger Pat Yeo scored in the first three minutes of the match. Forbes winger Neil Rees scored in the corner off a strong run and penalty kicks by Alan Groundwater and Ray Nicholson gave Forbes the win.

Forbes' 7-3 victory surprised the majority of fans' Dubbo CYMS stalwarts were reported to be offering five points start to Forbes in the match.

To CYMS' disappointment a late try was disallowed which would have given them the match. CYMS players were certain they had scored however the referee had the final say no try, forward pass.

Article from: The Forbes Advocate, 1970. Republished courtesy of ACM/Forbes Advocate.

Magpies Meet CYMS in Muddy Grand Final
CYMS—They hold the title

Back Row: N. Bahr, G. Yeo, N. Dodd, P. Yeo, C. Parkes, M. Wilson, P. Brown.
Middle Row: K. Murray, A. Kelly, R. Patton.
Front Row: G. Miller, K. McMullen, K. Brown.
Inserts: M. Pelly and B. O'Sullivan.

Courtesy of: Dubbo CYMS Old Boys, 1970 Grand Final Program.

Forbes—They want the title

Back Row: D. Redfern, A. Groundwater, R. Wilson, N. Rees, A. Slacksmith (Captain),
A. Constable, A. Bell, P. Kennedy.
Front Row: A. Smith, M. Cain, G. Douglas, R. Nicholson, B. Turner.

Courtesy of: Dubbo CYMS Old Boys, 1970 Grand Final Program.

Flashback Action Scenes

THE LAST TIME THEY CLASHED: Some action from the second-round encounter between today's Grand Finalists Forbes and CYMS.

Courtesy of: Dubbo CYMS Old Boys, 1970 Grand Final Program.

Forbes in Grand Final

Canowindra centre Len Hamilton is well held by Forbes half Brian Turner and second rower Alan Bell in last Sunday's final at Forbes.

Forbes defeated Canowindra and advanced to the Grand-Final at Victoria Park Dubbo the following Sunday to play CYMS.

Courtesy of: Dubbo CYMS Old Boys, 1970 Grand Final Program.

Hooking His Way to Fame

Group 11 this year provided three players to wear the sky blue of NSW Laurie Wakefield (Parkes), Les Hutchings (Condobolin) and Kel Brown (CYMS).

Of the trio, only Brown remains in Group 11 and he will be right in the thick of things in the grand-final.

Wakefield has joined the Parramatta Club in Sydney while Hutchings is with Canterbury. Brown is one of Dubbo's best footballing sons. He was born, bred and learned all his football in Dubbo.

Brown started his career as a half and it was not until he joined CYMS that he was tried in the hooking position.

He was not outstanding in CYMS juniors and did not really start to blossom as a hooker until last season.

Brown dominated the scrums last year and it was his initial year in representative football.

He represented Group 11 and then on to represent Western Division in the country championships. This year he started off again in Group 11, went to Western Division and then to the Country team to tour New Zealand.

On his return from New Zealand, he was the number one Country hooker and played for Country firsts against City firsts on the Sydney Cricket Ground.

He then returned to the CYMS team and like a bolt out of the blue, was selected in the NSW team to play Queensland in the return series on the SCG.

Courtesy of: Dubbo CYMS Old Boys, 1970 Grand Final Program.

Kel Brown in action

Ken McMullen Wallaby to League

Ken McMullen was a talented and tigerish halfback who had the misfortunate for his career to coincide with that of Ken Catchpole, one of the all-time greats. With his fiery red hair and a penchant for sharp darts around the fringes, McMullen genuinely threatened Catchpole and at one point it was seriously considered that McMullen be shifted to fly half in order to accommodate the talented pair in the same side. McMullen was also a more than handy cricketer who played for Country against touring West Indian and England teams.

McMullen went on and played for Eastern Suburbs (1964-1967. In 1968 he accepted the position as captain-coach Dubbo CYMS and retired in 1972.
Source: Classic Wallabies'. Rugby League Project.

MUDBATH

But Forbes were the mudlarks

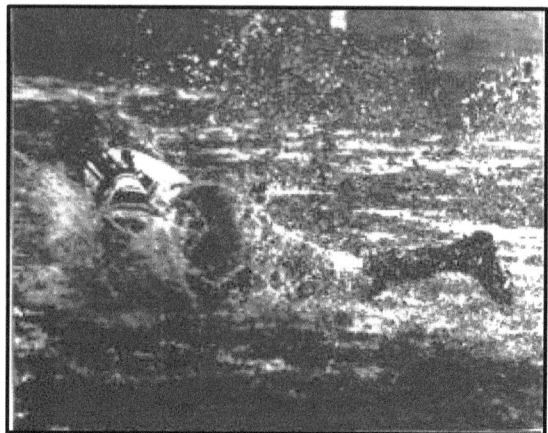 

Forbes defeated minor premiers CYMS 7-3 in the Group 11 Rugby League grand final at No.1 Oval yesterday.

September 1970

The game was played under shocking conditions with No. 1 Oval a mudheap and under water in most places.

Veteran referee Norm Johnson described the conditions as the worst he had experienced in 25 years of refereeing.

As well as mud, players had to combat heavy showers which fell during the afternoon.

No. 1 Oval was a quagmire and Dubbo City Council's Parks supervisor (Gordan Tindall) and a Council representative are today investigating the extent of the damage on No. 1 Oval.

Forbes sprang a big upset in downing CYMS and they handled the conditions far better than the minor premiers.

They tackled CYMS out of the game and were by far the better side on the day as they lifted their game more than CYMS.

Forbes' win was a team effort and full credit must go to captain-coach Tony Slacksmith who at 23, is the youngest captain-coach in the Group.

Forbes had a very young side with the average age 22 and their enthusiasm won the day.

CYMS were disjointed in both attack and defence and it was one of the team's worst performances of the season.

Article from: The Dubbo Daily Liberal, Monday, September 28, 1970. Republished courtesy of ACM/Dubbo Daily Liberal.

FORBES JUST TOO STRONG

Forbes won the 1970 Group XI Rugby League first grade premiership by defeating minor premiers CYMS 7-3 in a grand final played under appalling conditions at No.1 Oval yesterday.

September 1970

Torrential rain made the ground a quagmire with mini lakes of water on the ground.

Although conditions made good football virtually impossible Forbes thoroughly deserved their win because they were the better team it was as simple as that.

In a tremendous display of defensive football, Forbes tackled CYMS out of the game from almost the opening whistle.

CYMS seemed lethargic and their handling, as compared with that of Forbes, was dismal to say the least.

It was one of the minor premiers' worst displays of the season and the writing was on the wall at half time.

Forbes led only 5-3 at half-time but they were clearly superior and except for a momentary flash of attacking football in the last five minutes CYMS were doomed to defeat after only 15 minutes play.

Surprisingly Forbes hooker Daryl Redfern shaded NSW hooker Kel Brown in the first half.

However, in the second half Brown came right back into his own and gave CYMS a glut of possession with which they should have won the game.

The game was only four minutes old when Neil Dodd gave CYMS supporters heart for the first and only time of the day.

Dodd sidestepped past his opposition Gordon Douglas and broke away clear into the open.

When cornered by Forbes fullback Ray Nicholson, Dodd passed to winger Pat Yeo and raced away to touch down in the corner.

Fullback Geoff Miller was called up for the conversion and the ball only travelled about 10 feet in the air.

Still CYMS had their tails up and for the next 10 minutes pounded the Forbes try line.

But gradually CYMS started to wilt and Forbes after initial nerves, settled into the groove.

Exploiting the age old CYMS weakness against forward play up the centre Forbes pounded the CYMS line. Finally, winger Neil Rees gained a slight overlap five yards out and he crashed over in the corner.

Prop Alan Groundwater made a top class attempt at goal but the ball just fell short and the scores were tied at three all.

Forbes gained heart from the try while the CYMS team started to become disjointed in attack and defence.

McMullen was being very closely marked by Forbes and he could not get going at all in this period.

Referee Graham Barby was being very severe on McMullen and Brown and gave Forbes several penalties from scrum infringements.

From one of these 35 yards out and on a slight angle, Groundwater kicked a great penalty to give his team the lead.

Only superb defence by second rower Peter Brown and hooker Kel Brown kept Forbes at bay.

Peter Brown gave a tremendous display of tackling and at one stage tackled five Forbes players in a row while the other CYMS players stood and watched.

McMullen gave his players a verbal lashing at half-time, but the effects were not shown in the second half.

CYMS lost second rower Mick Wilson who was replaced by Bryan O'Sullivan while Forbes remained intact.

However Forbes prop Alan Groundwater was forced off the field midway through the second half and replaced by Don Parslow.

Shortly after Groundwater went off CYMS second rower O'Sullivan was penalised near his own line and fullback Ray Nicholson landed the goal to give his team a 7-3 lead.

In a series of incidents which could have cost CYMS the match (a) McMullen made a strong run from the scrumbase and was pulled down only feet short from the line and (b) winger Gary Yeo dropped the ball twice when the line was wide open.

The match finished with Forbes well in CYMS half and back on attack as was the case for most of the game.

It was a real team effort by Forbes and it is hard to single out players in the team.

However special mention must be made to captain coach Tony Slacksmith who was in everything and half Brian Turner had a class match.

CYMS were best served by Peter Brown who played magnificently while prop Norm Barber and centre Neil Dodd never gave up trying.

Scores: Forbes 7 (N. Rees try: A Groundwater, Ray Nicholson goals) defeated CYMS 3 (P. Yeo try).

Article from: The Dubbo Daily Liberal, Monday, September 28, 1970. Republished courtesy of ACM/Dubbo Daily Liberal.

After the Game

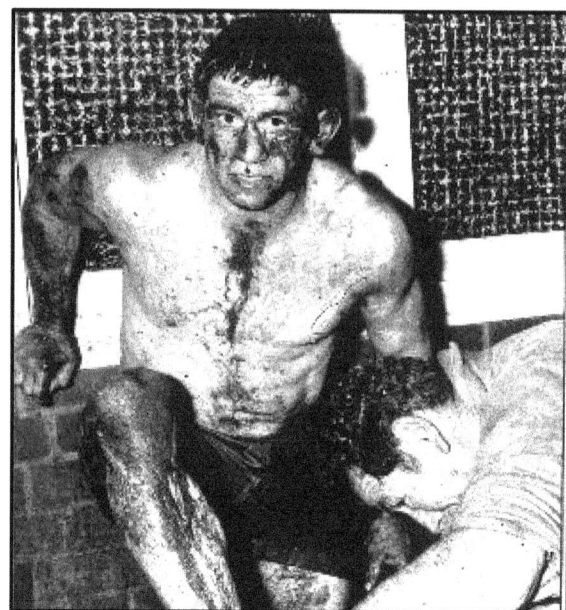

Above: Mud splattered Forbes centre Peter Kennedy is helped with his bootlaces by Forbes' strapper Leo Martin after the grand final yesterday. Kennedy, third place getter in the Daily Liberal Best and Fairest competition, played very strongly in CYMS premiership demise. Kennedy played through the match with a broken hand which was heavily taped before he went on.

CYMS Patron Fr. Smith with Ken McMullen

Article from The Dubbo Daily Liberal, Monday, September 28, 1970. Republished courtesy of ACM/Dubbo Daily Liberal.

1970 Forbes Rugby League Team Group 11 Premiers

The Forbes first grade team after their big win over Dubbo CYMS in the Group 11 Rugby League grand final on Sunday.

Forbes team:
Back Row: J. Corliss (Committeeman), B. Turner, A. Smith, R. Wilson, A. Constable, A. Slacksmith (Captain), D. Parslow, A. Groundwater, N. Rees, A. Bell.
Front Row: D. Redfern, M. Cain, G. Douglas, P. Kennedy.

Article from: Celebrating a Century of League Our Grand Final Glory – Forbes Advocate, June 3, 2019. Republished courtesy of ACM/Forbes Advocate.

Article from: Peak Hill & District Times, 18th, September 1970. Republished courtesy of ACM/Peak Hill & District Times.

1971 Season

Captain Coach Graham "Muncher" Kennedy was the major force behind the Parkes club's re-emergence as a country footy force. Larger than life, the prop forward added discipline, authority and commitment to his coaching and led Parkes to the Grand Final only to be beaten in extra time by Dubbo CYMS.

Looking over the performances of the Parkes rugby league team in recent weeks, I think it is only fair to mention the outstanding form of utility player, Dennis Finn.

Dennis, as you may recall, was one of Parkes' top juniors several seasons ago but was forced into premature retirement due to a nagging leg injury.

All and sundry thought they had seen the last of this fine young prospect but he has burst back onto the scene this year, bigger and better than ever.

After four years on the sideline, he has made a spectacular comeback with perhaps his best performance being recorded against Dubbo Macquarie two weeks ago.

Finn's two tries in this vital game enabled Parkes to defeat Macquarie and maintain a tight hold on their fourth semi-final position.

On his present form, Dennis must be rated the top five-eighth in Group 11, a fitting reward for his determination to get back into the game.

Article from: The Parkes Champion Post, March, 1971. Republished courtesy of ACM/Parkes Champion Post.

1971 Cobar Rugby League Team Group 15 Premiers
Cobar Roosters 33 defeated Bourke 6

Cobar Roosters win Group 15 consecutive premierships and Clayton Cup (1971/1972).

Back Row: M. Ralph, "Gidgee" Robinson (Strapper), John Josephson, Neil Basedow, Ray Hamilton, Peter Bannister, Tom Knight, Brian Lawrence (Captain Coach).

Front Row: Barry Grace, Stan Ralph, Bob Clark, Les Houghton, Jim Ralph, Jim Goonrey, George Greer, Brian Heap.

Courtesy of: John Collins, The Crowing of The Roosters, from Bob Clark Collection.

First Home RL Match on Sunday

The Parkes Rugby League selectors have made an interesting change in the hooker position for the match against Condobolin at Pioneer Oval on Sunday.

June 1971

Selectors have experimented in shifting second rower Ray Neilsen to take over the hooking role.

The move is an important gamble aimed at giving the team more possession than it has been getting in earlier games.

Neilsen is not entirely new to the position, as he has had spasmodic games as hooker.

Selectors intend to give Neilsen concentrated training on hooking this week.

Neilsen has been preferred to regular hookers, Alan Kelly and Reg Davison.

Davison, who transferred from Trundle and has been plagued with minor injuries, has been unable to get into top condition.

Kelly and Davison will be partners in the reserve grade front row on Sunday.

Second rower Chris Millwood, who has had first grade experience, has been brought in to the second row in Neilsen's place.

The only other change made in the side is in the fullback position.

Dennis Finn replaces Alfie Davies who is unavailable.

Finn, a former first grade centre and five-eighth, is resuming this year after an enforced spell because of ankle injuries.

The team's Western Division representatives, five-eighth Jim Bonus and lock Wayne Hetherington are returning to the side.

The team is at near full strength and its performance against Condobolin is full of interest.

Condobolin last Sunday showed it cannot be under-rated.

Condobolin last week beat Dubbo CYMS 26/22.

In the first round Dubbo CYMS beat Parkes 14/13.

Condobolin will be led by former St. George player Dennis O'Callaghan (lock).

He joined St. George in 1967 and played with them for two years before going to Eden as coach there in 1970.

Article from: The Parkes Champion Post, June, 1971. Republished courtesy of ACM/Parkes Champion Post.

PARKES TO TEST CYMS

June 1971

CYMS big match brilliance will get a severe testing from Parkes rugged side. The game should be decided in the forwards.

Parkes, a great winning pack of forwards, have come under fire even in their own camp for their lack of defence in the forwards.

Phil Gibbs, Peter Barnes and Reg Davison are all fine attacking players but much of the defensive work about the rucks has fallen on skipper Graham Kennedy, prop Rob Atkinson and five-eighth Dennis Finn who has been doing a "Bill Smith" around the rucks for most of the season.

Not that CYMS have been exactly starring themselves in the tackling department in the forwards.

If CYMS repeat the sluggish defence work they showed here against Macquarie they can expect Graham Kennedy will send Gibbs and Atkinson through the gaps.

If there isn't some determined stuff shown by the pack this week some of the regular names might not be looking at the first grade match the following week.

They have allowed only 102 points against them and the nearest effort to that is Forbes with 131.

On the other hand, Parkes has scored more points than anyone else and they have the potential match winners in brilliant Jim Bonus, Charlie Glapiak, Bob Jayet and Phil Gibbs.

Kennedy himself has been playing fine football. He is a reformed character this season and his couple of stints before the judiciary have turned him into a strong leader, though still a rugged defensive player.

CYMS have outstanding big match players in Tony Kelly, Col Parkes, Neil Dodd and Nelson Smith.

Wingers Pat and Gary Yeo are in striking top form and will certainly give Parkes a great duel.

Dodd will handle Bonus in his usual quiet style and if new five-eighth Peter Whale provides the service to Dodd, the experienced centre will give big bustling Peter Walkom the chances he has been starved of this season.

CYMS have abundant try scoring material in the backline and they can match Parkes' backline in every position.

Finn has more experience than Whale and the youngster has a big test ahead of him. Finn played very well against Macquarie here and could be a danger man.

Wighton is not worried about McMullen's reputation and he can be relied on for a big 80 minutes effort.

CYMS v PARKES

CYMS:
FULLBACK: N. Smith
WINGERS: G. Yeo, P. Yeo
CENTRES: P. Walkom, N. Dodd.
FIVE-EIGHTH: P. Whale.
HALF-BACK: K. McMullen.
LOCK: C. Parkes.
SECOND ROWERS: B. O'Sullivan, P. Brown.
PROPS: A. Kelly, J. Yeo.
HOOKER: G. Negline.

PARKES:
FULLBACK: R. Davies.
WINGERS: C. Glapiak, R. Jayet.
CENTRES: R. MacDonald, J. Bonus.
FIVE-EIGHTH: D. Finn.
HALF-BACK: D. Wighton.
LOCK: B. Shean.
SECOND ROWERS: G. Kennedy (Captain), P. Barnes.
PROPS: R. Atkinson, P. Gibbs.
HOOKER: R. Davison.

REFEREE: Mr. N. Johnson

Article from: The Parkes Champion Post, June 9, 1971. Republished courtesy of ACM/Parkes Champion Post.

PARKES IN FOURTH POSITION

Gibbs Guides Team to Vital Victory

The Parkes Rugby League team edged into clear fourth position following its 20-17 win over Narromine in an evenly fought clash at Pioneer Oval yesterday.

June 1971

Article from: The Parkes Champion Post, June 27, 1971. Republished courtesy of ACM/Parkes Champion Post.

Canowindra wins Caltex K.O. title

Group XI Rugby League team Canowindra played brilliant football to win the Western Division Caltex $1000 knockout carnival at Parkes yesterday. Canowindra defeats Narromine in the final

July 1971

The top 16 teams from Groups 10, 11, 14 and 15 competed and the carnival saw Group 11 teams end decisively Group 10's previous domination of the knockout.

The final was an all Group 11 affair in which Canowindra defeated the surprise team of the Carnival Narromine in the final by 17 points to 8. Canowindra won $600 and Narromine $300. The beaten semi-finalists Dubbo Macquarie and Coonabarabran each received $50.

However, Canowindra which stood out as the best team of the carnival had to produce its best football to down the courageous Narromine side.

Dubbo Macquarie showed splendid form to eliminate second team Oberon 7-2 while Canowindra put the writing on the wall when it bowled over Orange Ex-Services 16 nil.

Canowindra's play at times provided real champagne football with the team using its speed and size splendidly.

Stars of the Canowindra side were forward Peter Ryan and fullback Pat Clyburn.

Ryan's bursts directed by the captain-coach Greg Hay repeatably put the brilliant Canowindra attacking machine into action.

Clyburn's amazing speed earned him two magnificent tries and he was always dangerous.

Greg Hay was also in top form and his clever combination with half Fisher, several times completely fooled the opposition. Hay scored three tries.

Narromine side led splendidly by coach Alan Gill knocked out the top Group 10 and 11 teams Cowra and Wellington.

Narromine's best were the hard-working Malcom Dawes, Alan Gill and centre Pat Smith.

In the semi-finals Canowindra defeated Coonabarabran and Narromine defeated Dubbo Macquarie.

Above: Rugged Parkes centre, Rod MacDonald bursts through a gap during Parkes' clash with Coonabarabran. Second rower Wayne Hetherington, supports MacDonald.

Article from: The Parkes Champion Post, July 5, 1971. Republished courtesy of ACM/Parkes Champion Post.

1971 Canowindra Rugby League Team Divisional Caltex Knockout Winners and Competition Leaders

Back Row: Ian Jeffery, Bill Gollen, Eddie Clyburn, Bill Hilton, Greg Hay (Captain Coach), Allan Carrol, Robert Hilton, Jack Rice, Trevor Simpson, Derry Hines, Peter Ryan.

Front Row: Danny Seal, Pat Clyburn, Tod Fisher, Jack Earsman, Gary Carpenter, Brian McClintock.

The Canowindra Tigers, defeated Narromine in the final of the Western Division Caltex Knockout at Parkes, July 1971.

During the 1971 season, Hay was in charge again and this time they were clear ladder leaders at the end of the competition. Fate befell them again when Greg Hay broke his leg in the final and, for the second year in a row, the Tigers missed the decider.

Courtesy of: Geoff Mann, Sports Journalist, Dubbo.

Parkes' Great Second Half Recovery in R.L.

July 1971

The Parkes rugby league first grade team got up off the "floor" to defeat old rivals Forbes at Forbes yesterday.

The win was a vital one for Parkes who have maintained their lead in the semi-final battle for fourth position.

Two of yesterday's heroes, Phil Gibbs and Dennis Finn, leave the field after the bruising encounter.

Article from: The Parkes Champion Post, July 30, 1971. Republished courtesy of ACM/Parkes Champion Post

Parkes v Forbes	Parkes v Wellington 1971 Semi Final

Parkes little general Russell Worth in action against Forbes last week. Barry Shean and Dennis Finn in the background.	Wellington captain coach Robin Turner tries to break through the tackle by Parkes second rower Ray Neilsen during the first semi-final at Canowindra yesterday which Parkes won 20 – 12.
Article from: The Parkes Champion Post, July 30, 1971. Republished courtesy of ACM/Parkes Champion Post.	*Article from: The Dubbo Daily Liberal, August 16, 1971. Republished courtesy of ACM/Daily Liberal.*

FORBES GALLANT BUT DEFEATED

The Parkes Rugby League team finished strongly to snatch a narrow 19-15 win over Forbes in a traditional, hard struggle at Forbes yesterday.

July 1971

A memorable try by second-rower Phil Gibbs two minutes from the end enabled Parkes supporters to breathe freely for the first time in the match.

Parkes led only 16-15 when Gibbs with sheer strength and speed sent the Forbes defence sprawling in a powerful 60-yard burst to score an amazing try.

Gibbs and lock Dennis Finn were Parkes' outstanding players.

Finn's all round display was first class and he scored the try which started Parkes' fight back in the second half.

Article from: The Parkes Champion Post, July 26, 1971 Republished courtesy of ACM/Parkes Champion Post.

Grand Final Fever Hits
Parkes 23 Canowindra 20

Parkes defeated Canowindra in extra time in the Group 11 pre-liminary final. Parkes have now earned the right to meet the powerful Dubbo CYMS side in the grand-final, to be played at Pioneer Oval in Parkes next Sunday.

Graham Kennedy insisted that his team head to the entry gate and clap the Canowindra team as they left the ground.

CYMS tipped to win two grand-finals, Dubbo Dominant

Canowindra captain coach (Greg Hay) last night tipped CYMS to win two out of three grades in the Group 11 Rugby League grand-finals next week at Pioneer Oval Parkes.

August 1971

Parkes centre Jim Bonus crashes Canowindra centre Jack Earsman to the ground during yesterday's final which typified the toughness of the match.

Article from: The Dubbo Daily Liberal, August 13, 1971. Republished courtesy of ACM/Daily Liberal.

PARKES TO WIN

ARRANGEMENTS IN HAND FOR 'GRAND FINAL DAY'

Given fine weather, one of the biggest crowds ever assembled in the central west could gather at Pioneer Oval, Parkes, on Sunday for the grand finals of the Group XI Rugby League competition.

August 1971

The Parkes Rugby League Football Club has arrangements well in hand to cater for an expected huge influx of people.

Parkes Rugby League President, Mr. Ron Harrison, who is also president of Parkes Sports Council, said yesterday that special rope fences would be erected on the oval, 30 yards back from the playing area, to allow patrons to sit on the grassed area inside the boundary fence.

"Spectators are quite welcome to sit on the oval, as long as they remain seated," he stated.

Mr. Harrison added that the playing surface will be in "tip top" condition and that efforts are currently being made to arrange an early fixture between a combined Parkes/Trundle/Peak Hill under eight team.

"Gates to Pioneer Oval will open all night and Parkes residents will be able to park their vehicles as early as they wish," he concluded.

The Parkes team to play CYMS in the first grade final had a novel training run early Thursday morning, pictured above.

Coach Graham Kennedy took his boys for an "18 hole run" over the Parkes Golf Course at 6 a.m. and they returned to the club house for a breakfast of steak and orange juice.

Article from: The Parkes Champion Post, August 22, 1971. Republished courtesy of ACM/Parkes Champion Post.

1971 Group 11 Grand Final

Neil Dodd, Kel Connelly and Tony Kelly.

Colin Parkes and Neil Dodd.

Graham Kennedy (Parkes) and Ken McMullen (CYMS). Dubbo CYMS defeated Parkes: 23 to 20.

Article from: The Dubbo Daily Liberal, September 13, 1971. Republished courtesy of ACM/Dubbo Daily Liberal.

1971 Grand Final Shield

Tony Kelly after 1971 Grand Final

Ken McMullen and Ron Harrison.

Tony is pictured above with his two sons after the 1971 Grand Final at Pioneer Oval Parkes.

Courtesy of: Blast From the Past, Dubbo CYMS Old Boys.

1971 CYMS Rugby League Team Group 11 Premiers

The Mighty Greens

Back Row: P. Walkom, B. O'Sullivan, I. Burke, P. Brown, C. Parkes, G. Yeo.

Middle Row: A. Kelly, G. Negline, N. Dodd,

Front Row: K. Connolly, K. McMullen (Captain Coach), G. Miller.

Courtesy of: Blast From the Past, Dubbo CYMS Old Boys

Dubbo CYMS

Player	Age	Height	Weight	Occupation
G. Miller	24	5' 8"	13.0	Clerk
G. Yeo	26	6' 0"	13.0	Carpenter
P. Yeo	24	5' 11"	12.7	Technician
N. Dodd	25	5 10"	12.10	Carpenter
P. Walkom	19	5' 8"	13.2	Teller
K. Connoly	24	5' 9"	12.0	Clerk
K. McMullen	29	6' 1"	11.10	Sales Manager
C. Parkes	20	6' 0"	14.5	Builder
B. O'Sullivan	28	6' 2"	14.0	Van Salesman
P. Brown	21	6' 2"	13.7	Labourer
A. Kelly	23	6' 1"	14.0	Deputy Town Clerk
G. Negline	28	5' 11"	15.0	Insurance Inspector
L. Burke	21	6' 3"	14.7	Radio Technician

AVERAGE AGE 24 and WEIGHT 13.4

Parkes

Player	Age	Height	Weight	Occupation
R. Davies	21	5' 10"	10.0	Salesman
C. Glapiak	21	5 '8"	11.8	Welder
R. Jayett	22	5' 11"	12.4	Labourer
J. Bonus	27	5' 10"	13.4	Labourer
R. MacDonald	22	5' 9"	12.7	Draughtsman
D. Finn	22	5' 8"	13.0	Clerk
R. Worth	18	5' 5"	10.7	Teller
D. Hodges	22	5' 10"	12.8	Salesman
C. Millwood	20	5' 10"	12.7	Welder
W. Hetherington	23	5' 10"	13.0	Labourer
R. Davison	22	5' 10"	13.8	Garage Employee
G. Kennedy	26	5' 11"	14.4	Plumber
R. Neilsen	22	5' 9"	13.6	Council Worker

AVERAGE AGE 24 and WEIGHT 12.9

Courtesy of: Blast From the Past, Dubbo CYMS Old Boys.

1971 Dubbo CYMS v Parkes

CYMS player Pat Yeo out runs Parkes player Dennis Finn.

Colin Parkes getting the ball to his supporting players

Courtesy of: Blast From the Past, Dubbo CYMS Old Boys.

1971 Parkes Rugby League Grand Final Team

Back Row: Geoff Spiller, Jack Hetherington (Selectors), Bob Jayet, Jim Bonus, Graham Kennedy (Captain Coach), Phil Gibbs, John Hodge, Russell Davies, Wayne Hetherington, Dennis Finn, Charlie Glapiak and Ron Harrison (President).
Front Row: Russell Worth, Rod MacDonald, Ray Neilsen, Chris Millwood, Reg Davison, Ray Bonham, David Hodges and Barry Shean.

Courtesy of: Roseanne Finn.

1971 Coonamble Rugby League Team Group 14 Premiers

On The Buses
During the sixties and seventies, the most common mode of transport for football teams was bus.

Left: Coonamble team in front of the bus.

The advantage of a bus was that all three teams, first, reserves and junior grades could fit in the one bus.

Coonamble Bears defeated Coonabarabran 31-8
Back Row: Frank Fish, Ray Pickering, Ray Cleary, Barry Smith, George Algozeri (Captain Coach), Mick McEntyre, Bruce Jackson, Alwyn Shone.
Front Row: Shane Horan, Gordan Hunt, Paul Kennedy, Mervyn Smith, Noel Lane, (absent-Peter Kennedy).
Courtesy of: Coonamble Rugby League Club, Paul Wheelhouse.

1971 Grand Finalists Clash in First Trial

Last year's Group XI Rugby League grand-finalists Parkes and Dubbo CYMS, will meet in the first official round of Group XI trial games at Pioneer Oval on Sunday.

March 1972

Both sides have undergone only slight changes since last season and Sunday's clash, which is Parkes' first home trial game this season, could produce an entertaining match.

The match will be watched by Group selectors and following the second-round trials the following Sunday, the Group 11 team to play in the Western Division trials at Dubbo on April 2, will be announced.

In other official trials on Sunday Canowindra is at home to Wellington, Macquarie plays Narromine at Dubbo and Forbes will travel to Condobolin.

Parkes will face a tough game against Ken McMullen's 1971 premiership side.

Dubbo CYMS have already shown that they will be a force again this year with a 32-9 win over Wellington at Wellington last weekend.

Apart from McMullen (half-back), CYMS players from last year who have shown promising form early are Tony Kelly (front row), centre Peter Walkom and John Yeo (second row).

Last year's lock, Colin Parkes trialled with Newtown earlier this season but is reported to have returned to CYMS.

CYMS have added thrust in the backs this year with the acquisition of former brilliant Wellington full-back, Nelson Smith.

The Parkes side has a few positions to finalise. The half-back berth is open and former Condobolin half Doug Wighton, could be contesting the position with locals Ross Stevens and John Fawkner.

The Parkes side has a few positions to finalise. The half-back berth is open and former Condobolin half Doug Wighton, could be contesting the position with locals Ross Stevens and John Fawkner.

Centre, Rod MacDonald is another who could be considered, as he sometimes played in the position for Orange Ex-Services two years ago.

However, MacDonald will probably be retained in the centres with Jim Bonus, as these two proved a very good pair last season.

Bonus and solid five-eighth Dennis Finn, are in good early season form and must be in line for Group and W.D. selection.

Last year's Parkes forwards Graham Kennedy, Reg Davidson, Phil Gibbs, Ray Neilsen and Chris Millwood have been joined by Harry Parker (former Parkes lock) and former Condobolin prop Rob Atkinson and the pack should be a tough one this year.

Parkes should have fair depth as the reserve grade side has trialled some promising players, including newcomer John Davoren (front row).

Okeydokey, Landscapes

Article from: The Parkes Champion Post, March 20, 1972. Republished courtesy of ACM/Champion Post.

THE BIG LEAGUE
By Graham Gorrel
Today: Narromine

March 1972

There are ominous signs for Group 11 clubs that Narromine is on the way back.

The Narromine Rugby League machine in the 1950's won three premierships in four years.

Their last was in 1968 under Bob Weir the man that the Narromine committee has charged with the task of winning this year's premiership.

The man at the helm of the club is Ted Barber, highly regarded as a Group 11 official and back in the "hurly burly" of League administration once again.

Ted Barber doesn't take kindly to "knockers" and a month ago in Narromine there were plenty of them.

"It did not look too good but the win over Macquarie at Dubbo did wonders for the club ". Ted Barber said this morning.

The gate last Sunday of £207 (which was for a trial match) was bigger than any of the competition matches last season.

We are not too concerned about last week's loss particularly as Weir was injured.

I think we'll give the top clubs something to think about before the season is over.

We realise we have to strengthen the backs and Weir, who has been playing front row, will probably have to go back to the centres. We are, however looking for a top centre.

On top of this we have the Englishman Chris Harding sitting on the sidelines.

The Country Rugby League is trying to get a clearance through for him and once he plays the backline will be lifted and it will enable Brian Walsh to go back to the forwards.

Malcolm Dawes, Joe Dougherty, Alan Hutchinson and Neil Skalenars form the basis of a very good pack even if Bob decides to go back to the centres.

We have some good young backs coming up and if we can secure another centre we will do alright.

Two of the youngsters are the halfback Phil Phillips and Mr Barber's son Robert.

It is certain that Narromine will have plenty of strength up front.

The loss of Bob and Pat Smith however left the backline weakened.

Harding will give it a big shakeup once he returns to the field. As well the little Englishman has taken over coaching the juniors who are likely to develop into a good team.

Like the first-grade side, the club has big strong forwards in the juniors, 15-year-old Brad Ryan and props Alan Coventy and Des Anthony will be appearing for the Group team on Sunday.

Mr. Barber said the team had been beaten well in two matches but they were late getting together.

Harding is now getting the team into a workmanlike combination and the talent starting to show should serve Narromine well for many years to come.

Weir is quite happy with progress so far. Weir has never been known to panic and his calm but tough approach will be felt by his opponents before the grand-final comes around in September.

Veteran Mal Dawes has lost little of his skill and we expect him to play a vital part in the team's campaign.

Most Narromine supporters and a good many of opponents rate Joe Dougherty the top hooker in the group and in the two trials to date he has shown excellent form.

Strong centre Norm Newman, who was injured last Sunday, will appreciate another good player alongside him.

If Narromine can secure that player in the next few weeks and a clearance is gained for Harding quickly, Narromine will open the season at home on April 16 against Parkes with tremendous vigour.

And for those who like to reflect, the omens for Narromine are all good ones, Weir is back after winning a premiership in his last year, Mr. Barber is back in harness as president and when he was there last, Narromine also won the grand-final.

To top it off Barber was the team's mascot when Narromine won those three premierships in the 1950's.

Narromine will be wearing their old colours of green with two gold v's and black shorts this season.

Article from: The Daily Liberal, Thursday, March 30, 1972. Republished courtesy of: ACM/Dubbo Daily Liberal.

PARKES WIN HARD CLASH
Parkes 18 Macquarie 15

May 1972

Sheer power by Parkes forwards and a brilliant display by five-eighth Dennis Finn kept the team's unbeaten record intact against Dubbo Macquarie yesterday at Number One Oval.

Parkes won 18/15 in a see sawing match in which the under-estimated Macquarie forwards tackled their hearts out against a Parkes pack backed with a huge share of the ball.

Parkes deserved to win with four tries to one but they came perilously close to losing it in the last minute when Ken Rodwell made a dash for Macquarie and the movement halted 20 yards out.

Rodwell, who had one of the quietest matches all season, kept the Blues in the match with six goals from seven attempts.

It was a match with plenty of brilliant rushes, great personal games from Finn and Macquarie coach Kevin Kind and with excellent defence.

In the end it was Parkes persistence in attack with their big men Phil Gibbs, Rob Atkinson and the five-eighth Dennis Finn which started to create gaps in otherwise solid Blues defence.

There is no doubt that Parkes are going to be a tremendously hard team to beat.

Equally as certain is that the Blues are going to be no pushover.

They gave a gutsy performance yesterday and if they could have got an equal share of the ball, I think they would have won.

Hooker Peter Stephens lost the scrums 7/4 in the first half and 11/3 in the second.

Kind left the field four minutes before the finish but he played tremendous football before a badly cut eye forced him off.

The game was only two minutes old when Rodwell opened the scoring with a penalty goal from 30 yards out in front when Parkes were off side. Macquarie led 2 nil. In the seventh minute centre Jim Bonus "ironed" Geoff Hartley with a stiff-arm tackle and was cautioned by referee Barry Kitch.

In the 10th minute Rodwell kicked a great goal from 52 yards out when Kitch ruled Atkinson had received a deliberate forward pass, but it was a highly controversial decision from the side-line. Macquarie led 4 nil.

Parkes winger Charlie Glapiak scored the first try of the match after 13 minutes when Bonus threw a 15 yards pass to Glapiak on the wing which cut out two players. Bonus missed the kick Macquarie 4 Parkes 3. In the 21st minute Parkes hit the front when Barnes was caught offside and at a wide angle, Bonus kicked, the penalty goal. Parkes 5 Macquarie 4.

Atkinson made a break after getting a Bonus pass from a ruck and Wighton was sent through a gap to the line. He fired a pass at right winger Bernie Wilson who knocked on with the line wide open.

In the 29th minute Wighton was penalised and Rodwell kicked his third goal for Macquarie to regain the lead 6/5.

Four minutes later Atkinson infringed when he interferred with Pat Smith who shortkicked and followed on. Rodwell kicked his fourth successive goal and Macquarie led 8/5.

Bonus levelled the scores, two minutes from half time when he dummied to Glapiak then stumbled through a gap, reached out of the tackle and touched down wide out. Bonus failed with the conversion attempt. The score at half time was 8-all.

Bonus had a bad day with the boot and missed a vital kick early in the second half.

After six minutes Kind started a rush on halfway when he slipped a pass to Gary Giddings who raced 30 yards and was about to be tackled by Russell Davies but was able to slip the ball to winger Pat Smith who scored. Rodwell missed the kick, Macquarie 11 Parkes 8.

After 11 minutes Robert Pilon gave away a penalty kick when he interfered with the play the ball and Bonus kicked an easy goal. Macquarie 11 Parkes 10.

Parkes then gave away two easy penalties in the 13th and 15th minutes. First Davies was cautioned for illegal play then MacDonald was caught off side in front of the posts. Rodwell kicked both penalty goals to make it Maquarie 15 Parkes 10.

Parkes was beginning to storm back and Finn, Wighton and Atkinson were beginning to burst the first line, which had held so well.

After several minutes of pressure the ball went to centre Peter Barnes who dummied to Wilson and scored wide out. Bonus landed the goal and the scores after 23 minutes were level again at 15 all.

A minute later Barry Shean put Parkes in front after two thrilling sorties by his team.

From well inside their own half Finn made a burst to halfway, passed to Atkinson, Finn backed up to get the ball again and passed to hooker Reg Davison who was tackled 25 yards out.

Continued following page

Article from: The Dubbo Daily Liberal, Monday, May 1, 1972. Republished courtesy of ACM/Dubbo Daily Liberal.

PARKES BEAT THE BLUES

May 1972

Continued from previous page

Quickly the play the ball pass went to Atkinson who sent lock Shean racing through the gap for the line and he scored handily. Bonus missed the conversion. Parkes 18 Macquarie 15.

In the 36th minute Kind left the field with blood pouring from a cut over his eye.

The game was not over and the Parkes defence, hardly worried at all by the normally smart moving Rodwell, let him go on halfway.

Rodwell got the ball away and in a short passing burst Bill Mulholland finally had the ball knocked from his grasp with an overlap in the offering.

The final whistle went with Parkes winning a vital scrum on their own 25-yard line and in winning that one the story was virtually told.

Parkes had nearly a 3/1 share of the ball from set scrums and they wore down their opposition.

It was a thrilling match and no one could have gone away unhappy.

Five-eighth Finn was grand in attack and defence and in my book is already a better player than his brother Bruce.

He completely kept Rodwell out of the match, except for Rodwell's kicking.

Wighton at halfback, had a grand match. He was sharp in attack, elusive and backed up well.

Parkes captain-coach Graham Kennedy played the second half in a daze after being heavily tackled in the first half but resumed in the second half, directing his men well and keeping the pressure on his opponents.

Kennedy might not be the idol of the opposition crowds but he is an effective player and as proved yesterday a good skipper.

Macquarie forwards with Kind showing by example with some splendid tackling, kept Phil Gibbs and company quiet for most of the match.

Kind had another fine game and he got through an enormous amount of work.

Second rower Gary Giddings also played tremendous football and was always prominent with the ball.

Prop Peter Barnes did some good work in defence whilst the outside backs got limited chances because of the shortage of ball.

Finn, Wighton, Shean, Atkinson, Davison, Barnes and Davies all had good matches for Parkes.

Bonus has played more brilliant games but he was responsible for both of Parkes first half tries and did some clever work in attack.

Wighton had his best match of the season. His opponent Robert Pilon left the field in the second half with only 15 minutes to go and Alan Willoughby replaced him.

Scores:

PARKES 18 (C. Glapiak, J. Bonus, P. Barnes, B. Shean tries, J. Bonus 3 goals) defeated

MACQUARIE 15 (P. Smith try, K. Rodwell 6 goals).

THE BATTLE IS OVER:

The battle finished four minutes before the end for Macquarie's coach Kevin Kind seen leaving the field after turning in a great performance for his side against Parkes.

Blood pouring down his face Kind staggered to the sideline to get temporary attention from ambulance men before he had four stitches inserted in this wound over his right eye.

Doctors also found a leg injury which needed six stitches which Kind was oblivious to, during the second half.

His opposing coach, Graham Kennedy, of Parkes had to be helped to his car after the match and was still dazed from a heavy tackle just before halftime.

It was a torrid "no beg pardons" affair.

Kevin Kind

Article from: The Dubbo Daily Liberal, Monday, May 1, 1972. Republished courtesy of ACM/Dubbo Daily Liberal.

TRIBUTE TO MACKA

August 1972

It's all over for valiant Macka

Football supporters cheered the magic of a battered Ken McMullen for the last time yesterday.

McMullen played his last game in the Green and White jumper he has brought from obscurity.

Despite a severe head cut that would have put most men in hospital, a broken nose and two black eyes, "The Digger" stayed on the field to spur his depleted team.

He tried everything to get his team into the grand final and he failed.

He went down for the eight count twice and valiantly climbed off the floor to stay with his team.

Despite his injuries, the arrow-straight passes the flashing cover tackles and magic left boot that have made him a household name in Dubbo were still there.

It was a somewhat tragic ending to a great career that started in a Wagga Rugby League team 10 years ago, and blossomed to an Australian representative and then two premierships and four grand final appearances with Dubbo CYMS.

Battered, bleeding and beaten he could still manage to smile as his players shouldered him through the No. 1. Oval crowd after the match.

And this morning he held nothing against Macquarie for the injuries he had received. "It's all in the game," he smiled.

IN ACTION

Top: McMullen is shouldered off the field by his CYMS team as Macquarie players look on.

Above left: McMullen early in the match charges into action.

Above right: Kevin Kind, Ken McMullen and Graham Kennedy sharing a drink.

Article from: The Dubbo Daily Liberal, Monday, August 14, 1972. Republished courtesy of ACM/Dubbo Daily Liberal.

Blues March into Grand Final with a Win over CYMS

August 1972

Dubbo Macquarie yesterday marched into the Group 11 Rugby League grand-final with a hard fought 24-16 victory over a weakened CYMS side. Macquarie will meet Parkes in the decider at Pioneer Oval.

Atkinson let off:

Parkes Rugby League prop Rob Atkinson has had his two-week suspension waived by the Country Rugby League.

The shock lifting of suspension will allow Atkinson to play in Sunday's grand-final against Macquarie.

At the weekend Atkinson flew to Sydney and appealed to the Country Rugby League over his suspension following his dismissal from the field for a head high tackle against CYMS last weekend.

Country Rugby League Secretary John O'Toole told the Daily Liberal this morning that the CRL had dismissed Atkinson's appeal but had varied the sentence from a suspension to a $50 fine.

Article from: The Dubbo Daily Liberal, Monday, August 15, 1972. Republished courtesy of ACM/Dubbo Daily Liberal.

"ALWAYS A BRIDESMAID" NOT THIS YEAR!   *PARKES WILL WIN*

The Parkes Rugby League Team is favoured to win its first Group XI premiership since 1954 when it meets Dubbo Macquarie in the grand-final at Pioneer Oval on Sunday.

August 1972

In 1954 Parkes created a Group record when it took out all three grade premierships.	**Trump Card:** Little do Dubbo Macquarie realise that Parkes have the trump card and it is Dennis Finn, opposing five eighth to Barney Chandler.
Although it has contested grand-finals since, it has always been a case of "always a bridesmaid and never a bride."	
Parkes has been unsuccessful in three Group grand-finals in the last four years, but the team is confident it can end it's run this Sunday.	Chandler was reported in the Daily Liberal as the best five eighth in the Group and would over shadow Finn, however history tells us more about Dennis Finn as a first class five eighth

Article from: The Parkes Champion Post, August 18, 1972. Republished courtesy of ACM/Parkes Champion Post.

Pioneer Oval Ready for the Big Game

Courtesy of: Parkes Rugby League Club, Tony Dwyer President.

Country Rugby League Football of NSW Group XI First Division

Courtesy of: The Parkes rugby League

1972 GRAND FINAL
Parkes v Dubbo Macquarie
Sunday, 20th August, Pioneer Oval Parkes. Admission 60c

First Grade Teams

Position	Parkes (White with Red and Blue V)	Dubbo Macquarie (Sky Blue)
1. Full-back	R. Davies	K. Rodwell
2. Winger	C. Glapiak	C. Cooke
5. Winger	R. Jayet	J. Etcell
3. Centre	J. Bonus	R. Smith
4. Centre	P. Barnes	P. Smith
6. Five-Eighth	D. Finn	B. Chandler
7. Half-Back	D. Wighton	R. Pilon
8. Lock	D. Hodges	R. Shanks
9. Second Row	R. MacDonald	G. Giddings
10. Second Row	B. Shean	K. Kind (Captain)
11. Front Row	P. Gibbs	R. Pilon
12. Hooker	R. Atkinson	M. Lowe
13. Front Row	G. Kennedy (Captain)	G. Hartley

Referee: Mr. G. Barby; Touch Judges: R. Wiegold and W. Wilkes

July 20th 1969 Man Lands On The Moon

Moon Landing

Parkes Radio Telescope

Parkes Rugby League Teams became the Parkes Spaceman.

Parkes Radio Telescope played a major role sending signals of the landing back to NASSA.

On July 20, 1969, American astronauts Neil Armstrong and Edwin "Buzz" Aldrin became the first humans ever to land on the moon. About six-and-a-half hours later, Armstrong became the first person to walk on the moon. As he took his first step, Armstrong famously said, "That's one small step for man, one giant leap for mankind."

Source: https://en.Wikipedia.org/wiki/Apollo 11

BLUES CAN DO IT
Grand Final Fever Hits Dubbo

August 1972

If Macquarie can weather the first half bombardment by Parkes, their brilliant play can win them the match.

However, Macquarie will find the going tougher than last Sunday when they ousted CYMS with a 24-16 win.

Parkes have the experience and size which CYMS boasted plus speed which was missing from the CYMS lineup.

Parkes, like Macquarie, have speed to burn.

The minor premiers enter the match as favourites. There has not been a team as favoured to win a grand final for years.

Parkes hold the key to success with big men Rob Atkinson, Phil Gibbs and Graham Kennedy. Gibbs in particular will relish the challenge of the Macquarie pack.

Most supporters are shuddering at the thought of what they will do to Macquarie up the middle. However, they can be stopped.

Macquarie, after smothering opposition forwards all season, will have to go low early around these big men.

If they move up and put them on the ground Barney Chandler style then the match will be played in the backs.

Macquarie have three trump cards up their sleeve that Parkes did not have to worry about when they struggled to beat CYMS 13-11 in the semi.

Fullback Ken Rodwell has hit his best form and will be itching for another big one in his last match.

Five eighth Barney Chandler is the best pivot man in the group and he should shade Parkes' Dennis Finn and therefore give the Blues' backs a good look at the ball.

Five eighth Barney Chandler is the best pivot man in the group and he should shade Parkes' Dennis Finn and therefore give the Blues' backs a good look at the ball.

The Blues also have a solid half in Bob Pilon and a better lock in Rob Shanks.

With these advantages it is up to big men Geoff Hartley, Kevin Kind and Garry Giddings to bring the Parkes pack to ground. It will be the most crucial task in the Grand Final.

Record crowd tipped

And it is an operation that will keep referee Graham Barby fully occupied.

Parkes pack is one of the roughest in the west and they know all the tricks of the trade.

If it does get rough it is to be hoped that Mr. Barby does not hesitate in dealing with offenders.

Penalties and chit chat with players are definitely not enough even if it is a grand final.

The image of Rugby League will be hanging on the line before an estimated crowd in excess of 7,000 people at the Grand Final.

It should be one of the best grand finals for a long, long time.

Okeydokey, Landscapes

Article from: The Dubbo Daily Liberal, August 18, 1972. Republished courtesy of ACM/Dubbo Daily Liberal.

1972 Grand Final Action Shots Pioneer Oval Parkes

Left: One of the successes of the grand-final was Parkes' tireless five eighth Dennis Finn. He always gets through an enormous amount of tackling in a match and the grand-final was no exception. Finn and Doug Wighton combined to keep a firm hold on an opposing player, Barney Chandler.

Below: Dennis Finn and Peter Barnes prepare to "sandwich" Dubbo's five-eighth, Barney Chandler, as he attempts to make a break with the ball.

Article from: The Parkes Champion Post, August 21, 1972. Republished courtesy of ACM/Parkes Champion Post.

1972 Grand Final Action Shots Pioneer Oval Parkes

Left: Parkes' strong tackling five-eighth, Dennis Finn, prepares to give his opposite number, Barney Chandler, the "don't argue" as he makes a strong attacking run. Barry Shean, left, one of Parkes' most improved players this year, and Kennedy, are pictured in the background.

Below: It's Macquarie's turn to attack as centre Bob Smith positions winger Etcell. Jim Bonus has Smith well covered as Dennis Finn and Rob Atkinson move across to claim Etcell.

Article from: The Parkes Champion Post, August 21, 1972. Republished courtesy of ACM/Parkes Champion Post.

The 1972 Group XI Premiership Winning Parkes Spacemen
Parkes v Dubbo Macquarie
Grand Final Pioneer Oval

Captain Coach:
Graham (Muncher) Kennedy

Lured to the Spacemen in 1971 by an energetic committee under the direction of the late Ron Harrison (Croker) after Parkes ran last in 1970, Kennedy was a major force behind the clubs' re-emergence as a country footy force.

With a larger-than-life prop forward adding discipline, authority and commitment up front, the Spacemen edged out Canowindra 23-20 in extra time at Dubbo in the Group 11 preliminary final.

Ironically Parkes were beaten by Dubbo CYMS by the same score in the 1971 grand-final at Pioneer Oval.

The 1972 grand-final, also at Parkes, provided the opportunity for the Spacemen's first title since winning all grades in 1954.

Kennedy's men did not disappoint with the Champion Post reporting the 21-12 victory in the following terms:

Parkes outclassed Macquarie for the first 60 minutes of the game during which time they brilliantly progressed to a 21-2 lead to seal the 1972 premiership.

However, the Parkes side then appeared to relax its pressure and as its play wilted.

Macquarie, who tried hard throughout, staged a spirited fightback to keep the match alive.

In the closing stages, Macquarie played their best football and added two converted tries to make the score fairly respectable.

Parkes, however won quite comfortably with a full-time score of 22-12.

The lack of dirty play was a tribute to the coaches, Graham Kennedy and Kevin Kind, who had their sides concentrating on playing football rather than the man.

Parkes' premiership win capped a great season in which the side won the Caltex $1,000 Knockout as well as taking out the Group 11 minor premiership.

In convincingly defeating Macquarie 21-12 in the grand-final, Parkes established itself as the top Group 11 team of the season.

The side was beaten only twice in the season by Dubbo CYMS and Condobolin in the second round.

Kennedy, Phil Gibbs and Robert Atkinson spearheaded one of the toughest forwards packs in the group, while halves Doug Wighton, Dennis Finn and centres Jim Bonus and Peter Barnes formed the backbone of one of the fastest and most competent set of backs.

One of the outstanding features of the game was the performance of Dennis Finn who completely outclassed Barney Chandler at five-eighth.

Phil Gibbs

Article from: The Parkes Champion Post, August 21, 1972. Republished courtesy of ACM/Parkes Champion Post.

1972 Victory Lap Group 11 Shield

Above: Victory lap after Grand-Final win. Dennis Finn and Charlie Glapiak holding the shield with fans.

Article from: The Parkes Champion Post, August 21, 1972. Republished courtesy of ACM/Parkes Champion Post.

Graham (Muncher) Kennedy holds the Group X1 Premiership winning shield.

Group X1 Minor-Major Premiers 1st Grade 1972 Blazer.

Courtesy of: Roseanne Finn.

1972 Parkes Rugby League Team Group 11 Premiers

Back Row: Robert Atkinson, Phil Gibbs, Reg Davison, Bob Jayet, Ken Taylor, Bernie Coleman, Jim Bonus, Alan Kelly.
Middle Row: Rod MacDonald, Peter Barnes, Graham Kennedy (captain/coach) and mascot Scott Kennedy, Dick Hogan, David Hodges, John Davoren.
Front Row: Peter Thomas, Doug Wighton, Dennis Finn, Charlie Glapiak.
Absent: Russell Davies and Barry Shean.

Courtesy of: Parkes Shire Library. One Hundred Years of Local Government.

1972 Cobar Rugby League Team Group 15 Premiers

Cobar wins back-to-back Premierships 1971-1972.

Back Row: Les Houghton, Harry Marshall, Peter Shanahan, John Josephson, Robert Gordon, Peter Fox, Brian Heap.

Front Row: Peter Bannister, Brian Lawrence, (Captain Coach), John Stephens, Bob Clark.

Cobar Roosters 23 defeated Walgett 2
Courtesy of: John Collins, The Crowing of The Roosters.

1973 A Big Year for Canowindra Tigers

Above: Tom Clyburn Oval, home of the Canowindra Tigers
Courtesy of: Canowindra Historical Society & Museum Inc.

Canowindra News
Moves to make ground name official
Canowindra Football Oval

In 1995 the Canowindra Apex Club erected signage at the Canowindra Recreation Ground or Oval as it was also referred to honouring the late Tom Clyburn.

Despite the signage, the ground was never officially ratified by appropriate authority, the NSW Geographical Society Names Board as the Tom Clyburn Oval.

The Clyburn family is attempting to rectify the field oval complex oversight.

They have put an application to the Cabonne Council and are waiting for an official reply to enable the football ground and not the sporting complex to be renamed the "Clyburn Family Ground"

Prior to 1995 the area in question was simply referred to as "The Oval".

Article from: The Canowindra News. Republished courtesy of ACM/Canowindra News.

Finn Family Five-Eighths

February 1973

It looks as though the sorely depleted Parkes Rugby League team could lose another two of last season's premiership winning first grade side.

It is understood that Canowindra who lost nearly all its players to Orange Group 10 teams are very interested in Parkes five-eighth Dennis Finn and another player noted for his great cover defence.

The loss of these two players would be another body blow to the Parkes side which reached great heights last season.

If these players go, it will end a long sequence of the Finn family five-eighths for Parkes.

Since 1965 onwards, from juniors to first grade, either Dennis or his brother Bruce Finn has been five-eighth for one of the Parkes sides.

Bruce left Parkes to join the Balmain Tigers (gold and black guernseys).

If Dennis goes to Canowindra, it will be an unusual coincidence in club colours as Canowindra have the same colours as Balmain.

Article from: The Parkes Champion Post, February 14, 1973. Republished courtesy of ACM/Parkes Champion Post.

Out to break 26 year long drought

The Canowindra Rugby League team will be striving to break a 26-year drought of Group XI premierships when it meets Parkes in the grand-final at Pioneer Oval on Sunday.

August 1973

Canowindra last won the premiership in 1947 the year after Group XI was re-formed.

In that year, Canowindra, led by veteran 15 stone forward S. (Pongo) Hodge, defeated Forbes, (led by Joe Huggett) in the grand final at Spicer Park, Parkes.

The gate of £220 ($440) was a record one. Admission was about two shillings (20c).

Since then Canowindra has had a pretty lean time but had its best chance in 1971 when under coach Greg Hay, the side won the Group minor premiership.

However Parkes, led by tough captain coach Graham Kennedy knocked Canowindra out when it beat the minor premiers 23-20 in the final at Dubbo.

In that stirring struggle, the scores were 15-all at full time and Parkes gained the upperhand in extra time to beat the Tigers.

The teams in that final were:

PARKES:
A. Davies C. Glapiak, R. MacDonald, J. Bonus, B. Jayet, D. Finn, R. Worth, D. Hodges, C. Millwood, W. Hetherington, G. Kennedy, (Captain), R. Neilsen, R. Davison.

Parkes reserves: P. Gibbs (injured leg), P. Barnes (forward), B. Shean, R. Bonham.

CANOWINDRA:
G. Traves, I. Jeffries, D. Hines, T. Simpson E. Clyburn, W. Hilton, W. Fisher, G. Hay (Captain), R. Hilton, J. Earsman, J. Rice, W. Gollan, A. Carroll, D. Finn.

Referee: D. Levick Parkes.

Article from: The Parkes Champion Post, February 14, 1973. Republished courtesy of ACM/Parkes Champion Post.

Tigers Set for Good Season

The dwindling ranks of local players in the Canowindra Rugby League side could be offset this year by the acquisition of players from other centres including two, possibly three from Parkes.

February 1973

Over recent years, Canowindra has lost a lot of players to neighbouring towns in Group 10, such as Cowra and Orange.

Included in Canowindra's top-line players to go are Len Ryan, Jack Earsman, Derry Hines and Bob Hilton.

However, this season things appear to be swinging Canowindra's way.

It is believed that a split has occurred in the Cowra Rugby League Club over the appointment of Bobby Camden as captain-coach, and this has resulted in Canowindra gaining five top players.

The players include second rower, John Nicholls, who played for Group 10 in the Western Division trials last year.

Canowindra officials are already tipping a big year for the Tigers following the clinching of the five players. The players, two forwards and three backs, will continue to live in Cowra but will travel to Canowindra twice a week to train.

The signing will be a great boost to the Canowindra club which was struggling to field one team at the end of last season.

Canowindra are now strong final contenders under coach Reg McCulla.

Canowindra has also gained the services of two of Parkes key players, five-eighth Dennis Finn and lock forward, David Hodges.

A third Parkes first grader, Ray Neilsen, a top class utility forward, is also likely to join Canowindra.

Canowindra is also reported to have acquired two players from Brewarrina and five from Gooloogong.

The Tigers have also gained the services of Trevor Simpson who had a shoulder operation last year and missed most of the season.

Article from: The Canowindra News, February 21, 1973. Republished courtesy of ACM/Canowindra News.

1972 Premiership Blazers Presentation

Parkes Rugby League Football Club presented members of the 1972 Group XI Premiership side, Parkes, with their blazers at a special presentation dinner/dance at the Parkes Leagues Club last Friday night.

June 1973

The evening was a great success with well over 160 people attending.

A delightful smorgasbord supper was provided and the music was provided by the GTK Quartet of Orange.

The majority of the premiership side were present at the function. Apologies were received from last year's coach Graham Kennedy, Phill Gibbs and Doug Wighton who were unable to attend.

Present: Rob Atkinson, Barry Shean, Peter Barnes, John Davoren, Russell Davies, Ken Taylor, Bernie Coleman, Alan Kelly, Rod MacDonald, Peter Thomas, Dennis Finn, Reg Davison, Dick Hogan, Charlie Glapiak, David Hodges and Jim Bonus.

Article from:: The Parkes Champion Post, June 1st 1973. Republished curtesy of ACM/Parkes Champion Post.

1973 Parkes Overcome the Loss of Kennedy

In 1973 Parkes overcame the loss of Kennedy and several other key players from the 72 campaign to retain their premiership in convincing fashion. Leading by example at half back was new captain coach Gary Jeffrey, lured to Parkes after legendary service with Tumut Blues in Group 9. The defection to Canowindra by key local products Ray Neilsen and Dennis Finn added further to the pre-season intrigue.

Under Jeffrey's shrewd tactical approach, the Spacemen were able to emulate the magnificent deeds of the 1972 side by winning the coveted Caltex Knockout/Group Premiership double. By beating Mudgee 10/0, Narromine 11/0, Wellington 5/2 and Bathurst St Pats 8/6, Parkes sent its home supporters into near riot in the Caltex promotion.

The Parkes squad comprised:
Gary Jeffrey (Captain Coach), Rod MacDonald, John Cooper, Peter Barnes, Chris McNaughton, Charles Glapiak, Ron Jackson, Ken Taylor, John Rodwell, Reg Davison, Barry Shean, David Hodges, Terry Brown, Gary Knowles, Keith Scott, Stewart Dines, Allan Kelly.

Courtesy of: Parkes Shire Library. One Hundred Years of Local Government.

1973 First Grade Rugby League Points Score
How they finished in the comp

TEAMS	W	L	D	F	A	Pts
PARKES	12	2	0	307	187	24
CANOWINDRA	8	4	2	252	247	18
CYMS	8	6	0	211	188	16
NARROMINE	7	6	1	232	204	15
FORBES	6	7	1	172	144	13
WELLINGTON	8	8	0	236	277	12
MACQUARIE	3	10	1	223	290	7
CONDOBOLIN	3	10	1	196	257	7

Courtesy of: Geoff Mann, Sports Journalist, Dubbo.

Parkes Leagues Club

Parkes Leagues Club was the retreat for the players and supporters after the games where the game would be played over again.

The club was packed after home games and grand finals.

Courtesy of: Parkes in Photos of Years Gone Past.

1973 Dubbo CYMS Rugby League Semi Final Team

Dubbo CYMS are pictured after a recent training run at Dubbo's No. 2 Oval. CYMS beat Narromine 13-10 in the first semi.

Courtesy of: Geoff Mann, Sports Journalist, Dubbo.

Tim was the star junior

JOHN MUNDAY

Group XI's top junior Tim Keith bowed out for 1973 in Sunday's semi-finals in reserve grade.

Tim was given his chance by Parkes officials after Parkes juniors had been knocked out of running by CYMS in the junior minor semis.

On Sunday in reserves he came on at halftime and had a good game considering he had to mark two very experienced centres in Bob Rich and David O'Neil.

Rich has played for Group 11 and O'Neil is a Sydney grade player.

Parkes are ever ready to give their youngsters a chance and they have found another star in Keith.

Tim won the John Munday award this season for his efforts in the Parkes junior backline.

Courtesy of: Geoff Mann, Sports Journalist, Dubbo.

Above: Tim Keith

Country Rugby League Football of NSW Group XI First Division 1973 Grand Final

Parkes v Canowindra

Sunday, 2nd September, Pioneer Oval Parkes. Admission 60c

First Grade Teams

Position	Parkes	Canowindra
1. Full-back	P. Bishop	G. Carpenter
2. Winger	C. Glapiak	R. Burges
5. Winger	R. Jackson	H. Osker
3. Centre	J. Cooper	T. Simpson
4. Centre	P. Barnes	G. Webb
6. Five-Eighth	R. MacDonald	R. McCulla (Captain)
7. Half-Back	G. Jeffrey (Captain)	W. Fisher
8. Lock	D. Hodges	R. Haddin
9. Second Row	G. Wright	R. Neilsen
10. Second Row	B. Shean	J. Nichols
11. Front Row	G. Knowles	A. Carroll
12. Hooker	R. Davison	J. Haddin
13. Front Row	R. Atkinson	M. McKenzie

REPLACEMENTS:
PARKES: K. Taylor, C. McNaughton, A. Kelly, J. Rodwell, T. Brown, K. Scott.
CANOWINDRA: D. Finn, B. McClintock, Pete Sargent, Phil Sargent, D. Wright, J. Cousins.

Referee: Mr. G. Barby, Touch Judges: P. McCarten and P. Williams

Fourth successive grand final

September 1973

Top Group 11 referee, Graham Barby, will control his fourth successive Group 11 grand final when he officiates at the Parkes v Canowindra game on Sunday.

Barby a school teacher at East Parkes Primary School, has established himself as one of the country's leading referees with his displays over a number of years.

Graham Barby

Article from: The Parkes Champion Post, September 19, 1973. Republished courtesy of ACM/Parkes Champion Post.

PARKES DO IT AGAIN

Brilliant 21-6 victory in Group XI RL grand final

The Parkes Rugby League team took out its second successive Group XI premiership with a brilliant 21-6 win over Canowindra in an entertaining grand-final at Pioneer Oval yesterday

September 1973

The win gave Parkes its second big season double of the Western Division Caltex and the Group title in a row.

The win also gives Parkes the Marlboro Shield for the second year in succession.

No other team in the Group has recorded these feats and to achieve this year's honours after losing so many of the last year's players is a tribute to Gary Jeffery's Parkes team.

Yesterday's match was closer than the scores indicate as it was only in the closing stages that Parkes really got on top.

The exciting first half produced some brilliant football and the teams were locked together 6-all at half-time.

Although Parkes went to an 11-6 lead midway through the second half it was still anybody's game until Canowindra started to wilt in the last ten minutes.

Parkes maintained its pressure throughout and added 15 points in the last 20 minutes (10 in the last five) to race away with the game.

Parkes coach Gary Jeffery said after the game that the match was just as tough as the side expected and he would not like to play it over again.

"We were not greatly concerned at half time," said Jeffery, "but after 15 minutes in the second half we were becoming very worried."

"We then felt we had to really knuckle down and pull something out of the fire or we could lose."

"The whole team responded strongly in those closing minutes," added Jeffery.

The Parkes forwards lifted their game to get on top of their big hard running opposition and it was Parkes players who were running up the centre in the finish.

The Parkes forwards spearheaded by hooker Reg Davison, front rower Rob Atkinson, second rower Barry Shean and lock David Hodges turned in first class efforts.

Davison had a great game which inculded winning the scrums 16-13. He made ground in attack and his defence was solid.

Atkinson did a lot of work both in defence and attack and his fire helped put Parkes on top.

Best of the Canowindra pack were John Nicholls and Malcolm McKenzie.

Parkes halves Gary Jeffery and Rod MacDonald had a great tussle with opposites Warren Fisher and Reg McCulla for most of the game but the Parkes pair took the honours for the match.

Parkes crack centres John Cooper and Peter Barnes had the better of a tough duel with Trevor Simpson and Greg Webb. Barnes scored two tries.

Parkes winger Charlie Glapiak had a strong game while on the other flank Ron Jackson was somewhat shaky but did not stop trying.

Fullback-junior Phillip Bishop, again came through a tough ordeal in great style. Bishop's cool handling under pressure and his running with the ball stamp him as a player with a future.

The match opened in tense and typical grand final atmosphere with both sides testing each other out in fierce clashes in the forwards.

In the 11th minute Canowindra centre Trevor Simpson brilliantly pulled in a high pass and raced across wide out to score the first points of the match.

Carpenter missed the coversion attempt and Canowindra led 3-nil.

Continued following page.

Article from: The Parkes Champion Post, September 19, 1973. Republished courtesy of ACM/Parkes Champion Post.

PARKES DO IT AGAIN
Brilliant 21-6 Victory in Group XI Rugby League Grand Final

September 1973

Continued from previous page.

Parkes lost a scoring chance in the 16th minute when MacDonald missed with a simple shot at penalty goal.

In the 20th minute Parkes evened the scores at 3-all when Atkinson sent centre Peter Barnes skirting the defence to score in the corner.

Parkes unwound some brilliant open football and had the Canowindra side defending desperately.

Atkinson crossed the Canowindra line after receiving a late pass from Davison but referee Barby recalled play and penalised Davison for passing the ball "off the ground".

In the 29th minute Parkes' sustained attack was rewarded when Rod MacDonald raced across to score in a handy position.

The attempt at conversion failed and Parkes led 6-3.

Three minutes later Canowindra hit back and clever work by Reg McCulla from a scrum near the Parkes line put winger Henry Oscar over in the corner.

The scores remained 6-all at the break.

Canowindra centre Trevor Simpson was replaced by former Parkes player Dennis Finn after half-time.

Parkes lost several scoring chances early in the second half when players lost possession right on the Canowindra line at vital stages.

However after 20 minutes of hard exciting football, Parkes went to a 11-6 lead with a well deserved try by front rower Gary Knowles.

Receiving the ball 20 yards out from the Canowindra line Knowles crashed through several tackles with a powerful run to score in a handy position. Parkes captain Jeffery took the conversion kick and was successful.

Parkes second rower Geoff Wright was obviously suffering from the stomach injury received in the final against CYMS the previous week and was replaced by Keith Scott.

Canowindra's big veteran prop Allan Carroll was replaced by David Wright.

Parkes was starting to get on top and front rower Atkinson broke the defence with a strong burst up the centre from half way.

Davison ran up in support, received the ball and sent Barnes over between the posts.

Jeffery converted and Parkes had the match sealed with a 16-6 lead and only five minutes left of play.

Parkes maintained its pressure and David Hodges who had a strong game pulled in a difficult pass from Cooper only seconds from the full time bell.

The bell went before Jeffery had placed the ball for the conversion attempt and the excited crowd swarmed onto the field.

Despite the crowd on the ground Jeffery kicked the goal from touch to give Parkes the premiership 21-6.

RESULTS:

PARKES: 21 (P. Barnes 2, G. Knowles, R. MacDonald, D. Hodges tries; G. Jeffery 3 goals) defeated:
CANOWINDRA: 6 (T. Simpson, H. Oscar tries).

Parkes hooker Reg Davison won the scrums 16-13 while penalties favoured Canowindra 9-6.

Article from: The Parkes Champion Post, September 19, 1973. Republished courtesy of ACM/Parkes Champion Post.

Parkes Over Ran Canowindra in the First Grade Grand Final Yesterday

September 1973

Minute by minute rundown of the match is:

8 mins- McCulla split the blindside defence and passed to Simpson who dived over in the corner. Carpenter missed 3-0.

10 mins- Simpson cautioned for a head-high tackle.

15 mins- Tigers offside but MacDonald missed penalty.

19 mins- Atkinson ran blind and slipped a pass to Barnes who scored in the corner. MacDonald missed 3-3.

29 mins- Parkes were running all over the Tigers when Cooper ran wide near the posts and sent MacDonald over near the posts.

Both Atkinson and Jackson had tries disallowed during this period of pressure. Barnes took over the kicking but missed 6-3.

31 mins- McCulla flicked the ball back to lock Hadden from the scrum. He passed to winger Oskar who scored. McCulla missed 6-6.

At half time Finn replaced Simpson for the Tigers. Scrums 7 all, Penalties Parkes 3-2.

10 mins- Atkinson out for a head high tackle caution.

12 mins- Knowles ripped out of a tackle and galloped 15 metres to score. Jeffery converted 11-6.

25 mins- Wright (hernia) replaced by Scott for Parkes.

26 mins - Carroll replaced Wright for Canowindra.

36 mins- Davison flicked a pass to Barnes who scored under the posts. Jefferey converted 16-6.

38 mins- Backline move to Hodge who spun out of a tackle to score. Jeffery converted 21-6.

Tigers coach Reg McCulla

Article from: The Parkes Champion Post, September 19, 1973. Republished courtesy of ACM/Parkes Champion Post.

1973 Grand Final Pioneer Oval Parkes

Above Left: Dennis Finn moves towards Rob Atkinson who passes the ball to a fellow team player. During the second half both teams try to establish their superiority.

Above Right: Dennis Finn supporting Canowindra centre Joe Nichols with Rod MacDonald moving in to make the tackle.

Article from: The Parkes Champion Post, September 3, 1973. Republished courtesy of ACM/Parkes Champion Post.

OSKAR DIVES OVER

Canowindra winger Henry Oskar dives over in the corner with a Parkes defender trying to push him into touch. The try was contrived by Tigers coach Reg McCulla. He ran the blind side from a scrum and flicked the ball behind him to lock Ross Haddin. Haddin passed to the winger who scored to make it 6/all.

Article from: The Parkes Champion Post, September 3, 1973. Republished courtesy of ACM/Parkes Champion Post.

1973 Parkes Rugby League Team Group 11 Premiers Western Division Knockout Champions

Back row: John Rodwell, Alan Kelly, Terry Brown, Barry Shean, Gary Knowles, Peter Barnes, Ken Taylor, John Andrew, Geoff Wright, Charlie Glapiak.
Front row: Terry Savage (strapper), Rod MacDonald, Phillip Bishop, David Hodges, Gary Jeffery with mascot Steven Cooper, Reg Davison, John Cooper and Keith Scott.
Absent: Rob Atkinson, Chris McNaughton and Ron Jackson.

Courtesy of: Peter Barnes and Alan Macdonald.

1973 Group 15 Rugby League Team

Norm Armstrong went on to represent Western Division against Great Britain in 1974 and a member of the 1974 AMCO Cup team winning the final against Penrith. Norm was referred to as the Cobar Flash.

Jim Goonrey, Brian Heap and Brian Lawrence played in the 1971 and 1972 Cobar Group 15 Premiership Teams and went on to win the Clayton Cup in both years.

Back Row: D. Smith (President), N. Thorne, T. Ash, P. Cooper, R. Davis, G. Neale, J. Lovett (Secretary).
Middle Row: N. Miller, C. Williams, J. Goonrey, C. Ogilvy, A. McKenzie, B. Heap.
Front Row: B. Gibbs, N. Armstrong, B. Lawrence, D. Purcell.

Courtesy of: John Collins, The Crowing of The Roosters, Michael Bannister.

Few Suprises in Group Sides

Two Parkes Players Selected

Group XI Rugby League selectors have chosen a very strong side to take part in the Western Division group trials at Wellington next Sunday

March 1974

The team, which was chosen following the successful pre-season finals and East West knockout at Parkes on Sunday, contains few surprises.

Parkes has only one representative in the side, centre John Cooper.

Two former Parkes players are in the side. They are Dennis Finn and Ray Neilsen, who is a replacement forward.

Both had big games in Canowindra's 21-19 win over Wellington in the pre-season final on Sunday.

Captain-coach of the team is Dubbo Macquarie half-back, Noel Sing, who is a former Penrith player.

Selectors wisely brought the brilliant Nelson Smith of Wellington, into the side as fullback, in preference to Wellington's coach, John King, a former St. George and Australian star.

King had a very mediocre game at fullback in the final on Sunday, being caught out of position on a number of occasions.

The forwards chosen are all strong players and should be a tough lot to lead the fast and capable set of backs.

Front rower, Peter Leslie (Macquarie) is a newcomer to Rugby League. Leslie a former St. George and Gordon Rugby Union player, is sports master at Dubbo High School. He transferred to League only this year.

The first grade Group 11 side is:

Fullback: N. Smith (Wellington)

Wingers: P. Smith (Narromine), P. Frew (Dubbo CYMS)

Centres: T. Fahey (Wellington), J. Cooper (Parkes)

Five-eighth: D. Finn (Canowindra)

Halfback: N. Sing (Macquarie), Captain

Lock: C. Parkes (Dubbo CYMS)

Second row: J. Earsman (Canowindra), C. Smith (Wellington)

Front row: P. Leslie (Macquarie), E. Elwell (Wellington)

Hooker: B. Wilson (Dubbo CYMS).

Replacement backs: P. Walkom (Dubbo CYMS), M. Maude (Narromine).

Replacement forwards: R. Neilsen (Canowindra), K. Sloan (Condobolin).

Article from: The Parkes Champion Post, March 27, 1974. Republished courtesy of ACM/Parkes Champion Post.

1974 Group XI Finals
First Division Pre-season Competition and Second Division Knockout Competition
Canowindra v Wellington

Sunday, 24th March, Pioneer Oval Parkes. Admission 60c

First Grade Teams

Position	Canowindra	Wellington
1. Full-back	C. Carpenter	J. King (Captain Coach)
2. Winger	D. Shearwood	B. Douglas
5. Winger	E. Clyburn	G. Fahey
3. Centre	R. Haddin	T. Ellems
4. Centre	L. Wakefield	T. Fahey
6. Five eighth	D. Finn	B. Flanagan
7. Half-back	W. Fisher	T. Drew
8. Lock	J. Earsman	G. Lousick
9. Second row	R. Neilsen	C. Smith
10. Second row	J. Nichols	N. Smith
11. Front row	P. Sargent	E. Elwell
12. Hooker	J. Haddin	D. Hyde
13. Front row	C. Thompson	C. Hill

REPLACEMENTS:
CANOWINDRA: D. Seale, L. Green, B. McClintock, J. Marsh.
WELLINGTON: I. Miller, B. Lawson, B. Lassere, J. Lousick.

It was interesting to note the part played by ex-Parkes players in Canowindra's 21-19 win over Group 11's northern glamour team, Wellington, in the pre-season final at Parkes last Sunday.

Canowindra's first eight points came from former star local Parkes players, with Laurie Wakefield kicking a goal and Dennis Finn and Denny Shearwood scoring a try each.

Wakefield would have almost certainly been the Group's fullback had he not suffered a torn leg muscle.

Finn, deservedly, was chosen as Group five-eighth and another former Parkes player, Ray Neilsen (also with Canowindra), was selected as a replacement forward.

Canowindra punters got three points start in Sunday's final so the team's backers should be pretty financial.

Left to right 1974 team members: Denny Shearwood, Laurie Wakefield, Ray Neilsen and Dennis Finn.

(Pictured at Canowindra's One Hundred Year Reunion, 2021).

Article from: The Parkes Champion Post, March 29, 1974. Republished courtesy of ACM/Parkes Champion Post.

1974 Great Year For Dennis Finn

April 1974

Dennis Finn's success this season must have almost erased his memory of 1973, his worst year.

Finn is in the Western Division team to play the Rest on Sunday and if he continues the form he displayed last weekend, he should be a regular in the top rep side this seaon.

With the visit of the Great Britain team plus the Sydney knockout competition, Finn certainly has picked the right season to hit top form.

Yet this time last year Finn had little thought of playing any football at all.

After transferring to Canowindra Tigers from premiers Parkes, he snapped his leg in one of the first matches of the season.

Finn spent the remainder of the season on the sidelines, except for a brief performance as a lock during the finals.

This year, under the guidance of Laurie Wakefield, Finn has taken up where he left off with Parkes a season ago.

On Sunday he provided a perfect pairing in the halves with Noel Sing.

Former Parkes, and now Canowindra, rugby league player Dennis Finn is pictured in action during the Western Division group trials.

Finn capped a great display at five-eighth by being selected in the Western Division side to play "The Rest" in the final Western Division trial.

Article from: The Parkes Champion Post, April 3, 1974. Republished courtesy of ACM/Parkes Champion Post.

Western Division Comments

It's pleasing to see Rod MacDonald make the side. Brian Wilson was the best player on the paddock.

Dennis Finn had a great game. Welcome to the Western Division team Dennis. Keep training.

T. SAVAGE

Article from: The Parkes Champion Post, April 3, 1974. Republished courtesy of ACM/Parkes Champion Post.

1974 Jets are Group XI Champions

Bob Weir's Narromine Jets took out the 1974 Group XI Rugby League premiership on Sunday, downing Dubbo CYMS 18/12.

With Weir nursing a broken leg and cheering from the sideline, the Jets got right on top of arch rivals CYMS and at one stage led 15/0.

CYMS recovered to make it 15/12 but a great try by hooker Walls in the closing minutes sealed the game for Narromine.

After the game players and supporters celebrated at Narromine Golf Club and parties continued into the early morning.

The win capped a fine year for Weir who broke his leg in the last competition game.

The injury could end Weir's long career in Rugby League so it was fitting that a team he led so well all year should go on to take out the premiership.

Captain Coach: Bob Weir.

Article from: The Narromine News & Trangie Advocate, September 3, 1974. Republished courtesy of ACM/Narromine News & Trangie Advocate.

WE ARE THE CHAMPIONS

The Narromine side runs onto the field.

Murray Bouchier, of Narromine, and Brian Wilson, of Dubbo, size each other up at the start of the game.

Brian Walsh is speared into the turf by CYMS defenders.

Narromine winger Noel Gallagher takes a nose dive with the help of a CYMS player.

Article from: The Narromine News & Trangie Advocate, Tuesday, September 3, 1974. Republished courtesy of ACM/Narromine News & Trangie Advocate.

Pioneer Oval Parkes
Where all the Action takes place

Courtesy of: Parkes Rugby League Club, Tony Dwyer President.

1974 Group 11 Grand Final Pioneer Oval Parkes

Dennis Richie, who had a great game receives a caution from referee Graham Barby.

Narromine prop Dennis Ritchie makes a crashing run against CYMS.

Peter Walkom, a CYMS player brings down big Narromine prop Dennis Ritchie.

Article from: The Narromine News & Trangie Advocate, Tuesday, September 3, 1974. Republished courtesy of ACM/Narromine News & Trangie Advocate.

1974 Narromine Rugby League Team after the Grand Final

Narromine players sip a well-earned beer after their 18-12 grand final win yesterday. Coach Bob Weir holds the shield he last won in 1968.

Article from: The Dubbo Daily Liberal, Monday, September 2, 1974. Republished courtesy of ACM/Dubbo Daily Liberal.

1974 Narromine Rugby League Team Group 11 Premiers

Back Row: G. Purvis (Secretary), J. Gallagher, D. Richie, R. Cale, W. Woolfe (Manager).
Middle Row: D. Walsh (President), K. Riley, B. Walsh, J. Covency, M. Bouchier, B. Gillham (Treasurer), R. Cleary (Trainer).
Front Row: P. Barling, P. Smith, T. Blackhall, R. Weir (Captain/Coach), P. Walls, C. Harding, P. Phillips.
Courtesy of: Geoff Mann, Sports Journalist, Dubbo.

Blues best day for 12 seasons

Dubbo Macquarie supporters went wild at Parkes yesterday as their teams dominated the 1974 Group XI Rugby League grand finals.

September 1974

Dubbo Macquarie juniors after their big win in the grand-final at Pioneer Oval yesterday.

Macquarie Juniors:

Back Row: Joe Rodgers, Martin Churchill, Don Pilon, Glen Ivors, John Barden, T. Morris, Blue Young, Brian Currey, Bomber Forrestor, Merve Bourke, Dave Tink, Ross McDermott, Steve Carney.

Front Row: Brian Monro, Rick Hazell, Doug Moore, Allan Pilon, Les Thompson, Keith Brandy.

Dubbo Macquarie reserves begin their celebrations after the grand final win at Pioneer Oval yesterday.

Macquarie Reserves:

Back Row: Peter Leslie, Greg Rees, Tex Giddings, Col Saunders, Terry Pilon, Marshall Peachey, Butch Young, Barry Graham, Dick Speechley, Gary Hargraves, John Cole, Tom Greens.

Front Row: John Neals, John Etcell, Leode Brassak.

Macquarie Juniors, expected to have plenty of trouble holding the defending premiers Dubbo CYMS, had their match won in the first six minutes.

At one stage the Blues led 22-2 with a brilliant display of attacking football.

Final score: Dubbo Macquarie 25 defeated Dubbo CYMS 10.

Macquarie Reserves, strong favourites to run away with the match, had plenty of trouble holding a game Canowindra side in the closest match of the day. It took two bulldozing tries by hooker Butch Young to win the match for Macquarie in the final minutes.

Final score: Dubbo Macquarie 20 defeated Canowindra 12.

The reserves being the best game of the day.

Article from: The Dubbo Daily Liberal, Monday, September 2, 1974. Republished courtesy of ACM/Dubbo Daily Liberal

A SYDNEY COACHING TRIP FOR CYMS

January 1975

John McDonell

Dubbo CYMS' new coach John McDonell arrives in the city late this afternoon and has already announced a shock new plan to get the Greens into peak condition.

McDonell announced before leaving Sydney last night that he had booked Dubbo CYMS into a Narrabeen National Fitness Camp.

CYMS will travel to Sydney for a full weekend's training at the camp late January or early February.

He has enlisted the aid of a couple of Sydney's top fitness coaches to put CYMS through their paces.

CYMS officials expect McDonell to crack the whip over players right from the start.

McDonell is renowned for his fitness and there will be plenty of aching CYMS players around late Sunday morning.

McDonell's arrival completes a trio of four tough taskmasters in the northern Group 11 clubs.

Noel Sing has had Macquarie in full swing for more than two months and several players have benefitted greatly from a weight lifting course.

Wellington captain coach Johnny King has been preparing his players for a similar period and they will be in just as good a condition as they were early last season.

Bob Weir has yet to begin coaching premiers Narromine.

However the Jets will soon begin training twice a week and Weir will make sure they don't fall behind the other sides.

Noel Sing

Article from: The Dubbo Daily Liberal, Thursday, January 2, 1975. Republished courtesy of ACM/Dubbo Daily Liberal.

THE BIG LEAGUE—THE BIG LEAGUE—THE BIG LEAGUE

New Breed of Captain Coach
February 1975

Busy Period for Group 15 Players

Group 15 Rugby League players wishing to play rep football face a busy period in the weeks to come.

The pre-season comp kicks off on Saturday, February 15th with the big match between Bourke and the new-look Nyngan side at Bourke under lights.

The competition will continue until March 8 when the final will be played at Nyngan.

On March 23rd the possibles will play the probables in the Group trial game at Brewarrina.

Following that match a Group 15 team will be named for the inter-Group clashes at Dubbo on April 6th.

Centre Signs

The Parkes Rugby League Football Club has signed a classy Illawarra back.

He is Don Thorn (24) who played with Dapto last season.

Thorn is big, fast and can fill in either fullback or centre.

Newly appointed Parkes coach, John Bonham, played against Thorn last season and is reported to highly regard the newcomer. Thorn was selected in the possibles v probables match for the Illawarra district side last season and according to Bonham, had a "blinder."

Thorn started the match as a centre and later had to transfer to fullback when the original fullback was forced to leave the field. It Is understood Thorn has also played in the second row.

Another excellent gain by the Parkes club is the re-signing of five-eighth Dennis Finn.

Finn played all his football with Parkes until two seasons ago when he transferred to Canowindra. While with the Tigers last season, he was selected in the Group XI side.

Finn resides in Parkes and his aquisition will greatly boost the Parkes line-up this season.

The standard of Rugby League in Western Division was at its highest-level last season and judging by the build-up to this season, 1975 should be even better.

I think the major reason for this improvement particularly in Group 11 is that most clubs are now looking for better captain coachs' register.

By better, I mean they are looking for clubmen who will be a credit to the club both on and off the field.

For too many years football clubs in the west have gone for big name players who were failures as clubmen.

Even though these men may have won premierships they did nothing for their code in their clubs and in their town.

Dubbo CYMS started the ball rolling for better clubmen coaches when they selected Ken McMullen for their position in 1968. By the time McMullen hung up the studs in 1972, CYMS had three grades crammed with excellent young footballers and they had a club bubbling over with enthusiasm and goodwill.

I am not knocking some previous coaches who may have led previous Dubbo sides but McMullen was the first fulltime captain coach who performed just as well off the field.

In recent seasons this trend towards the clubman rather than the star player has continued.

Parkes little clubman Gary Jeffery was the king of that centre during his two seasons there.

Bobby Weir's reinstatement at Narromine after a year in the wilderness eventually led to a 1974 premiership with the Jets.

Johnny King's record with Wellington needs no unveiling here. He is the perfect clubman for the Reds if only some of their officials, players and supporters would realise it.

At Forbes, Tony Herring has already got the Magpies rearing to go.

Dubbo Macquarie's champion halfback Noel Sing is the keenest Blues coach I can remember both on and off the field.

And John McDonell has shown in a few weeks here that CYMS have signed yet another top-notch leader.

I mention the above cases because officials and supporters sometimes pass over a potential topline coach in favour of a star player, only to find in a year's time that they received little value for the investment.

Their argument at the start of the year was that a big game player will draw more people than the player coach who is not as well known.

Continued next page

Article from: The Dubbo Daily Liberal, Wednesday, February 5, 1975. Republished courtesy of AC M/Dubbo Daily Liberal.

THE BIG LEAGUE—THE BIG LEAGUE—THE BIG LEAGUE

Continued from previous page

Sure, people may go and watch a big-name player at the start of the year, but if his team loses consistently because of his inabilities as a coach, they soon desert the stands on Sunday afternoon.

But if a player-coach builds a good team and starts a winning streak, the people stay for the season.

One of the problems in country football is that committee men do not check an applicant thoroughly. They listen to too many whispers and uninformed reports and then act hastily.

This season a western club was chasing a well-known Sydney first grader.

I heard three very different reports about him from three supporters within one day. They were:

- "He's a great bloke, make an ideal coach."
- "Hasn't got a brain in his head. Plays well, but he's punchy mate."
- "He's a drunk. His club was going to let him go because he just couldn't be relied upon."

This is the sort of problem country clubs have to surmount when purchasing a $5000 a season coach.

I would like to see some sort of coaches' register set up in NSW Country League.

A player would have to apply to the CRL to be placed on this register.

His career from schoolboys through to the current season would be kept on file plus a confidential report on his attitude to his club, fellow players, coach and training.

All players on that file would have to hold NSW Rugby Leagues coaches' certificate.

Such a country coach's register would be an excellent guide for clubs, especially those who consistently sign captain coaches who do not produce the goods.

Ken McMullen

Noel Sing

Bob Weir

John McDonell

Garry Jeffery

Dennis Finn

Article from: The Dubbo Daily Liberal, Wednesday, February 5, 1975. Republished courtesy of ACM/Dubbo Daily Liberal.

CYMS 34 d Condobolin 7

The stars of Dubbo CYMS football team may be gone next year but yesterday they showed that they meant business in 1975 with a 34/7 walloping of Condobolin.

Feburary 1975

Above: Condobolin's veteran little halfback Dougie Wighton (7) attempts to stop a John McDonell pass during yesterday's match at No. 1 Oval.

Mc Donell had another excellent match and is playing his best football since signing with CYMS from Canterbury. Wighton, who played with Parkes in their premiership winning teams of the early 70's, says he will quit league at the end of this year after a long career.

Above: Andrew Hamblin, who has proved to be one of the finds of the season in the CYMS backline, has Condobolin's Ray Hocking well covered in the mud at No. 1 Oval.

- CYMS 34: (D. Grant 2, M. O'Neill 2, A. Hamblin, J. Mc Donell, R. O'Dea, W. Barnes tries and A. Hamlin 4 goals).
- CONDOBOLIN: 7 (H. Sanson try and I. Goolagong 2 goals).
- Scrums CONDO: 18 – 17.
- Penalties CONDO: 9 – 2.

Article from: The Dubbo Daily Liberal, Monday, August 11, 1975. Republished courtesy of ACM/Dubbo Daily Liberal.

CYMS CAN STARVE FAHEY IN THE SEMI

August 1975

McDonell is Confident

Dubbo CYMS captain coach, John McDonell is happy with the selection of Terry Fahey on the wing for Sunday's major semi-final at Kennard Park, Wellington.

"Wellington's move in selecting him on the wing suits us right down to the ground," he said this morning.

"We'll be able to block him out of the game simply by starving him of possession."

"Fahey will have his work cut out handling Robert Pedryez without worrying about roving around during the game," McDonell said.

Although the tactics in Wellington's back line held the lime-light this week, Sunday's major semi-final could be decided in the forwards.

	CYMS	WELLINGTON
FULLBACK:	R. O'Dea.	R. Hyde.
WINGERS:	R. Pedryez, M. O'Neil.	J. Hyde, T. Fahey.
CENTRES:	J. Wilson, A. Hamblin.	G. Fahey, B. Douglas.
HALVES:	M. Musgrave, S. Merritt.	B. Lawson, P. Phillips.
LOCK:	C. Parkes.	G. Lousick.
SECOND ROW:	W. Barnes, J. McDonell (C).	C. Hill, N. Smith.
PROPS:	D. Grant, P. Orbell.	N. Miller, D. Grant.
HOOKER	B. Wilson.	P. Stephens (C).

Pictured are the Dubbo CYMS First Grade team before training last night:
BACK ROW: Michael O'Neil, Neil Musgrove, Bob Pedyrez, Andrew Hamblin, Steve Merrit, Rick O'Dea, Peter Orbell, Bill Barnes, Brian Wilson.
FRONT ROW: John Wilson, Col Parkes, John McDonell (Captain), David Grant, Neil Dodd.

Article from: The Dubbo Daily Liberal, Friday, August 29, 1975. Republished courtesy of ACM/Dubbo Daily Liberal.

Greens Go Marching into Grand Final
CYMS FIGHT-BACK TAKES THRILLING SEMI
Dubbo CYMS defeated Wellington: 25-23

September 1975

Dubbo CYMS yesterday played their way into the Group 11 grand final and became a chance to win the Clayton Cup with their 25-23 win in the action-packed major semi-final at Kennard Park.

Rival wingers Terry Fahey and Robert Pedryez had an interesting clash when they marked each other yesterday. Both wingers finished even with a try a piece. In our picture left Fahey has the drop on "Pedro" but the cover defence of Johnny Wilson (out of the picture range) stopped a certain try early in the game.

Gate was record for Group 11

The gate of $2,849 yesterday at Kennard Park was a record for a Group 11 Rugby League match according to official records.

The previous highest gate was $2,837 for the Parkes CYMS grand final in 1971.
According to Group officials yesterday the third highest gate was $2,600 at the Macquarie-Parkes grand final in 1972.

Officials yesterday showed they had made a wise decision in allocating the major semi to Wellington.

The crowd was well-behaved.

Neil Musgrove (Left), Brian Wilson and Andrew Hamblin in the dressing rooms after beating Wellington 25-23. All three had good games with Hamblin kicking the winning goal from the sideline. Wilson tore shoulder ligaments and burst a blood vessel in his shoulder in the first tackle of the match. He stayed on the field to win the scrums 11-7.

Article from: The Dubbo Daily Liberal, September 1, 1975. Republished courtesy of ACM/Dubbo Daily Liberal.

CYMS THE BEST

September 1975

McDonell heaps praise on players, officials

RESULTS AT A GLANCE
FIRSTS: CYMS 20 d. Macquarie 7
RESERVES: Forbes 13 d. Macquarie 11
JUNIORS: Macquarie 12 d. Parkes 0

" Dubbo CYMS are the best country club in Australia," a jubilant captain – coach John McDonell said yesterday after leading the Greens to a 20-7 win in the 1975 Group 11 grand final.

"They told me CYMS were the best country club in Australia and today we went out and proved it." CYMS turned in one of the best displays ever seen in a Group 11 grand final when they led 8-7 at half time and then blotted the Blues completely out of the match in the second half.

Before a record crowd of 7,000 people, CYMS players chaired McDonell from the field and then ran a lap of honour after he had been presented with the premiership shield.

Later in the dressing shed a bruised and battered McDonell said it had been a tough grand final.
"It was hard alright. Macquarie gave us plenty in defence," McDonell, sporting bruises and cuts around the face, said.

Reluctant to single out individuals from a great team effort, McDonell named Col Parkes, Peter Orbell and Brian Wilson as the best players.

Wilson claimed after the match that Macquarie had been given a lot of latitude in the second half scrums.

"That match broke my duck as far as grand finals are concerned," Wilson said.

Colin Parkes had another great game in attack and defence and his cover tackles saved CYMS at vital stages.

CYMS tackled tenaciously for 15 minutes of the second half as Macquarie camped on their line.

They were superior to Macquarie in every department of the game and Macquarie were the first to admit it afterwards.

It was Dubbo CYMS' first premiership win in four years.

However, it was also their third grand final win in six years which speaks volumes for the club, its players and officials.

Article from: The Dubbo Daily Liberal, Monday, September 15, 1975. Republished courtesy of ACM/Dubbo Daily Liberal.

1975 Grand Final

Above Left: It was tough in yesterday's grand final as these action pictures show. Here, Macquarie's prop Nev "Gub" Thorne is dragged to the ground by Col Parkes, the man of the match David Grant coming over the top.

Above Right: Robert Atkins, Macquarie's prop, dives in for a tackle but CYMS skipper John McDonell gets a pass away.

Article from: The Dubbo Daily Liberal, Monday, September 15, 1975. Republished courtesy of ACM/Dubbo Daily Liberal.

1975 Group XI's Footballer Of the Year

Group 11 President Fred King awards the Footballer of the Year trophy to Colin Parkes. 2DU Manager (Mr Reg Ferguson) watches.

Col Parkes has been named Group 11 footballer of the year.

Parkes was presented with the trophy donated by radio station 2DU, at the grand final on Sunday.

Colin Parkes, CYMS second rower and Western Division representative, wasted little time in showing 7,000 fans why he won the award.

He gave a brilliant all-round performance in attack and defence to help CYMS win their third Group 11 premiership.

Parkes is reportedly going to join Canterbury Bankstown next season, scored a brilliant individual try when he three times dummied to dive over and score in the second half.

Article from: The Dubbo Daily Liberal, September 15, 1975. Republished courtesy of ACM/Dubbo Daily Liberal.

1975 Dubbo CYMS Rugby League Team Group 11 Premiers

Back Row: J. Wilson, G. O'Dell, C. Parkes, W. Barnes, M. Wilson.

Middle Row: M. O'Neill, P. Orbell, D. O'Sullivan (president) S. McFadden (Secretary), D. Merritt, R. O'Dea.

Front Row: N. Musgrave, D. Grant, J. McDonell (capt/coach). J. Piffero, A Hamblin, B Wilson.

Absent: P. Madden.

Insert: Robert Pedryez.

Article from: The Dubbo Daily Liberal, September 15, 1975. Republished courtesy of ACM/Dubbo Daily Liberal.

CLUB ROUNDUP

September 1975

DUBBO CYMS

CAPTAIN COACH John McDonell, formerly Manly, North Sydney, Canterbury, excellent first up season with the Greens.

Coached them to win in the West-Wyalong Knockout, but a shoulder injury side-lined him for representative games. Playing his best football in final games and is ideal ball distributor and defender in tight.

MOST CONSISTENT PLAYER: Halfback Steve Merrrit, who was unlucky to miss out on the representative sides. Former C.H.S. "Blue" winner, is big for a halfback, but he has good hands and is quick on his feet. At 20, he may move to the forwards or centres next year.

PLAYER TO WATCH: Prop David Grant, who has a big future in the game at 19 years of age. Has size and pace for the big time.

Above: CYMS top hooker Brian Wilson on the run.

CYMS RESULTS FOR THE SEASON:

Beat Wellington 32-24
Beat Canowindra 45-28
Beat Forbes 13-3
Beat Narromine 36-12
Lost Macquarie 27-17
Beat Condobolin 21-7
Beat Parkes 44-14
Lost Wellington 15-7
Beat Canowindra 46-11
Beat Forbes 44-14
Beat Narromine 35-11
Beat Macquarie 15-12
Beat Condobolin 34-7
Beat Parkes 47-8
MAJOR SEMI
Beat Wellington 25-23.

Article from: The Dubbo Daily Liberal, September 15, 1975. Republished courtesy of ACM/Dubbo Daily Liberal.

1975 Dubbo Macquarie Rugby League Team

WINNER GROUP 11 PRE-SEASON KNOCKOUT, WINNER WESTERN DIVISION KNOCKOUT CARNIVAL.

Back Row: Tom Moore (strapper), Jack Pearce, Frank Edwards, "Bomber" Forrester.
Middle Row: Robert Atkins, Barney Chandler, Nev "Gub" Thorne, Kimble Riley, Pat Smith.
Front Row: Marshall Peachey, "Butch" Young, Noel Sing (Captain Coach), Tim O'Connor, Mike Priddis.

Courtesy of: Geoff Mann, Sports Journalist, Dubbo.

Oberon Grand Final Wins

1970: Oberon Tigers defeat Cowra Magpies 7/6.
Mistakes robbed Cowra of their first premiership and presented Oberon with a ninth premiership in just 10 years.

1971: Oberon Tigers defeat Cowra Magpies 12/5.
A record attendance of 7,000 at the Bathurst Sportsground witnessed a sensational intercept try by Oberon winger Gordon Rawlings in the corner in the dying stages of the game to give the Tigers a 12/5 victory over the Magpies. If Rawlings had missed the intercept, Cowra lock Barry McColl would have scored the winning try.

1975: Oberon Tigers defeat Orange Ex-Services 17/4.
The crowd at Bathurst Sportsground witnessed Oberon Tigers take out their 11th premiership in 16 seasons in Group 10 rugby league competition.

BLUES RETAIN SIDE BUT WEIR TIPS JETS

September 1976

Dubbo Macquarie last night retained the team which beat Forbes, but former NSW star Bobby Weir still tips a Narromine win in Sunday's Group 11 Rugby League grand final.

Weir said this morning he believed Narromine would again prove too strong for Macquarie in the forwards.

He predicted Narromine would repeat their 15-5 win in the major semi-final.

"Of course I'll be cheering for Narromine," he added. Weir coached Narromine to their last premiership wins in 1974 and 1968.

He said he rated this year's Narromine team highly amongst the premiership teams of the past.

.Weir was having his first year out of juniors when he won a premiership for Narromine under Leo Nosworthy in 1955 and repeated the effort the following year.

"This year's team is a lot faster than the teams from the past it certainly was not as fast when I first started playing in first grade sides."

Macquarie last night had a relatively light training session under captain coach Noel Sing.

Sing's tapering off program follows a hard game against Forbes which should have the Blues at the peak of their condition.

All players trained soundly including centre Marshall Peachey, who had been troubled with a shoulder injury.

Macquarie reserves spent the night re-organising themselves.

The team most favored to win the premiership has a new forward pack following switches in the first grade side last week.

Macquarie have left hard-working prop Robert Atkins as a replacement.

Atkins will come on as a second half replacement
as he did against Forbes on Sunday.

Bob Weir

Dubbo Macquarie's grand final team
FIRST GRADE

Fullback: Kimball Riley

Wingers: Greg Hillard, Barry Graham

Centres: Marshall Peachey, Mike Priddis

Halves: Steve Hall, Noel Sing

Lock: Mark Forrester

Second row: Col Young, Tom O'Connor

Props: Bert Scott, Nev Thorne

Hooker: Max Lowe

Reserve: Robert Atkins.

Article from: The Narromine News & Trangie Advocate, Wednesday, September 8, 1976. Republished courtesy of ACM/ Narromine News & Trangie Advocate.

1976 JETS WIN GROUP Xl RUGBY LEAGUE PREMIERSHIP

The Jets pounded and ran their way to a great 24/16 victory over Dubbo Macquarie at No. 1 Oval yesterday.

Boetle was wrong, Macquarie was wrong and Pat Smith was right as the team with the best offensive and defensive record in the competition proved exactly that.

They were the best team. Man for man, position for position, they out maneuvered and out played the Blues in a brilliant grand final display.

Led by Pat Smith who played a magnificent game as captain and player, they recovered from an early set back with Macquarie scoring first and from the 15th minute in the first half were never headed.

Here for the record is how it happened:
6th minute: Forrester (Macquarie) try, unconverted, 0/3
15th minute: Mark Smith try, Harding goal, 5/3
20th minute: Rosser an unconverted try, 8/3
22nd minute: P. Walls try, Harding goal, 13/3
27th minute: Thorne (Macquarie) try, 13/6
31st minute: Hall (Macquarie) try, 13/9
41st minute: O'Connor (Macquarie) goal, 13/11
51st minute: L. Rosser try, Harding goal, 18/11
64th minute: P. Smith field goal, 19/11
66th minute: C. Harding goal, 21/11
69th minute: N. Smith try, 24/11
73rd minute: Forrester (Macquarie) try, O'Connor goal, 24/16.

So, there it is, five tries to four and the centres scored four of the Jets' tries while the much vaunted, best centre in the group from the blues never scored and never looked like scoring as Smith and Rosser dominated.

The whole team played above themselves and it seems offensive to pick out individuals but Phillips must have been the best player on the ground with quick breaks from the scrum base, backing up of his backs and forwards and fierce low tackles that so often stopped the big men with a grunting thump as they crashed to the ground.

Smith was the inspiring leader. Greg Barling showed in the menacing runs what a power he will be. Watts was his cool, admirable self. Harding dominated the back area with admirable control.

And then we come to the prime architects of the victory, that great pack of forwards led by the mighty "Dino". His damaging runs and alert ball distribution harried the Blues to abject surrender.

Cale played a blinder, totally exhausting himself with committed determination. Riley was everywhere in defence and the picking up and dropping of Thorne from a great height several times did seem to blunt "Gubber's" enthusiasm.

Players chair captain Pat Smith from the field.

Narromine did a lap of honour carrying the Group XI Shield after the match.

Article from: The Narromine News & Trangie Advocate, Wednesday, September 13, 1976. Republished courtesy of ACM/ Narromine News & Trangie Advocate.

1976 Grand Final Action Shots

Luke Rosser, Mike Watts and Ian Head move in to tackle Barry Graham of Macquarie.

This shot is typical of the tough defence from both sides. Macquarie's Blue Young dumps a Narromine forward.

Macquarie defender Max Lowe moves in to tackle Luke Rosser.

Courtesy of: Macquarie Regional Library (Narromine).

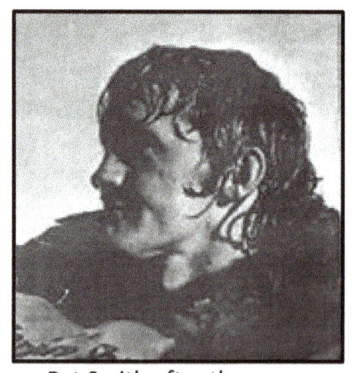

Pat Smith after the game

But one last word of congratulations must go to the mystery composers and singers of the "Song of the Jets," Jay Hughes, Ray Bohm and Brian Maher.

The chorus of the song tells the story:
The Jets have the crown,
They've beaten all the bigger towns
For many miles around.
They say we're only country boys
Who live out in the sticks,
But when it comes to football
We show them all the tricks

Courtesy of: Macquarie Regional Library (Narromine).and Narromine Jets Facebook

Jets League Champions

Courtesy of: Macquarie Regional Library (Narromine).

1976 Narromine Rugby League Team Group 11 Premiers

Back Row: W. Wolfe (Trainer), N Gallagher, T. Riley, R. Calder, R. Cale, D. Ritchie, T. Shennan (Treasurer).
Middle Row: K. Hollebone (President), M. Watts, W. Rosser, T. Mill, I. Rosser, G. Barling, B. Ball (Secretary).
Front Row: I. Head, P. Walls, P. Smith (Captain/Coach), C. Harding, M. Smith, P. Phillips.
Courtesy of: Geoff Mann, Sports Journalist Dubbo, Country Rugby League Yearly Book.

Eugowra created an enviable record in Group 11 Rugby League, boasting the best premiership feats in the group history. The "golden years" of rugby league in Eugowra commenced with the 1963 Eugowra All-Blacks winning five consecutive Group 11 Premierships from 1963 to 1967. It was a Group 11 record made in the 60s and still remains today.

- Eugowra won five consecutive Group 11 Premierships, 1963-1967.
- Rugby league commenced in Eugowra with the Eugowra Blues in 1921.
- Cargo first grade football team also won five premierships in Group 11 Eastern 1949, 1950, 1954, 1955 and 1958. However, Eugowra holds the Group 11 record, five in a row.
- The other teams to win consecutive premierships were Narromine 1955, 1956, Dubbo Macquarie 1959, 1960 and 1961 (They also won the Clayton cup in 1959) and Parkes 1972, 1973.

Images of players taken from: Mural at Eugowra. Courtesy of Roseanne Finn.

GROUP X1 1st DIVISION PREMIERS EUGOWRA
1963, 1964, 1965, 1966 & 1967

W. Adams	W. Haydon	I. Porch
B. Beath	J. Hobby	J. Porch
W. Beath	D. Jones	C. Pritchard
A. Bell	D. Madden	M. Rawsthorne
L. Bloomfield	I. McClintock	K. Smith
M. Cummings	M. McClintock	J. Taylor
A. Gilmore	G. McGrath	B. Toohey
D.J. Glasson	M. Mongan	V. Toohey
D.W Glasson	K. Norris	M. Toohey
F. Glover	N. Pengilly	B. Turner
D. Greenhalgh	R. Pengilly	

John Hobby, 1962-1965

The Eugowra Old Boys Spirit Lives On

November 2022 the small country town of Eugowra was changed forever after the devastating floods raced through and destroyed the majority of the town's buildings

The devastation affected the whole town and surrounding area including the local football club.

However, it may have destroyed buildings and memorabilia but it didn't erase the memories of a small communal country town which won five consecutive Group 11 Rugby League Premierships.

Among the washed-out roads and gutted homes there is still hope that the town will rebuild and retain its memorable history.

Article from: The Forbes Advocate. Republished courtesy of ACM/Forbes Advocate.

Group 11 Premiership Winning Team Results 1946 - 1976

1946: Wellington 11 d Forbes 4	1962: Forbes 16 d Wellington 4
1947: Canowindra 12 d Forbes 2	1963: Eugowra 13 d Forbes 10
1948: Wellington 4 d Forbes 2	1964: Eugowra 8 d Forbes 7
1950: Condobolin 16 d Dubbo 6	1965: Eugowra 28 d Narromine 2
1951: Peak Hill 12 d Wellington 0	1966: Eugowra 22 d Canowindra 3
1952: Dubbo 19 d Parkes 9	1967: Eugowra 14 d Parkes 3
1953: Narromine 25 d Wellington 8	1968: Narromine 12 d Dubbo CYMS 4
1954: Parkes 11 d Narromine 5	1969: Dubbo CYMS 16 d Parkes 12
1955: Narromine 27 d Wellington 2	1970: Forbes 7 d Dubbo CYMS 3
1956: Narromine 16 d Dubbo 7	1971: Dubbo CYMS 23 d Parkes 20
1957: Condobolin 20 d Parkes 8	1972: Parkes 21 d Dubbo Macquarie 12
1958: Forbes 16 d Cumnock 3	1973: Parkes 21 d Canowindra 6
1959: Dubbo Macquarie 15 d Narromine 11	1974: Narromine 15 d Dubbo CYMS 10
1960: Dubbo Macquarie 22 d Forbes 7	1975: Dubbo CYMS 20 d Dubbo Macquarie 7
1961: Dubbo Macquarie 23 d Forbes 11	1976: Narromine 24 d Dubbo Macquarie 16
1949 Results not recorded	

Records Set by Teams in Groups Nine-Ten-Eleven-Fourteen & Fifteen

- Eugowra wins five consecutive Group 11 premierships (1963-1967).
- Baradine Magpies wins five consecutive Group 14 premierships (1951-1955).
- Temora wins three consecutive Group 9 premierships (1957-1959).
- Cobar wins two consecutive Group 15 premierships (1971-1972).
- Coonamble Bears wins three consecutive Group 14 premierships (1957-1959).
- Dubbo Macquarie wins three consecutive Group 11 premierships (1959-1961).
- Narromine wins six Group 11 premierships (1953, 1955, 1956, 1968, 1974 and 1976).
- Forbes were runners up in eight Group 11 premierships.
- Orange CYMS wins three consecutive Group 10 premierships (1952-1954).
- Parkes wins all three premiership grades in Group 11, 1954.
- Dubbo CYMS wins all three premiership grades in Group 11, 1971.
- Dubbo Macquarie wins all three premiership grades in Group 11, 1979.
- Parkes and Dubbo CYMS were the only Group 11 clubs to win all three grades up until 1976.
- Oberon wins seven consecutive Group 10 premierships (1961-1967).

Forbes could have been considered unlucky not to have won more Group 11 premierships.

1960 Group 10 When Oberon Conquered the Central West

While St George were creating their own dynasty in the NSWRL, the Oberon Tigers were building a winning streak that would go unmatched in Country Rugby League.

From 1960 to 1969, Oberon featured in every single grand-final, winning eight of them. In the grand finals they won, the opposition rarely got close.

1963 Group 10 Premiers

Back Row: Rolf Trudgett, Jock Schrader, Ken Nicholl, Gary Harvey, Laurie Evans, Ron Brown.
Middle Row: Peter Richards, Barry Grady, Col Elwin, Gordon Rawlings, Don Elwin.
Front Row: Brian Harvey, Bill Fawcett, John Rush, Norm Brown, John Brien, Trevor Grady.

1966 Group 10 Premiers

Back Row: Alf Goodlett, Ray Rodwell, John Harvey, Ron Brown, Rolf Trudgett, Norm Hawken, Ken Nicholl, John Rush, Norm Delamotte.
Middle Row: Col Elwin, John Brien, Wally Hagerty, Norm Brown, Palmer Mitchell, Jock Schrader, Gordon Rawlings.
Front Row: Trevor Grady, Garry Fisher, Brian Harvey, Bil Fawcett, Gary Harvey.

Article from: The Oberon Review News. Republished courtesy of ACM/Oberon Review News.

1965 Oberon Tigers defeat Lithgow Workies 29-5

The Lithgow Workies Club were runners-up for the fifth consecutive year and, once again, didn't even get close to the red-hot Tigers side.

```
• FIRST GRADE GRAND FINAL
       To Start at 3.00 p.m.
WORKMEN'S CLUB        OBERON
(Colours: Green, Gold Bars) (Colours: Black and Gold Bars)
              FULL-BACKS:
1—BILL PARKER          1—BILL FAWCETT
              WINGERS:
2—PETER GLENDENNING    2—BRIAN HARVEY
5—TED ELLERY           5—GORDON RAWLINGS
              CENTRES:
3—JOE FISHER           3—KEN NICHOLLS
4—MICK HAWKEN          4—TREVOR GRADY
              FIVE-EIGHTHS:
6—ROY THOMPSON         6—JOCK SCHRADER
              HALVES:
7—TOM FRANCIS          7—NORM BROWN (Capt.)
              LOCK FORWARDS:
8—JOHN BAKER           8—GARY HARVEY
              SECOND ROW:
9—KEITH NORTHEY        9—JOHN BRIEN
10—GRAHAM HALL         10—JOHN HARVEY
              FRONT ROW PROPS:
11—KEITH KING          11—JOHN RUSH
12—KEITH GRAHAM (Capt.) 12—DON ELWIN
              HOOKERS:
13—JOHN BERRY          13—COL. ELWIN
    Referee: NOEL McALISTER (Lithgow).
Linesmen: Kevin Faulks (Orange), W. Marshall (Lithgow).
```

1969 Oberon Tigers defeat Orange Ex-Services 7-3

Oberon were lucky to qualify for the finals, let alone the decider in 1969.

Under the rules of the day, Oberon were required to play off against Orange CYMS for fourth spot, as teams that finished level on points were not separated by points differential.

Oberon defeated CYMS in the play-off, Workmen's Club in the semi-final and then Cowra in the preliminary final to qualify for an incredible 10th consecutive grand-final. They were up against minor premiers Orange Ex-Services and the conditions were quite unique.

The decider was played in a snowstorm at the Bathurst Sportsground and, at times, it was not easy to tell players apart.

Oberon showed what a great team they were completing a remarkable 1969 final series in winning its 10th premiership.

Article from: The Oberon Review News. Republished courtesy of ACM/Oberon Review News.

1960-1969 Oberon Record Breaking Summary

The following details the results of the mighty Oberon Tigers who set the bench mark in Country NSW Rugby League of eight Group 10 Premierships between 1960-1969 and runner up in two. Seven consecutive premierships created a record which still remains. In all, Oberon would win all but one Group 10 grand-final between 1961-1971.

- 1960: Lithgow Workies 12–11 Oberon Tigers
- 1961: Oberon Tigers 22–7 Lithgow Workies
- 1962: Oberon Tigers 14–7 Lithgow Workies
- 1963: Oberon Tigers 23–2 Lithgow Workies
- 1964: Oberon Tigers 30–2 Lithgow Workies
- 1965: Oberon Tigers 29–5 Lithgow Workies
- 1966: Oberon Tigers 23–10 Bathurst Charlestons
- 1967: Oberon Tigers 23–2 Bathurst Charlestons
- 1968: Bathurst St Pat's 9–8 Oberon Tigers
- 1969: Oberon Tigers 7–3 Orange Ex-Services.

Article from: The Oberon Review News. Republished courtesy of ACM/Oberon Review News.

1958 Grand Final Oberon Tigers

Above action: Left to right, John Rush, John Harvey, Jock Schrader, Neville Kelly, Norm Brown with the ball, Noel McAllister from Katoomba was the referee.

All the above Oberon players represented Western Division. Norm Brown represented Country NSW against the City team in 1964. Norm Brown was the captain.

John Rush created a record in playing in 13 grand-finals for Oberon Tigers winning ten Group Premierships.

Courtesy of: Kerry Gibbons, Oberon.

Kerry Gibbons:

One of Oberon's greatest country rugby league followers, describes rugby league during the golden years in the bush:

The town's people and the farming community got behind their local teams in the 50s, 60s and beyond. The 60s and 70s were a great period for country rugby league.

Kerry went on to say that he started to follow rugby league at the age of 10 and witnessed all Oberon grand-final games.

His dream was to wear the black and gold jumper but unfortunately a leg injury when playing at school ended his ambition. However, he went on to be as he stated, a football fanatic sharing the successes of his beloved Oberon Tigers.

In the 1958 season Oberon joined the Group 10 competition and went on to play in their first grand-final, losing to Orange CYMS. Kerry was there barracking for the Tigers and as he stated that the best was yet to come.

Courtesy of: Kerry Gibbons, Oberon.

1958 Oberon Tigers Rugby League Team Group 10 Premiers

Back Row: Ross Corby, Peter Richards, Kevin Ryan, Keith Hawken, Ron Brown, Don Elwin, Bobby King, Bob Ellington.

Front Row: Laurie Evans, Bob Cook, Gordan Rawlings, George Smith (Captain Coach), John Brien, Norm Brown.

Oberon team made it to the grand-final in their first year in the Group 10 rugby league first division competition.
Orange CYMS defeated Oberon in the 1958 Group 10 grand-final 17-6 after Oberon was leading 6-2 at half

Article from: The Oberon Review News. Republished courtesy of ACM/Oberon Review News.

1964 Oberon Tigers Caltex £500 Rugby League Knockout

July 9, 1964 Pioneer Oval Parkes

Oberon defeated Dubbo CYMS in the semi- final 6-2 and went on to defeat Lithgow Workies in the final 8-0.

Above: Dubbo CYMS centre Tim Smith puts his boot to the ball during the semi-final match against Oberon in the Caltex £500 Rugby League knockout competition at Parkes. Following through are team-mates Ray Hardie and John Kempston.

Courtesy of: Blast From The Past, Dubbo CYMS Old Boys July 9, 1964.

1925-1936 Royal & Tourist Hotels Oberon

The Original Royal Hotel left and the Tourist Hotel Oberon. The Original Tourist Hotel was destroyed by fire.

Courtesy of: Noel Butlin Archives, Australian National University.

SECTION 2:
Representative Teams - International Games and Amco Cup

International opponents Eric Weissel and Jonathan Parkin

Table of Contents for Section 2

	page
England Football Team Defeats Orange 1920.	209
Australian and English Football Teams 1921-1922.	210
England's Combined Play Resulted In Cootamundra Defeat 1924.	211
Group 9 plays New Zealand 1925.	212
Far Western Rugby League Representative Team 1927.	212
Great Britain Touring Team / England v Far West, Parkes 1928.	213
England v South Western Districts Cootamundra 1928.	215
Second Australian Rugby League Test Team 1928.	216
N.S.W Rugby League Team 1928 / Queensland State Football Team at Dubbo 1930.	217
City v Country and Country Triumph 1928.	218
1929 Western Districts Football Representative Team	219
Southern Districts Representative Team, Country Week, 1929.	220
Australian Test Team 1929-30.	220
Great Britain v Western Division History 1924-1974.	221
Australian First Test Team 1932 / Group 9 Representative Team 1934.	222
England vs Western Division Parkes 1936.	223
N.S.W. Rugby League Team 1945.	224
Western Team Plays Englishmen Wade Park Orange 1946.	224
Country Rugby League Blazers 1947.	224
Sydney v Country 1949.	225
N.S.W. Country Rugby League Trials 1950.	226
Western Division Team Plays Great Britain Forbes 1950. Opening of Spooner Oval.	227
Western Division Team Plays French Touring Team Forbes 1951.	229
Country vs City 1953.	230
Western Division vs Great Britain 1954.	231
Western Division Selection Group Trials 1955.	233
French Touring Team Plays Western Division Parkes 1955.	235
City v Counry 1956. West Holds UK League Side to Draw 1958.	236
N.S.W. Country Rugby League Firsts Representative Team 1959.	237
A Boy's Dream Comes True.	237
Western Division defeats Eden Monaro 1961.	238
Three in a row, Western Division Caltex Country Rugby League Champions 1961,62 and 63.	239
Great Britain plays Western Division 1962.	240
Country City Firsts Rugby League Teams 1962.	241
Paskins Captains Western Division and City vs Country Firsts 1962.	242
New Zealand vs Western Division Parkes 1963.	243
In the Group XI Team, Western Division Side 1964.	247
Country Rugby League Championships 1964.	249
N.S.W. Country First and Second Rugby League Teams 1964.	253
Western Division v France Wade Park Orange 1964.	254
Country Inter Group Trials and Caltex Country Rugby League Championship 1965.	258
Know Your Sportsmen, Bob Weir.	262
Leo Nosworthy's Story.	263
Western Division v Great Britain Parkes 1966.	264
Trials at Wellington and Western Division Plays Southern Division 1969.	269
Combined Country Team New Zealand Tour and Country Seconds v Sydney 1970.	271
England Plays Western Division Bathurst 1970.	272
N.S.W. Team Includes Group XI Players 1970 / Reunion Day for Dick Huddart.	279
Best Side Ever Group XI, Inter Group and Western Division Trials 1972.	280
Caltex Country Divisional Trials and Champions 1973.	283
Western Division Trials Selection and Western Division plays Monaro 1974.	284
Western Division Plays Great Britain Orange 1974.	287
Western Division Wins AMCO Cup 1974.	295

REPRESENTATIVE TEAMS, INTERNATIONAL GAMES AND AMCO CUP

This section of the book journeys through the golden years of rugby league in the bush with representative and international games, players, teams and some of the great moments for the players, coaches, administrators and spectators.

Rugby league emerged as the major sport played on the weekends in regional NSW's smaller and larger towns who formed their own teams with competitions between rival towns extremely competitive and fierce.

Group and divisional representative teams were selected during the 1920s to play against English and New Zealand touring teams at Orange, Cootamundra and Parkes.

As the decades moved on many more matches against the English, New Zealand and French touring teams were played in various country towns. Players from Sydney clubs were contracted to coach country teams and a resurgence in player skills and teams made them formidable opponents.

The Country Rugby League Championships were held each year and Western Division won three consecutive titles in 1961, 1962 and 1963. Illawarra, Southern, Monaro, Riverina, Newcastle, Northern and Western Division competed for the title of NSW Country Champion.

The best country players were selected to play in the Country First and Second teams to play against their city rivals which became an annual event. Some great players from Southern and Western Divisions went on to represent NSW and Australia.

The Amco Cup showed the Sydney team players that the country players were up there with them. Western Division won the 1974 cup against all the odds, defeating Penrith in the final.

1920 England Football Team defeat Orange 36-8
Wade Park Orange

Football ENGLAND v ORANGE EASY WIN FOR VISITORS Wednesday 9th June, 1920	The Teams **English:**

Football
ENGLAND v ORANGE
EASY WIN FOR VISITORS
Wednesday 9th June, 1920

The presence of the English footballers in Orange was a means of arousing the keenest interest amongst sporting bodies and the attendance at Wade Park to witness the match on Wednesday afternoon, was one of the largest seen, being reminiscent of the good old days, when Lucknow was booming and football was at its highest.

Visitors were present from all parts of the west and the attendance was estimated at 3,000, close on £100 being taken at the gate.

The English team, accompanied by Mr. Wilson (Manager) and a trainer arrived by the mail train on Wednesday morning and during their stay here were located at Central Hotel. At 11.30am they were accorded a civic reception by the Mayor, Ald D. Treweeke and the president of the local league P. Ford and secretary J.P. Jaeger.

The Teams

English:

Fullback, A. Woods.
Three quarters, C. Stacey, D. Hurcombe, J. Doyle, J. Bacon.
Halves, E.W. Jones, R. Lloyd (Captain).
Forwards, H. Hilton, J. Cartwright, G. Skelhorne, J. Bowers, G. Rees, W. Reid.

Orange:

Fullback, O. Jaeger.
Three quarters, J. Bone, W. Keane, C. Plowman (Captain), T. Coyne.
Halves, D. Lawler, H. Hartley.
Forwards, P. Murphy, W. Murray, T. Dalton, A. Slonne, L. McIntyre, F. Reed.

Mr. E.H. Allan controlled the game excellently, although at times some of the Englishmen were heard to question his interpretation of the rules.

Article from: The Orange Leader, Friday 11, June, 1920. Republished courtesy of ACM/Orange Leader.

Australian-English Football Teams 1921-1922

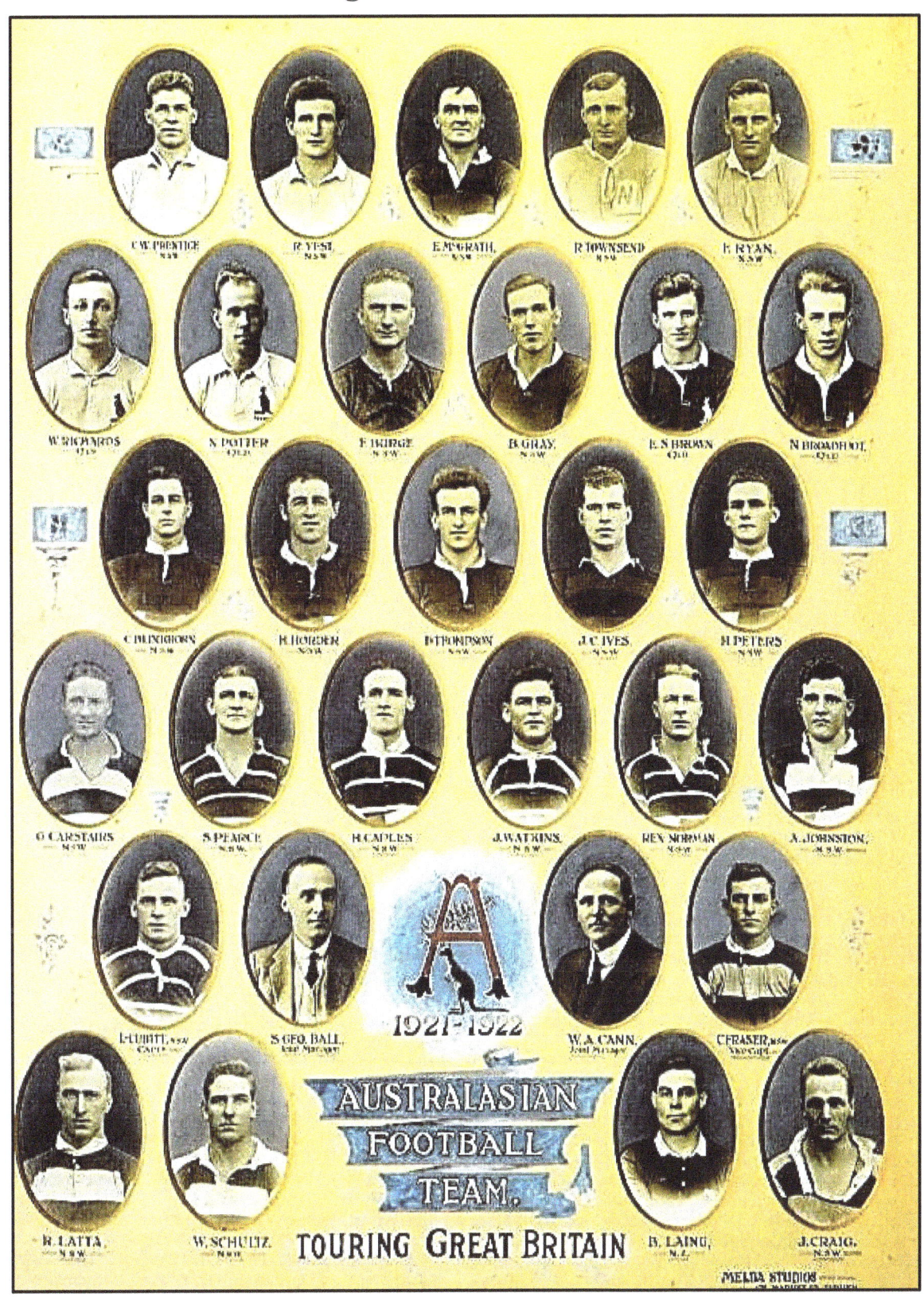

Harry Caples and Rex Norman moved to the bush as paid players and coaches. Harry was contracted to Wagga for £19 and Rex moved to Canowindra in 1926 on a contract of £8 plus free lodging.

Courtesy of: Terry Williams. (NRL).

1924 England Plays Cootamundra

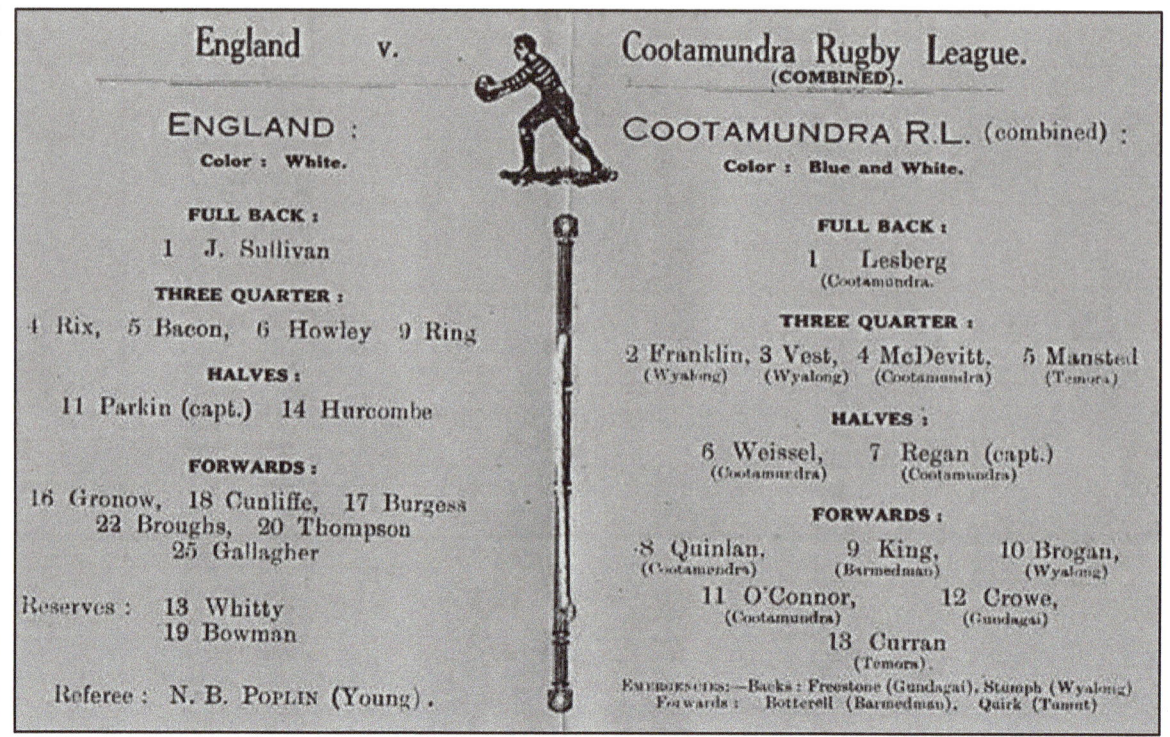

Article from: The Cootamundra Herald, Wednesday, May 28, 1924. Republished courtesy of ACM/Cootamundra Herald.

1924 England's Combined Play Resulted In Cootamundra Defeat

31 to 4 Victory

LOCALS' FINE STANCE AGAINST SUPERIOR FORCE

The English internationals, in their first game in N.S.W. at Cootamundra yesterday, by their superior combination and dashing individual play and also their superior and heavier pack, gained a complete victory over the locals by 31 points to 4.

The game was regarded with the utmost importance, both locally and by league headquarters. Roughly, nearly six thousand spectators came from near and far, by special trains and by road. Many travelled over a hundred or more miles in distances with league representative and followers of the game also attending from Sydney.

Fisher Park Cootamundra

Article from: The Cootamundra Herald, Wednesday, May 28, 1924. Republished courtesy of ACM/Cootamundra Herald.

1925 Group 9 v New Zealand

Date: Wednesday, August 19th 1925
Referee: Larry O'Malley
Venue: Fisher Park (Cootamundra)

3.15pm
Come and see the local lads beat the All-Blacks

GROUP 9 TEAM:
1. G. Robinson, (Cootamundra)
2. Eric Freestone, (Gundagai)
3. Jack Brown, (Young)
4. Peters, (Griffith)
5. Jack McCarthy, (Wagga)
6. Eric, Weissel, (Cootamundra)
7. Jim Cornett, (Leeton)
8. Gerry Crowe, (Gundagai)
9. Gerry Quirk, (Tumut)
10. R. Mulvihill, (Tumut)
11. Jack Wunsch, (Wagga)
12. Bill Brogan, (West Wyalong)
13. Ted Curran, (Temora)

SOUTHERN DISTRICTS DEFEAT NEW ZEALAND A BRILLIANT GAME

Weissel's Day Out

A combined Southern Districts defeated the New Zealanders by 26 points to 25, at Cootamundra yesterday

Southern Districts 26:
Tries: Jack Wunsch (2), Bill Brogan, Eric Freestone.
Goals: Eric Weissel (7).

New Zealand 25:
Tries: Jack Kirwan (2), Edwin Ellis, Francis Henry, Stanley Webb.
Goals: Thomas Mouat (5).

Eric Weissel led the Group 9 team and was the master in defeating the All Blacks 26/25 in front of a crowd of approximately 3,000. The Kiwis were paid a guaranteed £62.

Article from: Cootamundra Daily Herald, August, 20, 1925. Republished courtesy of ACM/Cootamundra Daily Herald.

1927 Far Western Football Representative Team

Back Row: A. Stammers (Mandurama), W. Marsh (Cowra), J. McLeish (Cowra), K. Kinghorne (Mandurama).

Middle Row: R. Make (Cowra), J. McDonald (Bourke), N. Quinn (V Captain) Parkes, J. Clancy (Parkes), S. Maker (Dubbo), C. Willard (Mandurama).

Front Row: F. King (Dubbo), J. Kelly (Parkes), J. P. Sheahan (Manager Parkes), R. Buckley (Captain) Parkes, P.C. Rose (Manager) Dubbo, C. Friend (Dubbo), G. Fletcher (Parkes).

Courtesy of: Macquarie Regional Library. "Melba Studios 65 Market St. Sydney.

Wouldn't be a game without the ball

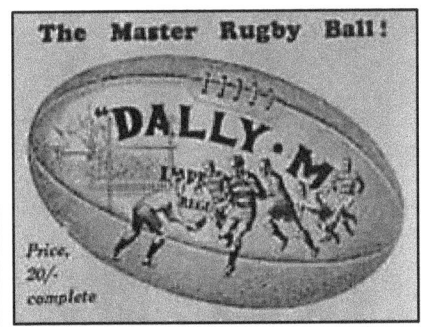

Courtesey of: NSW Rugby League. The Rugby League News, April, June, 1928.

1928 Great Britain Australian Touring Team

Back Row: M. Bentham, A. Ellaby, W. Bowman, J. Thompson, O. Dolan, W. Williams, J. Brough.

Third Row: J. Evans, R. Sloman, A. Young, A. Fildes, W. Burgess, W. Horton, J. Sullivan, R. Halfpenny.

Second Row: F. Bowen, J. Oliver, A. Fredsham, G.F. Hutchings (Secretary Manager), J. Parkin (Captain), E. Osborne (Team Manager), T. Gwynne, W. Gowers, M. Rosser.

Front Row: B. Evans, L. Fairclough, D. Murry (Trainer), G. Askin, B. Rees.

Courtesy of: NSW Rugby League, The Rugby League News, June, 1928.

1928 ENGLAND v FAR WEST
Spicer Park Parkes

10,000 SPECTATORS SEE GREAT MATCH
FAR WEST SURPRISE
STIRRING FOOTBALL STRUGGLE
ENGLAND BEATEN IN SECOND HALF

The titanic struggle for football supremacy between Far West and England has come and gone, yet although the home team suffered defeat, they were by no means disgraced and gave a splendid exhibition of both defensive and offensive football.

In the first half of the game the great players of England got going and soon established their superiority by leading at the interval by 17-3.

But the Far West combination showed greatly improved form in the second term and on points actually, had the better of the encounter, scoring six points to England's five. Final score 23-8.

Fine weather and a warm sun enticed residents from all parts of the countryside to Parkes yesterday to witness the international match between England and a team representative of Far West. They came by special train, by motor and whatever means they could, and when the time scheduled for the big match arrived there were 10,000 spectators eager to witness the fray. The gate was 871 pounds.

Few in that gathering, which smashed all previous records for a football match in Parkes, expected that Far West would win. Few indeed thought that they would put up the sterling performance that they did;

indeed, a lesser number expected that Far West would actually hold the Englishmen in the latter stages of the game. But it was in the closing stages of the match that Far West played and showed their best. Their defence was all and more than was expected while they actually held the Englishmen penned in their own half.

Realising the valiant efforts that the home team were making the crowd yelled its appreciation and spurred them on to further achievements.

Article from: The Western Champion NSW, 1928 p.11. Republished courtesy of ACM/Parkes Champion Post.

1928 English Lions Series Spicer Park Parkes

GAME 15		
Date:	Wednesday, May 19th, 1928	
Kick off.	3:15 PM (local time)	
Referee:	William "Webby" Neill	
Venue:	Spicer Park (Parkes)	
Crowd:	10,000	
Match Stats	Far West 8	England 23
Halftime Score:	3	17
Tries:	J. Carolan (2) A. Sloane	Harold Bowman Les Fairclough Mel Rosser Joe Thompson
Goals:		Joe Thompson (5)
Teams:		
Fullback	1. Ted Taplin (Captain)	1. Walter Gowers (Captain)
Wing	2. Jack Kelly	2. Emlyn Gwynne
Centre	3. J. Carolan	3. Jim Brough
Centre	4. Gordon Fletcher	4. Mel Rosser
Wing	5. Cec Willard	5. Alf Frodsham
Five-Eighth	6. L. Coates	6. Les Fairclough
Halfback	7. A. Azar	7. Bryn Evans
Front row	8. Stanley Maker	8. Billy Williams
Hooker	9. C. Friend	9. Oliver Dolan
Front row	10. A. Sloane	10. Harold Bowman
Second row	11. R Gilmour	11. Joe Thompson
Second row	12. Norman Quinn	12. Ben Halfpenny
Lock	13. Rees Duncan Sr	13. Harold Young

Jonathan Parkin 1928 Great Britain Team Captain

Courtesy of: NSW Rugby League.
The Rugby League News, June, 1928

Eric Weissel 1928 South Western Districts Team Captain

Courtesy of: Wikipedia. Eric Weissel, Australian Rugby League.

1928 England v South Western Districts

England v.	South-Western Districts (GROUP IX)
ENGLAND Color: White, with Red and Blue V **FULL BACK** 1—J. SULLIVAN (Wigan) **THREE-QUARTERS:** 7.—A. ELLABY (St. Helens) 8—A. FRODSHAM (St. Helens) 5.—J. OLIVER (Batley) 6.—J. BROUGH (Leeds) **HALVES:** 11.—J. PARKIN, (Capt.) (Wakefield) 14—N. FAIRCLOUCH (St. Helens) **FORWARDS:** 15—M. BENTHAM (Wigan) 19—W. BURGESS (Barrow) 20—H. BOWMAN (Hull) 22—A. FILDES (St. Helens) 23—R. SLOMAN (Oldham) 26—H. YOUNG (Bradford) Reserves: 9—T. Gwynne (Hull) 17—W. Williams (Salford) Referee: MR. W. NEILL. Touch Judges: Messrs A. NAYLOR & N. H. POPLIN.	**SOUTH-WESTERN DISTRICTS** GROUP IX Color: Cerise and Blue **FULL BACK** 1.—W. PHILLIPS (Cootamundra) **THREE-QUARTERS:** 2—R. MAKER (Temora) 4—T. D ENGLISH (Wagga) 3—S. HALL (Young) 5—L. SMITH (Barmedman) **HALVES:** 6—E. WEISSEL (Capt.) (Temora) 7—N. ROBINSON (Cootamundra) **FORWARDS:** 8 J. KINGSTON (Cootamundra) 9 G. HINTON (Cootamundra) 10—G. TORPY (Cootamundra) 11—BEEGLING (Tumut) 12—CURRAN (Temora) 13 W. BROGAN (Wyalong) Reserves: 14—J. Lawrence (Barmedman) 15—G. Crowe (Gundagai) Early Match 1.45 p.m. TEMORA SCHOOL BOYS v. DE LA SALLE BOYS.

Article from: The Cootamundra Herald, Wednesday, May 28, 1928. Republished courtesy of ACM/Cootamundra Herald.

1928 Fisher Park Cootamundra

Courtesy of: Neil Pollock, Maher Cup author.

1928 England Plays South Western Districts

GAME 1		
Date:	Wednesday, May 30[h] 1928	
Referee:	William "Webby" Neill	
Venue:	Cootamundra Sports Ground (Cootamundra)	
Crowd:	8,000	
Match Stats	**South Western** 14	**England** 14
Scrums:	15	12
Sent off:		Harold Bowman
Tries:	L. Smith (2) A. Sloane	Alec Fildes Bob Sloman
Goals:	W. Phillips (4)	Jim Sullivan (4)
Teams:		
Fullback	1. W. Phillips	1. Jim Sullivan
Wing	2. R. Maker	2. Alf Ellaby
Centre	3. S. Hall	3. Alf Frodsham
Centre	4. L. Smith	4. Joe Oliver
Wing	5. Tom English	5. Jim Brough
Five-Eighth	6. Eric Weissel (Captain)	6. Jonty Parkin (Captain)
Halfback	7. Norm Robinson	7. Les Fairclough
Front row	8. Bill Brogan	8. William Burges
Hooker	9. J. Curran	9. Nat Bentham
Front row	10. L. Beegling	10. Harold Bowman
Second row	11. R. Hinton	11. Alec Fildes
Second row	12. George Torpy	12. Bob Sloman
Lock	13. Jack Kingston	13. Harold Young

1928 Second Australian Football Test Team

Back Row: C. Pearce (NSW), H. Steinohrt (NSW), G. Treweeke (NSW), V. Armbruster (Q), D. Dempsey (Q), P. Maher (NSW).

Middle Row: J. Kingston (NSW), C. York (NSW), J. Craig (Q), T. Gorman (Q), J. Busche (NSW), A. Justice (NSW), H. Byrne (NSW).

Front Row: E. Weissel (NSW), N. Hardy (NSW).

Courtesy of: NSW Rugby League, The Rugby League News, July 1928

1928 NSW Football Team

The NSW Football team of 1928 was a fine achievement for a country town like Parkes. Two Parkes players Norman Quinn and Gordon Fletcher were selected in the State team, following a good showing from Parkes at the Country Week carnival in Sydney.

Both men were born and raised in Parkes although Quinn represented the State three years earlier when he played for the now defunct Sydney University team in the Sydney premiership competition. Quinn was one of the stars of the team in 1928 and one Queensland report credited him with a better match than his legendary second row partner, George Treweeke, in the first match at Brisbane. Following his selection with the 1928 NSW team, Fletcher moved to Sydney to play football.

Top Row: H. Bailey (Visitor), J. Kingston, N. Quinn, G. Treweeke, J. Mogridge, R. Clayton (Visitor).

Third Row: J. Busch, C. Pearce, S. Brain, C. Willard, M. Bailey.

Second Row: H. Kadwell, H. Byrne, W. Shankland, C. Cavanough, N. Hardy, J. Dempsey.

Front Row: C. York, A. Justice, H. R. Matthews (Joint Manager), P. Maher (Captain), E. Brolly (Joint Manager), R. Lindfield, G. Fletcher.

Courtesy of: Parkes Shire Library Parkes One Hundred Years of Local Government.

1930 Queensland State Football Team Dubbo Hotel

Queensland Football Team in Dubbo NSW. Three interstate games were played in 1930, two in Sydney and one in Brisbane. The tour coach can be seen on the left outside the Dubbo Hotel as the players and officials are photographed.

Eric Weissel played five-eighth and Jack Kingston played lock forward for NSW in the second game at the Royal Agricultural Society Showground

Saturday: 7th June, 1930.
Final-sore: NSW 16, Queensland 11

Source: Wikimedia Commons, Free Media Repository.

1928 CITY v COUNTRY

SPORTING NOTES

A COUNTRY TRIUMPH
City Football Team Defeated

BATHURST PLAYERS REMARKABLE DISPLAY

HUGHES' WONDERFUL DISPLAY

The outstanding personality was D. Hughes (Western) as full-back. He converted all the tries his side scored. Four of his kicks were taken from the 25 yards line, within a few feet of touch. Although his great goal kicking as it turned out, accounted for the victory, it was his robust play in attack and defence which repeatedly evoked clamorous applause from the crowd of about 10,000. Hughes is exceptionally hard to pull down. He has a habit of shaking off a genuine tackler and on brushing through unprepared defenders. He showed this in many a straight run, which was supported and spelt danger to the City line. Hughes has got great turn of speed.

D Hughes

Combined Country Triumph

Sydney May 9
Sydney Cricket Ground

The combined country team defeated the best available football players chosen from the city clubs by the narrow margin of a point, in the annual match at the Sydney Cricket Ground today. The scores were 35 to 34, but the margin does not reflect the overwhelming superiority shown by the country players during the second half in every department of the game. It was a triumph and recovery for the country as the city at one stage led by 11 points.

The match was virtually a final trial for positions in the State side. Apart from individual successes, there was clear proof that the game in the country centres had advanced, and intense coaching of yesterday's victors would produce a remarkable thirteen. There was a degree of consideration among the delighted crowd, if not among the selectors, at the skill revealed by the winners.

Final Score:
Combined Country defeated City 35-34.

Article from: The Lithgow Mercury, Thursday, May 10, 1928. Republished courtesy of ACM/Lithgow Mercury.

When Wests Met North West in Five Yard Rule

The five-yard rule is a question which finds a player continually at fault. The rule lays down that "a player within the five-yards radius cannot under any circumstances be placed on side."

Courtesy of: NSW Rugby League, The Rugby League News. June, 1927.

1928 City v Country

Date:	Wednesday, May 9th 1928	
Kick Off:	3:15 PM (local time)	
Referee:	William "Webby" Neill	
Venue:	Sydney Cricket Ground (Sydney)	
Crowd:	10,000	
Match Stats:	**New South Wales City Firsts** 34	**New South Wales Country Firsts** 35
Halftime Score:	18	10
Tries:	Ernie Lapham (2) Vic Lawrence (2) Benny Wearing (2) Eddie Root George Treweeke	Jack Dempsey (2) G Crawford Rees Duncan Sr Eric Freestone Frank Hawthorne Jack Kingston
Goals:	Benny Wearing (3) John McIntyre (2)	Don Hughes (7)
Teams:		
Fullback	1. Vern Deacon	1. Don Hughes
Wing	2. Benny Wearing	2. Frank Hawthorne
Centre	3. Vic Lawrence	3. Eric Freestone
Centre	4. Nelson Hardy	4. Pat Maher
Wing	5. Stan Brain	5. W Taylor
Five-Eighth	6. Jerry Brien	6. Eric Weissel (Captain)
Halfback	7. Alby Lane (Captain)	7. Jack Dempsey
Lock	8. John McIntyre	8. Jack Kingston
Second Row	9. George Treweeke	9. Norm Quinn
Second Row	10. Bob Lindfield	10. Rees Duncan Sr
Front Row	11. Ernie Lapham	11. G Crawford
Hooker	12. Eddie Root	12. Colin York
Front Row	13. Frank Spillane	13. C Plater
Bench:	14 Frank Matterson	

1929 Australian Rugby League Kangaroos Team

Source: Sporting Memorabilia.

Back Row: A. Justice, C. Fifield F. Laws, L. Sellars, A. Ridley, P. Madsen, W. Brogan, G. Bishop, A. Henderson.

Third Row: W. Prigg, D.V. Dempsey, G. Treweeke, L.V. Armbruster, A.S. Hennesy (Coach-Trainer), J. Kingston, H. Steinohrt, W. Shankland, W. Spenser.

Second Row: H. Finch, J. Upton, P. Maher (Vice-Captain), J. Lorne Dargan (Joint-Manager), H. Sunderland (Joint-Manager), T. Gorman (Captain), F. McMillan, E. Root.

Front Row: A.E.G. Edwards, E Weissel, J. Busch, J. Holmes, H. Kadwell.

Courtesy of: NSW Rugby League, The Rugby League News, July 1928

1929-30 Australia v England Ashes Series
Test 1 Saturday 5 October 1929

Venue: Craven Park, Hull
Referee: R. Robinson

England 8
Tries: Jack Feetham and Alf Middleton.

Australia 31
Tries: Bill Shankland (2), George Bishop, Wally Prigg, Bill Spencer, George Treweeke and Eric Weissel.

Goals: Joe Thompson.

Goals: Eric Weissel (5).

Teams:

Fullback	1.	Tom Rees
Wing	2.	Emlyn Gwynne
Centre	3.	Roy Kinnear
Centre	4.	Billy Dingsdale
Wing	5.	Alf Frodsham
Five Eighth	6.	Les Fairclough (C)
Halfback	7.	Bill Rees
Front-Row	8.	Harold Bowman
Hooker	9.	Nat Bentham
Front-Row	10.	Joe Thompson
Second-Row	11.	Bill Horton
Second-Row	12.	Alf Middleton
Lock.	13.	Jack Feetham.

Teams:

Fullback	1.	Frank McMillan
Wing	2.	Bill Spencer
Centre	3.	Cec Fifield
Centre	4.	Tom Gorman (Captain)
Wing	5.	Bill Shankland
Five Eighth	6.	Eric Weissel
Halfback	7.	Joe Busch
Front-Row	8.	Peter Madsen
Hooker	9.	George Bishop
Front-Row	10.	Bill Brogan
Second-Row	11.	Viv Armbruster
Second-Row	12.	George Treweeke
Lock.	13.	Wally Prigg.

Wikipedia.org/wiki/1929-30, Kangaroo Tour of Great Britain.

1929 Southern Districts Football Representative Team

Country Week, Sydney

Courtesy of: The Wal Galvin Collection.

Back Row: A. Bussey (Trainer), Viv Marsh (Tumut), Alan Ridley (Queanbeyan), Jack James (Cootamundra), Charlie Cornwell (Temora), Tom Forbutt (Tumut), Bob Cooke (Canberra).

Middle Row: Jack Kingston (Cootamundra), Warren Bradley (Queanbeyan), A. Bowers (Manager), Eric Weissel Captain (Temora), Sylvester Keyes (Gundagai), Tom O'Connor (Queanbeyan), Charlie York (Yass).

Front Row: Frank Blundell (Queanbeyan), Reg Maker (Temora), George Purcell (Cootamundra).

1929-1930 Australian Rugby League Team

With their bus in England.

Eric Weissel

Source: Wikimedia.org/Wikipedia/Commons

1929 Western Districts Football Representative Team

Country Week, Sydney 1929

Back Row: G. Whittaker, R. Barry, D. Hughes, V. Schiener, J. Flowman, R. Brady.

Middle Row: H. Summerfield (Manager), J. Green, W. Taylor, R. Miller (Captain), R. Elliott, V. Cleary, R. Clayton.

Front Row: P. Green, N. Schiemer, G. Hughes, B. Clifton.

Courtesy of: Macquarie Regional Library. "Melba Studios 65 Market St. Sydney."

1924-1974 Great Britain v Western Division

In 1924 Orange centre Phill Bagwill played against Great Britain, who won 42-23.

The 1928 side that played at Parkes against the Poms were beaten 22-9, with local players including centre Fletcher and lock Norman Quinn.

In 1936 Great Britain beat Western Division 33-16 at Parkes, with full back 'Spec' O'Donnell captaining WD, supported by prop Bob Wethered.

In 1946 at Orange Great Britain won 33-2 against a Western side that included Norm Miskell, of Bathurst, the man who later coached Parkes.

Peter Braken, the former St. George star who led Parkes to its 1954 premiership, captained Western Division against Great Britain at Bathurst in 1954 when the tourists won 29-11.

The sensational 24-24 draw in 1958 at Orange involved a young back Jim Smith, a paid player from Sydney, who died in Parkes not long after that match.

In 1962 Great Britain won 24-10 at Bathurst against a Western side which included prop Bill Byrnes, now back in town as a police sergeant and Allan Jones, at that time with Wellington.

In 1966 at Parkes when the Poms again won comfortably, Allan Jones was the sole local representative.

At Bathurst four years later however, Jones joined Laurie Wakefield, Terry Scurfield and Bruce Finn in the side beaten 40-11.

Centre Rod MacDonald represented in 1974 at Orange when the tourists won 25-10 after two Western players had been sent from the field. MacDonald was also a member of the Amco Cup side that beat Penrith 6-2 in the inaugural final of the popular mid week competition.

Courtesy of: Parkes Shire Library. Parkes One Hundred Years of Local Government.

Above: Right
ONLOOKER: *"What's the referee like Bill"?*
PLAYER: *"The best I've ever played against".*

Courtesy of: NSW Rugby League, The Rugby League News, May, 1924.

1932 June-July Australian Rugby League Team

Back Row: Alex Burdon (Manager), Wally Prigg, Mick Madsen, Dan Dempsey, Joe Pearce, Cliff Pearce, Unidentified Official.

Middle Row: Harry Sunderland (Manager), Eric Weissel, Ernie Norman, Herb Steinhort (Captain), Hec Gee, J. Little, Unidentified Official.

Front Row: Frank McMillan, Fred Laws, Joe Wilson.

Courtesy of: Wikipedia. Eric Weissel, Australian Rugby League.

Sydney Cricket Ground

Source: Wikipedia.org/Wiki/Sydney Cricket Ground. Courtesy State Library.

1934 Group 9 Rugby League Representative Team

Back Row: A. Phair (Junee), Bill Newcombe (Young), Reverend Dudley Leggatt (Young), Jack James (Cootamundra), Bill Thompson (Grenfell), Jack Whitty (Junee), Norman Bland (Temora, President).

Front Row: Bert Williams (West Wyalong), Bill Kearney (Young), Tom Stanford (Temora), Eric Weissel (Temora Captain), Jim Woods (Temora), Sid Hall (Young), Jack Melrose (Temora). Officials Unknown.

Courtesy of: Jim Woods, 1932 and 1934 photos.

Back Row: B. Brogden, H. Woods, G. Davies, F. Harris, N. Bilock, A. J. Risman, H. Ellington.
Third Row: L. Troup, T. Armitt, M. Hoddgson, J. Arkwright, H. Beverley, H. Jones, M. Exley, B. Hudson.
Second Row: H. Field, A. Atkinson, J. Miller, R.F. Anderton, (Business Manager), J. Brough (Captain), W. Popplewell, (Team Manager), H. Belshaw, J.G. Morley, A.S. Edwards.
Front Row: W. Watkins, E. Jenkins, T. McCue, S. Smith.

Courtesy of: NSW Rugby League, The Rugby League News, May, 1970.

1936 Western Division v England

Date:	Wednesday, June 11th 1936	
Referee:	Alex Spankie	
Venue:	Spicer Park (Parkes)	
Crowd:	7,000	
Match Stats:	**Western Division** **16**	**England** **33**
Halftime Score:	4	10
Tries:	J. Frost A. Williams	Alan Edwards (3) Artie Atkinson Stan Brogden Barney Hudson
Goals:	L. O'Donnell (5)	Billy Belshaw (6)
	Teams:	
Fullback:	1. L. O'Donnell	1. Billy Belshaw
Wing:	2. Mick Rankine	2. Barney Hudson
Centre:	3. H. Stubs	3. Artie Atkinson
Centre:	4. A. Williams	4. Gus Risman (Captain)
Wing:	5. Cec Willard	5. Alan Edwards
Five-Eighth:	6. Sid Mannix	6. Stan Brogden
Halfback:	7. Eric Mork	7. Tommy McCue
Lock:	8. E. Kemp	8. Joe Miller
Second Row:	9. J. Frost	9. Harry Field
Second Row:	10. V. Hodge (Captain)	10. Harry Woods
Front Row:	11. R. Wethered	11. Hal Jones
Hooker:	12. Don Gulliver	12. Mick Exley
Front Row:	13. Jack Huxle	13. Harold Ellington

1945 NSW Country Rugby League Team

Back Row: M. Penn (Sydney Morning Herald), W. H. Corbett (Sun Newspaper.)

Third Row: J. Jorgenson, J. Spenser, A.V. Johnston (Coach), L.W. Cooper., R. Bailey.

Second Row: J. Hampstead, T.M. Bourke, R. Johnson, A.C. Clurs, F.M. Farrell, E. Bennett.

Front Row: C. Kennedy, G.T. Watt, H. Russell (Co-Manager), H. Narvo (Captain), G. Fahy (Co-Manager), W. Wylie, T. N. White

Played Queensland 21st July 1945
Courtesy of: NSW Rugby League, Rugby League News.

1946 Western Team Played Englishmen

Full Back: O. Kennerson (Bathurst),

Three-quarters: E. Parkes (Wellington), P. Reynolds Captain, (Cumnock), F. McGarry (Bathurst), N. Miskell (Bathurst),

Halves: C. Turvey (Wallerawang), W. Flynn (Forbes),

Forwards: J. Huggett (Forbes), C. Hallam (Lithgow), J. West (Orange), C. Hartas (Dubbo), A. Simmons (Yeoval), F. Bell (Lithgow).

Reserves: S. McCauley (Orange), J. McDermot (Dubbo).

1946 AT ORANGE
Courtesy of: John Hugget, Memorabilia, Wellington.

1947 Combined Country Rugby League Blazer & Guernsey

Courtesy of: NSW Rugby League.

1949 Sydney v Country

Country Prepares

Hundreds of miles from Sydney, matches will be played this week-end in the first-round trials which will culminate in the Country v Sydney fixtures at the Show-ground a month hence.

Trials will be staged each week-end until the two Country teams to oppose the cream of talent available in the 10 Sydney clubs are selected.

This means that Country players who win through to the Showground will be the best available and they will be in fit condition to last right through a hard 80 minutes' non-stop football.

In the past the Country has provided many of the brightest stars in Rugby League history and it is quite natural to assume that further new stars will be unearthed this season.

Sydney-Country matches always are a feature of the football year and the fact that they give the fans the first glimpse of potential internationals under big-match conditions each season maintains this interest.

This year the Sydney-Country match will be under somewhat different conditions from the Country angle, in as much as the players from "the bush" will have every chance to be in as good condition as their opponents.

The later date for the big match this year also will allow country selectors in various Groups to sort out their out-standing players and this factor should assist in raising the Country standard.

The presence in the country of so many grade players and Kangaroos as coaches also cannot fail but be beneficial to the prospects of Country.

In Sydney the metropolitan selection committee is studying the form of local players, a member of the committee being sent to each of the five matches weekly.

These men all have had experience in big football and know what is required to build this year's teams.

Supporters of every club can pick out players whom they expect to be among the stars of Sydney Country. The next few weeks will tell whether their fancies are to make the grade this year.

Keith Tull played for Cootamundra and Nevyl Hand was Captain Coach of Gundagai in 1949.

NEXT SATURDAY
SYDNEY v. COUNTRY
At Showground. 2.30 p.m.

In front of a crowd of 24,332

City defeated Country 23-2

Sydney: Les Cowie, Fred De Belin, Ron Roberts tries and Matt McCoy seven goals.

Country: Ron Rowles one goal.

1949 NSW Country Firsts Team

Back Row: S. Frost (Trainer), E. Dawson, P. Pritchard, N. Woods (Trainer).

Middle Row: W. Flanagan (Manager), R. Diamond (brother of Peter Diamond) A. Miller, N. Hand, R. Bower, H. Nolan (Coach).

Front Row: N. Andrews, K. Tull, N. Mulligan, W. O'Connell (Captain), T. Pitman, R. Rowles, V. Bulgin.

Saturday June 4th 2:30 pm
Referee: Tom McMahon Jnr

Fullback	1.	Vic Bulgin
Wing	2.	Bobby Diamond
Centre	3.	Ned Andrews
Centre	4.	Keith Tull
Wing	5.	Ron Rowles
Five-Eighth	6.	Wally O'Connell
Halfback	7.	Perce Pritchard
Lock	8.	Noel Mulligan (Capt)
Second Row	9.	Angus Miller
Second Row	10.	Tom Pitman
Front Row	11.	Bob Bower
Hooker	12.	Ted Dawson
Front Row	13.	Nevyl Hand.

Article from: The Rugby League News, May 7, June 22, 1949. Republished courtesy of NSW Rugby League.

1950 NSW Country Rugby League Trials

Country Selectors at work

State-wide trials are being conducted this week-end as the Country Rugby League trials are advanced to another stage in preparation for the matches between combined Country and Sydney at the Cricket Ground on May 13.

NSW Country Firsts Team Selected to Play NSW City Firsts.
Saturday, May 13, 1950, Sydney Cricket Ground.

Fullback	Russ Naughton
Wing	Norm Jacobson
Wing	W. Bunt
Centre	V. Madge, (Captain)
Centre	Barry Redding
Five-Eighth	Jack McIntosh
Halfback	Col Donohoe
Lock forward	Bill Edwards
Second row	Arthur Collinson
Second row	K. Gray
Front row	Charlie Gill
Front row	Sid Hobson
Hooker	Ted Dawson

City Firsts 51 defeated Country Firsts 13 in front of a crowd of 45,699

Courtesy of: Geoff Mann, Sports Journalist, Dubbo.

Western District v Great Britain Team
Forbes June 7th 1950

Great Britain
Colours: (White Jersey with Red and Blue V)

1. Fullback	J. Legard
2. Wing	E. Daniels
5. Wing	W. Ratcliffe
3. Centre three quarter	T. Danby
4. Centre three quarter	J. Cunliffe
6. Five-Eighth	W. Horne
7. Halfback	A. Pepperell
8. Lock forward	K. Trial
9. Second row	D. Phillips
10. Second row	H. Murphy
11. Front row	D. Naughton
13 Front row	J. Featherstone
12. Hooker	F. Osmond
14. Reserve	R. Williams
15. Reserve	R. Ryan
REFEREE: E. McALPINE.	

Courtesy of: Geoff Mann, Sports Journalist, Dubbo.

Western Districts v Great Britain
Forbes June 7th 1950

Front Row:
Left to Right, P. Wilson (Oberon) W. Neale (Cobar) J. George (Wellington)
J. Cudmore, Capt. (Orange) R. Hutchinson (Lithgow)
K. McLean (Mudgee) F. Bell (Lithgow)

2nd Row: R.B. Campbell, Pres. (Mumbil) R. Cameron (Trangie)
B. Wright (Nyngan) L. Burke (Bathurst) J. Birnie (Coolah)
J.L. Donovan, Manager (Oberon)

Back Row: W. Ezzy (Bathurst) J. Welsh (Lithgow) L. Ley, Coach (Wellington)
K. Slattery (Canowindra) M. Kennedy (Bathurst)

Great Britain was to play Western Districts at Forbes NSW on June 7th, 1950. However, fog gripped the town's airport and the plane carrying the visiting team was unable to land and the match was cancelled. Western Division team players profile next page.

Courtesy of: Geoff Mann, Sports Journalist, Dubbo.

1938 Spooner Sports Oval Opening
Friday 2nd December 1938

The Minister for Works and Local Government Mr. Spooner, will visit Forbes on January 18th to officially open Spooner Sports Oval, formally known as the Cricket Ground, on which the sum of £4,000 has been spent in renovations and the building of a new brick grandstand. A new timber fence has been erected around the boundary with an inner fence surrounding a new banked cycle track.

The Forbes District Hospital and the Forbes Ambulance have combined to draw up a programme for a monster sport-carnival to mark the opening of the oval.

Article From: The Sydney Moring Herald NSW, 1842-1954. December, 2 1938.

1950 The Western Team Profile

From Blackheath to Bourke, from Coolah to Cobar, from Coonamble to Condobolin on through Canowindra to Orange, Mudgee, Bathurst and Lithgow, stretches the vast area (one third of the state) from which the Westerners have come for today's match.

Comprising the four Groups, 10, 11, 14, and 15, the Western Division contains within its boundaries the four cities of the Blue Mountains, Lithgow, Bathurst and Orange and 60 other centres where Leagues are functioning and flourishing. Over 150 teams take the field each weekend in regular competition football and regularly 40,000 fans view the game.

From the vast organisation, Messrs. Brazil (Group 10), Menchin (Group 10), Lay (Group 11), Frater (Group 14) and Sedgeman (Group 15) have selected the following men to oppose the might of Great Britain today.

J. CUDMORE, Captain and fullback. Age 23. Weight 13.10. Comes from Orange. An Ex-Newtown reserve grade player, he specialises in attack.	**W. NEAL**, Second-rower of Cobar is a miner from that centre. He also coaches the Cobar team. He came originally from Newtown reserves. Is 28 years of age and weighs 14 stone.
K. McLEAN, a winger from Mudgee, weighs just over 11 stone and is 18 years of age. A product of the local St. Matthew's Convent School, this lad impressed on each occasion he has been before the selectors.	His partner, **KEN SLATTERY,** is the sole Group 11 representative in the team. Ken hails from Canowindra and although outstanding in Country elimination games during the past three years has been overlooked. He will make the best of his chance today. Age 22. Weighs 13.9.
W. EZZY, from Bathurst, is the other winger. Weighs 12.7. He is a member of the Bathurst Railway team which had such a successful 1949 season.	**FRANK BELL,** of Lithgow is the front row prop. The father of the team. Frank is 32 years of age and weighs 14 stone. His performances in the past include captaincy of Country Firsts.
M. KENENDY, also from Bathurst, is a centre, age 22 years. Weighing 13 stone and strong in attack. His performance against the Englishmen should interest the crowd.	**R. WRIGHT,** of Nyngan, age 26 and weighing 14 stone, has raked for Nyngan for the past three years. A good rucker, he should find the tough Englishmen to his liking.
J. BIRNIE, of Coolah is a solicitor, 21 years of age and 12.2 in weight. He is an ex-Randwick Rugby Union player, having his first season of Rugby League. He is the other centre.	**R. CAMERON,** from Trangie, represented Canberra in 1949. He weighs 14.7 and has seen 26 summers.
L. BURKE, of Bathurst, 24 years of age, weighing 12 stone, has been knocking on the door of big football for a number of years. His chance comes today.	**JOHNNY GEORGE,** of Wellington is the reserve back. A youth of 18, he is very solid packing 13 stone into a height of just over 5 feet. This is his second season in first grade football.
R. HUTCHINSON, of Lithgow, impressed at the trials at Dubbo. Solid, weighing 11 stone, he is 24 years of age.	**P. WILSON,** of Oberon, given a chance to perform, should justify the confidence of the selectors. A Group 10 representative player, he is considered the type to mix it into hard rucking forwards.
J. WELSH, the Vice-Captain, also hails from Lithgow. He kicked his way into the Western team at Dubbo. A second row forward in recent Country versus City games. His age is 21 years and weight 13.8.	**REFEREE:** E. McALPINE
Courtesy of: Geoff Mann, Sports Journalist, Dubbo.	

1951 Western Division v France at Forbes

Date:	Wednesday, May 30th 1951	
Referee:	K. Rowan	
Kick Off:	3:05 P.M.	
Venue:	Grinsted Oval Forbes	
Crowd:	5,950	

Match Stats:	Western Division 24	France 26
Halftime Score:	9	16
Tries:	Rolf Trudgett (3) J. Birney (1)	Andre Beraud (2) Maurice Andre (1) Maurice Bellan (1)
Goals:	Oriel Kennerson (6)	Puig Aubert (7)
Teams:		
Fullback:	1. Oriel Kennerson	1. A. Puig-Aubert (Captain)
Wing:	2. Norm Jacobson (Captain)	2. Raymond Contrastin
Centre:	3. Leo Nosworthy	3. Ode Lespes
Centre:	4. J. Birney	4. Maurice Bellan
Wing:	5. M. Smith	5. Maurice Andre
Five-Eighth:	6. Rolf Trudgett	6. Rene Duffort
Halfback:	7. William Kelly	7. Jean Dop
Front Row:	8. J. West	8. Francois Rinaldi
Hooker:	9. Ian Walsh	9. Jean Audoubert
Front Row:	10. F. Hogan	10. Andre Beraud
Second Row:	11. L. Kable	11. Michel Lopez
Second Row:	12. Ron Kelly	12. Edouard Ponsinet
Lock:	13. Ken Slattery.	13. Francois Montrucolis.

1951 French Rugby League Touring Team

Back Row: J. Audoubert, M. Lopez, G. Galixte, E. Brousse, G. Delaye, R. Perez, A. Beraud, E. Ponsinet, O. Lespes.
Middle Row: P. Barhtoletti, J. Duhau (Coach), R. Duffort, R. Contrastin, L. Mazon, V. Cantoni, Antone Blain (Manager), A. Puig-Aubert (Captain), M. Andre, G. Geroud, F. Montrucolis, F. Rinaldi, P. Samatan (Coach).
Front Row: M. Martin, J. Merquey, M. Bellan, R. Caillon, J. Dop, J. Crespo, G. Comes.

Courtesy of: The Shire of Flinders, Queensland.

1953 City v Country Firsts

Date:	Saturday, May 16th 1953	
Referee:	Jack O'Brien	
Venue:	Sydney Cricket Ground	
Crowd:	46,936	
Match Stats:	City	NSW Country Firsts
	27	28
Tries:	Noel Pidding (2) Arthur Collinson Keith Holman George Martin	Don Schofield (2) Ron Battye Brian Carlson
Goals:	Noel Pidding (6)	Darcy Russell (8)
Teams:		
Fullback	1. Clive Churchill	1. Darcy Russell
Wing	2. Noel Pidding	2. Ron Battye
Centre	3. Keith Middleton	3. Harry Wells
Centre	4. George Martin	4. Robert Bartlett
Wing	5. Ian Moir	5. Jack Lumsden
Five-Eighth	6. Col Geelan	6. Rees Duncan
Halfback	7. Keith Holman	7. Bryn Evans
Front row	8. Peter Diversi	8. Noel Hill
Hooker	9. Ken Macreadie	9. Billy Williams
Front row	10. Arthur Collinson	10. Don Schofield
Second row	11. Roy Bull	11. Charlie Gill
Second row	12. Ken Kearney	12. Ernie Hammerton
Lock	13. Kevin Hansen	13. Bryan Orrock
		14. B. Carlson

1953 Country's Winning Rugby League Team

For the first time since 1942 Country beat Sydney in 1953 by the narrow margin of 28-27 after Noel Pidding had missed with a penalty shot from right on touch after the full-time bell. Hero of the match was Wollongong centre Bobby Bartlett, not long back from England. He did so well that he displaced Clive Churchill from the State captaincy against Queensland the following week.

Back Row: W. Stansbury (Manager), R. Duncan, D. Russell, R. Battye, A. Mannix (Trainer).
Middle Row: A. Folwell (Coach), H. Wells, A. Paul, B. Orrock, D. Schofield, C. Gill, R. Stehr.
Front Row: V. Roach (Manager), J. Lumsden, B. Carlson, R. Bartlett (Capt), E. Hammerton, N. Hill, R. Norman (Coach).

Courtesy of: NSW Rugby League, The Rugby League News, May, 1953.

1954 Western Division Rugby League Team

Great Britain v Western Division
Game 1- Bathurst Sports Ground, May 19, 1954. (Crowd- 5,218)
Final score: Great Britain 29 defeated Western Division 11.
Courtesy of: John Hugget, Memorabilia, Wellington.

1954 Western Division Team at Bathurst

1. Fullback:	R. Beaumont (Canowindra)
2. Wing:	P. Weldon (Trangie)
5. Wing:	J. Cohen (Wellington)
4. Three quarter:	L. Bourke (Bathurst)
3. Three quarter:	P. Marks (Warren)
6. Five-Eighth:	K. Deacon (Dubbo)
7. Halfback:	P. Bracken (Parkes, Captain)
8. Lock forward:	V. Corrish (Dunedoo)
9. Second row:	F. Hogan (Bathurst)
10 Second row:	R. Potter (Orange)
11. Front row:	R. Border (Coonabarabran)
13. Front row:	K. Fogarty (Forbes)
12. Hooker:	B. Cameron (Trangie)
Reserves:	P. Burns (Bathurst), R. Harden (Baradine)

Courtesy of: Geoff Mann, Sports Journalist, Dubbo.

"I Was Groggy and Punchy" Says Deacon After Battering by U.K. League Team in Bathurst Game

The UK Rugby League players in yesterday's match against Western Division at Bathurst were "experts at the art of short, stiff-arm tackling," Dubbo's captain-coach Keith Deacon said today.

Deacon said he felt like Sugar Ray Robinson after the match. "I was groggy and punchy".

The Western Districts forwards, he proudly said, stood up to the punishment meted out by the English pack and gave back all they received.

May 1954

Deacon played five-eighth against England and scored his team's only try against the tourists and made the following comments:

"The score of 29-11 in favour of the visitors was not a true indication of the game," Deacon said. " A return match would find the scores much closer."

The Western Districts had most of the play in England's territory and trailed 11-14 at one stage.

"The Englishmen's machine-like passing was a highlight of their play, together with the loose forward play, which enabled an overlap in the backline to give the fast flank men a scoring chance," Deacon said.

No Champion

English centre three-quarter, Lewis Jones, former international Rugby Union player, was outstanding, while Billy Boston proved a good winger.

"But Boston is a champion," Deacon said. "And he is certainly not another Harold Horder, as suggested in city papers."

"I have seen better wingers in Sydney. Both Barry Stenehouse (Canterbury-Bankstown) and Ian Moir (South Sydney) are more determined wingers. Boston has a habit of swinging infield off his right foot and he got away with it against a mediocre cover defence yesterday," Deacon said.

"But he will be cut down by any good cover defence sweeping across field in future games. In my opinion he lacks the quality needed by a big game winner."

"The English players are heading for much trouble over the play-the-ball rule. Yesterday they just rolled it between their legs," Deacon said.

Many critics cry out that it is the first match for the Englishmen and give the Western Districts little credit for a good display.

But it must be remembered that players in the Western team come from scattered areas from Forbes to Warren, Orange, Dunedoo and Parkes and are playing their first game together.

Final score: England 29 defeated Western Division 11.

Article from: National Library of Australia, Great Britain v Western Division, May 19, 1954.

1955 Group Trials Western Division Selection

NILON ONLY DUBBO PLAYER CHOSEN FOR GROUP XI TEAM

(By "Scrum Half")

July 1955

Dubbo League forward Alan Nilon is the only local player to gain selection in the Group 11 team to play Group 10 in the Western Division elimination trials at Dubbo on Sunday.

Representative teams from Groups 14 and 15 will meet in the other match.

At the conclusion of both games a Western Division team will be selected to play in the Country Week trial in Sydney.

There is a strong possibility that this team will also play the French Rugby League tourists at Parkes on July 20.

Former Balmain and Interstate hooker, Ken Fogarty, who is coaching Forbes for the second year will lead the Group 11 side.

Three other "name" players at present coaching Group 11 town teams are also included in the representative team.

Ex St. George winger Kevin Hole who represented City against the Englishmen last year and this season signed up with Condobolin will play on one flank and fleet-footed Joey Cohen of Wellington on the other. Cohen played in this position against the American All Stars at Dubbo two years ago.

Outstanding ex-Australian and Western Suburbs forward Kevin Hansen will add a touch of class and experience to the Group 11 pack.

Hansen is coaching Manildra in the second division Group 11 competition. Second row forward J. Borham (Eugowra) is also from this division.

Big Jock Weir from Narromine and promising Parkes lock, J. Gain are good selections and should do well.

Although he only recently recovered from a bout of sickness Wellington coach, Ces "Babe" Kelly was obviously selected on reputation for the half-back post.

His brief run with Wellington against Dubbo last Sunday was apparently enough to satisfy the selector present that he is a player of class.

Kelly recently returned from England where he played with the famed Wigan Club and also won selection in the Other Nationalities team which did so well in games against England, France and Scotland.

Parkes player, R. Aldrich, was the logical choice for full-back while former Eastern suburbs three-quarter Darcy Henry, has the vital five-eighth position.

It is not surprising to see Dubbo players conspicuous by absence from the Group team.

Despite the glowing reports of its success in trials so far this season, the team which is comparatively young has yet to face the acid test in competitive games.

Second row forward, Alan Nilon deserves his place as a replacement in the Group team, however, as he has displayed grand form in the trial games.

GROUP 11

Full-back: R. Aldrich (Parkes).

Three-quarters: J. Cohen (Wellington), R. Priestly (Parkes), W. Towers (Forbes), K. Hole (Condobolin).

Halves: D. Henry (Forbes), C. Kelly (Wellington).

Forwards: J. Gain, J. Perrin (Parkes), J. Borham (Eugowra), K. Hansen (Manildra), J. Weir (Narromine), K Fogarty (Forbes).

Replacements: R. Harding, M. McClintock (Canowindra), R. Walsh (Narromine), A. Nilon (Dubbo).

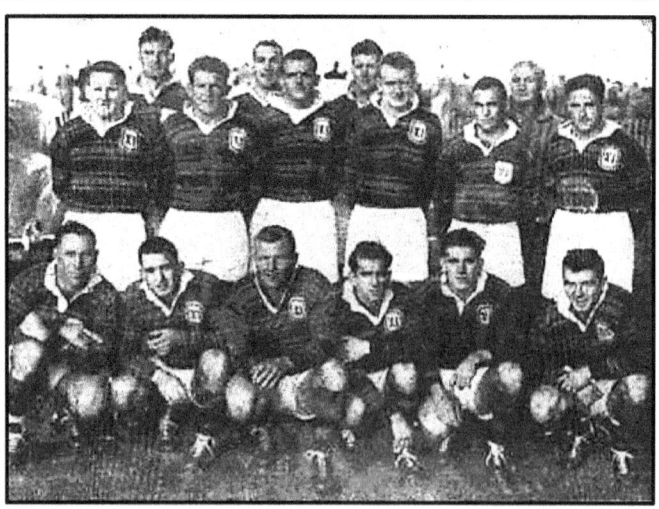

Above: Selected Group 11 Team 1955

Article from: The Dubbo Daily Liberal, Thursday, July 28, 1955. Republished courtesy of ACM/Dubbo Daily Liberal.

1955 Group Trials Western Division Selection

3.15 p.m. GROUP 11 (Black and Red)	GROUP 10 (Black and White)
1. Full-Back: N. Mckay (Parkes) 2. Left Wing: D. Parrish (Dubbo Macquarie) 5. Right Wing: R. Light (Dubbo Macquarie) 3. Outside Centre: R. Cremin (Dubbo CYMS) 4. Inside Centre: L. Sclori (Peak Hill) 6. Five-Eighth: A. Fanning (Eugowra) 7. Half-Back: J. McGarry (Narromine) 8. Lock: R. Lynch (Forbes) 9. Second Row: C. Hackett (Peak Hill) 10. Second Row: R. Weir (Narromine) 11. Front Row: G. Rossiter (Forbes) 13. Front Row: K. Hartin (Condobolin) 12. Hooker: Ian Walsh, Captain-Coach (Eugowra) Replacement Back: L. Willis (Condobolin) Replacement Forward: B. Perry (D Macquarie).	1. Full-Back: T. Paskins, Vice-Captain (Oberon) 2. Left Wing: G. Rawlings (Oberon) 5. Right Wing: B. Gorman (Cowra) 4. Centre: T. Hunt (Orange CYMS) 5. Centre: A. Hanson (Lithgow Workmen's Club) 6. Five-Eighth: L. O'Brien (Wallerawang) 7. Half-Back: C. Fahy (Orange CYMS) 8. Lock: K. King (Lithgow Workmen's Club) 9. Second Row: I. Fowler, Captain (Orange Emmco) 10. Second Row: D. Dwyer (Orange Emmco) 11. Front Row: H. Bonham (Bathurst Railway) 13. Front Row: R. Gilson (Lithgow Workmen's Club) 12. Hooker: K. Kelly (Orange CYMS) Replacement Forward: P. Commins (Orange CYMS) Replacement Back: Fitzpatrick.
	Referee: F. McAlpine. Linesmen: J. Tink and V. Ryan
1.30 p.m. GROUP 14 (Maroon and Gold)	GROUP 15 (Red, White and Blue)
1. Full-Back: W. Elwin (Gilgandra) 2. Left Wing: G. Frenth (Coonabarabran) 5. Right Wing: E. Manning (Coolah) 3. Centre: V. Everingham, Captain (Coolah) 4. Centre: N. Bryant (Coonamble) 6. Five-Eighth: C. Evans (Coonabarabran) 7. Half Back: R. Trudgett (Coonamble) 8. Lock: J. Hobby (Coolah) 9. Second Row: P. Keegan V. Captain (Coonabarabran) 10. Second Row: R. Palmer (Gilgandra) 11. Front Row: P. Condon (Mudgee) 13. Front Row: A. Head (Coonamble) 12. Hooker: B. Byrnes (Coonamble) Replacement Back: E. Harrison (Gilgandra) Replacement Forward: J. Candrick (Baradine).	1. Full-Back: A. Norton (Brewarrina) 2. Left Wing: J. Jermyn (Cobar) 5. Right Wing: K. Martin (Bourke) 3. Centre: J. Grant (Brewarrina) 4. Centre: K. Miskell (Cobar) 6. Five-Eighth: L. Darcy (Brewarrina) 7. Half-Back: K. Neale (Cobar) 8. Lock: R. Moore (Brewarrina Magpies) 9. Second Row: D. Beetson (Brewarrina) 10. Second Row: A. Buck (Brewarrina Magpies) 11. Front Row: S. Whitney (Brewarrina Magpies) 13 Front Row: A. Buck (Brewarrina Magpies) 12. Hooker: C. Beetson (Brewarrina) Replacement Back: H. O'Connel (Burke), B. Harvey (Cobar) Replacement Forward: L. Mackey (Burke), R. Pike (Cobar).

Referee: M. Leary. Linesmen: J. Tink and L. McCarthy

12 noon: DUBBO CYMS JUNIORS v ORANGE EMMCO JUNIORS

1955 Western Division Rugby League Team

Back Row: R. Patterson, J. Simpson, F. Bell (Coach), J. Border, J. Perrin, R. Aldridge, I. Walsh, K. Hansen, F. Thurn, R. Stanford, R. Priestly, R. Phillips (Manager).

Front Row: J. Gain, L. Nosworthy, R. Bowden, J. Holden (Captain), K. Hole, K. Lawrence.

Perrin, Priestly, Stanford and Gain all came from Parkes Rugby League Club.

Above: Western Division Team to play France at Pioneer Oval Parkes
Team chosen from Group trials matches between the following: Groups 10, 11, 14 and 15.

Courtesy of: Parkes Shire Library. Parkes One Hundred Years of Local Government.

1955 French Touring Team Plays Western Division

Wednesday, July 20, 1955 Pioneer Oval Parkes hosted a game between France Rugby League team and Western Division. Another coup for sports fans of the Parkes Shire, as the French Rugby League team were runners up in the 1954 World Cup (the first such event for either rugby code).

Les Chanticleers drew a crowd of 8,306 to the newly developed Pioneer Oval.
France Beat West 11-8 in a Torrid Game

France wins a rough game: The French Rugby League team beat the Western Division 11-8 at Parkes today in one of the roughest games on the tour. The standard of play was high in the first half, but after the interval the local team came on to the field determined to play destructive football.

There were several fights and at the end of the game. The French fullback, Jean Dop, lay on the ground after being kicked on the shin. However, he was not seriously hurt.

The Frenchmen scored three tries and a goal to Western Division four goals. Front-row forward Andrew Carrere was awarded a penalty try. Centre Fernand Canton and winger Maurice Voron scored fine tries after their brilliant movements.

The second half deteriorated into one of the most unedifying displays of the tour. Western Division forwards tore into the rucks. Their inside backs stood as close as possible and prepared to harass the opponents. Some of the French forwards quickly became excited and there was much scuffling.

Hookers Rene Moulis (France) and Ian Walsh (Forbes) continued a private fiery brawl that had begun to smoulder in the first half. They dealt with each other in and out of the scrums and both of them needed attention from the ambulance attendants.

Big Kevin Hansen, former New South Wales prop forward upset the Frenchmen by his vigour and determination in the rucks and by strong running with the ball.

Left: Andre Carrere

Article from: The Parkes Champion Post, July 21, 1955. Republished courtesy of ACM/Parkes Champion Post.

1955 French Rugby League Touring Team

The French rugby league team played Western Division at Pioneer Oval Parkes.

The team selected listed below:

1. Jean Dop, 2. Maurice Voron, 3. Victor Larroude, 4. Fernand Cantoni, 5. Andre Savonne, 6. Andre Delpoux, 7. Sylvain Menichelli, 8. Andre Carrere, 9. Rene Moulis, 10. Armand Save, 11. Jean Jammes, 12 Jean Pampbrun, 13. Roger Guilhem.

1955 France Rugby League Team: Source: Steve Ricketts, Site Covering All Things Rugby League.

May 19, 1956

Once again, we extend a cordial welcome to the Country teams here for the annual challenge to the pick of Metropolitan sides in their efforts to secure State and later Australian honours.

This season a lot is expected from the two Country teams. They have been carefully chosen after an exhaustive series of trials in some cases as old as the season itself.

Players have gone through test after test and those wearing the Country jerseys today have proved themselves.

The Country standards like that of the city, have risen in recent years and this year should be at its highest peak.

Big money has attracted talented players, including Test men to the country.

Apart from building up their town sides they also have made opponents play better football.

Crowd: 37, 396
Referee: Col Pearce
Results: City First defeated Country First 36-17.

Courtesy of: NSW Rugby League, The Rugby League News, May, 1956.

West Holds UK League Side to Draw
Orange 1958
West 24 UK 24

May 1958

ORANGE Wednesday More than 5,000 spectators at Orange today saw Western Division Rugby League team force a 24 all draw with Great Britain.

The Western side hurled themselves at the tourists' line for the last 10 minutes of the game in an effort to put the issue beyond doubt.

The British "Lions" lacked a first-class goal-kicker. Three kickers were tried, but only three goals were scored. One unsuccessful kick caused both linesmen to disagree but referee Lyons rightly ruled no goal.

Western Division kicker, Don Parish of Wellington, kicked six goals. The tourists met unexpected opposition from the Western side, which really played above themselves.

Article from: The Canberra Times, Thursday, May 22, 1958. Republished courtesy of ACM/Canberra Times.

Back Row: D. Maizey (Manager), D. Dwyer, B. Halloran, H. Bonham, T. Copeland, W. Towers, I. Fowler.

Middle Row: W. Elwyn, B. Tranter, D. Schiemer, R. Weir, W. Watson (Trainer).

Front Row: J. Smith, D. Parish, I. Walsh (captain), P. Kane, J. McGarry.

Scores: Western Division 24 (J. Smith, R. Weir, D. Schiemer, W. Elwyn, tries, Don Parish, six goals) drew with:
Great Britain 24 (A. Murphy 2, B. McTigue, R. Ashton, J. Challinor, K. Sullivan, tries, A. Murphy 3 goals.)

Courtesy of: Dave Kent, Orange & District Historical Society.

1959 NSW Country Firsts Rugby League Team

Back Row: R. Davies, R. Heanry, T. Beckett, J. Cann, S. Frost (Trainer).

Middle Row: P. Hagan (Manager), J. Monro, B. Olive, B. Hambly, T. Johnston, H. Hamilton (Trainer).

Front Row: J. Hattam (Manager), J. Kell, I. Walsh, A. Stauton, D. Parish, W. Owens, N. Mulligan (Coach).

City Firsts vs Country Firsts Sydney Cricket Ground, Saturday 23rd May, 1959
City Firsts defeated Country Firsts 37-7

Courtesy of: NSW Rugby League. The Rugby League News, May, 1959.

GIFTS TOTAL NEARLY £700
A Boy's dream come true says Don

September 1959

A crowd of 150 people representing nearly every sporting body in Dubbo, attended a civic farewell at the Royal Hotel last night to Dubbo's first Rugby League international, Don Parish, who leaves on Friday to join the Kangaroo tour party in Sydney.

During the evening, the Mayor, Ald. L. H. Ford, M.L.A. presented Don with a cheque for £473 / 6 / 0 raised in a week by public subscription. Additional gifts totaling £200 were acknowledged during the night.

They included £50 from Group 11, £25 from Western Division and £20 from Group 10.

To assist Parish in every way on the tour the Mayor of Dubbo presented him with a letter of introduction from the Municipal Council, under the seal of the Council, "on behalf of every citizen of Dubbo."

The president of the Macquarie Rugby League Club, Mr. Bob Pack, said that in his cricket and football Parish has always been held in esteem.

"To be among the first 26 of Australia's best footballers is the greatest thing that could happen to a boy like Donny," he said. " His selection is also a feather, in the cap of the Macquarie Club, since it's only been in operation for two years.

Secretary of Group 11 Mr. Ron Dobson, spoke highly of the honour Parish's selection has given the group and pointed out that of the four country players selected from the 22 groups in N.S.W. two came from Group 11.

Don Parish was one of those unique rugby league players considered good enough to be picked in an Australian team while still playing in the bush with Dubbo Macquarie

Don went on to play with Western Suburbs. An outstanding attacking fullback, pictured below on the burst against Easts at the Sydney Sports Ground.

Don Parish
Source: Terry Williams.

Article from: The Dubbo Daily Liberal, September 1, 1959. Republished courtesy of ACM/Dubbo Daily Liberal.

1961 Western Division Defeats Eden Monaro 31-15

RUGBY LEAGUE FOOTBALL

CALTEX £1000

WESTERN DIV.
v.
MONARO DIV.

Sunday, 14th May
Cowra Recreation Ground
PROGRAMME: 1/-
(Organised by Cowra Rugby League)

Cowra "Guardian" Print

Former N.S.W. back Tony Paskins led Western Division Rugby League team to a convincing 31-15 win over Monaro in the opening round of the Country Championships at Cowra today.

Paskins played an outstanding game scoring two tries and kicking five goals. Ian Walsh dominated the scrums and the Monaro team spent most of the 80 minutes defending.

Scores:
Western Division: 31, (T. Paskins 2, D. Bourke 2, I. Evans 2, J. George 1 tries, T. Paskins 5 goals).
Monaro: 15, (G. Bladen 2, Warren 1 tries, J. Carr 3 goals).

Western Division 31 Monaro 15

Western Division will meet Riverina in the first semi-final at Parkes next Sunday and maintain the same team that defeated Monaro.

May 21st 1961 Semi-final Pioneer Oval Parkes:
One Point Victory Over Riverina

A record crowd of over 5,000 saw Western Division score a one-point victory over Riverina, in a Rugby League thriller, at Parkes on Sunday. Western Division snatched victory as the final bell sounded to win 15 points to 14.

A penalty right on fulltime saw G. McMillan of Lithgow raise the flags as the bell sounded to end the match.

Scores:
Western Division: 15, (A Paskins, J. George, M. Nairn tries, McMullan 3 goals).
Riverina: 14, (Roots, Williams tries, J. Jones 4 goals).

Western Division 15 Riverina 14

Western Division
(Green, double white v)

FULLBACK:
Tony Paskins Captain (Oberon)
WINGERS:
Don Burke (Peak Hill), Jim Tierney (Lithgow Workmen's)
CENTRES:
Dennis Cubis (Gilgandra), Bobby Hansen (Coolah)
FIVE-EIGHTH:
Doug Moore (Dubbo Macquarie)
HALF-BACK:
Johnny George (Dubbo Macquarie)
LOCK:
George Smith (Peak Hill)
SECOND ROW:
Brian Halloran (Bathurst Railway), Mick Nairn (Condo)
FRONT ROW:
Laurie Evans (Oberon), Athol Curry (Dubbo Macquarie)
HOOKER:
Ian Walsh (Eugowra)
RESERVES
FORWARD: Barry Harris (Dubbo CYMS)
BACK: Ross Everingham (Bathurst Railway)
MANAGER: Mr. Kevin Devenish
REFEREE: Mr. Keith Lyons (Lithgow).

Courtesy of: Geoff Mann, Sports Journalist Dubbo.

Monaro Division
(White jumper, red inscription)

FULLBACK:
John Cunningham (Goulburn United)
WINGERS:
John Pilley (Captain's Flat), Barry Devlin (Goulburn Workers)
CENTRES:
Paul Slater (Jindabyne), John Carr (Goulburn Workers)
FIVE-EIGHTH:
Bernie Nevin Vice-Captain (Goulburn Workers)
HALF-BACK:
Don Burge (Yass)
LOCK:
Terry Mooney (Cooma Rovers)
SECOND ROW:
Garry Bladen (Captain's Flat), Bob Warren Captain (Cooma Public Service)
FRONT ROW:
Keith Crapp (Moruya), Stanford Dixon (Goulburn Workers)
HOOKER:
Gordon Thompson (Cooma St Pats)
RESERVES
FORWARD: Vince Duffy (Goulburn Workers)
BACK: Ken Murphy (Tathra)
MANAGER: Mr. Max Thorogood.

Western Division Win Three in a Row

28th May 1961
NEWCASTLE SPORTS GROUND
WESTERN DISTRICTS GREAT LEAGUE WIN
R L Title Goes to Wests; Paskins Star:
………………………………………………………..Inspired by 3 first half tries, by Tony Paskins, Western Division gave Newcastle a football lesson on Saturday in the final of the Caltex knockout Country Rugby League Championship.

Locals fail to cross line

Western Division in the Caltex Rugby League Country championships' final at Newcastle yesterday thrashed Newcastle far more thoroughly than the score of 19-10 indicated.

Western Division: 19 (A Paskins 3 tries, G. McMillan 5 goals)
Newcastle: 10 (L Johns 5 goals).

Western Division 19 Newcastle 10

7th May 1962
PIONEER OVAL PARKES
WESTERN DIVISION TAKES COUNTRY AGAIN

A record crowd in the vicinity of 10,000 paid £1,609 at Pioneer Oval Parkes to see Western Division withstand a determined second-half bid by Newcastle to win the Country Rugby League Championship by 15 points to 13.

After leading 15/0 at half-time West had to use its guile to withstand a second half onslaught.

Star of the match was Lithgow Workman's Club winger Greg McMillan who scored a brilliant try and kicked three goals from six attempts to score nine of Western Division's points.

Western Division: 15 (Greg McMullan, Vince Everingham, Kevin King tries, Greg McMullan 3 goals).
Newcastle: 13 (Bill Owens, Don Williams, John Williams tries. Les Johns 2 goals).

Western Division 15 Newcastle 13

6th May 1963
WOLLONGONG
RUGBY LEAGUE TITLE TO WEST

Wollongong Sunday a goal was disallowed three minutes from full-time which cost Southern Division its first £1000 Country Divisional Country Rugby League Championship. Western Division claimed its third consecutive Country Championship when it defeated Southern Division 9-8.

Western Division 9 (Keith King try, Peter Thompson 3 goals).
Southern Division 8 (Dennis Laverty, Des Tobin tries, Richie Lumsden 1 goal).

Western Division 9 Southern Division 8

Courtesy of: Geoff Mann, Sports Journalist Dubbo.

1962 Western Division Caltex Rugby League Team
Country Rugby League Divisional Champions

Back Row (heads showing): A. Jones (Wellington) reserve, J. Brophy (Mudgee), A. Curry (Dubbo), B. Harris (Dubbo), G. Smith (Lithgow).

Middle Row: M. Nairn (Condobolin) reserve, A. Burke (Bathurst), K. King (Lithgow), V. Everingham (Oberon), W. Byrnes (Parkes).

Front Row: N. Brown (Oberon), G. McMillan (Lithgow), A. Paskins (Oberon) Captain, E. Harrison (Gilgandra), K. Negus (Cowra).

W. Burns of Parkes replaces I Evans of Oberon who had to withdraw from an injury.

The Western Division team to play Great Britain today was chosen after Western Division defeated Newcastle at Pioneer Oval Parkes in the Caltex Country Divisional Championship final.

Courtesy of: Geoff Mann, Sports Journalist, Dubbo.

1962 Great Britain Rugby League Touring Team

Back Row: Gary Cooper, John Shaw, Don Fox, Bill Sayer, Brian McTigue, Frank Carlton, Ike Southward, Eric Frazer, Mick Sullivan.

Middle Row: Billy Boston, Neil Fox, John Taylor, Gerald Round, Lawrence Gilfedder, Jack Wilkinson, Ray Evans, Peter Small.

Front Row: Arthur Walker (Assistance Manager), Norman Herbert, Dick Huddart, Eric Ashton (Captain), Stuart Hadfield (Manager), Derek Turner (Vice Captain), Brian Edger, Ken Noble, Colin Hutton (Trainer).

Sitting: Alec Murphy, Dave Bolton, Harold Paynton.

Courtesy of: NSW Rugby League, The Rugby League News, June, 1962.

1962 Great Britain v Western Division

Sunday, May, 27th, 1962, Crowd: 10,000.
Great Britain defeated Western Division 24 points to 10 at the Bathurst Sports Ground

GREAT BRITAIN	WESTERN DIVISION
FULL-BACK	**FULL-BACK**
Gerald Round	Tony Paskins
WINGERS	**WINGERS**
Billy Boston, Ike Southward	Greg McMillan, John Brophy
CENTRES	**CENTRES**
Lawrence Gilfedder	Tony Burke, Vince Everingham
FIVE-EIGHTH	**FIVE-EIGHTH**
Harold Paynton	Earl Harrison
HALF-BACK	**HALF-BACK**
Don Fox	Norm Brown
LOCK	**LOCK**
Derek Turner Captain	George Smith
SECOND ROWERS	**SECOND ROWERS**
Dick Huddart, John Taylor	Keith King, Barry Harris
FRONT ROW	**FRONT ROW**
Ken Noble, Jack Wilkinson	Athol Curry, Bill Byrnes
HOOKER	**HOOKER**
Stephen Shaw	Kevin Negus
RESERVES	**RESERVES**
Mike Sullivan, Roy Evans	A Jones, M. Naim

WESTERN TEAM SWAMPED BY ENGLISHMEN

(By "Observer")

The touring Great Britain Rugby League team yesterday swamped Western Division by 24 points to 10 at Bathurst.

The Englishmen gave a superlative display of power football combined with snap passing and precision movements, which left the Western Division team bewildered.

May 1962

Spearheaded by its large pack of forwards, England kept Western Division on the defence for practically all the match.

Stars of the England team were second-rower Dick Huddart and five-eighth Harold Paynton.

Huddart's crashing bursts split the Western Division defence on several occasions.

Paynton gave a great display in the pivot position and kept his team on the attack with clever switching of play.

Practically none of the Western Division team did any good in attack.

George Smith was regarded as the best player on the field.

His outstanding defence was an example for the Englishmen and Western Division players.

All his tackles were low and effective and his cover defence was outstanding.

Barry Harris of Dubbo turned in another great performance but was inclined to hang on too much, especially during the first half.

However, his barging runs and crashing tackles were a feature of the match.

Harris was a tower of strength and required two and three English defenders to drag him down.

One of the tries he scored in the second half of the match was a beauty. He broke through a ruck on the Western Division 25-yards line and raced almost 50 yards, without support, before being pulled down.

From the play-the-ball Ken Negus broke through an opening and as a he was tackled flipped a pass infield. Harris backing up brilliantly, snapped up the ball and dived over for a well-earned try.

Western Division wingers Geg McMillan and Jim Brophy turned in good all-round displays.

Full-back Tony Paskins had a quiet day. His line kicking and defence was solid but his attacking moves were few.

Athol Curry of Dubbo played well in the front-row position but faded during the second half because of a shoulder injury.

Centres Alan Burke and Vince Everingham played well, especially in defence.

SPECIAL AWARDS

Following the match English five-eighth Harold Paynton and Western Division lock George Smith were presented with wrist watches for being the best players on the field.

Article from: The Dubbo Liberal, Monday, May 28, 1962. Republished courtesy of ACM/Dubbo Daily Liberal.

1962 Country Firsts Rugby League Team

Back Row: L. Griffin (Trainer), J. Kelly, P. Jackson (Coach), R. Honeysett, E. George (Trainer).

Middle Row: G. McMillan, R. Courley, B. Harris, G. Smith, G. Langlands, W. Owens.

Front Row: L. Armstrong (Manager), J. Richards, K. Negus, A. Paskins (Captain), R. Smith, C. Kentwell, J. Wroe (Manager).

May 12, 1962
Crowd: 15,541
Country Firsts 18 defeated City firsts 8.
Referee: Col Pearce.

Courtesy of: NSW Rugby League, The Rugby League News, May, 1962.

1962 Western Division Captain

TONY PASKINS
Oberon player, Tony Paskins is captain of the Western Division team.

He is the best Captain Western have boasted in recent years and he has twice led them to championship honours.

Paskins is a fast, elusive player. He is always a danger to the opposition when in possession of the ball.

It is his sparkling play and intelligent tactics which have made him the present No. 1 contender for the Australian Test Captaincy.

Paskins began his football as a college Rugby Union star.

After he switched to league, he played for seven years in England with Warrington Town Club.

He gained valuable experience there and this could be a telling factor in his appearances against the Englishmen.

He gained valuable experience there and this could be a telling factor in his appearances against the Englishmen.

Tony Paskins went on to captain Country Firsts against the City Firsts winning 18-8 at the SCG.

Tony Paskins playing for Forster-Tuncurry in 1970, retiring at the end of the season after winning the grand-final.

One of the greatest Country Rugby League players of his time.

Article from: The Central Western Daily, May 26, 1962. Republished courtesy of ACM/Central Western Daily.

1962 City v Country Firsts

Date:	Saturday, May 12th 1962	
Referee:	Col Pearce	
Venue:	Sydney Cricket Ground	
Crowd:	15,541	

Tony Paskins

Match Stats	New South Wales City Firsts 8	New South Wales Country Firsts 18
Tries:	Ken Irvine (2)	Barry Harris Tony Paskins
Goals:	Brian Carlson (1)	George McMullin (6)
Teams:		
Fullback	1. Brian Carlson	1. Changa Langlands
Wing	2. Eddie Lumsden	2. Charlie Kentwell
Centre	3. William Bischoff Jnr	3. Tony Paskins (Captain)
Centre	4. Don Parish	4. John Kelly
Wing	5. Ken Irvine	5. George McMullan
Five-Eighth	6. Tony Brown (Captain)	6. Bob Honeysett
Halfback	7. Arthur Summons	7. Bob Smith
Lock	8. Ron Lynch	8. George Smith
Second Row	9. Graham Wilson	9. Bill Owen
Second Row	10. Norm Proven	10. Barry Harris
Front Row	11. Ron Crowe	11. Bruce Olive
Hooker	12. Ian Walsh	12. Kevin Negus
Front Row	13. Elton Rasmussen	13. R. Gourley
Bench:		14. Vince Everingham
Coach:	Harry Bath	Phill Jackson

Civic Welcome Planned for Kiwis Football Team

A Civic Reception in Chamberlain Square will form the official welcome to Parkes for the New Zealand Kiwis and their first opponents for their 1963 Australian tour, Western Division Rugby League side.

May 1963

Charlie Dwyer Receives Recognition

Article from: The Parkes Champion Post, May 15, 1963. Republished courtesy of ACM/Parkes Champion Post.

Official Opening of The Chas. Dwyer Pavilion

Prior to the main game, Western Division v. New Zealand, the mayor of Parkes, Ald. A. C. Moon, MBE, will officially open the new Chas Dwyer Pavilion.

May 1963

The Pavilion has been erected by Parkes Municipal Council, with generous assistance from the Parkes Leagues Club and is being named after one of the best known, Rugby League Administrators in the State.

Mr. Dwyer was one of the founders of Rugby League away back in 1920 and has been actively associated with the code since that date.

In that time, he has built up a record which few men can equal and is serving his twelfth successive term as President of Group 11.

He is a Vice-President and Past-President and Post-President of Western Division.

A life member of Group 11 Referees Association.

Past President and life member of Parkes Rugby League. President and life member of Parkes Leagues Club. The honour being bestowed on Charlie Dwyer offers sincere congratulations to him.

Article from: The Parkes Champion Post, May 15, 1963. Republished courtesy of ACM/Parkes Champion Post.

Pictures From RL Game

Our cameraman was at Parkes yesterday for the New Zealand /Western Division game, won by the tourists 36/11.

May 1963

New Zealanders give their famous "Haka".

Western fullback (partly obscured) sends the ball goal-wards. This was his third successful penalty kick and brought the score to 6 all.

Article from: The Dubbo Daily Liberal, May 23, 1963. Republished courtesy of ACM/Dubbo Daily Liberal.

Fullback In Fast Dash

Garry Phillips, the Kiwis' full-back, making one of his many brilliant runs at Parkes yesterday, when the visitors beat Western Division 36-11.

Article from: The Dubbo Daily Liberal, May 23, 1963. Republished courtesy of ACM/Dubbo Daily Liberal.

1963 NEW ZEALAND v WESTERN DIVISION
Pioneer Oval Parkes

May 1963

NEW ZEALAND	WESTERN DIVISION
COLOURS: BLACK, WHITE V & KIWI EMBLEM	COLOURS: GREEN, DOUBLE WHITE V & MONOGRAM
FULL-BACK	**FULL-BACK**
G. Phillips (11).	P. Thompson (1).
THREE-QUARTERS	**THREE-QUARTERS**
B. Reidy (12) R. Bailey (3) G. Kennedy (9) N. Denton (5)	J. Brophy (2), K. Smith (5) R. Weir (3) R. Rushworth (4)
FIVE-EIGHTH	**FIVE-EIGHTH**
J. Bond (4)	D. Shead (6)
HALF-BACK	**HALF-BACK**
W. Snowden (2)	N. Brown (7)
FORWARDS	**FORWARDS**
M. Cook (11) Captain R. Ackland (16), E. McMaster (25) M. Emery (20), J. Butterfield (18), S. Edwards (19)	J. Hobby (8) K. King (9) Captain, A. Gillespie (10) R. Gilson (11), A. Curry (12), K. Negus (13),
RESERVES	**RESERVES**
K. McCraken (10), R. Hammond (23).	R. Taylor (14), C. Piper (15).
Managers: G. G. Grant and W. E. Desmond. Coach: W. Telford and Trainer: H. Somerville.	Manager: Mr. N. McLean (Orange) Coach: R. Trudgett (Oberon) and Trainer: Mr. W. Baker
REFREE: K. Lyons (Lithgow), LINESMEN: K. Dwyer and K. McCrae. BALL BOYS: R. Harrison and R. Neilsen.	

Brilliant Kiwis Swamp Western Division at Parkes

(BY MALCOLM McKAY)

A brilliant New Zealand Rugby League team overwhelmed Western Division in the opening match of the tour at Parkes yesterday.

Before a crowd of 4000 at picturesque Pioneer Oval, New Zealand ran away to a 36-11 win after leading 11-9 at half time.

May 1963

NEW ZEALAND TEAM:
Fullback: G. Phillips.
Three quarters: Brian Reidy, Roger Bailey, Graham Kennedy, Neville Denton, Ken McCraken.
Five-eighth: Jim Bond.
Half-back: Bill Snowden.
Forwards: Mel Cooke (Captain), Ron Ackland, Don Hammond, Maunga Emery, Jock Butterfield, Sam Edwards, Colin McMaster.

WESTERN DIVISION TEAM:
Fullback: P. Thompson.
Three quarters: K. Smith, R. Weir, B. Rushworth, J. Brophy.
Five-eighth: D. Shead.
Half-back: N. Brown.
Forwards: J. Hobby, K. King (Captain), A. Gillespie, R. Gilson, K. Negus, A. Curry.

Fourteen of the fifteen NZ players named for the match have represented New Zealand in Tests and the fifteenth forward Colin McMaster has been a reserve forward for four Tests.

Western Division matched the Kiwis' play in the first half, but in the second session the tourists' teamwork was given full play and they swamped the Country side.

Their backing up and handling thrilled the crowd and left the Western Division players standing.

Most of the spectators left the ground with a great opinion of the New Zealand team work and a leading Sydney sportswriter said that the standard of play was better than that displayed by the Englishmen on their last tour.

A goal-kicking duel between rival full-backs Phillips and Peter Thompson of Lithgow, had the score six-all.

Kiwis went on to lead 11-9 at half time. Following McCracken's try, winger Kerry Smith of Forbes, scored for Western New South Wales a minute before half time.

Smith's try in which Lithgow centre Barry Rushworth did the spade work, was a beauty. Thompson failed to covert and at half time the scores were 11/9.

The Kiwis machine started to function in its full glory immediately in the second half with Western Division scoring only two points in the second half with a good goal from Thompson. New Zealand ran up 25 points which included five tries.

Centre Rushworth, second-rower Keith King of Lithgow and Kevin Negus of Cowra, were Western Divisions best players.

Final Scores:
New Zealand 36 (K. McCracken 2, R. Bailey, G. Kennedy, M. Denton, J. Bond tries; G. Phillips 9 goals) defeated Western Division 11 (K. Smith try; P. Thompson 4 goals).

Article from: The Dubbo Daily Liberal, May 23, 1963. Republished courtesy of ACM/Dubbo Daily Liberal.

In Group XI Team
1964

Dubbo CYMS Ray McTiernan and Macquarie front-rower Barry Perry have been selected in the Group XI team to play in the Group trials at Wellington on Sunday. Macquarie coach Bill Hansen has been named as a replacement forward for the team.

April 1964

Ray McTiernan

COUNTRY RUGBY LEAGUE
WESTERN DIVISION

Inter-Group Trials

KENNARD PARK, WELLINGTON

Sunday, 14th April, 1964

GAMES 40 MINUTES DURATION

Group 14   v.   Group 11
Group 11   v.   Group 10
Group 10   v.   Group 14

The points scored for each team is divided by points against that team. The highest answer is the winner.

Programme organised by Group XI.

C. J. DWYER, President.
R. B. MIDDLETON, Treasurer.
R. S. PHILLIPS, Hon. Sec.,
29 Fifth Avenue, Narromine.

Nº 1921

Group 11
Colours: Black and Red

FULL-BACK
M. Mc Cintock (1)

THREE-QUARTERS
K. Smith (2) K. Talbot (5)
A. Jones (3) A. Packham (4)

FIVE-EIGHTH
R. McTiernan (6)

HALF-BACK
C. Burrows (7)

FORWARDS
J. Hobby (8) Captain
J. Gartshore (9), A. Gillespie (10)
R. Beath (11) B. Wright (12), B. Perry (13)

RESERVES
D. Shead (14), D. Hansen (15).
Manager Coach: N. Gordon (Parkes).

Group 10
Colours: Blue

FULL-BACK
F. Fawatt (1)

THREE-QUARTERS
B. Harvey (2) G. Rawlings (5),
T. Gradey (3), J. Sokora (4)

FIVE-EIGHTH
J. Schrader (6)

HALF-BACK
N. Brown (7)

FORWARDS
K. King (8) Captain
J. Hanning (9), A. Cashin (10)
J. Arrow (11) G. Elwyn (12), J. Rush (13)

RESERVES
R. Lidden (14), J. Gersbach (15).

Group 14
Colours: Maroon and Gold

FULL-BACK
K. Condon (1)

THREE-QUARTERS
M. Schiemer (2) D. Kennard (5)
R. Hansen (3) B. Running (4)

FIVE-EIGHTH
E. Harrison (6) Captain

HALF-BACK
B. Graham (7)

FORWARDS
T. Cook (8)
V. Schiemer (9), J. Estens (10)
R. Gilson (11), N. Edwards (12), R. Walton (13)

RESERVES
M. Wright (14), W. Campbell (15).

Article from: The Dubbo Daily Liberal, April 13, 1964. Republished courtesy of ACM/Dubbo Daily Liberal.

1964 Group 11 Rugby League Team

![1964 Group 11 Rugby League Team photograph]

Back Row: from left: A. Packham, K. Talbot, J. Gartshore, W. Beath, A. Curry, R. Weir, J. Hobby, N. Gordon (manager, Parkes), R. Hansen.
Front Row: C. Burrows, R. Smith, A. Jones, J. McClintock, A. Gillespie, B. Wright, R. McTiernan.

Article from: The Dubbo Daily Liberal, April 13, 1964. Republished courtesy of ACM/Dubbo Daily Liberal.

1964 Curry & Weir in Group 11 Team

Curry, Weir Picked

April 1964

Eight Group 11 players, including Dubbo Macquarie front-row forward Athol Curry are in the Western Division team.

Yesterday's Group trial games were successfully conducted at Kennard Park, Wellington, where a crowd of about 3,000 paid a near record £540 to see the games.

Western Division will play Northern Division at Tamworth next Sunday in the £1,000 Country Rugby League championships.

TRIAL RESULTS

Group 11 defeated Group 14, 6/0
Group 10 defeated Group 11, 10/3
Group 10 defeated Group 14, 18/2

Western Team

The following is the Western Division team to play Northern Division at Tamworth on Sunday:

Fullback:
K. Condon (Mudgee)
Wingers:
K. Smith (Forbes), B. Harvey (Oberon)
Centres:
R. Weir (Narromine), M. Wright (Baradine)
Five-eighth:
E. Harrison (Gilgandra)
Half-back:
N. Brown (Oberon) Captain
Lock:
J. Hobby (Eugowra)
Second row:
J. Gartshore (Parkes), K. King (Lithgow)
Front row:
B. Beath (Eugowra), A. Curry (Macquarie)
Hooker:
J. Arrow (Bathurst)
Reserves: A. Gillespie (Narromine), K. Talbot (Parkes).

Article from: The Dubbo Daily Liberal, April 20, 1964. Republished courtesy of ACM/Dubbo Daily Liberal.

COUNTRY RUGBY LEAGUE CHAMPIONSHIPS

SIX KEY CHANGES IN RIVERINA TEAM TO PLAY WEST

Riverina has made six changes in its team to play Western Division at Parkes on Sunday in the semi-final of the country rugby league championships.

Western Division has made one change only in its team. Col Elwyn of Oberon will replace Jack Arrow of Bathurst as the hooker.

WEST-RIVERINA RL CLASH DOMINATES WEEKEND SPORT

Western Division, holders of the Country rugby league championships since 1961, will meet the powerful Riverina team at Parkes on Sunday in the semi-final of the 1964 country championships.

Article from: The Dubbo Daily Liberal, Wednesday, April 29, 1964. Republished courtesy of ACM/The Dubbo Daily Liberal.

CALTEX Country Rugby League Championship Semi-final

Western Division v. Riverina

Sunday, 3rd May, 1964
PIONEER OVAL, PARKES

Riverina Team
Colours: Maroon and Gold

FULL-BACK
L. Moraphi (1)

THREE-QUARTERS
Bob Cheney (2) Kevin, O'Connor (5)
Roger Ludkin, (3) Mick Redden (4)

FIVE-EIGHTH
Fred Strutt (6)

HALF-BACK
Barry Casey (7)

FORWARDS
Dick Smith (8) Captain
Warren Glanville (9), Bernie Walsh (10)
Ron Crowe (11), Ron Cooper (12), Fred Jones (13).

RESERVES
Fred Norden (14), Terry Baker (15)

Coach: Greg Haywick; **Manager:** Bruce Maitland.

Western Division Team
Colours: Green, Double White V

FULL-BACK
Ken Condon (1)

THREE-QUARTERS
Kerry Smith (2) Brian Harvey (5)
Robert Weir (3) Mervyn Wright (4)

FIVE-EIGHTH
Earl Harrison (6)

HALF-BACK
Norm Brown (7) Captain

FORWARDS
John Hobby (8)
Keith King (9), Jock Gartshore (10)
Athol Curry (11), Col Elwin (12), Barry Beath (13).

RESERVES
Keith Talbot (14), Arnold Gillespie (15)

Manager: Mr. Bob Middleton.

Referee: J. Arnold. Touch Judges: K. Dwyer and K. MacRae.

Western Division defeated Riverina: 20 points to 5 in the semi-final at Parkes

Brilliant Victory by Western Division Team Unchanged to Meet Newcastle

May 1964

Western Division moved a step closer to its fourth consecutive Country rugby league championship yesterday, defeating Riverina convincingly 20-5 in the semi-final at Parkes.

Newcastle defeated Southern Division 24-5 in the other semi-final and will meet Western Division in the final at Newcastle next Saturday.

Article from: The Dubbo Daily Liberal, Monday, May 4, 1964. Republished courtesy of ACM/ Dubbo Daily Liberal.

1964 John Hobby Western Division

John Hobby with the ball, moves away from a Newcastle would be tackler in one of the games in the Country Championships.

Courtesy of: Barry Ross, March 23, 2017 (an article from "Family of League").

WESTERN DIVISION TOO SOLID FOR NORTHERN TEAM

The Caltex Country Division Champions, Western Division, finished too solidly for the Northern Division in a very interesting and keenly contested elimination match at Tamworth's No. 1 Oval yesterday.

April 1964

Western Division Coach: Rolf Trudgett	Northern Division Coach: Bill Sorenson
1. Ken Condon (Mudgee) 2. Kerry Smith (Forbes 3. Bob Weir (Narromine) 4. Merve Wright (Baradine) 5. Brian Harvey (Oberon) 6. Earl Harrison (Gilgandra) 7. Norm Brown (Oberon) 8. John Hobby (Eugowra) 9. Keith King (Lithgow) 10. Jock Gartshore (Parkes) 11. Athol Curry (Dubbo) 12. John Arrow (Bathurst) 13. Barry Beath (Eugowra) 14. Reserve: Keith Talbot (Parkes) 15. Reserve: Allan Gillespie (Narromine).	1. Mick Flannagan (Guyra) 2. David Burns (Quirindi) 3. Doug Ricketson (Inverell) 4. Bill Sorenson (Glen Innes) 5. Dudley Towers (Walcha) 6. Trevor Barnes (Warialda) 7. Barry Kellam (Boggabri) 8. Jim Payne (Warialda) 9. Kevin O'Toole (West Tamworth) 10. Bill Smith (Narrabri) 11. John O'Neil (Gunnedah) 12. Greg Barnphrett (Quirindi) 13. John Love (Walcha) 14. Reserve: Trevor Menzies (Merriwa) 15. Reserve: Don Woods (Guyra).
Manager: Mr. Bob Middleton	**Manager:** Mr. John Quinn

Game:

Western Division, which led 2-nil at half-time, won by 13 points to three.

The first half produced some rugged football, with the defence of both sides being thoroughly tested.

Early in the second half, the northern team led 3-2 after Dudley Towers had scored and at this stage, the visitors looked a beaten combination.

The Test five-eighth Earl Harrison of Gilgandra although well watched by Northern lock Jim Payne and five-eighth Trevor Barnes gave a polished display.

Harrison set up most of the visitor's scoring movements the last try scored by the visitors he cut North's defence to ribbons before transferring the ball to Smith who then gave lock John Hobby a clear run for the line. Smith missed the conversion.

Game results:

Over all scrums favoured Western Division 12-7

Western Division 13 (N. Brown 2 and J. Hobby tries and K. Smith 2 goals), defeated Northern Division 3 (D. Towers try)

Referee: Noel Sophr, Newcastle.

Final Score 13-3 in favour of Western Division.

Article from: The Dubbo Daily Liberal, Monday, April 27, 1964. Republished courtesy of ACM/Dubbo Daily Liberal.

1964 Bubble Bursts In The Final

Newcastle, Sunday. Newcastle yesterday ended Western Division's undefeated record in the Country Rugby League championship.

Newcastle's 16-5 win broke a sequence of three title wins by Western Division. Western had beaten Newcastle in the 1961 and 1962 finals and a 1963 semi-final.

1. S. Nelson
2. Jim Perry
3. Gordon Doyle
4. Dave Brown
5. Bob Horne
6. Ron Madge
7. Bill Giles
8. Norm Wilkinson
9. David Hayburn
10. Alan Thompson
11. Brian Smith
12. Alan Buman
13. Jim Morgan
14. Warren Bell
15. Barry Dunlop.

Newcastle Representative Rugby League Team 1964, winner of State Championship Final.

Article from The Newcastle Herald.com.au/story, 1964. Republished courtesy of ACM/Newcastle Herald.

1964 Western Division Rugby League Team

Back Row: Bob Middleton, Earl Harrison, Bob Weir, Barry Beath, Jock Gartshore, John Hobby, Kerry Smith, Keith King, Athol Currey, Keith Talbot, Rolf Trudgett (Coach).
Front Row: Mervin Wright, Ian Condon, Norman Brown, Col Elwyn, Brian Harvey, Arnold Gillespie.
Newcastle 16 Defeated Western Division 5, May 17, 1964.

Courtesy of: Geoff Mann, Sports Journalist Dubbo.

1964 NSW Country Firsts Rugby League Team

Back Row: D. Barsley, R. Hopper, L. Griffin (Trainer), D. Brown, T. Barnes.

Middle Row: W. Baker (Trainer), D. Hayburn, D. Ricketson, K. Horne, W. Petley, P. Jackson (Coach).

Front Row: P. Katsooles (Manager), W. Sullivan, R. Crowe, N. Brown (Captain), J. Morgan, J. Gartshore, P. Kennedy (Manager).

Country Firsts Team played City at the SCG on Saturday, May 16, 1964 in front of a crowd of 29,924. City defeated Country Firsts 27-4.

Courtesy of: NSW Rugby League, (Melba Studios).

1964 Country Seconds Rugby League Team

Back Row: M. Wright, L. Moraschi, R. Madge, J. Hobby, A. Thomson, W. Giles, R. Stewart.

Middle Row: W. Baker (Trainer), R. Thomas, J. O'Neill, B. Smith, C. Wiseman, R. Weir (Captain), B. Carlson (Coach), L. Griffin (Trainer).

Front Row: P. Katsoolis, (Manager), P. Wilson, R. Cheney, N. Wilkinson, J. Armstrong, A. Curry, P. Kennedy (Manager).

Courtesy of: Geoff Mann, Sports Journalist, Dubbo.

May 16-17, 1964

Once again, we extend a cordial welcome to the Country teams here for the annual challenge to the pick of City teams.

This season a lot is expected from the two Country teams. They have been carefully chosen after an exhaustive series of trials in some cases as old as the season itself.

Crowd: 28,924

Results:
City Firsts 27 defeated Country Firsts 4
Referee: Fred Erickson.

City Seconds 29 defeated Country Seconds 2
Referee: Keith Lyons.

Courtesy of: NSW Rugby League, The Rugby League News, May, 1964.

1964 Western Division v France Wade Park Orange

Western Division Team
(COLOURS: GREEN / WHITE V)

Fullback:
Ken Condon 1, (Mudgee).

Wingers:
Mervyn Wright 2, (Baradine), Brian Harvey 5, (Oberon).

Centres:
Robert Weir 3, (Narromine), Keith Talbot 4, (Parkes).

Five-eighth:
Earl Harrison 6, (Gilgandra).

Half-back:
Norm Brown 7, (Oberon).

Lock Forward:
John Hobby 8, (Eugowra).

Second Row:
Keith King 9, (Lithgow), Arnold Gillespie 10, (Narromine).

Front Row:
Athol Curry 11, (Dubbo), Barry Beath 13, (Eugowra).

Hooker:
Colin Elwyn 12, (Oberon).

Reserves: Ron Lidden 14 (Bathurst), Jock Gartshore 15, (Parkes).

Manager: Mr. Bob Middleton (Cudal).

French Touring Players:
1. Carrere, Andre
2. Etcheberry, Jean
3. Boule, Michel
4. Fabre, Bernard
5. Mantoulan, Claude
6. Lecompte, J. Pierre
7. Bourrell, Andre
8. Castel, Henri
9. Savonne, Gerard
10. Blo, Pierre
11. Villeneuve, Jean
12. Garnung, Roger
13. Verge, Louis
14. Bertrand, Georges
15. Panno, Jean
16. Faletti, Laurent
17. Sabathie, Christian
18. Mas, Francis
19. Duseigneur, Edouard
20. Graciet, Jean
21. Ailleres, Georges
22. Eramouspe, Robert
23. Estieu, Serge
24. Bardes, Michael
25. Larrue, Herve
26. Azalbert, Pierre
27. Chamorin, Henri
28. Lapoterie, Joseph

French Team
(COLOURS: RED, BLUE & WHITE V)

Fullback:
A. Carrere 1.

Wingers:
M. Boule 2, J. Etcheberry 5.

Centres:
J. Lapoterie 23, A. Bourrell 4.

Five-eighth:
G. Savonne 15.

Half-back:
R. Garnung 7.

Lock Forward:
H. Chamorin 13.

Second Row:
S. Estieu 11, G. Ailleres 27.

Front Row:
L. Faletti 8, C. Sabathie 10.

Hooker:
J. Graciet 9.

Reserves: H. Castel 17, J. Panno 21, E. Duseigneur 25.

Referee: Mr. A. Byrnes (Wollongong), Touch Judges: K. Faulks, H. Hammond.

Source: Official Souvenir Program, 1964.

1964 Western Division Team

K. CONDON, Mudgee: Age 27, weight 12 ½ stone. Rep, Western Division 1960. Safe handler, reliable defender.

KERRY SMITH, Forbes: Age 22, weight 13 stone, Rep Country and Western Division 1963. Penetrating winger, good goal-kicker.

ROBERT WEIR, Narromine: Age 28, weight 14 ½ stone. Rep Country 1960, Western Division 1960-64. Straight, hard running centre.

MERVE WRIGHT, Baradine: Age 22, weight 12 ½ stone. South Sydney President Cup player. Rep Country 1964. Sharp in attack, solid defender.

BRIAN HARVEY, Oberon: Age 21, Weight 11 ½ stone. First major fixture. Good useful winger.

EARL HARRISON, Gilgandra: Age 24, weight 12 stone. Rep Australia against New Zealand and South Africa. Toured England and France 1963 played nine straight Tests. Top class player.

NORM BROWN, Captain, Oberon: Age 26, weight 12 stone, Rep, Western Division 1962-63. Captain Country 1964.

JOHN HOBBY, Eugowra: Age 26, weight 14 stone, Rep Country 1961, 1963 and 1964, Western Division 1961 and 1963. Experienced player, good cover defence.

KEITH KING, Lithgow: Age 30, weight 14 stone. Rep Country 1962 and 1963, Western Division 1961-62-63. Good open forward.

JOCK GARTSHORE, Parkes: Age 25, weight 14½ stone. Rep Northern Division, 1963, Country 1964. Solid second rower, hard runner.

ATHOL CURRY, Vice-Captain, Dubbo: Age 28, weight 15 stone. Rep Country 1961, 1962 and 1964, Western Division 1961, 1962 and 1963. Good scrummager, tight forward.

COLIN ELWIN, Oberon: Age 28 years. Rep Western Division against Newcastle 1963. Former Group 14 player.

BARRY BEATH, Eugowra: Age 19, weight 15 stone. Rep Country 1964. Very promising player, solid in defence and attack.

KEITH TALBOT, Parkes: Age 23, weight 13 stone. First major fixture. Group 11 winger with ability.

ARNOLD GILLESPIE, Narromine: Age 22, weight 14 stone. Rep Western Division 1963. Solid forward.

BOB MIDDLETON: Manager.
ROLF TRUDGETT: Coach.

Source: Copy, Official Souvenir Program, 1964.

1964 French Rugby League Touring Team

Courtesy of: NSW Rugby League, Rugby League News, July, 1964.

FAR WEST TEAM BEATS FRENCHMEN

Orange, Thursday: A crowd of 2,200 yesterday braved icy weather to watch strong finishing Western Division overpower France in their Rugby League match at Wade Park.

The crowd saw inspired first-half display by the Frenchmen in which they scored two tries and a goal to lead Western Division 8-5 at the interval.

But the tourists could not sustain their form in the second half, and wilted to be beaten 17-11. Gate Takings: £261,00.

May 1964

The number two country team and former country champions thus repeated the success of the 1960 side, which defeated France 14-7 at Dubbo before a crowd of 5,446.

Throughout yesterday's match, Wade Park was swept by intermittent showers. Poor weather severely affected the gate.

After yesterday's defeat, the Frenchmen were at a loss to explain the result.

Some blamed overtraining with exercises which they said had tired them and just left them jaded.

Tour manager, Mr. Jean Barres, also found the defeat unexplainable.

Through an interpreter he said the team had been told it must win if it was to lift its morale and improve chances for coming matches. Mr. Barres said the tourists could be expected to play 50 percent better football when they found cohesion.

France would now concentrate on developing cohesion by retaining as far as possible, the same players in the next few matches.

The tourists do not lack determination. Despite their string of defeats as they have not won a match in Australia this tour, they are adamant that they will perform better against the strong Newcastle team whom they meet on Saturday.

The only players missing were centre three-quarter Bernard Fabre, centre-partner Claude Mantoulan the 26-times international who was injured against City at the SCG on Saturday and 29-year-old second-rower Robert Eramouspe.

Western Division, one of the glamour sides in Country R.L, produced a sustained second half burst of attacking football to turn a half-time deficit of 5-8 into its winning score.

France in the first half gave the impression that it was on its way to its first winning score. Playing its best football of the tour, the team showed amazing ball control with the slippery ball.

Its combination bore no resemblance to that shown in its pathetic and humiliating defeat at the hands of the Test-strength combination City side at the SCG on Saturday.

If France can continue to show improvement and sustain its form in the second half, the results of future matches will be closer.

France's hopes in yesterday's match were dashed early in the second half when Western Division piled on seven points within five minutes of the resumption.

Western Division inside backs, who included the Kangaroo's reliable five-eighth Earl Harrison (Gilgandra), tackled strongly and were aggressive with the ball.

Harrison was supported by Combined Country half-back Norm Brown (Oberon) and centres Bob Weir (Narromine) and Keith Talbot (Parkes).

RESULTS:
WESTERN DIVISION 17
(R. Weir, N. Brown, B. Harvey tries and K. Condon 4 goals). Defeated:
FRANCE 11
(M. Boule 2 tries and J Etcheberry 1 J. Villeneuve, goal).

Article from: The Dubbo Daily Liberal, Thursday, May 28, 1964. Republished courtesy of ACM/Dubbo Daily Liberal.

French Rugby League centre Andre Bourreill gets his pass away after being tackled by a Western Division rival and Bob Weir right coming over the top at Orange, yesterday.

Courtesy of: The Central Western Daily, 1964.

1965 COUNTRY RUGBY LEAGUE
WESTERN DIVISION
INTER-GROUP MATCHES VICTORIA PARK, DUBBO
SUNDAY, 18th APRIL 1965

Positions:	Group 15 First Grade	Group 11 First Grade
Fullback	1. F. Ralph (Cobar)	1. I. Gunn (Parkes)
Wing	2. B. Barrett (Goodooga)	2. K. Talbot (Parkes)
Centre	3. J. Woodcock (Goodooga)	3. R. Weir, Capt (Narromine)
Centre	4. T. Southern (Cobar)	4. D. Gough (Dubbo Macq)
Wing	5. B. Harvey (Cobar)	5. I. McClintock (Eugowra)
Five-Eighth	6. H. O'Connell (Nyngan)	6. Ken Smith (Eugowra)
Halfback	7. W. Wakefield (Bourke)	7. L. Bloomfield (Parkes)
Lock	8. M. Carter (Bourke)	8. J. Hobby (Eugowra)
Second row	9. R. Green (Goodooga)	9. A. Gillespie (Narromine)
Second row	10. E. Good (Cobar)	10. B. Beath (Eugowra)
Front row	11. F. Douglas (Bourke)	11. M. Dawes (Narromine)
Hooker	12. D. Gibson (Warren)	12. J. Wallace (Dubbo Macq)
Front row	13. W. Constable (Goodooga)	13. A. Curry (Dubbo Macq)
Reserve Back	14. K. Markwell (Brewarrina)	14. T. Smith (Dubbo CYMS)
Reserve Forward	15. J. Griffith (Nyngan).	15. J. Gartshore (Parkes).
COACH:	J. Woodcock (Goodooga)	R. Phillips (Narromine)

REFEREE: N. Johnson / LINESMAN: J. Tink and K. McRae

Positions:	Group 15 Under 18	Group 11 Under 18
Fullback	1. R. Jeffree (Brewarrina)	1. A. Phillips (Narromine)
Wing	2. J. Goonery (Cobar)	2. D. Hodge (Forbes)
Centre	3. K. Manohy (Nyngan)	3. R. Smith (Narromine)
Centre	4. J. Piesley (Bourke)	4. C. Keed (Peak Hill)
Wing	5. T. Newman (Bourke)	5. P. Ashton (Forbes)
Five-Eighth	6. C. Allan (Warren)	6. C. Balfour (Dubbo CYMS)
Halfback	7. C. Wright (Brewarrina)	7. J. Carney (Dubbo Macq)
Lock	8. C. Robinson (Bourke)	8. N. Norman (Dubbo CYMS)
Second row	9. D. Greenaway (Warren)	9. L. Ryan (Canowindra)
Second row	10. T. Gordan (Brewarrina)	10. C. Hatch (Dubbo Macq)
Front row	11. K. Brennan (Warren)	11. M. O'Toole (Forbes)
Hooker	12. M. Moore (Cobar)	12. J. Storgh (Dubbo Macq)
Front row	13. D. Richards (Cobar)	13. R. Wilding (Forbes)
Reserve Back	14. R. Ingram (Nyngan)	14. D. Finn (Parkes)
Reserve Forward	15. R. Saunders.	15. P. Atkinson (Dubbo Macq).

REFEREE: V Ryan / LINESMAN: J. Tink and K. McRae.

1965 Group 15 Rugby League Team

Group 15 smashed by Group 11

1965 Group 15 played Group 11, the game was fairly even at half-time with Group 11 leading 13-5.

However, in the second half, Group 15's lack of training showed through and Group 11 put on another 35 unanswered points for a 45-5 drubbing.

Back Row: B. Harvey, R. Green, K. Markwell, T. Southan, N. Hines (Manager), S. Douglas, B. Gibbs, D. Gibson, M. Carter (Vice Captain).
Front Row: H. O'Connell, B. Barrett, L. Mason, I. Woodcock (Captain), S. Ralph, W. Wakefield, J. Josephson.
Courtesy of: John Collins, The Crowing of the Roosters.

1965 Group 11 and Group 15 Trial Match

Left: Narromine player Malcolm Dawes, dives over to score a try for Group 11 as K. Lovett of Nyngan tackles him. K. Markwell of Brewarrina is also pictured.

Group 11 defeated Group 15 48-15.

Group 11 were undefeated in all three trial matches.

Article from: The Dubbo Daily Liberal, April 20, 1965. Republished courtesy of ACM/Dubbo Daily Liberal.

1965 Group Trial Teams	Group 10 First Grade	Group 14 First Grade
Fullback	1. B. Grady (Oberon)	1. J. Butcher (Gil)
Wing	2. T. Ellery (Lith Workers)	2. J. Slacksmith (Coona)
Centre	3. Sikora (Bath St Pats)	3. R. Nelson (Gil)
Centre	4. T. Grady (Oberon)	4. M. Schiemer (Coolah)
Wing	5. B. Harvey (Oberon)	5. B. Kennaugh (Mudgee)
Five-Eighth	6. J. Schroeder (Oberon)	6. E. Harrison Captain (Gil)
Halfback	7. N. Brown Captain (Oberon)	7. R. Kellam (Coona)
Lock	8. J. Sinclair (Lith Workers)	8. R. Meyers (Gil)
Second row	9. K. King (Lith Workers)	9. A. Slacksmith (Coona)
Second row	10. R. Heffernan (Bath Rail)	10. M. Coggan (Coona)
Front row	11. J. Rush (Oberon)	11. L. Casbell (Gil)
Hooker	12. F. Kelly (Orange CYMS)	12. R. Dawson (Dunedoo)
Front row	13. K. Graham (Lith Workers)	13. M. Sparks (Dunedoo)
Reserve Back	14. R. Lidden (Bath Rail)	14. R. Milson (Coona)
Reserve Forward	15. P. Sikora (Bath Pats).	15. R. Murphy (Mudgee).
COACH:	T. Trudgett (Oberon)	E. Harrison (Gilgandra))
REFEREE: K. Dwyer / LINESMAN: J. Wilkins and C Andrews		
1965 Group Trial Teams	**Group 10 Under 18**	**Group 14 Under 18**
Fullback	1. C. Harvey (Oberon)	1. I. Bell (Mudgee)
Wing	2. W. Priest (Orange CYMS)	2. M. Hawkins (Bara)
Centre	3. W. Rodwell (Cowra)	3. C. Nelson (Gil)
Centre	4. R. Noonan (Bath St Pats)	4. A. Brien (Coona)
Wing	5. R. Gill (Lith St Pats)	5. R. Gawthorne (Mudgee)
Five-Eighth	6. R. Priest Captain (Orange RSL)	6. R. Field (Coona)
Halfback	7. E. Sewell (Bath St Pats)	7. B. Horeman (Gil)
Lock	8. R. Thompson (Lith Workers)	8. A. Bull (Dunedoo)
Second row	9. R. Dove (Bath Rail)	9. M. Fish (Coona)
Second row	10. W. Gibbs (Oberon)	10. J. Palmer (Dunedoo)
Front row	11. J. Shawcroft (Lith Workers)	11. B. Wade (Dunedoo)
Hooker	12. K. Connors (Bath St Pats)	12. R. Clark (Dunedoo)
Front row	13. M. Buckmaster (Cowra)	13. R. Dow (Coona)
Reserve Back	14. B. Sharpe (Orange RSL)	14. B. Martin (Bara)
Reserve Forward	15. B. McGee (Bath High School).	15. M. Preston (Coolah).
REFEREE: A. Smith / LINESMAN: B. McWhirter and J. Wilkins.		

CURRY AND GOUGH IN WESTERN TEAM TO PLAY NORTH

Five Group XI players, including Athol Curry and Danny Gough of Dubbo Macquarie, have been included in the Western Division team to play North Coast in the opening round of the Country rugby league championships at Bathurst next Sunday.

April 1965

Curry a regular member of the Western Division team, takes up his usual position in the front row. Gough is a reserve back.

Other Group 11 players in the team are Bob Weir (Narromine) and John Hobby and Barry Beath of Eugowra.

The shock omission is Group 10 lock forward John Sinclair, who turned in a fine game on Sunday.

He was slightly over-shadowed by Hobby as a lock, but should have gained a berth in the forwards.

Barry Beath did not have a good game for Group 11 and must be considered lucky to gain a position ahead of Sinclair.

Curry did not have a good game on Sunday, but his reputation and size for a front row berth stuck to him.

Actually, there were no impressive front-row displays in the trials.

Gough, despite scoring three tries for Group 11 failed to impress the selectors enough to secure a berth in the top 15.

With more experience, improved handling and a few pointers on defence and positional play, he could develop into a really good winger.

Norm Brown, who did not play in the trials, has been selected as the team half-back and captain.

Brown was unfit for Sunday's trial and will represent Western Division provided he survives a fitness test on Tuesday.

Selectors did not name a replacement for Brown if he is not fit, but his place would probably be taken by Bob Kellam of Coonamble.

Group 14 hooker R. Dawson must be considered unlucky to lose the position to Group 10 hooker Ted Kelly.

Dawson out-hooked Kelly but apparently the latter's general play must have been more impressive.

Champion Oberon centre Trevor Grady has at last been given a chance to prove his ability.

Ted Ellery was a certain to gain selection on the wing following a spirited display for Group 10.

Gough was considered a likely partner for him, but the selectors decided to play Brian Harvey, who is more experienced.

The selection of Bob Weir in the centre was a "must" following his excellent display for Group 11.

Following selected WD Team to play North Coast next Sunday

FULL BACK: R. Lidden (Bathurst Railway).

WINGERS: B. Harvey (Oberon), E. Ellery (Lithgow Workers).

CENTRES: T. Grady (Oberon), R. Weir (Narromine).

HALVES: E. Harrison (Gil), N. Brown (Oberon).

LOCK: J. Hobby (Eugowra).

SECOND ROW: R. Heffernan (Bathurst Railway), B. Beath (Eugowra).

FRONT ROW: A. Curry (Dubbo Macquarie), J. Rush (Oberon).

HOOKER: E. Kelly (Orange CYMS).

RESERVE BACK: D. Gough (Dubbo Macquarie).

RESERVE FORWARD: K. King (Lithgow Workers).

Article from: The Dubbo Liberal, April 20, 1965. Republished courtesy of ACM/Dubbo Liberal.

WESTS TOO STRONG FOR NORTH COAST R.L.

BATHURST: Superior Western Division outclassed North Coast 33-11 at Bathurst Sports Ground in the opening round of the Caltex Country Rugby League Championship. Only a small crowd of 1500 saw Western Division mesmerise North Coast with speed, clever passing and backing up.

Article from: The Dubbo Daily Liberal, April 17, 1965. Republished courtesy of ACM/Dubbo Daily Liberal.

Changes in Western Division Team

Western Division has made three important changes in its team to play Newcastle in the Country Rugby League final at Parkes on Sunday.

May 1965

Keith Talbot, of Parkes, replaces Ted Ellery on the left wing, Jack Sinclair, of Lithgow Workman's, replaces John Rush in second row and Jock Schroder goes into the centres in place of Terry Grady.

Grady who was made reserve back, did not pass a fitness test on Tuesday and his place has been taken by Dubbo's Danny Gough.

The only other likely change in the team is in the front row. Barry Beath, who was injured last Sunday, is still suspect.

He passed a fitness test on Tuesday, but must come through another severe test this afternoon at Parkes.

If he fails the test, his place will probably be taken by the reserve forward, Keith King who is experienced as a front rower.

Western Division will be spearheaded by one of the best pack of forwards ever to represent it.

Lock John Hobby needs no introduction, he is, without doubt the best lock in the Western Division.

Second-rowers Jack Sinclair and Bob Heffernan, are tough men who have years of experience with leading Sydney clubs.

Athol Curry and Barry Beath in the front row have been regular members of Western Division for several seasons and are excellent footballers.

John Kelly is a capable hooker and a tigerish forward.

Newcastle will need a really powerful lineup to match these. The possible weakness in the team could be centre Jock Schroder who is playing out of position.

Schroder is the Oberon five-eighth and may find it strange in the centres.

Bob Weir, the Narromine coach, has been the driving force in the Western Division backline.

He will undoubtably be heavily marked on Sunday.

Halves Norm Brown and Earl Harrison have a good understanding and should keep their backline functioning freely.

Keith Talbot and Brian Harvey have speed and determination and have a good defence.

If either does not go well in the first half Danny Gough will replace them at half-time.

Ian Gunn a slightly built but impressive attacking player completes the line-up as fullback.

Wests have tough opposition in Newcastle.

Last year Newcastle decisively defeated Western Division in the final at Newcastle.

On Sunday the Western team is determined and confident it can reverse last year's defeat and regain the title.

Athol Curry

OUTSTANDING PERFORMANCE FOR WESTERN DIVISION IN THE FINAL AT PIONEER OVAL PARKES

Sunday May 9th

Despite an impressive performance in the Country R.L championship final yesterday Dubbo Macquarie rugby league front-rower Athol Curry surprisingly missed out on a berth in the New South Wales combined team to tour New Zealand.

In a thrilling match Newcastle defeated Western Division by 18 points to 12.

Article from: Dubbo Daily Liberal, May 10, 1965, Republished courtesy of ACM/Dubbo Daily Liberal.

KNOW YOUR SPORTSMEN

He is Group Hope

Bob Weir was chosen this week to captain Country Seconds in the annual rugby league fixture against City.

May 1966

Bob Weir

One of the best-known footballers in the country, Bob is making his fourth appearance with Country.

Last year, when he was selected in the New South Wales side, Bob reached the highest point in his career, a career that began to take shape when he made his first appearance with the Narromine first grade team in 1955 at the age of 18 years

In 11 years with the Narromine first grade team Bob has rarely missed a game except during the 1961 season when he was forced to stay out because of a back injury, but he came back the following year as good as ever.

In 1963 he took over as coach of the club and led the team to a place in the semi-finals each year since.

Last season the team reached the grand final only to be defeated by Eugowra.

Representative honours first came Bob's way in 1958 when he won selection in the Group 11 side and went on to represent Western Division.

In the same year he played against the touring English team at Orange.

He has been in the group team almost every year since then and has played for Western Division as well.

Bob is best known as a centre, yet his first big chance came as a lock, the position he occupied against the English team in 1958.

He first played for Country in 1962, when he was selected as a centre in the seconds.

Selected as captain of the Country Seconds in 1964

In 1965 he went into the firsts and went on to play for New South Wales.

He toured New Zealand with the country team last year and was one of the big successes of the tour, his success leading to state selection

In his seasons with Western Division, he has played against England, France and New Zealand.

Western Division were eliminated early from the country championships series this season and Bob had few chances to press his claims for selection in the country team, but the selectors have not forgotten his great games last season and have named him as captain of the 1966 seconds.

All football followers in the west will wish Bob well on Saturday.

Courtesy of: Macquarie Regional Library, Narromine (1966).

1965 Country Firsts Rugby League Team

Back Row: L. Moraschi, A. Thomson, P. Jackson (Coach), D. Schofield, D. Brown.

Middle Row: T. Sheppard (Trainer), B. Beath, M. Cooke, R. Ackland, A. Buman, W. Baker (Trainer).

Front Row: J. Sharpe (Manager), E. Harrison, C. Bryant, A. Summons (Captain), R. Weir, R. Horne, B. Maitland (Manager).

Results:
City Firsts defeated Country Firsts 32-2
Referee: Les Samuelson
Crowd: 31,721.

Courtesy of: Geoff Mann. Sports Journalist Dubbo.

Leo Nosworthy's Story

Leo Nosworthy started to play grade football for the Tigers in 1948 and by mid-June he was playing reserve grade and first grade at North Sydney Oval.

Leo played nine third grade, five reserve and six first grade games.
He continued to play first grade with the Tigers in 1949 and 1950.

In 1951 he accepted a captain/coaching role with Narromine and led them to the semi-finals.

Returning to the Tigers in 1952 Leo captained the team in his last season as a player with the Tigers. He played wing, centre, five eighth and lock in first grade and finished with 64 top grade games and 27 tries.

1953 Leo Heads Back to Narromine

Leo was back as captain coach of Narromine and stayed until 1958. During that period, he led Narromine to win three Group 11 premierships, 1953, 1955 and 1956.

In 1954 Narromine played Parkes in the Group 11 grand final only to be beaten by Parkes 11-5.

In fact, had they beaten Parkes he would have had four consecutive premiership wins with Narromine.

In 1957 Narromine came fifth on the points table and in the last round they defeated Dubbo to hold the Johnnie Walker Cup.

In 1958 they came fifth again and failed to reach the semi-finals.

Leo moved on to captain coach Dubbo Macquarie to three successive premierships in 1959, 1960, 1961.

In 1959 Dubbo Macquarie won the Clayton Cup as the best NSW country team.

He remained with Macquarie until 1962 when they were defeated by Wellington in the semi-final.

Wellington moved onto the grand-final and was defeated by Forbes.

Back to Balmain Tigers

Leo returned to Balmain in 1963 as a third-grade coach and was offered the reserve grade position in 1967 and coached the team to win the premiership.

1969 was to be his year at Balmain where he was appointed first grade coach and led them to grand-final victory defeating South Sydney 11-2.

Group 11 Greatest Coach

During his time in Western N S W, he played for Western Division against the touring Frenchmen at Forbes on the 30th May 1951 and at Parkes on the 20th July 1955.

His record speaks for itself with six Group 11 Premierships within a 10-year period and back to the Tigers to coach reserve grade and first grade teams to Premiership wins.

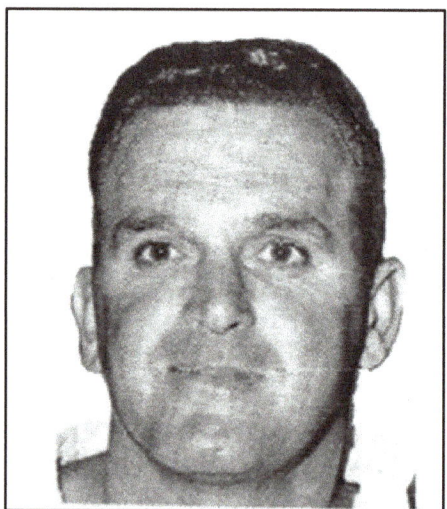

Leo Nosworthy

Article from: The Men of League. Republished courtesy of The Men of League.

1966 WESTERN DIVISION RUGBY LEAGUE
WESTERN DIVISION
v.
GREAT BRITAIN
PIONEER OVAL PARKES
SUNDAY, 17th JULY

Gates Open 8.30 a.m.
FIRST MATCH COMMENCES 10.00 A.M.
Main Game—Western Division v Great Britain
commences at 3.00 p.m.
ADMISSION: ADULTS 60c – CHILDREN 20c.

Aerial photograph of Pioneer Oval on the left.
Western Division v Great Britain, July 17th, 1966.

Article from: The Parkes Champion Post, July 18, 1966. Republished courtesy of ACM/Parkes Champion Post.

Kick Off & Game Started

Courtesy of: NSW Rugby League, The Rugby League News, July 1928

WELCOME GREAT BRITAIN

Parkes Champion Post, Friday, July 15, 1966

FIRST G.B.-W.D. CLASH IN GROUP X1 FOR 30 YEARS

A Rugby League tradition is developing when Great Britain plays Western Division within the boundaries of Group 11, the tourists play at Parkes, now the established "home" of major Rugby League in the West.

Article from: The Parkes Champion Post, July 15, 1966. Republished courtesy of ACM/The Parkes Champion Post.

Great Britain's Flying Winger Berwyn Jones

Jones, who has been playing league for only two years, in 1964 ran 10.3 seconds for 100 metres, the fourth fastest time ever recorded and better than the best Ken Irvine and Mike Cleary, Australia's league speedsters, can offer.

Berwyn Jones

Article from: The Parkes Champion Post, July 15, 1966. Republished courtesy of ACM/Parkes Champion Post.

1966 Great Britain Rugby League Touring Team

Back Row: Berwyn Jones, Arthur Keegan, Geoff Wriglesworth, Bill Burgess, Frank Myler, John Stopford, Carl Dooler, Paddy Armour (Masseur).

Third Row: Ian Brooke, Colin Clarke, Geoff Crewdson, Dave Robinson, Bill Romsey, Cliff Watson, Geoff Shelton, Alan Buckley.

Second Row: Terry Fegerty, Brian Edger, Ken Gowers (Vice-Captain), Mr. Will Speven (Manager), Harry Poole (Captain), Mr. Jack Erreck (Assistant Manager), Bill Bryant, John Meatle, Ken Roberts.

Front Row: Peter Flanagan, Willie Aspinall, Alan Hardisty, Tommy Bishop. Missing: Dan Watermark.

Courtesy of: NSW Rugby League, Rugby League News, July, 1966.

JONES IN
Greater Local Interest in WD-GB Clash

Parkes Rugby League centre Allan Jones has been brought into the Western Division team to play Great Britain at Pioneer Oval on Sunday.

July 1966

FIERY MATCH WATCHED BY 8,000 CROWD
Great Britain in Easy 38-11 Win

Allan Jones, Parkes (captain coach)

Article from: The Parkes Champion Post, July 15, 1966. Republished courtesy of ACM/Parkes Champion Post.

Two Parkes Juniors in Curtain Raiser

Two Parkes Juniors have been chosen in the Group 11 Junior Rugby League team to play Group 14 in the main early fixture before the England v. Western Division game at Parkes on Sunday.

They are Dennis Finn and Robin Houghton. Finn has been made captain of the side.
Group 11 Juniors were far superior to Group 14 side, winning by 20-2.

Article from: The Parkes Champion Post, July 18, 1966. Republished courtesy of ACM/Parkes Champion Post.

WILSON SCORES ONLY TRY FOR WEST R.L

A record crowd of more than 8,000 yesterday braved bitterly cold conditions to see Western Division rugby league team outclassed by the touring Great Britain side by 38 points to 11 at Parkes.

A plucky and determined Western Team thrilled the huge crowd with a never-say-die display against Great Britain forwards who coupled their weight superiority with a barrage of vicious head high tackling that angered the spectators.

July 1966

Great Britain scored eight tries to Western Division's one, flying winger Berwyn Jones dashing over for three plus a penalty try.

Most of the Western Division team, though soundly beaten, covered themselves with glory in their first ever "big" game.

Western Division's only try came just before half time when five-eighth Jock Schrader swung the ball across a ruck for Dubbo CYMS forward Mick Wilson to burst through a weak tackle by winger Sopford and go over in the corner.

Wilson was one of the best forwards. He turned in a vigorous display and at times had the defence stretched to the limit as he broke under head high tackles with determined running.

His front partner Bill Staines, also ran well and was not afraid to drive his shoulder into the giant Englishmen.

This pair did a lot of running from the rucks and made ground constantly.

Second rower John Brien though one of the smallest forwards on the ground was great in defence.

He continually brought the big men to ground with full-blooded tackles.

Lock Peter Sikora also showed out in defence and did a lot of running, once breaking clear away to reach the fullback before being brought to ground.

Malcolm Dawes played only in the first half and turned in a very competent display until slowed down by a heavy tackle that eventually caused him to be replaced.

Ted Kelly was beaten for the ball but did his share of hard work in the open.

Outstanding in the backs was Parkes centre Allan Jones, a last-minute selection in the team.

Jones was full of running and made several breaks through the defence to bring the crowd to its feet.

He tackled with great effect and was not overawed by the reputation of his opposing centres, test men Frank Myler and Geoff Shelton.

Condobolin halfback Les Hutchings had a great game.

He ran well, passed the ball cleanly and tackled with good effect throughout.

Gary Milsom showed great promise in attack running strongly whenever allowed to move at all, but he found the elusive Myler a hard man to pin down when the tourists had the ball.

Milsom could hardly be blamed for this, for Myler has proved more than a handful for our test men.

Winger Brian Harvey did not put a foot wrong all day.

He was very effectively bottled up, winger Stopford never allowing the speedy test player to move away, when he had the ball Harvey always did something constructive.

Fullback David Nicholls was very solid. He had a lot of work to do and was cool throughout under pressure.

The only blot on his game was a blatant tripping of Jones after the speedster had kicked through and was racing for the line.

This trip brought a heated protest from the tourists.

Nicholls scored eight of Western Division's points with four goals.

Jock Schrader had a quiet game in the pivot position, not once making a move to break through the defence but his passing and tackling were all solid as usual.

Mike Bryant had a luckless first half on the left wing and was replaced by Ken McKinnon at half time.

Bryant was marking the flying Jones and could not hold the speedster who scored two tries through a gaping hole in the defence in the first half.

McKinnon, coming on in the second half looked a better proposition and his determined running and sure tackling kept Jones busy for the remainder of the game.

Continued next page:

Article from: The Dubbo Daily Liberal, Monday, July 18, 1966. Republished courtesy of ACM/Dubbo Daily Liberal.

GREAT BRITAIN TOO CLASSY

Continued from previous page:

Ian Woodcock who replaced Malcom Dawes in the second row was too small and played too loosely.

He was always trying but was ineffective against the giant opposing players.

The tourists were too strong in every department.

They appeared to be playing well within themselves for most of the game and were never in danger of defeat.

The big forwards worked well together and went down the middle regularly with Bill Bryant and Geoff Crewdson.

Captain Harry Poole, though obviously not fully fit, showed clever use of the ball in sending his players through the gaps after standing up in tackles.

He slowed down in the second half and went out onto the wing.

Geoff Shelton left the field shortly after the interval with a gashed eye-brow and the tourists played the remainder of the match with only 12 men, though it made little difference.

They kept the ball moving about and had the defence running continually, but there were many periods of loose play during which they seemed to relax and lose concentration.

Vicious tackling marred their play throughout, many of the forwards seeming intent on crushing the Western Division players with brute force.

In the backs, half Carl Dooler and five-eighth Willy Aspinall did not impress.

Neither was very nippy and their defence was often suspect.

Myler, though he played in Saturday's test was by far the best of the backs.

He had little trouble creating overlaps for the men outside him and twice sent winger Jones flying down the touchline for tries.

Jones showed great speed, scoring two tries in the first half and adding two more in the second.

Both his second half tries were scored with surprise ease.

The first came when Jones raced through to intercept and trot away for a try under the posts and the second was a penalty try awarded after McKinnon tackled Jones as the two raced for the ball after a kick through.

There was no doubt that Jones would have scored and the referee had no hesitation in awarding the try.

Great Britain fullback Ken Gowers showed his class with some blistering runs in which he beat tackler after tackler.

Gower kicked six goals several from wide out and must be very unlucky to be out of the test side.

Great Britain's 38 points came from:
Tries by B. Jones (4), W. Bryant (2), C. Dooler and W. Aspinall. Six goals by K. Gowers and one by J. Stopford.

Western Division: M. Wilson scored a try and D. Nicholls kicked four goals.

Gate takings totalled $3,759, a record for the Division.

Article from: The Dubbo Daily Liberal, Monday, July 18, 1966. Republished courtesy of ACM/Dubbo Daily Liberal.

1966 Western Division Team

Fullback: D. Nichols (Bathurst), winger: B Harvey (Oberon), winger: M. Bryant (Gilgandra), centre: A. Jones (Parkes), centre: G. Milsom (Coonabarabran),
five-eighth: J. Schrader Captain (Oberon), halfback: L. Hutchings (Condobolin),
forwards: P. Sikora (Bathurst), J. Brien (Oberon), M. Dawes (Narromine), B. Staines (Lithgow), M. Wilson (Dubbo), T. Kelly (Orange).

Reserves: K. McKinnon (Forbes), L. Woodcock (Goodooga).

Great Britain defeated Western Division: 38-11

TRIALS AT WELLINGTON
GROUP 11 WINS THREE STRAIGHT

Group 11 emerged clear winners in the Rugby League round robin group trials played in Wellington on Sunday.

April 1969

Group gets seven in

Group 11 has gained seven representatives in the Western Division team to play Southern Division in Orange next Sunday.

Dubbo CYMS hooker, Kel Brown has been rewarded for his consistent play by gaining the hooking spot in the Western Division team.

The team is:

Fullback: Bob Priest (Orange Ex-Services)

Wings: Terry Scurfield (Parkes)
Greg Hanson: (Bathurst Railway)

Centres: Bob Weir (Narromine)
Mike Francisco (Cobar)

Five-Eighth: Ken Rodwell (Parkes)

Half-Back: Les Hutchings (Condobolin)

Lock: Allan Jones (Parkes)

Second Row: John Gahan (Orange CYMS)
Gary Harvey (Oberon)

Front Row: Brian Eakin (Canowindra)
Greg Worrell (Baradine)

Hooker: Kel Brown (Dubbo CYMS).

Reserve Back: Greg Milsom (Coonabarabran)
Reserve Forward: Earl Elwell (Wellington).

Group 11 played three matches and won each convincingly – they beat Group 15: 22-2, Group 14: 15-5 and Group 10: 14-6.

Although there were some bright patches, the standard of play generally was dull.

The highlight of the day came during the Group 11 and Group 14 match, when a brawl broke out among the crowd.

The free for all, involving 30 people, erupted on the hill.

In this fracas a youth was punched to the ground and kicked on the sideline.

Another youth was chased down the length of the field. He chose to make his escape along the length of the field of play and referee Terry Walters had to stop the game for two minutes while the fracas sorted itself out.

This diversion brought roars from the crowd and to many was probably the most stimulating moment of the day.

The day started off with Group 11 playing Group 15, a match in which Group 11 was superior in all departments.

Parkes winger, Terry Scurfield, scored two fine tries and his team-mate, Ken Rodwell, who had a wonderful day, kicked five goals.

Rodwell scored 30 points in three games a remarkable average of 10 points a game.

Other scorers for Group 11 in the first game were Les Hutchings and Allan Jones both with tries.

Kelly on the burst

Group 11 front rower, Tony Kelly, makes an attempt to burst out of Group 14 front rower, Don Martin's tackle. Group 11's Captain, Les Hutchings, is moving up to take a pass.

Article from: The Dubbo Daily Liberal, April 8, 1969. Republished courtesy of ACM/Dubbo Daily Liberal.

1969 Western Division Rugby League Team

Back Row: M. Nash (Manager), T. Scurfield, D. Milsom, R. Weir, G. Worrell, J. Harvey, E. Eakin and Trainer.
Middle Row: D. Abbot, J. Ganhan, M. Francisco, K. Brown, A. Jones, G. Hanson L. Hutchings, R. Priest.
Front Row: K. Rodwell.

Courtesy of: John Collins, Crowing of The Roosters, Mick Francisco.

1969 WESTERN DIVISION v SOUTHERN DIVISION
Played at Wade Park, Orange on 13th April, 1969
Referee: Mr. Graham Barby of Leeton.
Touch Judges: Messrs. M. Langham and B. Evers (Orange).

WESTERN DIVISION	SOUTHERN DIVISION
FULLBACK:	**FULLBACK:**
R. Priest (Orange Ex- Services).	I. Rigby (Nowra Warriors).
THREE-QUARTERS:	**THREE-QUARTERS:**
T. Scurfield (Parkes), R. Weir (Narromine),	R. Stewart (Gerringong), G. Wilkinson (Gosford),
M. Francisco (Cobar), G. Hanson (Bathurst Railway).	G. Cuthbert (Albion Park), T. Goovan (Gosford).
FIVE EIGHTH:	**FIVE-EIGHTH:**
K. Rodwell (Parkes).	C. Bagnall (Nowra Warriors).
HALF-BACK:	**HALF-BACK:**
L. Hutchings (Condobolin).	B. Poland (Bowral).
FORWARDS:	**FORWARDS:**
A. Jones (Parkes), J. Gahan (Orange CYMS),	G. Morris (Gosford), J. Cole (Mittagong),
J. Harvey (Oberon), B. Eakin (Canowindra),	R. Urquhart (Gosford), P. Quinn, Captain (Nowra),
K. Brown (Dubbo CYMS), G. Worrell (Baradine).	R. Corkery (Campbelltown), A. Haertsch (Bowral).
REPLACEMENTS:	**REPLACEMENTS:**
G. Milsom (Coonabarabran), E. Elwell (Wellington).	P. McGurran (Oakdale), W. Paillas (Shellharbour).

Southern Division defeated Western Division 28-7

Southern Division: Tries R. Stewart, J. Cole, R. Urquhart, B. Poland, G. Morris, A. Haertsch; Goals P. Quinn (4); Field Goal I. Rigby.
Western Division: Try K. Rodwell; Goals K. Rodwell (2).

Courtesy of: Geoff Mann, Sports Journalist, Dubbo.

May 16, 1970

Once again, we extend a cordial welcome to the Country teams here for the annual challenge to the pick of City teams.

This season a lot is expected from the two Country teams. They have been carefully chosen after an exhaustive series of trials in some cases as old as the season itself.

Crowd: 35,794

Results:

City Firsts 22 defeated Country Firsts 18
Referee: Mr. Don Lancashire.

City Seconds 24 defeated Country Seconds 13
Referee: B. Chapman.

Courtesy of: NSW Rugby League, The Rugby League News, May, 1970.

1970 Country Firsts Team v Sydney Firsts

Back Row: Ken Thompson, Bruce Stewart. Arthur Summons (Coach), Lionel Summons, John Cootes.

Middle Row: Paul Quinn, Kel Brown, Terry Pannowitz, Dennis Mount,

Front Row: Graham Lye, Laurie Wakefield, John Raper (Captain), Les Hutchings, Dave Grimmond.

Courtesy of: NSW Rugby League, The Rugby League News, May, 1970.

1970 Country Seconds Team v Sydney Seconds

Back Row: Terry McGurren (Trainer), Warren Kimberley (Manager), Frank Cleary, Michael Trypas, Dick Jeffery, Steve Dedes, Graham Kennedy (Coach), Les Griffin (Trainer).

Middle Row: Les McIntyre (Manager), Terry Scurfield, Eric Archer, Brian Bolte, Brian Sullivan, Karl Hutchinson, John Cole.

Front Row: Peter Cootes, Doug Crampton, Brian Burke, Paul Hassab (Captain), Glen Stewart, Peter Broad, Harry Cameron.

Courtesy of: NSW Rugby League, The Rugby League News, June, 1970.

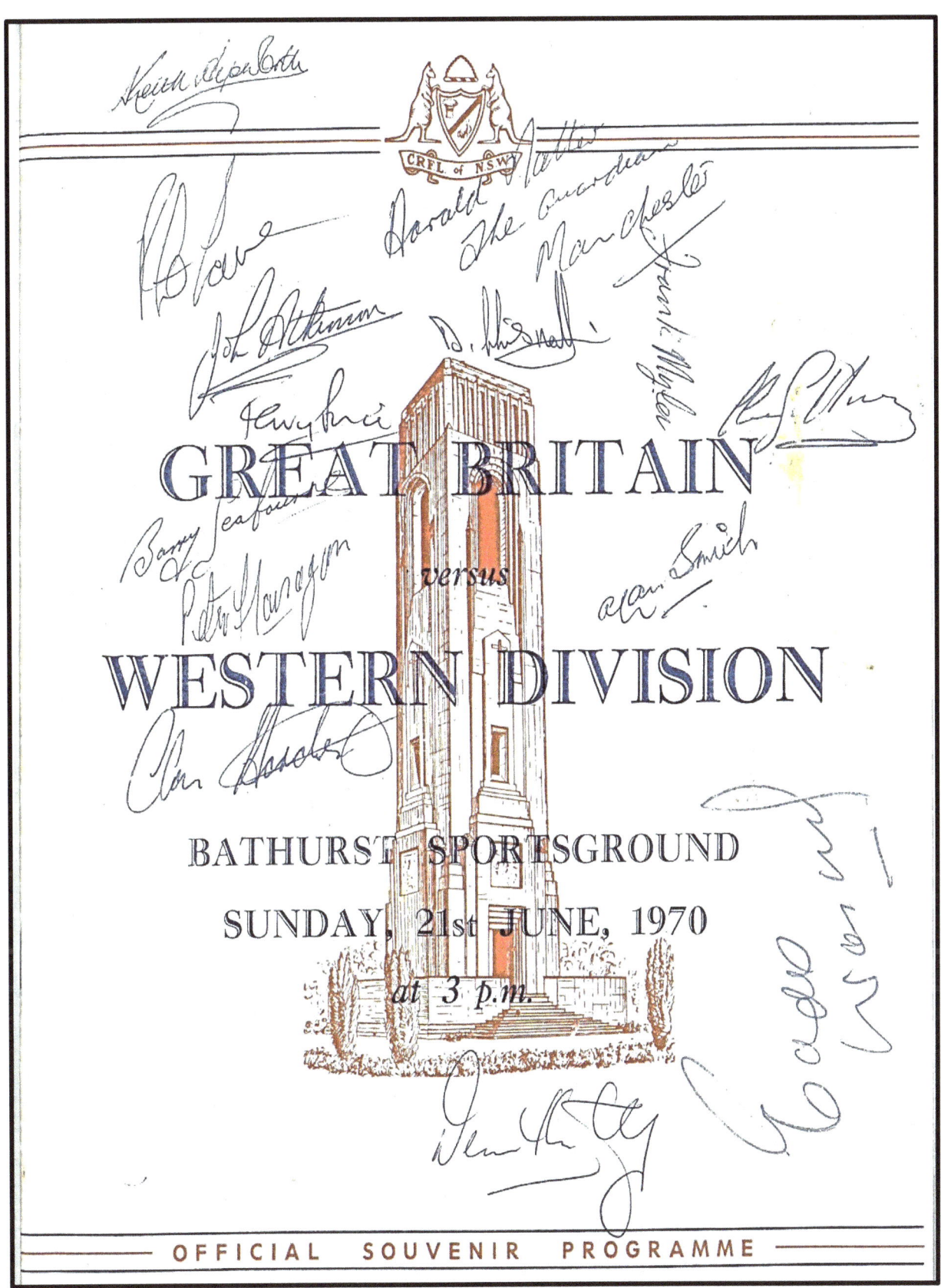

1970 Great Britain Rugby League Touring Team

Front Row: Ray Dutton, Dennis Hartley, John Harding, (manager), Frank Myler (captain), John Whiteley, (assistant manager), Phill Lowe, Cliff Watson.
Second Row: David Chisnell, Bob Irving, Clive Sullivan, Tony Fisher, Mike Shoebottom, Sid Hines.
Third Row: Barry Seabourne, Keith Hepworth, John Ward, Alan Hardisty, Derek Edwards, Peter Flanagan, Roger Millward.
Back Row: Malcolm Reilly, Dave Robinson, Alan Smith, Terry Price, John Atkinson, Doug Laughton, Jim Thompson, Chris Hesketh.
Courtesy of: NSW Rugby League. The Rugby League News June 1970.

Raid on the Parkes Back-line

Parramatta District Club, continuing its' big buying "spree" brought its recent acquisitions of young players from the Country to four with signing this week of two from Parkes Club: fullback Laurie Wakefield and winger Terry Scurfield.

Parkes bright backline has now supplied three players to Sydney clubs this season, the first transfer that of halfback and goalkicker John Bonham to Newtown.

Courtesy of: NSW Rugby League, The Rugby League News, June, 1970.

Laurie Wakefield   Terry Scurfield

N.S.W. Representatives:

Left: Laurie Wakefield (fullback) from Parkes and Les Hutchings (half-back) from Condobolin who were chosen to represent N.S.W.

They are pictured with Country Rugby League Secretary Mr. John O'Toole.

Courtesy of: Dubbo CYMS Old Boys, Official Souvenir Program.

1970 Great Britain v Western Division

WESTERN DIVISION

PROGRAMME

STARTING 3.00 P.M.

GREAT BRITAIN
(Colours: White, with Red and Blue V)

Team to be chosen from the following:

Full-Backs:
1. D. EDWARDS   2. T. PRICE   3. R. DUTTON

Wingers:
4. A. SMITH   5. J. ATKINSON   6. C. SULLIVAN

Centres:
7. S. HYNES   8. F. MYLER (Capt.)   9. C. HESKETH

Five-Eighths:
10. M. SCHOEBOTTOM   11. A. HARDISTY   14. R. MILLWARD

Half-Backs:
12. B. SEABOURNE   13. K. HEPWORTH

Lock Forwards:
25. M. REILLY   26. C. LAUGHTON

Second Row:
21. J. THOMPSON   22. D. ROBINSON   23. P. LOWE   24. R. IRVING

Front Row:
15. D. CHISNALL   16. C. WATSON   17. J. WARD   18. D. HARTLEY

Hookers:
19. P. FLANAGAN   20. A. FISHER

Manager: MR. J. HARDING
Assistant Manager and Coach: MR. J. WHITELY

WESTERN DIVISION
Colours: Green with Double White V)

Full-Back:
1. LAURIE WAKEFIELD (Parkes)

Wingers:
2. JOHN JEFFREY (Bathurst)   5. TERRY SCURFIELD (Parkes)

Centres:
4. PETER KENNEDY (Forbes)   3. NOEL HURFORD (Orange)

Five-Eighth:
6. BRUCE FINN (Parkes)

Half-Back:
7. LES HUTCHINGS (Parkes), Captain

Forwards:
8. CHRIS RECKIN (Bathurst)
9. ALLAN JONES (Parkes)   10. BRIAN AITCHESON (Coonamble)
11. BILL CAIN (Cowra)   12. GREG HAY (Canowindra)
13. KEL BROWN (Dubbo)

Reserves: 14. BOB PRIEST (Orange)   15. ERIC ELWELL (Wellington)

Coach: DON LEE (Nyngan)   Manager: W. MUNRO (Mudgee)

Referee: Tom Gustard (Newcastle)
Touch Judges: John Fitzpatric (Blue Flag), Vince Moase (Red Flag).
Ball Boys: Michael Single, Norman Matheson, Garry Dennis, Ian Hoppe.

Note the error in programme. Western Division Team player: 7, Les Hutchings, Condobolin.

Courtesy of: Dubbo CYMS Old Boys. Official Souvenir Programme.

Castleford Trio Coming Here

English League writers see the pictured pack of the scrum trio from Castleford (Yorkshire) club playing an important part of the matches on the coming tour.

For brilliant five-eighth Hardisty, it will be a second Australian tour. He was a star in the 1962 tests.

Alan Hardisty

Keith Hepworth

Malcom Reilly

Hepworth has been Hardisty's half-back partner for several years "at home". Lock-forward Reilly, is one of the big "hopes" of the tour.

The trio were among Castleford's five who were in the team that retained the Challenge Cup defeating Wigan 7-2 in the presence of 100,000 spectators at Wembley May 9, 1970.

Courtesy of: NSW Rugby League, The Rugby League News, June, 1970.

PEN PROFILES OF WESTERN DIVISION TEAM

LAURIE WAKEFIELD (Parkes). Fullback. Age 22. Former Parkes junior player with great future. Brilliant attacking player. Gained position for both Country Firsts and State teams this year.

JOHN JEFFREY (Bathurst Railway). Left wing. Age 21. Product of Bathurst St. Patrick's School. Played his senior football with Bathurst Railway and selected for Group 10 and Western Division for the first time this season. Extremely fast and elusive.

TERRY SCURFIELD (Parkes). Right wing. Age 21, played his early football with Forbes Marist Brothers before transferring to Parkes in 1969 and represented Western Division same year. A ball-and-all tackler, equally at ease in the centres. Played for Country this season.

PETER KENNEDY (Forbes). Age 23, 14 stone centre. Has represented Group 11 for the past two seasons. Very strong and hard running centre.

NOEL HURFORD (Orange Ex Services). Outside centre. Age 23. Graduated through Ex-Services junior teams to become Group 10 best player, 1969. Hard running centre and experienced goal kicker.

BRUCE FINN (Parkes). Five-eighth. Age 20, Parkes junior whose greatest attribute is a solid defence. First representative game.

LES HUTCHINGS (Condobolin). Half-back. Age 27. Tough pivot and captain-coach of Condobolin for third year. Represented Country Firsts in 1968, 1969. Key player in the side. Gained both Country Firsts and State half-back position this year.

CHRIS RECKIN (Bathurst Railway). Lock. Age 26. Former South Sydney President's Cup player. Represented Group 10 and Western Division 1968 and 1969. Tireless tackler and strong running ball carrier.

ALLAN JONES (Parkes). Left second row. Age 29, Western Division representative forward for the past five years. Regarded as the best 80 minutes footballer ever to play in the West. He has previously played against English Touring side, in 1966.

BRIAN AITCHESON (Coonamble). Right second row. Age 22. Former Inverell junior before joining Newtown. Transferred to Coonamble this year. Hard cover defender.

BILL CAIN (Cowra). Left prop. Age 26. Widely experienced most of his football forward. Played most of his football with North Sydney apart from two seasons in England. First year as a Western representative.

GREG HAY (Canowindra). Right prop. Age 27. Captain and coach of country teams for six years. Represented Riverina 1968 and 1969 and presently coaching Canowindra. Excellent ball distributor.

KEL BROWN (Dubbo CYMS). Hooker. Age 23. Leading hooker in Group 11. 1969, represented Western Division last year and besides winning possession proved a willing worker in the open. Represented Country Firsts and considered very unlucky to miss State selection.

BOB PRIEST (Orange Ex Services). Replacement back. Age 22. Product of Ex Services juniors. Versatile in any position in the three-quarter line fullback. Clever field goal and place kicker. Represented Western Division, 1969.

ERIC ELWELL (Welllington). Replacement forward. Age 25. Worthy substitute, who is at home anywhere in the pack.

WESTERN DIVISION PERSONALITIES

Pictured above left to right: Don Lee (Nyngan Coach), Bob Priest (Orange Outside Centre) and Chris Reckin (Bathurst, Lock Forward).

Courtesy of: Dubbo CYMS Old Boys, Official Souvenir Programme.

WALLOPING FOR WESTERN DIVISION SCURFIELD SHOWS OUT

BATHURST, Monday: England continued on her merry way by inflicting a 40-11 thrashing over Western Division in one-sided representative Rugby League fixture here yesterday.

June 1970

England were too big, too fast and too strong for Western Division who, apart from a golden 15-minute period in the second half, did not look like getting into the game.

The English team which ran on contained four players from the second Test team which gave Australia a hiding on Saturday.

The four were wingers Alan Smith and John Atkinson, second rower Jim Thompson and prop Dennis Hartley.

In addition, bogey man Cliff Watson came onto the field late in the second half as a reserve.

Although badly beaten there were two highlights from a Western Division point of view.

First there were three great tries to Parkes winger Terry Scurfield who shaded his Test rival Alan Smith on the day.

The first came at the start of the game when he cleverly snatched the ball off centre Peter Kennedy who had made a good break.

The second came at the start of the second half when he intercepted the ball on his own line and raced 90 yards to score in the corner.

The third came after the only real team effort of the day for Western Division when eight players handled before Scurfield dived over.

Scurfield is at present negotiating with Parramatta in Sydney for a transfer from his Parkes Club.

However, on his performance yesterday any chance of a light fee being placed on him by Parkes has gone by the wayside.

To score three tries in a game is a good effort, but it is a great one to score three against a touring side.

The other highlight for Western Division was the showing of CYMS hooker Kel Brown.

Brown broke even 16-all in the scrums against his highly experienced rival Peter "Flash" Flanagan

Flanagan paid his rival a high compliment after the game saying "the lad showed good promise".

"Once he learns to relax instead of pushing all the time he'll be a good rake," Flanagan said.

"He wastes a bit of energy pushing and pulling all the time, but he's got promise" the English hooker added.

"He didn't have anything in the front row helping him, so I think he's Sydney bound," Flanagan concluded.

England led 28-3 at half time and seemed set for a cricket score, but Scurfield's two tries brought a bit of interest back into the game.

For England the outstanding player on the field was young second rower Phil Lowe.

Western five-eighth, Bruce Finn (Parkes) and forwards, Bill Cain (Cowra) and Brian Aitcheson (Coonamble) were the best seen in defence.

Great Britain front rowers, Dave Chisnall, Dennis Hartley and 'Flash' Flannagan did rugged defence work.

All in all it was an entertaining game and the Englishmen gave the crowd of over 4,000 (gate $2,500) a feast of football.

SCORES:

England: 40 (J. Atkinson 2, P. Lowe 2, A. Hardisty 2, T. Smith, B. Seabourne, R. Irving, T. Price tries. Price 5 goals.) defeated

Western Division: 11 (T. Scurfield 3 tries, Hurford goal.)

Terry Scurfield

Article from: The Dubbo Daily Liberal, Monday, June 22, 1970. Republished courtesy of ACM/Dubbo Daily Liberal.

1970 Great Britain Western Division Action Shots

Above left: "Scurge of the West" that is what the opposition must have thought of him to be giant Great Britain lock, Phil Lowe, flings a one-handed pass away as Bill Cain ineffectually hangs onto his jersey. Chris Reckin is in the background.

Above right: Western star, Terry Scurfield fends off a Great Britain player with one hand after sending centre Clive Sullivan sprawling in his path in the match at the Bathurst sports ground yesterday.

Article from: The Western Advocate, June 22, 1970. Republished courtesy of ACM/Western Advocate.

LOOK AT LEAGUE
WITH JOHN BEGG

June 1970

Kel Brown

Down at Bathurst on Sunday night, I ran into the dean of English Rugby League commentators (Eddie Waring). Eddie is still sprightly as ever and still busting with confidence about England's prospects in the third test.

Eddie was critical of the way the English tour was set up and said the Englishmen should have come straight to Sydney and then gone to Queensland.

"It gave them a false sense of security and besides they hadn't recovered from travelling," Eddie said.

"Alan Smith told me he was still feeling the effects of the trip a week after they arrived" he added.

I hastened to inform the gentleman that the test was played three weeks later but he pressed on regardless.

"We can win it and we will win it—forget the first test as we weren't right," quoted the English scribe.

What with Jackson, Huddart, Watson and then Waring on my hammer it just wasn't my weekend.

A man who plugs around each week without getting the credit he deserves is CYMS hooker Kel Brown.

Brown's hooking record in the past six months has been very good yet it has passed virtually unnoticed by Sydney scribes.

Brown in the last six months has hooked against the cream of the world's hookers.

He has raked against the New Zealand hooker whom he beat 16-10 and the English hooker whom he drew 16 all with.

He hooked against the Australian rake Walters in the City-Country match and was beaten 14-12.

He should have beaten Walters, because he had the ball in the second row on numerous occasions, but the Country pack was pushed off it.

It's a terrific effort for a hooker without much experience and I think Kel Brown deserves' credit for it.

Article from: The Dubbo Daily Liberal, Tuesday, June 23, 1970. Republished courtesy of ACM/Dubbo Daily Liberal.

HUTCHINGS OFF TO CANTERBURY BUT FEE IS SECRET

CONDOBOLIN, Tuesday, Condobolin Rugby League committee have refused to disclose the transfer fee placed on captain-coach (Les Hutchings).

June 1970

Hutchings will join the Sydney Canterbury Club as replacement for suspended half-back Terry Reynolds.

The Condobolin committee last night met to discuss the transfer fee to be placed on Hutchings.

Condobolin committee-man (Fred Schneider) said this morning that the fee would not be disclosed by the committee.

"We discussed it in full last night and the fee was decided to be fixed by negotiation between Condobolin and Canterbury," he said.

"It was a committee decision to do things this way and not disclose the fee," he added.

Hutchings, the NSW and Western Division representative, has had overtures from Sydney clubs but last night decided to join Canterbury.

He is the centre of interest from Sydney clubs after replacing Billy Smith from the half-back position in the NSW team.

Canterbury came into proceedings after suspending regular half Terry Reynolds from the team for refusing to have his hair cut.

Hutchings, move has also left Condobolin in a quandary for a captain-coach for the remaining games of the season.

Condobolin are at present grimly hanging on to third place on the competition ladder with Wellington and Forbes.

However, it is expected that president (Neville Bell) and lock Nev Morris will run the team until a suitable replacement can be found.

Bell and Morris ran Condobolin when Hutchings was involved in representative fixtures with great success.

Hutchings, should come right into calculations for a third test spot if Billy Smith pulls out.

Smith injured rib cartilages in a club game last weekend and Hutchings seems the logical replacement if Smith is forced out.

Happy Night for New State Halfback

Les Hutchings, from Condobolin, the new State halfback, is congratulated by managing director of Caltex Oil (Aust.) Pty. Ltd, Mr. Dudley Braham, after being presented with the Country League's "Player of the Year" award at Caltex House.

On the left of the picture are Country Firsts' skipper, Johnny Raper and the coach, Arthur Summons.

Article from: The Dubbo Daily Liberal, Tuesday, June 23, 1970. Republished courtesy of ACM/Dubbo Daily Liberal.

1970 Combined Country Team Zealand Tour

Back Row: S. Dedes, K. Hutchinson, D. Mount, L. Simmons, T. Scurfield, A Summons (Coach).

Middle Row: G. Sloggett (Manager), K. Thompson, R. Jeffery, H. Cameron, T. Pannowitz, K. Walsh (Manager).

Front Row: G. Lye, K. Brown, L. Wakefield, J. Raper (Captain), L. Hutchings, D. Crampton, G. Stewart.

Absent: P. Quinn, D. Grimmond.

Courtesy of: NSW Rugby League, The Rugby League News, June, 1970.

1970 NSW Star Studded Rugby League Team

Back Row: Dave Grimmond (Queanbeyan), Jim Morgan (Souths), John Wittenburg (St George), Arthur Beeston (Balmain).

Third Row: John McDonald (Manly), Ron Cootes (Souths), Harry Bath (St George-Coach), Bob McCarthy (Souths), John Cootes (Newcastle).

Second Row: Laurie Wakefield (Parkes), John Brass (Easts), John King (St George), Ron Costello (Canterbury), Elwyn Walters (Souths), Les Hutchings (Condobolin).

Front Row: Monty Porter (Manager), Graeme Langlands (St George), John Raper (St George), Phil Hawthorne (St George), Fr ank Farrington (Manager).

Laurie Wakefield

Les Hutchings

Above right: Laurie Wakefield and Les Hutchings both Group XI representative players.

Courtesy of: Parkes Shire Library. Parkes One Hundred Years of Local Government.

REUNION DAY FOR DICK HUDDART

It was a day of reunions in Bathurst yesterday for the touring English Rugby League team.

Macquarie captain-coach (Dick Huddart) had an impromptu reunion with his old teammates in the Bathurst Leagues Club after the match.

Huddart toured on the 1958 and 1962 Australian tours joining the St. George Club in 1964.

He played for the St. Helen's Club in England and two of his teammates were Frank Myer, the English captain on the present tour and big prop Cliff Watson.

One of the highlights of yesterday's game was the performance of Phil Lowe, the young English second rower.

Lowe, the 20 year old from Hull Kingston Rovers, is being likened to Huddart at his peak.

He is built on similar lines to Huddart and runs very fast when taking the ball on the burst.

He is built on similar lines to Huddart and runs very fast when taking the ball on the burst.

Huddart spent the day with the English team and helped them out in the dressing room before and after the match.

Huddart was also a touring teammate of the English assistant manager and coach (John Whiteley).

"It was terrific to see the chaps again and we had a long discussion over old times," Huddart said.

"They are a good side and I think they'll take home the Ashes to England," he added.

"They have a good balance in forwards and backs and they are very confident now," Huddart said.

Huddart will be renewing further aquaintances in September when he will return to England for about five months.

Article from: The Dubbo Daily Liberal, Monday, June 22, 1970. Republished courtesy of ACM/Dubbo Daily Liberal.

1971 Country Seconds Rugby League Team

Back Row: T. Stevens, G. Foster, S. Day, G. Kennedy (Coach), M. Otton, W. Hetherington, R. McDermott,

Middle Row: G. Griffin (Trainer), R. McCullock, W. Randell, B. Sullivan, T. Andrews, W. Shirlaw, G. Dowing, L. Hennessy (Trainer).

Front Row: S. Sercombe (Manager), G. Hellyar, J. Adamson, R. Priest (Captain), K. Orr, J. Walsh, N. Gale (Manager

Results:
Crowd: 35,790
City Seconds 19 defeated Country Seconds 5.
Referee: B. Chapman.

Courtesy of: The Rugby League News, May, 1970.

Best group side ever

March 1972

Group 11 Rugby League coach Allan Jones believes Sunday's team is the best the group has ever fielded.

Group 11 will meet Group 14 in the main Western Division trial at No. 1 Oval Dubbo.

Jones said the backline was one of the best he had been given to coach.

"There are loads of experience in the team and if they all pull their weight they should win," Jones said.

"We'll be having a talk tomorrow night when the team gets together and I'll be concentrating on getting the forwards working together.

We'll have two runs on Saturday-one about 7am and the other later in the afternoon. I think the backline is an excellent one very experienced throughout."

Group 14 secretary Mr. Paul Devoy says the team is the strongest the Group could put on the field. Their officials are confident that hooker Mat Day of Mudgee, halfback Ron Gallagher and five-eighth Brian Conroy can win places in the Western Division trials at Orange on Sunday week.

Rival halfbacks Ken McMullen and Gallagher played at the same time at Eastern Suburbs.

The two senior trials should be a crowd pleasing fixtures.

Players in these four teams know they are not assured of places in the following week's trial. The selection can go outside the teams on Sunday if they feel the talent for various positions is not strong.

However, McMullen, McCulla, Bonus and Kennedy are an experienced combination.

Lock forward Colin Parkes has a big chance to win representative honours at divisional level for the first time and club mates Les Bourke and Graham Negline are strong candidates.

New Zealand international Bob Irvine will lead Group 15 against Group 10.

Group 10's team contains many surprises: They have a young backline but some experienced forwards.

Coach Jones Tips Victory

Allan Jones

Former North Sydney halfback Bob Camden leads the Group 10 team with last year's Country representative Bob Priest at five-eighth.

Group 10 should win this match.

The junior matches, as usual, will provide Rugby League at its best.

Some of the players to watch are:

Group 14 five-eighth J. Morrisey from Gulgong.

Group 11 players J. Hall from Trundle, Brad Ryan from Narromine, Gary Lasker of Macquarie and the five-eighth Neil Musgrove.

Group 10 players five-eighth Tony Trudgett, of Oberon, a son of former coach Rob Trudgett, and lock forward Ian Webber.

Gates will open on Saturday between 3pm and 7pm so that patrons can park their cars overnight. Owners should park their cars as close as possible to each other. The gates will be locked at 7pm.

The gates on Sunday will not be opened until 9am when the groundkeepers arrive from Parkes.

Okeydokey, Landscapes

Article from: The Daily Liberal, Thursday, March 30, 1972. Republished courtesy of ACM/Dubbo Daily Liberal.

1972 Group 15 Rugby League Team

Back Row: George Rose, Bob Clark, John Stephens, Paul Dowton, John 'Burra' Lovett (Manager) Geoff Thorne, Bob Irvine, Alan Hamilton, Jim Goonrey, Trevor Demmery.

Front Row: Denis Smith (President), Richard Davis, Lloyd Beetson, Greg McMullen, Ray Hamilton, Brain Heap, Tony McKenzie, Trapper Jeffery (Trainer).

Courtesy of: John Collins, The Crowing of The Roosters, Tony McKenzie.

1972 Inter Group Trials First Grade Teams

GROUP 14 Colours: Maroon and Gold
FULLBACK: (1) R. Lane (Mudgee).
THREE QUARTERS: (2) C. Sephton (Coonamble) (5) S. Chapman (Dunedoo), (3) T.Wotton (Coonabarabran), (4) R. Cover (Mudgee).
FIVE-EIGHTH: (6) B. Contoy (Mudgee).
HALFBACK: (7) R. Gallagher (Dunedoo), Captain.
FORWARDS: (8) G. Mukn (Mudgee), (9) L. Graham (Dunedoo), (10) D. Milsom (Coonabarabran), (11) K. Campbell (Baradine) Vice-Captain, (13) D. Abbott (Coolah) (12) M. Day (Mudgee).

REPLACEMENTS:
(14) B. Jackson (Coonamble), (15) W. Martin(Dunedoo).
COACH: R. Gallagher (Dunedoo).

GROUP 10 Colours: Sky Blue
FULLBACK: (1) W. Kifly (Cowra).
THREE QUARTERS: (2) P. Hope (Bath Railway), (5) J. Chapman (Bath. St. Pats), (3) N. Kelly (Oberon), (4) D. Peacock (Lithgow Workers).
FIVE-EIGHTH: (6) R. Priest (Orange CYMS).
HALFBACK: (7) R. Camden (Cowra), Captain-Coach.
FORWARDS: (8) J. Earsman (Orange Ex-Services), (9) C. Reekin (Bath Railway), (10) R. Chashen (Bath Charleston), (11) J. Rush (Oberon) Vice-Captain, (13) G. Fearnley (Cowra), (12) W Rose (Bath Railway).

REPLACEMENTS:
(14) M. Smith (Orange CYMS), (15) L. Raleigh (Portland).

GROUP 11 Colours: Red and Black
FULLBACK: (1) P. Clyburn (Conawindra).
THREE QUARTERS: (2) E. Clyburn (Canowindra), (5) R. Jayet (Parkes), (3) J. Bonus (Parkes), (4) P. Kennedy (Forbes).
FIVE-EIGHTH: (6) R.McCulla (Canowindra).
HALFBACK: (7) K. McMullen (Dubbo CYMS), Captain.
FORWARDS: (8) C. Parkes (Dubbo CYMS), (9) K. Constable (Forbes), (10) D. O'Callaghan (Condo), (11) L. Bourke (Dubbo CYMS), (13) E. Elwell (Wellington) Vice Captain, (12) G.Negline (Dubbo CYMS).
REPLACEMENTS:
(14) P. Walkom (CYMS), (15) P. Smith (Forbes).
COACH: Allan Jones (Parkes).

GROUP 15 Colours: Black and White
FULLBACK: (1) D. Downton (Nyngan).
THREE QUARTERS: (2) T. Deniery (Bourke), (5) G. Stemiens (Cobar), (3) A. Hamilton (Bourke), (4) G. Thorne (Walgett).
FIVE-EIGHTH: (6) B. Ziebell (Nyngan).
HALFBACK: (7) R. Irvine (Walgett), Captain.
FORWARDS: (8) A. McKenzie (Walgett), (9) B. Heap (Cobar), (10) R. Davis (Nyngan), (11) R. Hamilton (Cobar), (13) L. Beetson (Brewarrina) Vice Captain, (12) G. McMullen (Brewarrina).
REPLACEMENTS:
(14) G. Greer (Cobar), (15) J. Goonery (Cobar).
COACH: R. Irvine (Walgett).

Courtesy of: Geoff Mann, Sports Journalist, Dubbo.

Western Division Rugby League
INTER-GROUP TRIALS
VICTORIA PARK, DUBBO
Sunday, 2nd April 1972

JUNIORS:	SENIORS:
Time: 35 minutes each way with time off.	Time: 35 minutes each way with time off.
11 am-Group 11 v Group 15.	**1.30 pm-Group 10 v Group 15.**
Referee: B. Kitch. Touch Judges: E. Holland, A. Broadfoot.	Referee: D. Levick. Touch Judges: R. Wiegold, W. Wilkes.
12.15 pm-Group 10 v Group 14.	**3 pm Approx-Group 11 v Group 14.**
Referee: N. Johnson. Touch Judges: E. Holland, A. Broadfoot.	Referee: G. Barby. Touch Judges: R. Wiegold, W. Wilkes.

Admission 60 Cents

PAT SMITH, President

KEVIN HENNESSY, Hon Secretary

Courtesy of: Geoff Mann, Sports Journalist, Dubbo.

Teams for the Western Divison versus Riverina match at Griffith next Sunday April 16th 1972.

WESTERN DIVISION	RIVERINA
FULLBACK:	**FULLBACK:**
R. Large (Mudgee).	C. Moses (Wagga Kangaroos).
WINGERS:	**WINGERS:**
J. Chapman (Bath. St. Pats), T. Wotton (Coona'bran).	B. Stewart (Wagga Magpies), C. Roberts (Cootamundra).
CENTRES:	**CENTRES:**
P. Kennedy (Forbes), J. Bonus (Parkes).	J. Shea (Harden), R. Timbs (Turvey Park).
HALVES:	**HALVES:**
R. Priest (Orange CYMS), R. Camden (Cowra) Captain.	J. Mavroudis (Wagga Magpies), P. Fritsch (Temora).
LOCK:	**LOCK:**
C. Reekin (Bathurst Railway).	L. Gaffey (Holbrook).
SECOND ROWERS:	**SECOND ROWERS:**
L. Raeligh (Portland), D. Milsom (Coona'bran).	J. Bonetti (Griffith), P. Cretan (Junee).
PROPS:	**PROPS:**
L. Bourke (Dubbo CYMS), G. Negline (Dubbo CYMS).	G. Chambers (Wagga Magpies), Captain, W. Rake (Wagga Magpies).
HOOKER:	**HOOKER:**
M. Day (Mudgee).	R. Lynch (Tumbarumba).
RESERVES:	**RESERVES:**
W. Kiely (Cowra), G. Fearnley (Cowra).	N. McWilliam (Griffith Waratahs), I. Schofield (Yenda).

Courtesy of: Geoff Mann, Sports Journalist, Dubbo.

1973 Caltex Country Divisional Championships
Country League Programme

January 1973

The NSW Country Rugby League has made the draw for the opening round in the 1973 Caltex Country Divisional Championships as follows.

- Illawarra v Southern at Wollongong
- Newcastle v North Coast at Newcastle
- Western v Northern at Dubbo
- Riverina v Monaro at Wagga.

Provisional date for this round is April 15, with the semi-finals on April 22 and the final on April 29.

This is in anticipation of the NSW Rugby League agreeing to postpone the annual Sydney v Country matches from Anzac Day, April 25, to a date no later than May 19.

The CRL has accepted an invitation from Queensland League to play a three-match program in Queensland, including a night fixture at Lang Park, Brisbane.

(NSW Country v Brisbane or South Queensland), on Wednesday, May 9.

The Country team would leave Sydney on Saturday, May 5, and return after the third match, on May 13.

The 18 players will be selected immediately after the Caltex final.

It is anticipated that a feature of the Lang Park night would be the appearance of John Sattler for the home side.

Article from: NSW Rugby League News, January, 1973. Republished courtesy of NSW Rugby League.

1973 NEWCASTLE COUNTRY CHAMPIONS

May 1973

Newcastle one of the strongholds of Country Rugby League, triumphed in this year's Caltex Country Divisional Championships.

They defeated Southern Division 25-14 after trailing 6-13 at one stage.

Illawarra had won the title for the past two years but were knocked out by Southern Division in the first round.

Almost the whole of today's Country Firsts were engaged in the match, which was described as one of the finest in the history of the titles.

Back Row: K. Mogg (Manager), P. Cootes, A. Brown, K. Hutchinson, J. Hattam (Secretary), D. Schofield (Coach), P. Hewlett, M. Goldman, H. Wagner (Trainer).

Middle Row: B. Bourke, R. McDarmott, A. Thompson (Captain), D. Ward, R. Sneesby, N. Henderson.

Front Row: R. Burgess, R. Thomson, J. Battey, K. Myers.

Courtesy of: NSW Rugby League, The Rugby League News, May 1973.

1974 Western Division Group Trials

Juniors (1:30 pm) Seniors (3:30 pm)

SENIORS-(3.30pm)

WESTERN DIVISION
(Green and White)

FULL-BACK:
(1) N. Smith (Wellington).
WINGERS:
(2) K. Rawlings (Oberon), (5) P. Walkom (Dubbo CYMS)
CENTRES:
(3) T. Fahey (Wellington), (4) G. Milsom (Coonabarabran).
FIVE-EIGHTH:
(6) D. Finn (Canowindra).
HALF-BACK:
(7) N. Sing (Dubbo Macq) Captain.
LOCK:
(8) C. Parkes (Dubbo CYMS).
SECOND ROW:
(9) D. Milsom (Coonabarabran), (10) D. Fish (Coonamble).
FRONT ROW:
(11) K. Campbell (Baradine), (13) S. Grabtrec (Bath. St. Pats).
HOOKER:
(12) W. Rose (Bathurst Railway).

THE REST
(Maroon and Gold Bars)

FULL-BACK:
(1) I Toohey (Bath. St. Pats).
WINGERS:
(2) N. Armstrong (Cobar), (5) D. Dent (Orange EX Services).
CENTRES:
(3) K. McHugh, (Coonamble), (4) J. Cooper (Parkes).
FIVE-EIGHTH:
(6) P. King (Orange CYMS) Captain.
HALF-BACK:
(7) R. Pilon (Orange CYMS).
LOCK:
(8) R. McBarry (Bathurst Charleston).
SECOND ROW:
(9) J. Earsman (Canowindra), (10) D. Woolbank (Bath Railway).
FRONT ROW:
(11) P. Leslie (Dubbo Macq), (13). E. Elwell (Wellington).
HOOKER:
(12) B. Wilson (Dubbo CYMS).
RESERVES: R. MacDonald (Parkes), N. Ramien (Coonamble), C. Smith (Wellington), R. Webster (Orange EX Services).

JUNIORS-(1.30pm)

GROUP 14
(Maroon and Gold Bars)

FULL-BACK:
(1) G. Reynolds (Gilgandra).
WINGERS:
(2) J. Tritton, (Mudgee), (5) W. Cleary (Coonamble).
CENTRES:
(3) A. Buckley (Coonabaraban), (4) P.Mahon (Mudgee).
FIVE-EIGHTH:
(6) J. Newling (Coonamble).
HALF-BACK:
(7) F. Spicer (Gilgandra).
LOCK:
(8) P. Morris (Gilgandra) Captain.
SECOND ROW:
(9)) R. Maffio (Mudgee), (10) S. Copelin (Gilgandra).
FRONT ROW:
(11) I. Frost (Dunedoo), (13) J. Farragher (Gilgandra).
HOOKER:
(12) L. Jenner (Coonabarabran).
RESERVES: (14). C. Fitzgerald (Mudgee), (15) D. Day (Coonamble).

GROUP 11
(Red and Black Bars)

FULL-BACK:
(1) S. Vane (Dubbo CYMS)).
WINGERS:
(2) J. Rodgers (Dubbo Macq), (5) G. Barling (Narromine).
CENTRES:
(3) M. Smith (Narromine), (4) S. Hollaway (Forbes).
FIVE-EIGHTH:
(6) J. Strudwick (Tullamore).
HALF-BACK:
(7) K. Brandy (Condobolin).
LOCK:
(8) R. McDermott (Dubbo Macquarie).
SECOND ROW:
(9), M. Forrester (Dubbo Macq), (10) N. Ashdown (Narromine).
FRONT ROW:
(11) M. Churchill (Dubbo Macq), (13) C. Young (Dubbo Macq).
HOOKER:
(12) W. Bishop (Parkes).
RESERVES: (14). R. Barrett (Wellington), (15) W. Wakefield (Parkes).

'74 A VINTAGE YEAR FOR GROUP XI!

April 1974

Group XI has produced many star-studded combinations over the years, but this one (pictured left) fielded in 1974 would surely have taken some beating.

That side in fact formed the nucleus of the Amco Cup-winning WD side of the year, with Fahey, Walkom, MacDonald and Nelson Smith and later Rob Pilon and Greg Lousick members of that famous side.

The side played its part in maintaining Group 11 domination of Western Division football by convincingly winning the divisional trials played at Wellington that year.

In view of the current interest in the group and divisional representative proceedings, Group 11 believed it appropriate for this photograph to be published today.

Pictured is that 1974 side no doubt you will find plenty of familiar faces:

Bach Row from left to right.

- Mr. Jim Fawkner (current Group 11 Western Division Secretary).
- Terry Fahey (former Wellington and Australian winger, now with South Sydney).
- Ray Neilsen (now coaching the Parkes under 18 side).
- Cliff Smith (former Wellington forward).
- Colin Parkes (ex-Western Division, Manly first grader, former with Dubbo CYMS and now captain coach of Dunedoo in Group 14).
- Peter Walkom (former WD player, now back with Dubbo CYMS after a stint on the north coast).
- Peter Leslie (former Dubbo Macquarie and Western Division prop).
- John Cooper (ex-Parkes now with Wollongong where he has represented the Division).

Kneeling:

- Dennis Finn (ex-Parkes, Canowindra and Western Division, now committee man at Parkes).
- Peter Frew (still with Dubbo CYMS although struggling to overcome injury).
- Jack Earsman (former Canowindra, Orange Ex-Services stalwart, now retired).
- Pat Smith (Western Division, Riverina and captained Country Firsts from Gundagai last year, now leading Maitland in the Newcastle competition).
- Earl Elwell, (former Wellington forward who played that year for Western Division).

Front Row:

- Terry Savage (WD and country trainer).
- Rod MacDonald (ex-Parkes, Forbes and Taree where he is now a committee member of Taree Old Bar).
- Noel Sing (ex-Penrith, still coaching Macquarie with plenty of success).
- David Hodges (ex-Parkes, Peak Hill and now captain coach of North Belconnen in the Canberra competition).
- Brian Wilson (ex-Country and Manly rake still with Dubbo CYMS).
- Nelson Smith (former Western Division and Wellington forward).

Article from: The Parkes Champion Post, April 12, 1974. Republished courtesy of ACM/Parkes Champion Post.

1974 Group 11 Rugby League Team

The 1974 Group 11 team — BACK: Peter Leslie, John Cooper, Ray Neilsen, Noel Sing (captain-coach), Pat Smith, David Hodge, Jack Earsman, Rod MacDonald, Terry Fahey. FRONT: Nelson Smith, Colin Parkes, Cliff Smith, Brian Wilson, Dennis Finn, Earl Elwell.

Courtesy of: Roseanne Finn.

MONARO DIVISION V WESTERN DIVISION
Played at Seiffert Oval, Queanbeyan, on 14th April 1974
Referee: Mr. T. Spain (Cootamundra)
Touch Judges: Messrs. T. Pass, D. Pickard (Canberra)

MONARO DIVISION	WESTERN DIVISION
FULL-BACK: I Moore (Canberra Tigers).	**FULL-BACK:** N. Smith (Wellington).
THREE QUARTERS: R. Moncrieff (Queanbeyan United), P. Rands (Canberra Tigers), P. Ryan (Goulburn Workers), T. Edwards (Goulburn United).	**THREE QUARTERS:** K. Rawlings (Oberon), T. Fahey (Wellington), G. Milsom (Coonabarabran), N. Armstrong (Cobar).
FIVE-EIGHTH: J. Ballesty (Queanbeyan United).	**FIVE-EIGHTH:** D. Finn (Canowindra).
HALFBACK: S. Hewson (Queanbeyan United).	**HALFBACK:** N. Sing, Captain (Dubbo Macquarie).
FORWARDS: D. Mackay (Goulburn United), B. Bourke (Queanbeyan United), C. Clearahan (Queanbeyan United), T. Parker (Canberra Tigers), J. Jones (Queanbeyan United), J. Morgan, Captain (Queanbeyan United).	**FORWARDS:** C. Parkes (Dubbo CYMS), D. Milsom (Coonabarabran), R. McGarry ((Bathurst Charlestons), P. Leslie (Dubbo Macquarie), B. Wilson (Dubbo CYMS), E. Elwell (Wellington).
REPLACEMENTS: J. Stone (Queanbeyan United), R. Belford (Belconnen United).	**REPLACEMENTS:** F. Fish (Coonamble), R. MacDonald (Parkes).

Monaro Division 23: Tries T. Edwards 2, R. Belford P. Ryan, R. Moncrieff. Goals I. Moore 4. Defeated Western Division 2: Goal N. Smith.

Courtesy of: Geoff Mann, Sports Journalist, Dubbo.

WESTERN DIVISION
versus
GREAT BRITAIN

AT THE HOME OF GROUP 10 FOOTBALL

WADE PARK, ORANGE
WEDNESDAY, 26TH JUNE, 1974

1974 GREAT BRITAIN TOURING TEAM

FRONT ROW (left to right): Alan Bates, John Bevan, David Eckersley, Paul Charlton, Ken Gill, Jim Challinor (asst. manager), Chris Hesketh (capt.), Reg Parker (manager), Roger Millward, 'Keith' Bridges, Steve Nash, David Watkins.

BACK ROW: Kevin Ashcroft, David Redfearn, Michael Nicholas, John Gray, Les Dyl, John Atkinson, Colin Dixon, Eric Chisnall, Jim Mills, Stephen Norton, John Bates, David Willicombe, Paul Rose, Terry Clawson, George Nicholls, John Butler. Absent is Jim Thompson who took the place of Michael Nicholas just before the team left.

OFFICIAL SOUVENIR PROGRAM — 20c

Courtesy of: Dave Kent, Orange & District Historical Society.

1974 Great Britain & Western Division Ready

Above Left: Great Britain's little halfback Steve Nash gets a pass away at training yesterday afternoon on Wade Park, as coach Jim Challinor comes in to try and stop it. Big Jim Mills is on the left and he will be in the front-row today.

Above Right: The Western Division Rugby League team looked keen at training yesterday as they wound up their preparation for today's game against Great Britain. Here the "Cobar Flash", winger Norm Armstrong gets a pass away. Other players in the side from left are Nelson Smith, Billy Ross, Robert Pilon, Dave Ross, Ian Toohey and Dennis Ritchie.

Courtesy of: CWN Negative Collection, Orange and District Historical Society.

Set for the kick-off

RECORD CROWD AT BIG GAME

A record Orange Rugby League crowd of 6,200 people crammed into Wade Park yesterday afternoon for the "game of the year" between Great Britain and Western Division. Above is a view of Wade Park from 1000 feet up yesterday afternoon. The record crowd can be seen around the perimeter of the ground. It was the biggest crowd to attend a football fixture at Wade Park since the visit of the Springboks in July 1971.

Cars were packed within three to four-blocks of Wade Park.

Note: the players on the field.

Courtesy of: Michael Downey, (Orange CYMS), Reunion Book.

WESTERN DIVISION'S KEY PLAYERS

ROBERT PILON, Orange CYMS half-back who will be one of the key players in today's game.

PAUL DOWLING, Bathurst St. Patrick's captain-coach and captain of Western Division today. His judicious kicking from five-eighth spot could be a problem for Great Britain.

DAVE ROSS, Orange CYMS lock, who is a new face on the Western Division scene this year.

PAUL SAMS, Bathurst St. Patrick's fullback, who is another newcomer to the Western Division scene this season.

GREG FEARNLEY, Cowra prop, who will lead the forwards today. A big game from him could lead to success.

BILLY ROSE, Bathurst Railway hooker, who will need to win an equal share of the ball today to give his team a chance. A tireless worker in the open.

Courtesy of: Geoff Mann, Sports Journalist, Dubbo.

Western Division v Great Britain June 26 1974
Wade Park Orange
Game Results:

Great Britain: 25 (Ken Gill 2, Steve Norton, David Redfearn, Les Dyl tries; John Gray 5 goals) defeated:

Western Division: 10 (Norm Armstrong try; Nelson Smith 3 goals; Bob Pilon field goal).
Referee: Kevin Honeybrook

Western Division - Great Britain Teams:

Western Division Team: Paul Sams, Dave Kent, Peter Walkom, Rod Macdonald, Norm Armstrong, Paul Dowling (captain), Bob Pilon, Dave Ross, Nelson Smith, Ted Ellery, Greg Fearnley, Billy Rose, Dennis Richie.
Reserves: Ian Toohey, Peter Frew. Coach: Johnny King.

Great Britain Team: Paul Charlton, David Redfearn, Chris Hesketh (captain), Les Dyl, John Atkinson, Ken Gill, Alan Bates, Steve Norton, John Gray, Eric Chisnall, Jimmy Thompson, Keith Bridges, Jim Mills.
Reserves: David Willicombe, John Butler. Coach: Jim Challinor.

Article from: The Western Magazine, August, 1974. Republished courtesy of ACM/Western Magazine.

1974 Great Britain & Western Division Teams

Great Britain and Western Division teams stand before the match for the National Anthem.
Courtesy of: CWN Negative Collection, Orange and District Historical Society.

Did Great Britain Underestimate Again?

GREAT BRITAIN DEFEATED WESTERN DIVISION: 25-10

The scene at Orange last Wednesday with big Jim Mills on the run for Great Britain.

Left: John Butler, the Great Britain back, gets stopped in his tracks by an unorthodox tackle from Robert Pilon.

Right: Test prop forward Jim Mills on one of his many strong runs during the game. Mills was always hard to pull down.

Courtesy of: CWN Negative Collection, Orange and District Historical Society.

Bob Pilon drags down Eric Chisnall. Western Division players are Dave Ross number 8, Greg Fearnley, Ted Ellery, Dave Kent and Billy Ross.

Courtesy of: CWN Negative Collection, Orange and District Historical Society.

Western Division players moving in on Great Britain player with the ball, left Ted Ellery, Geoff Lousick making the tackle and Paul Dowling.

Courtesy of: CWN Negative Collection, Orange and District Historical Society.

Referee Kevin Honeybrook cautions Great Britain's Keith Bridges.

Ted Ellery

Courtesy of: CWN Negative Collection, Orange and District Historical Society.

Above Left-Right: Geoff Lousick, Greg Fearnley, Nelson Smith (kicking penalty), Paul Sams, Ted Ellery.

Courtesy of: CWN Negative Collection, Orange and District Historical Society.

1974 Great Britain v Western Division

All-in brawl during Western Division v Great Britain played at Bathurst reputed to be one of the toughest rugby league games ever played.

Courtesy of: CWN Negative Collection, Orange and District Historical Society.

Great Britain's brilliant half-back Chris Hesketh with the ball.

Courtesy of: CWN Negative Collection, Orange and District Historical Society.

Amco Cup
KING WINDS OUR BOYS UP FOR CUP GAME

August 1974

Ted Ellery, Western Division's shock weapon, will be coach Johnny King's trump card again tomorrow night in the Amco Cup grand-final against Penrith at Leichhardt Oval.

"All our players will get a run at some stage of tomorrow night's game," King said this morning.

He remains non-committal on the tactics Western Division will use against Penrith but he isn't likely to deviate much from those used successfully against Auckland, Canterbury and Manly.

Although King doesn't like to single out players Ellery has been such a commanding player and demanded so much respect from the opposition, that his entrance into the game could be a mental barrier for Mike Stephenson's men to overcome.

King, speaking from the Shore Motel, Artarmon this morning, had just returned from a light training run.

"There are no injuries. Nelson Smith has trained very well and there are absolutely no doubts about him playing tomorrow night, none in the world", King said.

"We'll wrap it up with our main session this afternoon and then it'll be talks with the players from there."

Penrith secretary, Mr. Roger Cowan, said selectors would not finalise the team until tonight.

There are injury problems with Stephenson, prop Tim Sheens and winger Terry Quinn.

Ted Ellery

Article from: The Dubbo Daily Liberal, Tuesday, August 20, 1974. Republished courtesy of ACM/Dubbo Daily Liberal.

Penrith Line Up for Tonight's Amco Cup

Penrith had a setback last night when outstanding lock Peter Langmark dropped out.

The selectors switched Dennis Tutty to lock and named young David Hodge and Glen Stolzenhein as the second-rowers.

Back in the side after being out injured is experienced centre Grahame Moran who should provide a formidable centre combination with rugged Glen West.

Terry Geary came off the bench to replace Tim Sheens during the game.

Coach Jack Clare believes his team will have a fraction too much over all experience for the Western Division side.

The selected Penrith team is:
Phil Jelley, Ross Gigg, Grahame Moran, Glen West, Terry Quinn, Ritchie Thornton, John Wilson, Dennis Tutty, David Hodge, Glen Stolzenhein, Tim Sheens, Mike Stephenson (Captain), Bruce Ward.

Reserve: Terry Geary

Courtesy of: Terry Williams. (NRL).

A MILLION TO WATCH OUR WILD WEST BOYS

More than one million television viewers will watch tonight's Amco Cup grand final thriller between Western Division and Penrith at Leichhardt Oval

August 1974

Special television linkups will carry the game to stations throughout NSW and Queensland for what promises to be two hours of electrifying football. Western players have suddenly become the toast of Sydney in the past two days with pressmen and photographers clambering for interviews with the "Wild West" boys.

At midday today, the entire forward pack appeared on the top-rating Mike Walsh show on Channel 10. Walsh invited the pack on his show so that they could demonstrate the art of packing a scrum and tackling. He also presented a special interview with Rugby League's biggest celebrity of the moment Ted Ellery, also known as "Bald Eagle", "TV Ted"," Mad Dog" and "Crazy Horse".

From the Shore Motel in Sydney this morning, coach Johnny King said his team was fighting fit, except for Nelson Smith.

Smith still has a slight hamstring injury and has volunteered to have a run this afternoon. If he is fit enough, he will play King said.

However, Penrith will be a very tough nut to crack. They thrashed Country Championship finalists Northern Division and then knocked over the crack Eastern Suburbs team.

West's style of percentage football, with continual up the middle probes does not lend itself to large scores.

All West's games have been close affairs with Green and White gaining ascendency in the final quarter.

Penrith players will no doubt spot Ted Ellery when he makes his appearance. But this will ease the pressure on the other West players for the final 20 minutes.

Norm Armstrong
Photo: Mick Bannister

Western Division's first game of the competition where they were not expected to win a single game was against Auckland at Leichhardt Oval. Western Division won 13-7 and Norm Armstrong scored a try. A Sydney journalist dubbed him the "Cobar Flash." A name which stuck with him.

Article from: The Dubbo Daily Liberal, Tuesday, August 20, 1974. Republished courtesy of ACM/Dubbo Daily Liberal.

IT WAS BOBBY'S NIGHT OF NIGHTS

August 1974

Western led all the way:

Ageing centre Barry Rushworth and rising young star Bobby Pilon were the outstanding players in last night's thrilling Amco Cup victory.

Western Division won the match 6-2 with veteran captain Paul Dowling picking up all west's points with a clever side-stepping try, a field goal and a penalty goal.

However, it was the greying-former Kangaroo centre Rushworth and long-haired Pilon who captured the imagination of the crowd.

Rushworth's stone wall around the legs defence completely blotted Penrith's Glen West and Graham Moran out of the game.

Rushworth claims he feels 22 again when he takes the field with Western. He made three clean breaks last night by running on to the ball.

Pilon drew the crowd to its feet with his uncanny 70 metre touch-finders and his sharpness around the scrums and rucks.

Lock Geoff Lousick and prop Greg Fearnley also had very big games.

Lousick gave a non-stop display in cover defence and made four clean breaks which could have easily led to tries had he been supported.

Fearnley once again showed that he is at the forefront of the Australian prop forward lineup with another 80 minutes display which had the Sydney clubs talking to him after the game.

Fullback Sams and wingers Fahey and Armstrong defended very well, but did not get a chance to attack.

Trevor Simpson in the centres was again sound as was Dowling, who was closely spotted by Penrith.

Nelson Smith suffered a re-occurrence of a calf muscle injury in the first quarter and missed three shots at goal before he had to leave the field.

Des Milsom had his best game of the season and troubled Penrith around the rucks.

Big Dave Abbott once more took on much of the heavy work and came out with his reputation enhanced.

Hooker Billy Rose and Ken Campbell were unbeatable in defence. Ted Ellery had a fairly quiet game, but did his job well in defence.

Referee Laurie Bruyeres may have also won himself a final spot ahead of Keith Page by turning in a good display.

He made a couple of mistakes, but kept the game flowing and managed to keep heated moments to a minimum.

West led 4-0 at quarter time, 6-0 at halftime, 6-2 at three quarter time and 6-2 at fulltime.

West had many chances to throw the ball around as Pilon's line kicks kept the ball deep in Penrith territory.

But King's instructions were to play safe and keep probing around the rucks.

This gave Penrith no chances in loose play.

Scrums favoured Penrith 17-11 and penalties also favoured Penrith 12-9.

Article from: The Dubbo Daily Liberal, Friday, August 23, 1974. Republished courtesy of ACM/Dubbo Daily Liberal.

You Were Great Mike

"That's the best tackling side I've ever played against" a bruised and battered Mike Stephenson admitted at Leichhardt Oval last night as he visited the Western Division dressing rooms.

Stephenson was congratulating Western Division coach Johnny King. The former English Test star also congratulated the Western players and had a special handshake for opposing skipper Paul Dowling.

"Your lads were tremendous in defence, I've never seen a team tackle like they did. We never had a chance of getting into action around the rucks. "

Stephenson was very disappointed that he had failed to lead his team to victory.

"That's the way it goes, I hope the Western Division boys have a great drink-up."

King wished Stephenson an equally successful evening at the Drummoyne Rowing Club where Penrith had planned their victory celebrations. Stephenson replied rather sadly, "We'll have a good drink-up, but not for the same reasons as your side."

The Penrith skipper had a grand game for the Panthers in defence and was covered from head to toe in thick red dust after the match.

Mike Stephenson

Article from: The Dubbo Daily Liberal, Friday, August 23, 1974. Republished courtesy of ACM/Dubbo Daily Liberal.

How the Panthers Were Tamed
August 1974

Three orange peels and a handful of ice cubes last night earned Western Division Rugby League team $16,000 at Leichhardt Oval.

Coach Johnny King used the orange peels and ice cubes in an emergency tactics discussion at halftime in the big game.

King was trying to outline the Penrith tactics to West, at the same time drilling in counter tactics for the Western side.

I realised it would be a lot easier to show my players what to do rather than tell them, so I scooped up the peels and the ice cubes and put them on the table. The cubes were Penrith and we were the orange peels.

I showed my players what Penrith were doing in attack and then moved the orange peels about to counter those moves.

"Once they got back on the field, it worked like magic and every player knew his exact role."

King said the use of the cubes and peels came to him on the spur of the moment.

King also set down a scrum in the dressing room to work out why West were losing the scrums.

I told the boys to pack tight and hold. When the ball came into the scrum, they were to push forward 18 inches. It certainly worked.

Rivals on the field, pals off it. Penrith captain, former English test star Mike Stephenson and Western skipper Paul Dowling share a couple of cans after the battle.

Article from: The Dubbo Daily Liberal, Friday, August 23, 1974. Republished courtesy of ACM/Dubbo Daily Liberal.

Amco Cup

Celebrations after the Amco Cup win.

Article from: The Dubbo Daily Liberal Sport, 1974. Republished courtesy of ACM/Dubbo Daily Liberal.

Man of The Match: Last night the Dubbo born and bred halfback Bob Pilon was visibly moved when he was named man of the match, the award is worth $1,000 to Pilon more than he will earn all season with CYMS.

Above Left: Western Division Winger Norm Armstrong known as the "Cobar Flash" tackled by Penrith's Glen West during the 1974 Amco Cup final.

Above Right: Bob Pilon (Man of the Match) with father Bryan at the presentation after the final, flanked by two of rugby league's greatest wingers, Ken Irvine and Western Division coach Johnny King.

Article from: The Dubbo Daily Liberal Sport, 1974. Republished courtesy of ACM/Dubbo Daily Liberal.

Amco Cup Semi Final celebrations and results

Champagne time for Penrith in the dressing room after winning the semi-final.

Roy Masters holds court at quarter-time in the 1974 Amco Cup Final.

The semi-final results confounded all critics. Western Division drew 12-all with Manly, winning the match on a penalty count. Western Division had beaten Auckland and Canterbury in earlier rounds.

Penrith reached the final in style with a 10-9 victory, beating Easts for the second time that year. In most circumstances down the ladder Penrith would have been the underdog in any final. This time Western had the tag and they were a promoter's dream.

Most of the critics believed Western Division had their day and could not maintain the form that stopped Manly.

TV Ted Ellery, a balding second rower who was released on the opposition in the second half usually with devastating results, had captured the hearts of the television watching public. Almost singlehandedly, he had given the competition impetus.

Critics wrong: 1974 Western Division Amco Cup Winners
Western Division 6: Paul Dowling try, 2 goals (one goal and field goal).
Penrith 2: Bruce Ward (one goal).

Courtesy of: Penrith Rugby League Club.

1974 Western Division Amco Cup Winners

Back Row: B. Baker (Trainer), I. Toohey (Bathurst St Patricks), T. Fahey, (Wellington), G. Fearnley (Cowra), D. Ritchie (Narromine), T. Ellery (Lithgow Workmens), John King Coach (Wellington), C McDonnell (Manager).

Middle Row: P. Walkom (Dubbo CYMS), N. Smith (Wellington), P. Dowling, Captain (Bathurst St Pats), W. Rose (Bathurst Railway), P. Sams, (Bathurst St Pats).

Front Row: Dave Ross (Orange CYMS), Norm Armstrong (Cobar), Rob Pilon (Orange CYMS), Frank Fish (Coonamble), Rod MacDonald (Parkes).

Absent: G. Lousick (Wellington), K. Campbell (Baradine), R. Rushworth (Lithgow), T. Simpson (Canowindra), D. Abbott (Dunedoo), D. Milsom (Coonabarabran).

They won the final with a solid brick-wall defence that never offered the Panthers a single inch of territory.

A crowd of more than 20,000 squeezed into Leichhardt Oval, while a million or more cheered on television. Final score Western Division 6, Penrith 2.

'TV Ted' Ellery is the name mentioned first by just about everyone of a certain generation when the subject of Western Division and the events of 1974 come up. Ted, a knockabout miner from Lithgow, did more than any other individual to put the Amco Cup on the map.

Article from: The Western Magazine, June 24, 1974. Republished courtesy of ACM/Western Magazine.

1974 Penrith Rugby League Team

Back Row: Roy Masters (Co-Coach), Peter Langmark, Roy West, Peter Swanson, Bill Ashurst, Dennis Tutty, Glen Stolzenhein, Doug Bayly, Jack Clare (Coach), Tom Wilson (Co-Coach).

Front Row: Wayne Moore, Zac Olejarnik, Reg Walton, Jersey Komorowiski, John Wilson, Glen West.

Absent: Mike Stephenson

Courtesy of: Penrith Rugby League Club.

SECTION 3:
Maher, Jack Hore, Johnnie Walker and Clayton Cups

Phil Regan (second row left) captain of the undefeated Temora Maher Cup Team in 1923.

MAHER, JACK HORE, JOHNNIE WALKER & CLAYTON CUPS

Football in Western and Southern NSW was well on its way by the 1920s as the major sport played on weekends. The introduction of challenge cups became the main focus of attention and conversation in country communities, fostering intense local rivalries. Supporters would travel from near and far in large numbers to witness their teams in action.

This section includes the Maher, Jack Hore, Johnnie Walker and Clayton Cups. Articles of great players, teams and images describe how the game influenced regional NSW during the golden years of rugby league in the bush.

Hotels became the meeting place before and after the game, planning and replaying their team's victory and or loss.

Players were appointed from Sydney clubs as paid coaches improving the overall skills of the country NSW players and teams. Great players emerged and went on to represent their regions, state and Australia.

The challenge cup music finally died by mid 1970s and group competitions replaced them.

Tumut Birth Place of The Maher Cup

Tumut is both the place of origin and the place of rest for the cup. Cootamundra was the heart of Maher Cup football and was clearly the dominant side. It was also the geographical and administrative centre of the Maher Cup and Group 9 football. There were close to 729 calculated challenges between 1920 and 1971 for the Maher Cup.

Play was fierce and every week was like a grand-final. Even a draw meant a loss for the challenging team.

Courtesy of: NSW State Achieves. Tumut Main Street

'Old Tin Mug' a symbol of country rugby league for 50 years.

Creating madness within the Maher Cup Challenges. It was also responsible for bringing grown men to tears.

Many playing-coaches of State or International repute have often found to their sorrow that when they played Maher Cup football, they buried their reputations. It was said to be the toughest football in Australia. This statement was confirmed by an extract from the New South Wales "Rugby League News" April 14, 1956.

Article from: NSW Rugby League, The Rugby League News.

The Birth of the Maher Cup

Mr. E. J. (Ted) Maher
Donated the Maher Cup

Known as E.J. or simply Ted, and aged 32 he was a busy bloke going places. Within a year he had ticked off the following: donated a football cup in his name, captained a local football team, appointed chairman of the Tumut Ramblers Football Club, refereed and ran the line, led the change from union to league, joined the committees of the agricultural society, the turf club and a tennis club, shot at the Tumut Rifle Club, purchased the local Tattersalls (Wynyard Hotel) License and played cricket.

Courtesy of: Neil Pollock, Maher Cup author

Wynyard Hotel, purchased by E.J. Maher

Source: Archives, Australian National University.

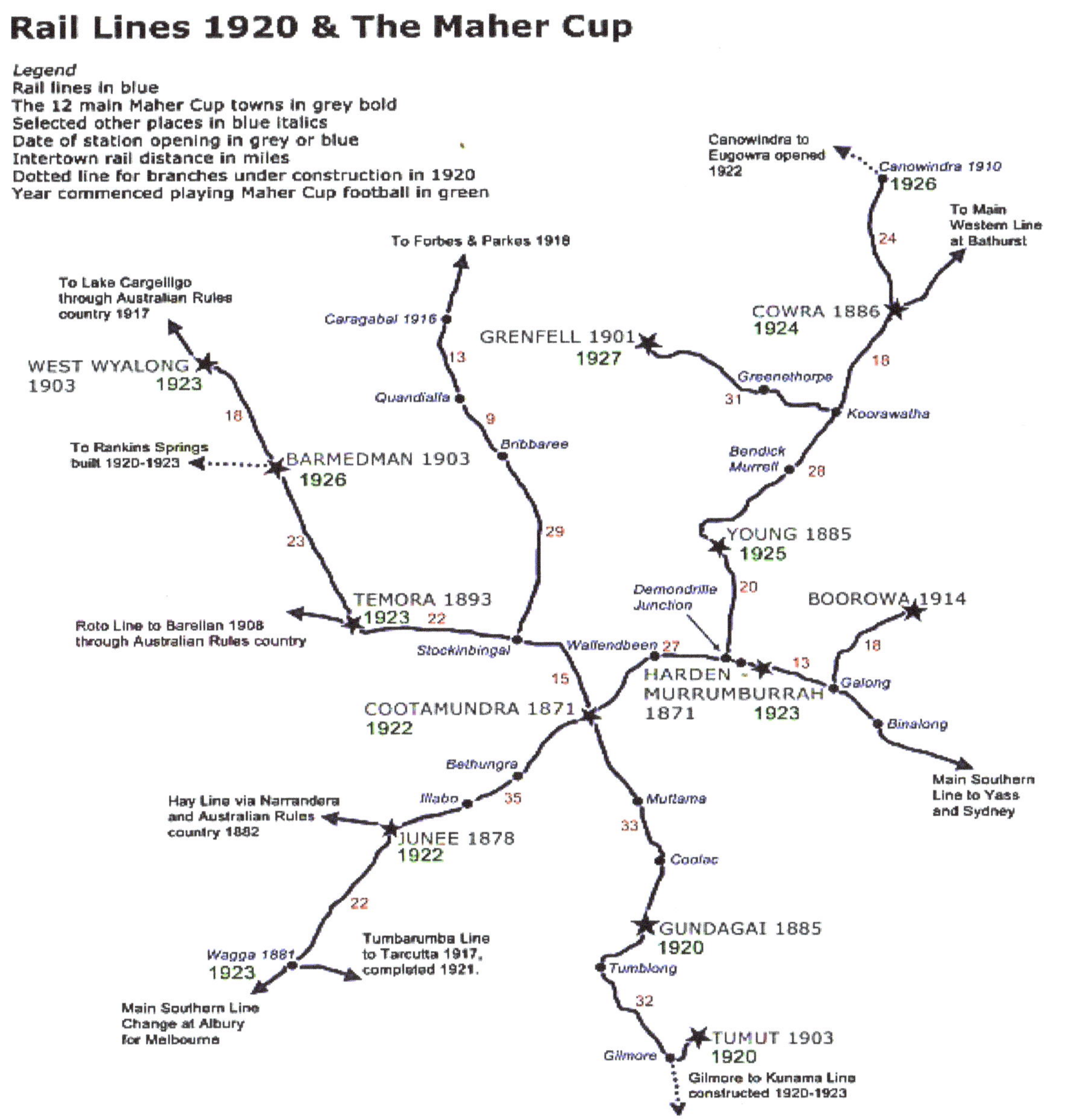

Rail Lines 1920 & The Maher Cup

Legend
Rail lines in blue
The 12 main Maher Cup towns in grey bold
Selected other places in blue italics
Date of station opening in grey or blue
Intertown rail distance in miles
Dotted line for branches under construction in 1920
Year commenced playing Maher Cup football in green

The rail network provided transportation for Maher Cup team supporters.
Courtesy of: Neil Pollock, Maher Cup author.

Junee Railway Station

Junee Railway Station opened 6th July 1890
Courtesy of: Junee Historical Society.

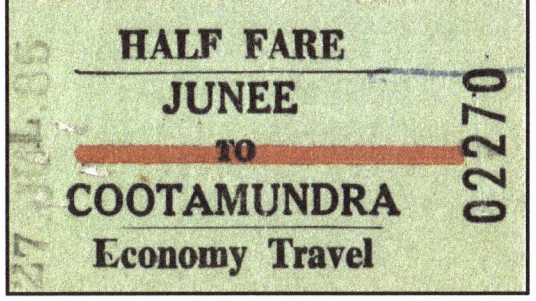

Railway Ticket
Courtesy of: Powerhouse collection. "Gift of Julian Hollis, 1986." Photographer Belinda Christie.

Trains play a part in the Maher Cup History

Steam trains played a big part in moving spectators to Maher Cup matches from the twenties to the fifties.

Courtesy of: Brian Hughes & Temora Independent.

1928 Australian Football Third Test Team

Australia defeated England, 21-14

The Two Greatest Maher Cup Players

Eric Weissel and Jack Kingston two of the greatest Group Nine players during the 1920s. Eric was a five-eighth and Jack lock forward. Both went on to play for Australia and toured England with the Kangaroos.

Back Row: E. Mead, H. Flegg, A. Burdon, J. Tennison, J. Stephensen, H. Sunderland.
Middle Row: Nelson Hardy, Jack Kingston, Herb Steinhort, George Treweeke, Vic Armbuster, Dan Dempsey.
Front Row: Eric Weissel, Cliff Pearce, Joe Bush, Tom Gorman (Captain), Jimmy Craig, Benny Wearing, Arthur Justice.

Courtesy of: Neil Pollock, Maher Cup author.

1920 Junee Rovers Local Competition Premiers

Back Row: Bob Phair, Gil Maroney, ? Davidson, Peter Edwards, Paddy Heaton, George Sutherland, Ernie Turner, Alf 'Soldier' Markham, Edward Wealands, Dave Robinson, Charlie Turner.

Middle Row: Herb Howard, (Unknown), A. Wenkie, Clive Turner, Percy Day, Cecil 'Doody' Porch.

Front Row: Jack Brown, Ron Fraser, Frank Champness, Peter Guerin.

Courtesy of: Neil Pollock, Maher Cup author and Geoff Edwards.

Eric Weissel in Temora Guernsey

Cootamundra's Eric Weissel is one of the greatest five eighths to play our game and he was named one of Australia's greatest 100 players. Born on 16th February 1903, Eric was the 11th child of railway fettler Edward Weissel.

He was born in the tiny village of Brawlin just south of Cootamundra and attended the local Cootamundra school, where he established himself as a top-class athlete as a young boy.

Eric came to the Cootamundra team at 19 years of age, for his first Maher Cup game on 30th August, 1922 when the team beat Tumut 20-5. Altogether, Eric finished with 45 Maher Cup matches for Cootamundra, winning 39, drawing one and losing five.

Courtesy of: Family of League.

1922-1923 Cootamundra Football Team

Back Row: M.J. Ryan (selector), Mick Tuncheon, P.J. Kiley, (Hon Secretary), Bill Lesberg, Bob Condon, Charlie Swartzel, D. J. Rand (President), Bernie Kinnane, Walter Farrer (Vice President), Frank Delaney (Referee).

Middle Row: Fred Hayward, Jack Watson, Phil Regan (Captain-Coach), Ray Sheedy, L.T. 'Dadie' Quinlan.

Front Row: C.H. Inson (Hon Treasurer), Brian O'Connor, Curtis 'Dick' Pellow, Eric Weissel, Tom 'Dipper' McDevitt.

Absent Players: Wal Franklin, Phil Freestone, Tom Ryan, L. Large, J. Kelley, Percy Mills, Charlie Schofield.

Courtesy of: Neil Pollock, Maher Cup author.

Eric Weissel

Eric Weissel "The Master"

Eric Weissel, the greatest footballer Group 9 has produced and arguably the greatest Country Rugby League player of all time.

Weissel played Maher Cup football from 1921 to 1933.

While captain-coach of Temora, he was chosen to play for Australia and in 1929/30 toured England with the Kangaroos.

Courtesy of: Brian Hughes & Temora Independent.

1924 Temora Football Team

Back Row: Slender O'Leary, Andy Naylor (Referee), Tom McAlister, Ernie Green, Rex Thwaite, Hector Curran, Allan Forbes, Ted Curran, George Jordan, Dinny Crowley.

Front Row: George Richards, Peter McSullea, Sid Mansted (Coach), Harrold Thomas, George Elliott, Llyod Smith, Cyril Meehan, Triffe 'Trizzie' Prior (Ball boy).

Courtesy of: Neil Pollock, Maher Cup author.

1928 Temora Football Team

Back Row: Walter 'Casey' Jordan, Artie McShane, Charlie 'Buck' Bray, Charlie Cornwell, Reg Maker, Horace Anthony.

Middle Row: Norm Bland (President), Joe Constable, Leo Curran, Eric Weissel (Captain Coach), Alan 'Snowy' Lynch, Bill Boyd, Les Pool (Secretary).

Front Row: Harrold 'Macca' Thomas, Jack 'Slender' O'Leary.

Courtesy of: Neil Pollock, Maher Cup author.

1927 Gundagai's Famous Football Team

Back Row: G. Owen, T. Lindley, J. McIntyre, T. Woodbridge, H. Worldon, H. McGairt, L. Lynch.

Middle Row: A. Perry, G. Woodbridge, J. Milller, C. Fraser, J. Donnelly, V. Carberry, D.P. Turner (President).

Front Row: P. Freestone, V. Freestone.

1927 team won the Maher Cup from Young and successfully defended it from Barmedman, Grenfell and Wagga. The Gundagai 1927 Maher Cup team coached by "Chook" Fraser. In front are two famous football bothers, Phil and "Bluey" Freestone. The latter went on to represent Australia.

Courtesy of: Brian Hughes & Temora Independent.

1930 Cootamundra Rugby League Team

Left to right:
Jack Kingston (Captain Coach),
Alf Tasker, Gordon Torpy, Jack Jame,
Gordon Hinton, Jack Schumack,
Jacky Walkom, Leo Sheedy,
Bill 'Chips' Phillips, Alby Winter,
Jack Watson, Frank Blundell,
Jack Dempsey.

Courtesy of: Neil Pollock, Maher Cup author.

Cootamundra Railway Station

Source: Wikimedia.org/wikipedia/commons.

1935 Tumut's Rugby League All Local Team

Back Row: Bill McGowan, Col Hargreaves, Bobby Banks, Joe Wilkinson (Non-Playing Coach), Jack Cruise, Tom Kirk, Clare 'Bill' Hargreaves, Clem Roddy (President).

Middle Row: Jack Blackeney (Secretary), Reg Baker, Jack Duncan, Bobby Dowing (Captain), Bede Madigan, Bob Silvester, Max Ibbotson (Referee).

Front: Row: Jack Smart, Douglas 'Jim' Lyell, Don Innes.

CLERGYMEN PLAY

This year Temora also held the Jack Hore Gold Cup which was competing strongly against the Maher Cup for popularity. For this cup Temora received challenges from Barmedman, Orange, Junee, Tumut, Canowindra (the original holders) and even from Wellington but they forfeited and never played.

Forbes also played for the Jack Hore Gold Cup that year. One of their stars being a young lad-Archie Crippen, who was later to play for Australia at the age of 18.

During the "thirties" two outstanding Maher Cup players were clergymen. One of them was Father John Morrison, now parish priest at Boorowa, and Dudley Laggett a Presbyterian minister. Both were members of the Young team that was prominent during that period. An example can be seen in the famous 1934 team: Rev. Dudley Leggett, Roy Hall, Sid Hall, Abe Hall, Father John Morrison, Clarence 'Jum' Miller, Bill Kearney, Mick O'Rourke, Norman 'Ben' Hall, Merv Torpy, Jack Brown, 'Blue' O'Malley, Jack Richens.

Courtesy of: Brian Hughes & Temora Independent.

1936 Temora Rugby League Team

Back Row: Jim Woods, Theo Witts, Tom Stanford, Cal Lynch, Ginger Lynch, Ron Wheatley, Alan Moroney, Eric Curran (Injured).
Front Row: Jim Winter, Jack Melrose, Snowy Lynch (Captain), Harold Thomas, Bill Pinney, Frank Blundell.
Courtesy of: Neil Pollock, Maher Cup author.

1935 The First Rugby League Air Transport

On 23 June, 1935 the Cootamundra team flew on two Butler Air Transport planes to challenge Forbes for the Jack Hore Gold Cup. The Cootamundra Herald thought the team would make history as being "the first to make use of this modern method of travel."

"The team members to fly were Bill Argaet, Jock Hetherington, Jim Winter (pictured front left row), Ray Ward, Clem Scrivener, Fred Thompson, Alf Tasker, W. Ayers, Charlie Rowe, Leo Sheedy, Noel Walpole and Pat Muffett.
Other passengers were Mrs Wally Hayded, Brian O'Connor, Ike Hennessey, Eric Nash, Frank "Tax" Ponting, Arthur Young and mascot Keith Starr. "Snowy" Martin refused to fly and drove to Forbes." *(Pollock, Neil, A Pictorial History of Cootamundra Rugby League To 1971, November 25, 2015)*
Courtesy of: Neil Pollock, Maher Cup author.

Bill Kearney

Bill Kearney right played Maher Cup football for Young from 1932-1946. An astute leader and tactician he gained Group 9 representation honours. He came from Queanbeyan to Young as a paid player for £2/10/-a week and board.

Although famous as a fullback, goal kicker and five-eighth, he gained even greater fame as a scrum half in combination with Bill Kinnane as five-eighth when the combined brilliance of their play earned them the titles of "The Wizards" or "The Terrible Bills".

Bill was cast in the same mould as Eric Weissel and perhaps one of the most outstanding personalities in Group 9 and other country areas.

1938 Young Rugby League Team
Mick O'Rourke, Mark Keogh, Lindsay Spencer, Jim Murden, Abe Hall,
Yank (Dr. Stan) Smith, Bill Hanley, Merv Torpy, Jack O'Connor, Bill Kinnane (Captain), Bill Kearney,
Sid Hall. Ken or Kevin Dillon, Tom Briggs.

Courtesy of: Brian Hughes & Temora Independent.

1938 Grenfell Rugby League Team

Back Row: J. Upton (Secretary), Bill 'Sorlie' Crowe, Bill Pike, Albert 'Dutchy' Stokes, Jack Batty, Bill Batty Merv McCelland, W. Thompson (President).
Middle Row: A. Burton, Pat Jeffries, Jenkins, Tom Bensley.
Front Row: Frank 'Googler' Brown, Mick Crowe, Sam Hamilton.

Courtesy of: Brian Hughes & Temora Independent.

1945 Cowra Rugby League Team

In 1945 Maher Cup football resumed. Young, as the Cup holders, won the first game and held it for twelve games with local players until beaten by Cowra 5-2 when Cowra had most of its players selected from the big army camp at Cowra.

Cowra won the last five games that season and started the 1946 season with nine wins in a row. Tumut then made its mark by winning the last nine games of 1946 after beating Cowra 5-2.

Back Row: G. Gledhill, Alan Hodge, Norm Weekes, Bill Maizey (Coach), J. Nicholas, W. Hughes (President).
Middle Row: H. Casson (Manager), K. Abrahamson, Allan Murphy, Arch Anderson (Captain),
Bert 'Curley' Hewitt, Jim Quinn, J. Caldwell (Secretary).
Front Row: Arthur "Blue" Roberts, Harry Chong Sun, R. Casson (Mascot), Reg Swilkes, Ray Kelly.

Courtesy of: Brian Hughes & Temora Independent.

1947 Cootamundra Maher Cup Rugby League Team

Back Row: Walter Cowled (Committee), Russel Cohen, Neil McDonell, Doug Wall, Stan McAlister, Bob Gehrig, Bob Hobbs, Kevin Chuck, Harold Thackeray, Frank Schurmer, Geoff Rogers.
Front Row: Ken Mulrooney, Jack Walsh (Committee), Alf Broughton, Jack 'Onion' Bell, Barry Fuller (Ball Boy), Herb Narvo (Captain Coach), Lance Penny (President), Jim Crowe, Les Wood (Selector).

Courtesy of: Neil Pollock, Maher Cup author.

1946-1956 Cootamundra Player Mick Howse
Typical Country Footballer

Mick Howse started playing for Cootamundra as a front rower at the age of seventeen in 1946, played 208 games and retired at the end of 1956.

During his career he played in Cootamundra's Maher Cup teams. In particular, the 1954 team defeated the Young Cherrypickers for the Cup.

Mick mentioned that his success was due to Herb Narvo who was Cootamundra's first grade coach and a great mentor.

Mick played in five winning premiership teams for Cootamundra: 1947, 48, 50, 51 and 54 and played in the 1953 grand-final.

The following details Cootamundra as Group 9 Premiers and runner-up in 1953:

Year:	Premiers:	Runner-up:	Score:
1947	Cootamundra Bulldogs	Young Cherrypickers	50 - 10
1948	Cootamundra Bulldogs	Young Cherrypickers	14 - 9
1950	Cootamundra Bulldogs	Junee Diesels	11 - 5
1951	Cootamundra Bulldogs	West Wyalong Mallee Men	16 - 13
1953	Young Cherrypickers	Cootamundra Bulldogs	9 - 7
1954	Cootamundra Bulldogs	Temora Dragons	21 – 7

Article from: Mick and Stephen Howse.

1950 Grenfell Maher Cup Winners

Back Row: Kevin Shepherd, Les McClelland, Arthur 'Ossie' Coleman, Noel Gavin, Don Bruce, Alf Aston, Quenton 'Quint' Graham.

Middle Row: Stan Lunken, Bill Parker, Jack 'Johnny' Clare, Clem Kennedy (Captain-Coach), Edward 'Barney' Hines, Brian Power.

Front Row: Ball boys W. Foote, Doug McClelland.

Courtesy of: Neil Pollock, Maher Cup author.

Evacuated From Ground

Crowd leaving Anzac Park, Gundagai, June, 1952, after a sudden rise in the Murrumbidgee River had marooned over 6,000 spectators. The match was played between Gundagai and Young.

Courtesy of: Brian Hughes & Temora Independent.

1951 Barmedmen Rugby League Team Maher Cup Holders

Back Row: A. Kelly (Vice President), T. Parker (Secretary), I. Curran (Referee), F. Kelly (Selector), C. Myott (President), L. Mangelsdorf, B. Rollison, J. Lawrence, W. Towers, A. Regan, F. Harvey, K. Steele, C. Quinlan, J. Harriott (Strapper, B. Walker, R. Barrett (Treasurer), K. McDonald, P. Kelly (Assistant Treasurer), E. Wirth (Vice-Captain).
Front Row: L. Cornwall, D. Lawrence, J. Berg, T. Kirk, N. Pierce (Captain-Coach, R. Moir, R. Gorham, Mascot Kevin Steele.

Courtesy of: Brian Hughes & Temora Independent.

1952 Cootamundra Rugby League Team Group 9 Premiers

Back Row: Ian Reid, Tony Howse, Neil McDonell, Keith Henniker, Mick Howse, Kevin Chuck.

Middle Row: Keith Duffey, Kevin Wheatley, Roley McDonell (Captain-Coach), Jim Crowe.

Seated: Vern Taylor, 'Digger' Fuller, Ball Boy, Peter Kirkby.

Courtesy of: Neil Pollock, Maher Cup author.

1952 Gundagai Tigers Rugby League Team

The famous Ferocious Gundagai Tigers in 1952, the team which held the Maher Cup for 22 consecutive games.

Back Row: Peter Reardon, Harry Gibbs, Stan Crowe (President), Noel Goodself, Cliff Attwood, Kevin Warden.

Second Row: George Ballard, Des Fields, Jack Plater, Len Koch, Owen Hourn, Paul Butz.

Front Row: Bryan Longhurst, Ron Battye, Nev Hand, Bill Gardiner, Wally Towers.

Seated: Trevor Lawson, John Ryan.

Courtesy of: Brian Hughes & Temora Independent.

Gresham Hotel Gundagai

"Dogs may sit on Tucker Boxes at Gundagai" but sportsmen, supporters and all others who like better service head to Gresham Hotel Gundagai.

Source: Archives, Australian National University

1955 Cootamundra Rugby League Team.

Back Row: Noel Crowe, Terry Paul, Wal Galvin, Charles Sedgwick, Ted Stanton, Denis Howse, Mick Howse.

Front Row: Lal Louttit, Bill Bell, Don Bowtell, Max Bell, Colin Yates, Larry Thamos, Barry Fuller (Ball Boy)

Source: Cootamundra Facebook

1957 Temora Rugby League Team Group 9 Premiers

Back Row: Barry Roberts, Brian Matthews, Len Henman, E. Coleman, (President), Peter McGrath, L. McMullen, Barney Roberts, Kevin Malby.

Middle Row: J. Stephenson (Selector), E. Curran, Ray 'Squeaker' Kerry, Les Gillard (Captain), Don Winbank, A. Lynch, S. Barrington (Selector).

Front Row: B. Howe (Masseur), Jim Broad, R. Allen, John Milton (Mascot), R. Smith, Don McKenzie, F. Meale (Treasurer).

Courtesy of: Brian Hughes & Temora Independent.

1935 Queensland Hotel Temora

The Queensland hotel was the place where the Temora team and their supporters would gather after Maher Cup games.

A victory would be followed by speeches and congratulations and the old cup would be passed around among the supporters who showed their appreciation by donating £1 and 10/- notes into the overflowing cup.

The proceeds would be shared equally among the players.

Hotels were the main meeting place after the game where players and spectators would celebrate their teams' victories, how the game was played and the referees' decisions. Blow by blow action replay.

Source: Archives, Australian National University

1959-1960 Harden-Murrumburrah Record Holders

The great team which held the Maher Cup for the whole of the 1959 season and for eleven matches in the 1960 season a total of 27 consecutive Maher Cup wins.

Back Row: R. Day, T. Apps, Garry Lanham, Matt Grenfell (Captain), Bernie Nevin, Frank Todd, I. Ellison.

Front Row: N. Cullen, Tex Steele, B. Robinson, E. Kuhn, K. Negus, John Dowd.

Courtesy of: Michael Greenwood.

1960 Maher Cup Game Referees Appointment

Group 9 Referees' Association

Patron:
G. CRONIN (Cootamundra)

President:
J. O'REILLY (Young)

Hon. Secretary-Treasurer:
W. RAY WARD (Cootamundra)
Phone 523.

Go to it.

"YOLANDE,"
71 KENT AVENUE,
COOTAMUNDRA 19-4- 1960.

J. Livermore.

You have been appointed to control "Maher Cup" Fixture between Harden and West Wyalong. at Harden on SATURDAY 23-4-60

Courtesy of: Neil Pollock, Maher Cup author.

1963 Gundagai Rugby League Team

Back Row: Phil Carberry, Brian Walsh, Warwick Randall, Bruce McCarthy, Rob Smith, Col Coulton, Roger Ludkin, Dick Smith.

Middle Row: Reg Hawthorne, Fred Norden, John Bronc Jones (Captain-Coach), Ian Sheather, Eddie Reardon.

Front Row: Allen Lewis, Paul McCarthy, Michael Maher.

Courtesy of: Brian Hughes & Temora Independent.

1963 Gundagai Prepare for Maher Cup Challenge
Harden Humiliated in Tough and Torrid Game

In a ferocious and fierce Maher Cup encounter last Saturday, Gundagai not only thrashed Harden-Murrumburrah, but humiliated them, bringing the Magpies to a complete subjection to the will of the Tigers.

It was a terrific game of power and might and in the clash the Black and Gold men rose to glorious heights and regained possession of the Cup that counts by the big margin of 24 points to 2.

The game was fierce and tough but contained very little of the spectacular, yet Gundagai's scoring moves were gems of speed and pace and the swiftness of the attack was something for which Harden had no counter.

Above Left: The Gundagai Tigers' skipper "Bronc" Jones (far right) discusses plans for the game prior to last Saturday's Maher Cup match with team members, Dickie Smith, Phill Carberry and Bruce McCarthy. In front the team's mascot, Paul McCarthy.

Above Right: Gundagai's big Ted Tout bursts away, winger Smith comes across, but Tout burst through his tackle and went on to score.

Article from: The Gundagai Independent, September 12, 1963. Republished courtesy of ACM/Gundagai Independent.

1965 Tumut First Grade Rugby League Team

Back Row: Graham Pearce, Mick Redden, John Stuckey, Terry Stuart, Ken Eggleton, Barry Webb, Greg Hay (Captain-Coach), Geoff Brian, Robert Giddings, Neil Ballard, Ray Bryan, Garry Jeffery, Vern Ree.

Front row: Peter Jeffery, Barry Madigan and (Ballboy).

Courtesy of: Michael Greenwood.

The Two Clubs to Play in the Final Maher Cup Game
5th June 1971 Young Football Ground

1971 TUMUT:
Back Row: Herb Gaul (President), Neil Bulger, Mick Cullen, Dick Smith, Robert Giddings, Bert Scott, John Hobby (Captain/Coach), Geoff McIntyre, Ron Pendergast.
Front Row: Ron Sutton, W. Elliott, Keiran Butler, Neil Richards, Garry Jeffrey, Ray Beavan, Terry Sturt, David Hobby (Ball-boy).

1971 YOUNG:
Back Row: Bob Weir (Coach), Martin Dorian, Max Gilbert (Captain), John Schofield, J. Hobson, I. Schofield, Adrian Saines, Alan McMahon, Michael Fairall, Terry Casey.
Front Row: Bernard Powdery, Barry Martens, Colin Blizzard, Don Jenkins, Noel Ashton, Terry Ricketts, "Noisy" McLachlan (Ball-boy).

Young defeated Cootamundra 17-14 at Young to hold the Maher Cup on the 29th May, 1971.

The final Maher Cup Challenge held on the 5th June 1971 went to the club where the great trophy started, Tumut. Tumut, who were playing their first game in six years, were destined to write themselves into the Cup's final year history.

A gate of $422.40 drew a crowd of 800 people, who were on hand to see Tumut give the holders a football lesson, defeating Young 43-4. In this *historical* game point scorers were:

Tumut G. McIntyre 2 tries, T. Sturt 2 tries,
R. Sutton 1 try J. Hobby 1 try, N. Richards 1 try, R. Beavan 1 try, M. Cullen 1 try, R. Sutton 6 goals
Young B. Martens 2 goals.

Without knowing it, the last Maher Cup match was played and the famous trophy was to slip into history after 50 years of great excitement and plenty of controversy. The cup returned to where it was born, Tumut.

Courtesy of: Brian Hughes & Temora Independent.

The Old Pot Finally Laid to Rest at Young
June 5th 1971

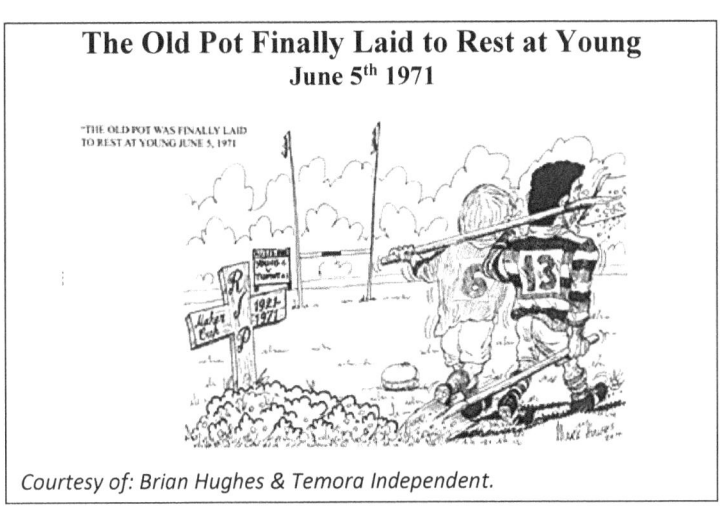

Courtesy of: Brian Hughes & Temora Independent.

Canowindra where the Jack Hore Memorial Gold Cup was Born

Canowindra formed its first rugby league team in 1920 and Jack Hore played fullback up until his sudden death on 4th March 1926.

On the 10th April 1926, a committee expressed interest in plans for a Jack Hore Memorial Cup. The committee collected money from the town's people to purchase a suitable cup. The response was immediate and a little over a month later, on the 28th May 1926, the Jack Hore Memorial Cup was displayed in the Canowindra Jeweler's shop window.

In those days when rugby league teams were the pride and joy of all the residents, the Jack Hore Memorial Cup soon ranked with the Maher Cup as one of the most prestigious trophies in challenge cup football. Towns throughout the Central Western and Southern regions would challenge for the honour of holding the cup.

Change was on its' way with the telephone replacing the bush telegraph, farming moving on and Saturday night at the picture theatres.

Gaskill Street, Canowindra in 1929.
Source: NSW State Archives Collection.

Jack Hore Gold Cup.

T.J. O'Brien's Royal Hotel, Canowindra 1924.
Source: Archives, Australian National University.

Deacon's Victoria Hotel, Canowindra 1925.
Source: Archives, Australian National University.

Royal Hotel, Canowindra 1949.
Source: Archives, Australian National University.

Victoria Hotel, Canowindra 1949.
Source: Archives, Australian National University

Jack Hore Sudden Passing

March 1926

Jack had a personality which many do not possess and everyone with whom he came in contact with could not help but like him and it was for this reason that his loss is keenly felt on all sides. On the field of sport, he was exceedingly popular and only last year it will be remembered that by his exploits he thrilled many a large crowd of spectators on the local football field and on other grounds. In the position of fullback for his side he fought for victory all the time and in many a match he received such punishment that he was almost compelled to leave the field but with his great heart, he always came up smiling and with a lightening spirit unequalled, stuck to his run. Jack was skipper of the local football team.

Jack Hore
Courtesy of: Canowindra Historical Museum Inc.

Jack also played for the Canowindra cricket team and was a dashing and valuable batsman. He was the life of the team, both on our ground and away from Canowindra and on occasions, he created many a laugh by his witty expressions but when we had to knuckle down with our backs to the wall, our late colleague was always to the fore and many a time he broke dangerous partnerships with his tricky delivery. Jack also played against Parkes and Grenfell in the Grinsted Cup.

The innumerable qualities of the late Jack Hore are embedded deep in the memory of everyone who knew him and he can never be forgotten.

His legacy continues in Canowindra to this day.

At the annual meeting of the Canowindra Rugby League Club on March 11, 1926, a minute's silence was held in his memory. On the 10th April 1926, a committee expressed interest in plans for a Jack Hore Memorial Cup. The committee, which included Tom Campbell and Tom Hough, was formed to collect money from the town's people to purchase a suitable cup. The response was immediate and a little over a month later, on the 28 May 1926, the Jack Hore Memorial Cup was displayed in the window of the shop of Mr Berbman, a Canowindra Jeweler. It proved to be a cup well worthy of the late Jack Hore. Many admirers had donated money for its purchase.

Some donations were only two shillings but the final amount of 130 pounds allowed for the cup purchase and a gift of a cot for the Canowindra Soldiers Memorial Hospital.

Jack Hore died suddenly on March 4, 1926 at Canowindra from a spinal complaint, myelitis. A requiem mass was held in St Edwards Catholic Church, Canowindra, on Friday, March 5, 1926. The service was conducted by his old friend, the Reverend Father O'Kennedy. Jack was buried in the Cowra cemetery. He was 25 years old at the time of his death.

Article from: The Canowindra Star, March 12, 1926. Republished courtesy of Canowindra Star.

Better Off To Catch The Next Train

Source: Donald Alfred Riach Collection.

Jack Hore Memorial Gold Challenge Cup

Over the years, not all clubs winning at the end of each season took advantage of the 1926 Rule 35 to have their names engraved at their own expense on the small shield. Those that are engraved are:

1926, Canowindra; 1927, Canowindra; 1928, Canowindra; 1929, Canowindra; 1930, Temora; 1931, Junee; 1932, Temora; 1933, Forbes; 1934, Forbes; 1937, Parkes; 1954, Cargo; 1955, Yeoval; 1956, Cumnock; 1959, Molong.

In those days when Rugby League teams were the pride and joy of all the residents, the Jack Hore Memorial Cup soon ranked with the Maher Cup as one of the most prestigious trophies in challenge cup football.

Other cups played for were the David Crawford Cup, the Denton Cup, the Hutchinson Cup, the Collison Cup, the Martin Cup, the Peters Cup, the F. & G. Cup and the Johnnie Walker Cup.

Courtesy of: Canowindra Historical Society & Museum Inc. (Jack Hore Memorial Cup, Ron Worboys, 1992, p. 8).

Canowindra Started to Employ Coaches

The first coach to come to Canowindra was Ponto Ryan, who came from Bathurst in 1924, and was a former Western Suburbs (Sydney) footballer, and who was paid by the players themselves. The following year, "Massa" Johnson came to Canowindra.
He was an original All Black of New Zealand, and coached the men on vacant land behind Finn's Store, and where the Commonwealth Bank now stands.

Canowindra was moulded into a fine team, and defeated teams from Grenfell who were coached by Frank Burge, and Cowra coached by Rex "Rocker."

Norman, a man who had the distinction of bowling the great Bradman, on the Canowindra oval, for a 'duck'. Rex was lured to Canowindra in 1926.

Canowindra players, under Norman, developed and had one of the finest teams produced in the country, and as one man said, in 1926 to 1929, we were in the 'Golden Age' of football here only losing one match in three seasons of football, and then winning the cup back the week following its loss.

During these years, all football was in the form of challenge matches for the Jack Hore Gold Cup, a cup donated by the people of Canowindra and District to perpetuate the memory of a very likeable personality, who died at Canowindra in March, 1926.

Article courtesy of: Canowindra Historical Society & Museum Inc.

Manildra Police Station Telephone Connection

Leader Orange NSW Monday 16th 1922

The Hon. J. C. L. Fitzpatrick has received the following communication from the Chief Secretary's Office: "In reply to your representation in relation to the request that the Manildra Police Station be connected by telephone with the local exchange, I desire to state that the Inspector General of Police, to whom the matter was referred, reports that the advantages of having all police stations throughout the State connected with the telephone service is realized by the police authorities, but the absence of funds, it is regrettable that the connection of the police station at Manildra with the local exchange must remain in obeyance for the present.

Old Police Station

Article: Courtesy of Orange Leader 16th October 1922. Page 2

The Canowindra Star

1926 FOOTBALLERS' BALL

September 1926

The annual ball of the Canowindra Football Club always a very bright affair took place on Tuesday night last. There were about 150 couples present, visitors coming from all the surrounding centres and towns, Cowra and Eugowra being well represented, while there were some from Orange and Grenfell. The Strand Theatre Hall was very nicely decorated with streamers of delicate hue, while baskets and balloons were suspended among the streamers. At the entrances from the ballroom to the pathways between the seats at the rear of the hall were built representations of goal posts on which were hung footballs and flags all done in the colours of the club black and gold. The decorations were carried out by Mr. Clarrie Boyd and members of the football club. They produced a pleasing and delicate effect.

Owen's Orchestra supplied the music, while some extras were also played by some of the dancers.

Not very many of the dancers came in fancy costumes. We understand that a good many costumes ordered went astray and could not be obtained in time for the ball. The outstanding characters were those of Mrs. W. Best, as a modern flapper, who was hailed as "Miss Australia" and Mr. J. W. Lowick as a "coster."

Supper was served in cafeteria fashion all partaking of refreshments just as they felt inclined between 10.30 and 12.30. Mrs. J. Larkin was entrusted with the catering, the refreshments being very well prepared.

During the evening opportunity was taken to present to the Club the Jack Hore Memorial Gold Cup, which had been held right through the season. Mr. Walter Murray made the presentation to Mr. A. H. Grant, President of the Club and he stated he wished to compliment the players on their magnificent victories.

He said that not one member of the team could be accused of wishing to hurt any playing opponent if they had to do that to win then they would sooner lose.

He went on to say that it had started in other towns that the rules governing the Hore Cup were unfair Cowra in particular.

There they were supposed to have great respect and regard for the late Jack Hore but had done most to injure his memory by unfair criticism of the cup which was in his memory.

They had done a fine thing in collecting £130 for the cup. He was certain the cup would be in play for very many years the unborn generation would talk of the Jack Hore Cup which was a memorial to a most exemplary young man.

Mr. A. H. Grant, in accepting the trophy, said, speaking of Jack Hore, he had been with him in sport, pleasure, work and in the house and there was not a better boy in Australia.

Mr. E. Murray gave some figures in connection with matches played during the season. Six had been played for the Hore Cup, the total scores being 128 points against their opponents' 30. They had played a total of 18 matches in first grade football, only being defeated twice, with a total of 321 points against 128 by the opposing teams.

The individual scores for the Jack Hore Cup matches were: R. Norman 40, L. Abberton 15, H. Turner 11, J. McLeigh 17, M. O'Neil 6, Eddie Grant 15, T. Sullivan 15, Arthur Grant 3, Ken Grant 3, E. Cassidy 3.

All matches:
Peter Grant 3, R. Norman 94, T. Sullivan 62, N. Cox 3, Arthur Grant 9, H. Turner 22, Reg Grant 18, M. O'Neil 9, Eddie Grant 30, W. Marsh 12, Ken Grant 10, Reg Goodacre 3, L. Abberton 26, J. McLeish 17, E. Cassidy 3.

Occasion was taken to present to Mr. O'Neil a medal which was for the best all-round player for the season awarded after a ballot had been taken among the public.

In returning thanks, Mr. O'Neil said he would treasure it, while he thought he was lucky in receiving it, as it could have been given to any one of a half dozen of the members of the team without doing an injustice. Dancing resumed and continued to about 2.30 am.

Mr. E. Murray, as secretary of the club, had the organisation of the ball well carried out, bringing the football season here to a happy ending.

Mr. Murray has done excellent work as organiser for the club in arranging so many attractive matches, which the public have thoroughly enjoyed.

Article from: Canowindra Star, Friday, September 3, 1926. Republished courtesy of Canowindra Star.

Canowindra Plays for the Jack Hore Gold Cup

Canowindra had a very good team at that time and was the holder of the 150 guineas Jack Hore Gold cup. This magnificent trophy was presented by the public in memory of a great sportsman, Jack Hore, who died in Canowindra at the age of twenty five. For some years this trophy competed very strongly with the Maher Cup for popularity, but the Maher cup with Its longer history ended as the winner.

An example of Canowindra's standard can be gauged from the fifth match played for the Jack Hore Cup against Young at Canowindra Showground on Sunday, July 25, 1926.

The teams were:

Canowindra: fullback, J. McLeish; three-quarters, L. Abberton, Rex Norman (captain and ex international), H. Turner, T. Sullivan; five-eighth, Ancil Grant; half-back, M. O'Neil; forwards, Eddie Grant, Ken Grant, Arthur Grant, J. Grant, N. Cox and W. Marsh.

Courtesy of: Canowindra & District Historical Society Inc.

Young: fullback, R. Hall; threequarters, J. Brown, L. Joyce, S. Hall, W. Douglas; five-eighth, E. "Teddie" Taplin (captain and coach); half-back, Armour; forwards, Tholry, Keogh, Phillips, Watts, Collins and McIntyre.

Canowindra won by 20 to nil. Opponents of Sunday football were very strong at that time so when a Young player and a Canowindra player started fighting with two minutes to go, it looked as if the critics would have some good ammunition. The Bathurst referee stopped the game and without any qualifications ordered the two fighters to shake hands. The unexpectedness of the order compelled them to do this. As one observer said, "It was like two man-eating tigers meeting."

One can understand then why Cootamundra, which had the main say in the rules, refused to have the Maher Cup at stake in its game. Canowindra then fielded an ordinary team and lost.

For the last game against Temora in that year of 1926, the Temora Municipal Council granted its employees a half holiday. There had been a lot of hot arguments about the referee and about anything else that could cause trouble, so general feeling was very tense.

Courtesy of: Brian Hughes & Temora Independent. (The Famous Maher Cup, 2010, page 20).

Canowindra Railway Station

Courtesy of: Donald Alfred Riach's Collection.

JACK HORE GOLD CUP

If a Group 9 team had won the Maher Cup and then won back the Jack Hore Gold Cup the same season, it could claim with truth that it was the best football team west of the Dividing Range.

Several teams, including, Temora, Barmedman and Young won this trophy at various times. For example, the Forbes team held the Cup for two years, they had won it from the Temora team led by Eric Weissel on July 9, 1933, by 17 points to 7.

On Sunday, July 7, 1935, Young added a new lustre to its fame by winning the Cup from Forbes by 12 points to 11. Twenty of the 23 points scored during this game came from goals with Forbes recording the only try just as the signal for full time was given.

Bill Kearney kicked five goals from all angles to score ten of Young's winning lead of 12 points.

In its report "The Western Sun" said, "It was a match of giants, but the deeds of Bill Kearney, of Young and Clifton, of Forbes, made the stars of the day."

Bill Kearney

Courtesy of: Brian Hughes & Temora Independent, (The Famous Maher Cup, 2010, P. 77).

Jack Kingston Rugby League Great

Cootamundra product first represented NSW in 1928 while playing for Young. A speedy lock forward and fine cover defender Kingston made his Test debut in Australia's Third Test win over England in the 1928 Ashes series before touring with the 1929-30 Kangaroos. He played in 26 matches on tour, including the Third Test draw and historic Fourth Test against England. Kingston, who scored the most tries by a forward on the tour (18), crossed for 4 tries in the Kangaroos' 42-19 win over 'The Rest' on his return to Australia. A member of Cootamundra's Maher Cup team Kingston continued to represent NSW until 1934 when he decided to try his luck in Sydney with Wests.

Jack Kingston died at the age of 49 in 1957, having collapsing at the wheel of his car while driving his children to school. The children were unharmed as his wife was able to take control of the vehicle.

1929 Jack Kingston

Source: Wikipedia, the free encyclopedia

The First Match

The first match for the Cup was played between Canowindra and Young on the 27 June, 1926. Canowindra won 4-nil with Rex Norman kicking two penalty goals. He was an outstanding sportsman who had come to Canowindra to play cricket. Rex captained and coached the Canowindra League team for a number of seasons. He was a great coach and football player who achieved outstanding results. He was paid 8 pounds a week and given free board at Fogart's Hotel, Canowindra, now the Hotel Canowindra.

The teams for the Jack Hore Memorial first match are shown in the souvenir programme below.

Canowindra won the match defeating Young 4 nil with Rex Norman kicking two penalty goals. *It is interesting to note that there were six Grants in the Canowindra team.*

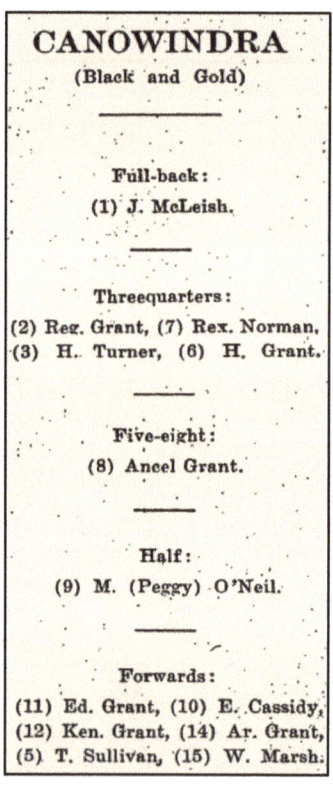
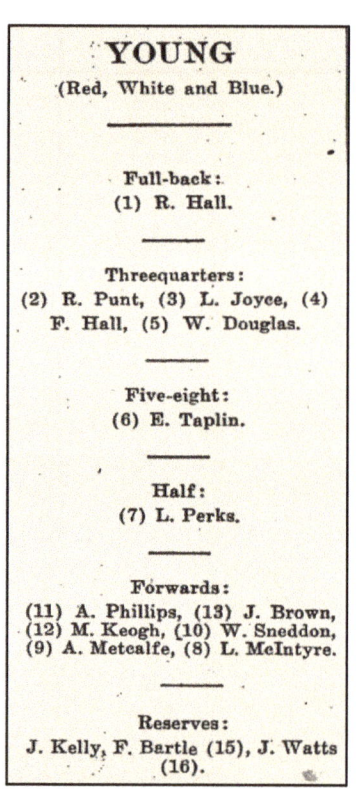

Courtesy of: Canowindra Historical Society & Museum Inc. (The Jack Hore Memorial Gold Cup, Ron Worboys, 1990.

Jack Hore Gold Cup Winning Blazer

Courtesy of: Robert Rice Canowindra.

1926 First Canowindra Football Team to Challenge Jack Hore Memorial Gold Cup

Players, Back Row: Cecil Press (white pullover), Tom Sullivan, Arthur Grant, Rex Norman, Wilf Marsh, Ed Grant, Reg Grant.

Front Row: Ancel Grant, "Peggie" O'Neil, Tom Barnes, Horace Turner, Ken Grant, Eddie Cassidy, Jack McGliesh.

Canowindra played Young at the Show Ground Canowindra, June 27, 1926.
Canowindra defeated Young 4-0.

Courtesy of: Canowindra Historical Society & Museum Inc.

Original Riach Farm House Gregra

Early in 1874 my great grand-parents Richard and Annie Riach travelled over the mountains by bullock-wagon with their three children and all their possessions which included seeds, tools, a single-furrow plough and various other pieces of small machinery.

In 1901 they planted about 12 acres of citrus trees on the property and were a well-known district orange grove. In the orange season, visitors from many miles around would come to purchase their citrus fruit. Richard had a bullock wagon and a team to cart produce to Sydney and return with supplies for his family and other settlers in the district. The return trip would take from six to eight weeks.

Original Farm house, Kurrajong.

Source: Donald Alfred Riach's Collection.

1873 Original Agricultural Receipt Richard Riach

Source: Donald Alfred Riach's Collection.

1927 Canowindra Football Team

Back Row: Arthur Patterson (President), Norm Cox, Tom "Bull" Sullivan, Arthur Grant, Val Conlen (Secretary), Hector Laranche.

Middle Row: Roddy Gilmour, Peter Reid, Mick Abberton, Rex Norman (Captain-Coach), Ken Grant, Wally Bowd, Horace Grant.

Front Row: Ancel Grant, Horace Turner, Teddy Grant.

Courtesy of: Canowindra Historical Society & Museum Inc.

1928 Jack Hore Gold Cup Challenges

The results of games played in 1928 are listed below. This was the greatest year ever for the Canowindra team, which held the Cup for eleven challenges. It is interesting to note that on many occasions the games were controlled by the top Sydney referees.

20.05.28	Canowindra V Cowra	Won 15-7
27.05.28	Canowindra V Carcoar	Draw 8 all
10.06.28	Canowindra V Orange Old Boys	Won 20-8
17.06.28	Canowindra V Wellington	Won 17-13
24.06.28	Canowindra V Grenfell	Won 9-5
22.07.28	Canowindra V Young	Won 17-6
29.07.28	Canowindra V Cowra	Won 13-10
05.08.28	Canowindra V Carcoar	Won 17-2
12.08.28	Canowindra V Bathurst Waratahs	Won 51-12
19.08.28	Canowindra V Yeoval	Won 13-8
26.08.28	Canowindra V Wellington	Won 5-nil

In 1928 Canowindra also travelled to Cootamundra and won the Maher Cup by 24-8. However, they lost in a protest as Rod Gilmore was ruled to live outside the ten-mile radius of Canowindra. Three hundred people travelled on a special train for the match and a hundred people joined from intermediate towns on the way to Cootamundra.

Courtesy of: Canowindra Historical Society & Museum Inc. (The Jack Hore Memorial Cup, Ron Warboys, 1992, p. 21).

Rex Norman

NSW RL Cartoon

Left: Rex Norman remembered for his accurate goal kicking, one of the best in country NSW.

Courtesy of: Canowindra Historical Society & Museum Inc.

1930 Jack Hore Memorial Gold Cup Challenge Canowindra v Temora

In June things got complicated in a tussle over Eric Weissel. Temora wanted him for a big match at Canowindra on Sunday for the Jack Hore Memorial Gold Cup, a trophy that generated as much passion as the Maher Cup in some Central West and Northern Riverina towns. However, the NSWRL had selected him to captain the state against Queensland the day before.

The mercurial Fred Cahill stepped in and negotiated that Eric would play both games, being driven overnight from Sydney to Canowindra.

It was heavy going crossing the mountains and Danny Murray, who was a member of the party, said he had the shivers well after the trip. Danny had to referee the match at Canowindra.

Temora won the match 27-7, Weissel scored a try and with a 5000 crowd and a massive £200 gate it was the biggest football match to date at Canowindra.

Temora went on and defended the cup against Orange.

1930 Temora Rugby League Team

Back Row: Eric Curren, Charlie Bray, Norman Bland (President), George King, Reg Maker.

Middle Row: Leo Curren, Horace Anthony, Eric Weissel (Captain Coach), Norm Dundas, Alan (Snowy) Lynch, Bob Boyd.

Front Row: Joe Constable, Harold Thomas, Harry Owen, Jack Stephenson.

Courtesy of: Neil Pollock, Maher Cup author.

Ian 'Bunda' Breen a Bush Legend

'Bunda' Breen is a fourth generation of Breen's born in Canowindra. He has lived all his life in the same house on the farm that his family has owned for 118 years.

A typical farmer always willing to have a yarn, after visiting him on the family farm I realised how much should be recorded about his local history. His knowledge of rugby league was endless, naming players, coaches and administrators of the time. He talked about the golden years which included not only rugby league but farming and the communities throughout the region.

He is a life member of the Canowindra Tigers Rugby League Football Club and trustee of the famous Jack Hore Gold Cup.

Ian Breen

Ian went on to talk about the Annual Footballer's Ball being a classy event, the men wearing suits and the girls looking beautiful in their evening dresses. The woolshed dances and backyard barbeques held for players, supporters and committee men were legendary.

In 2020 the rugby league club held its One Hundred Year celebration at the Services Club Auditorium. It was attended by well over 300 guests with Ian the compere reflecting on the 1960s -1980s highlights of the game. Ian was the star performer and received a rousing applause from the audience.

Source: Ian Breen, Canowindra Historian.

Jack Hore Gold Cup
Retaken by Canowindra

Barmedman and Junee held the Cup during June and July and on the 27 July 1930, Canowindra defeated Junee 21-5, to regain the Cup. Both teams are listed below in the official program. The attendance, which was about 700, was the biggest seen in Junee on a Sunday. Rex Norman gave one of the finest displays of goal kicking at Junee, piloting six over the bars some of which were from further than half way. Cowderoy was out of kicking form, missing four attempts for Junee. Fifield led the Junee side and Fitzgerald, one of the side's best men was taken off the field hurt. The Hore Gold Cup was originally put into play at Canowindra. Temora took it off them, Barmedman took it from Temora and Junee took it from Barmedman.

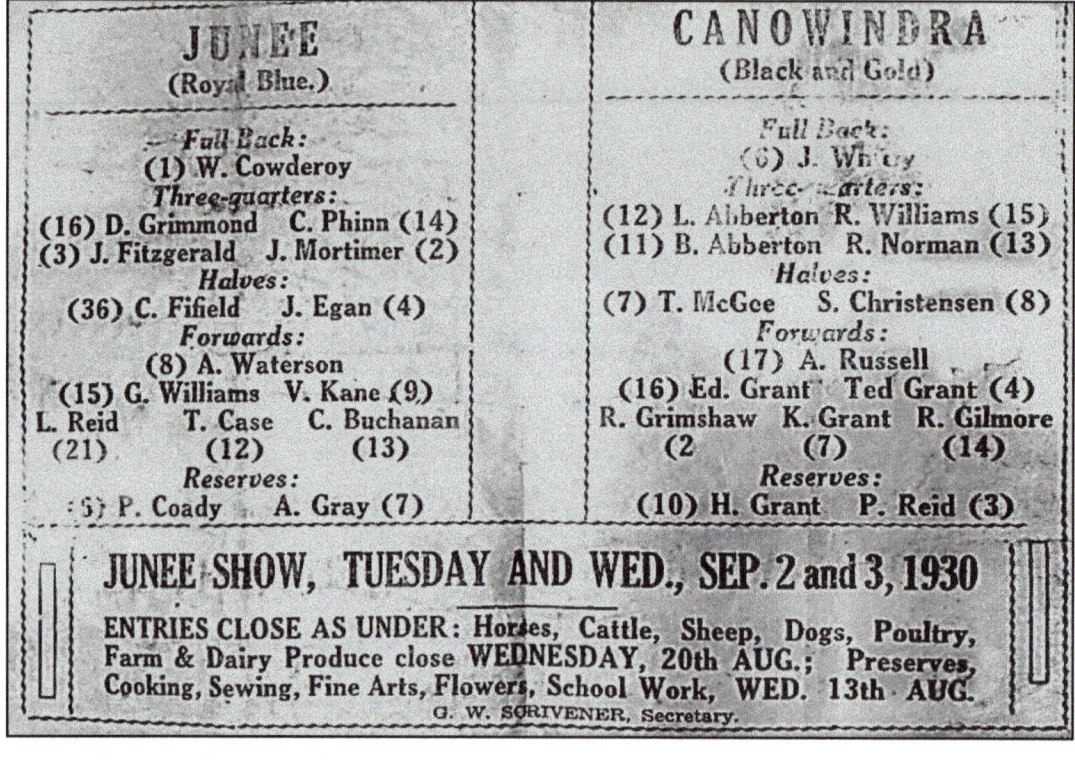

Courtesy of: Canowindra Historical Society & Museum Inc.

Bush Telegraph to Telephone

Some Services Your Telephone Can Render You

Emergency Calls - Time Service

Morning and Reminder Calls

Trunk Line Services, including Personal and Fixed Time Calls

Telephoning Telegrams

Calls to Non Subscribers

Overseas Radio Telephone Calls

For further particulars consult the front pages of your Telephone Directory

Source: Greg Riach Author

1930 Canowindra Jack Hore Gold Cup Team

From left to right: Tom McGee, Bertie Abberton, Rod Gilmore, Eddie Grant, Mick Abberton, Billy Smith, Horace Grant, Bob King, Jim Whitty, Peter Reid, Dick Grimshaw, Ken Grant, Rex Norman Coach).

Courtesy of: Canowindra Historical Society & Museum Inc

1932 Canowindra Jack Hore Gold Cup Team

From left to right: Albert Clyburn, Jack Stubbs, Bill Newcombe, Paddy Clyburn, Tom Clyburn, Stan Nichols, Cec Slatery, "Pongo" Hodge, Archie Thurtell, Fred Thurtell, Tony Lupton, Jack Ritchie, Dick Grimshaw, Rex Norman (Coach).

Courtesy of: Canowindra Historical Society & Museum Inc

1932 Manildra Amusu Theatre and Travelling Talkies

Saturday Night at the Pictures

Movies were first screened at Manildra around 1910. In 1914, they were shown in Fleeting's Hall, Derowie Street. Starting during the silent era, Allan Tom quickly adapted equipment for the "talkies". Known as a travelling picture show pioneer, Tom toured the central western and goldfields areas of New South Wales from the early 1920s into the 1940s to areas as far afield as Cobar, Bourke, Hillston, Trundle and Tullamore. Allan Tom pictured above right between the two trucks.

Courtesy of: Donald Alfred Riach's Collection.

The Canowindra Star Tells the Story May 15 1936

It is the long lane that has no turning was proved at Young last Sunday when Canowindra succeeded in defeating Young in the first Gold Cup match of the season. Six long years since the trophy left Canowindra. It was not to be wondered that the "town" literally went wild with excitement when news came to hand that the black and golds had defeated Young 8-4. A packed "house" greeted the players on their return. Even the engine driver of the special train, which the club had chartered for the occasion, joined in the spirit of celebration and the "Cock a doodle" of the whistle which began a few miles out of Canowindra did not cease until the train pulled into the station.

Next week's game will be welcomed by a crowd reminiscent of the days when Canowindra was fielding the greatest combination in the history of the locals.

Courtesy of: Canowindra Historical Society & Museum Inc, (The Jack Hore Memorial Cup, Ron Worboys,1992, p. 33).

1936 Canowindra Rugby League Team

Back Row: Archie Thurtell, Son Hodge, Albert Clyburn, Tony Lupton, Jack Stubbs, Ted Grant, Unck Ferner, Jack Day.
Front Row: Freddy Thurtell, Bob Richie, Tommy Clyburn, Dick Grimshaw (friend of Brian Grant), Ken Grant. Top Right: Albert and Tom Clyburn.

Courtesy of: Canowindra Historical Society & Museum Inc.

1952 Country Firsts v Sydney Firsts-R Norman Coach

Back Row: S. Frost (Trainer), C. Gill, R. Norman (Coach), N. Frazer, T. Downie (Trainer).

Middle Row: C. Miller (Selector), A. Paul, L. Burke, K. Mogg, R. Roberts, B. Smith, H. Gibbs, J.Sharpe (Referee).

Front Row: P.Osullivan (Manager), B. Corlson, B. Hewitt, N. Hill (Captain), H. Wells, C. De Lore, A. Delevere (Manager).

May 17th
Final Score: City Firsts 23 defeated Country Firsts 21.

Courtesy of: NSW Rugby League, The Rugby League News, September, 1952

Molong Retains Jack Hore Gold Cup

July 1939

Not for a great many years has any sporting fixture drawn such a crowd of spectators as that which witnessed play on Sunday when Yeoval played Molong for the coveted Jack Hore Gold Cup, the blue riband of western football.

The curtain raiser, by a Cumnock team versus Molong No. 2, proved an exciting prelude to the big game and it is safe to say that it held the interest of the spectators throughout and when the final whistle blew with the score at 5 to 8 in Molong's favour the bulk of those present had their appetites whetted for the clash of the giants to follow and they were not disappointed.

A special train, as well as numerous cars and a couple of lorries, brought the Yeoval team and their supporters to Molong, over 100 passengers boarding the motor train and trailer at Yeoval. Up till the time the Cup match started, 125 cars had arrived at the ground, after that our representative was too busy watching the play to count cars to do anything else except look and make notes.

Enthusiasm ran high, and neither team could complain of lack of encouragement from their supporters. The fair sex, who must have gathered "en masse" were certainly not sparing in their criticism of loose play, in fact there were several near the press table who were patently capable of umpiring a match as well as any mere male.

The curtain raiser was umpired by Mr. A. Dover in his usual capable manner and Mr. Les O'Donnell, of Parkes, carried out the responsible duty of controlling the big match in an impartial and painstaking manner

Play was fast and hard throughout, but clean, with an almost entire absence of foul tactics and both teams are to be complimented on the standard of football displayed.

The first half proved that the Molong men were definitely in the ascendant as far as the back division was concerned, while the visitors, because of the superior weight of their pack, were just as superior in forward play.

Throughout the match, Yeoval scored a large share of the ball from the scrums, but the advantage was countered by the dash and speed of our three-quarter line.

The team was led onto the field by Barrie Lee as a mascot, but the team needed more than luck to defeat their doughty opponents. It took courage, grit and dogged perseverance to achieve the desired end.

Molong fans were naturally delighted at the success of the result in winning seven to nil and are looking forward with intense interest to the contest on Sunday when they will meet the strong Parkes combination in defence of the trophy.

Outstanding players for Yeoval were McKeowan, N. Miskell, Housler and Brown, while for Molong Reg Hillan, Campbell, Connelly, Reynolds in the back division, played inspired football, whilst the forwards Lay, Garlick, Tomsett, Sloane and Woodbank struggled like heroes to prevent their weighty antagonists from pushing them right off the map. Ken Dunn at half, was on the job all the time, but seldom had a chance of getting his hands on the ball.

Final Score: Molong 7 defeated Yeoval nil.

Article from: The Molong Express, Saturday July 16, 1939. Republished courtesy of ACM/Molong Express.

The Mystery of the Stathis Cup

Many press items have been discovered in the National Library newspaper Trove mentioning rugby league teams in Boree Shire, playing for the Stathis Cup between 1924-1936. Towns mentioned include Grenfell, Woodstock, Lyndhurst, Cudal, Mandurama and Canowindra.

In 1909 at the age of 18, Panayiotis George Stathis, who later changed his name to Peter, migrated to Australia from Greece.

In 1920 Peter moved to Canowindra and operated a Fruit and Confectionary Shop or "Refreshment Rooms", called Garden Roses Café, firstly with Nicholas Calocherry, then on his own.

Reports indicated that the Cup was likely to have been donated by Peter Stathis as a marketing tool for his business.

The sponsorship of the cup competition may have included money to pay for uniforms, fees and maintenance of the grounds.

John Minchin has provided the information above in the hopes that someone may be able to provide details on the trophy or team photos, which may be sitting in someone's shed, lounge room or storage room, just waiting to be discovered.

Courtesy of: John Minchin.

Peter Stathis

JACK HORE CUP
Molong Protest Dismissed

July 1939

At a meeting of Group X1 judiciary committee at Parkes last night, Molong's protest in connection with the Hore Gold Cup match last Sunday was dismissed and the trophy was handed over to Parkes.

Molong alleged that the timekeepers had rung the final bell 10 minutes too soon.

The Judiciary committee reported that it could find no proof of the short time. It pointed out that the Molong timekeeper made no complaint to the Parkes timekeeper regarding any short time.

The case was heard before Messrs H. Triblett (Forbes), M. A. O'Neil (Dubbo) and H. J. Abberton (Canowindra).

Article from: The Dubbo Liberal and Macquarie Advocate, Tuesday, July 18, 1939. Republished courtesy of ACM/Dubbo Liberal and Macquarie Advocate.

1940 Canowindra Rugby League

Dick Grimshaw 1929

Canowindra, 27 June, 1940
Mr. R. Grimshaw
Canowindra.

Dear Sir:
Members of the Committee of the above club have asked me to congratulate you on refereeing your first Jack Hore Cup Match last Sunday. We understand this is the first occasion, in which a certificated referee from Canowindra has had the destination of controlling a Jack Hore Cup Match. It is also pleasing to note that both teams were satisfied with your capabilities, and we look forward to you handling many more games of importance.

Yours faithfully
Secretary Jack Pearce

Dick refereed the Gold Cup match in Forbes in 1940.

Courtesy of: Canowindra Historical Society & Museum Inc. (Jack Hore Memorial Cup, Ron Worboys, 1992, p. 30-31).

1941 Canowindra Jack Hore Cup Rugby League Team

Back Row: "Spec" Elliott, Lindsay Rice, Tony Lupton, Fred Thurtell, Tommy Clyburn.

Middle Row: Bill Newcombe, Jack Day, Son Hodge (Captain), Jack Grant, Cec Slattery, Albert Clyburn.

Front Row: Jack "Peggy" Clyburn, Stan Nicholas.

Courtesy of: Canowindra Historical Society & Museum Inc.

1946 Canowindra Jack Hore Gold Cup Rugby League Team

Back Row: Alan Green, Ken Slattery, Reg Garfourth, Tommy Lupton, Dick Grimshaw, Fred Thurtell, Tommy Clyburn (injured).
Middle Row: Bill Kelly, Cec Slattery, Son Hodges (Captain), Albert Clyburn, Jack Grant.
Front Row: Bob Leggett, Milty Wilkins.

After World War 2, Group football took control and the number of challenges fell away. When the rules were changed, only Group 11 teams could play for the Cup and the larger centres lost interest. Cup football was not to be played on most Sundays during the season and the main support came from the Group 11 2nd Division Clubs. Competition matches took over and the Jack Hore Cup Challenges ceased in 1948, 49, 50, 51.

In 1953 the Jack Hore Cup was back in play and it was a successful year for Canowindra. Players were: Arthur Sargent, Denny Clyburn, Nev Henderson, Dick Westwood, Bill Rue, Barry Grant, Eugene Marsh, John Marsh, Dick Marsh, Col Delaney, Jack Butler, Morris McClintock, Jack Newland, George Carpenter, Alan Green, Owen Kelly, Erroll Thurtell and Joe Jorgenson (Captain Coach).

In the first game of the season against Cargo, Canowindra lost 11-10. Cargo then defeated Tullamore 9-2 and Cumnock 4-3 before Canowindra regained the Cup from Cargo on the 27th of June, 1953. Canowindra won the next seven games only to lose to Cargo in the last match of the season.

Courtesy of: Canowindra Historical Society & Museum Inc. (The Jack Hore Memorial Cup, Ron Worboys, 1992, p. 41).

1953 Canowindra Jack Hore Cup Rugby League Team

Left to Right: Arthur Sargent, Denny Clyburn, George Henderson, Dick Westwood, Bill Rue, Barry Grant, "Boo" Marsh, Jack Marsh, Dick Marsh, Col Delaney, Jack Butler, Morris McClintock, Joe Jorgenson (Captain Coach).
Courtesy of: Canowindra Historical Society & Museum Inc.

Johnnie Walker Cup

June 1922

The Johnnie Walker Cup was inaugurated at a meeting in Dubbo on 28 June, 1922 and inaugurated officially on the 22 July, 1922 when the Cup was presented to Dubbo Rugby League by the Johnnie Walker alcohol company.

In August 1922, Gilgandra became the first challenger.

Dubbo won the first eight challenges before a combined Geurie, Wongarbon and Arthurville team upset the holders in August 1924.

During the 1930s, when the Johnnie Walker Cup became the most prized trophy in the Western Districts, Warren was one of the few teams who could compete with Dubbo.

The Johnnie Walker Cup was played as a local then regional competition right through until the 1940s when it was shelved in that format as Group competitions grew in strength and introduced their own cups like the Boronia Cup (Group 14).

Group 11 teams then played for the Cup based on the winner defending on their home ground. It continued fairly successfully until the mid-1980s when interest started to wane.

Article from: The Dubbo Daily Liberal, republished courtesy of ACM/Dubbo Daily Liberal.

FORBES FOOTBALLERS DEFEAT DUBBO
JOHNNIE WALKER CUP

**Home Team on Top in Second Spell Lack of Finish Spoilt Several Opportunities
Dubbo Downed After Great Game Forbes 20 Dubbo 4.**

September 1934

Before a large attendance, the much-discussed match between Dubbo and Forbes eventuated at the Show Ground on Sunday, when after a stirring game, the visitors downed the Johnnie Walker Cup champions 20-4. It was a fast and stirring tussle from whistle to whistle and although the second spell was characterised by battles between the forwards for possession, there were frequent bright and spectacular movements. On the day, the better team won, but play in the second half indicated that the final score was not a true indication of the merits of the sides. Dubbo was beaten, and well beaten, but had a little more initiative been shown when the home team had the advantage, the scoring deficit could have been considerably smaller.

The game was well controlled by Mr. T. McMahon of Sydney.

Article from: The Dubbo Liberal and Macquarie Advocate, Tuesday, September 4, 1934. Republished courtesy of ACM/Dubbo Daily Liberal and Macquarie Advocate.

1920 Macquarie Street Dubbo

Source: historicalaustraliantowns.blogspot.com

FOOTBALL

Dubbo After Johnnie Walker Cup

Hard Match At Canowindra Tomorrow
BY "TOUCHLINE"

July 1939

At Canowindra tomorrow Dubbo probably will have its hardest match of the season. When these teams last met here the local representatives won 12-8, but Canowindra led until 10 minutes before the final whistle and when Dubbo wiped out the deficit the visitors were without the services of one of their best forwards.

Canowindra always is hard to beat on its own ground and in view of that stern struggle when these teams clashed a few weeks ago, a win by Dubbo tomorrow will be the crowning achievement of the season.

If Dubbo can produce the fireworks of which it is capable, the Johnnie Walker Cup will be back here. The locals are not noted for their consistency, however, and unless they play at their top from the first whistle they will have no chance of beating Rex Norman's men on their own battling ground. If Dubbo does make the pace from the start, however, it will topple the cup-holders. It is up to every man in the side to make a special effort for this game, for the "Johnnie" must be brought back to the West where the traditions surrounding it were established.

A good team has been selected, but in the opinion of this column the backs should have been left in the same positions as they were before the game at Parkes. Clymo was taken from centre to his old position as full-back, Woods was put centre, Sing on the wing and Patman centre. The rearrangement was a failure, according to those who saw the Parkes clash.

Apparently the selectors did not think so, for the only alteration for tomorrow is that Patman will play on the wing and Sing will be centre. Clymo is said to have played an excellent game as fullback at Parkes. If he can repeat this performance tomorrow, all should be well, for when he is on his game, Russell has few equals in the country. Provided he realises his responsibilities tomorrow and produces the form of which he is capable, Dubbo's chances will be enhanced considerably.

The forwards will be a better pack than the one that met Parkes. Owens is back again and will play in the lock position. It is the first time this season that he has played there, but he should make a success of the job and give good protection to the half back. O'Reilly and Frost will be joined in the second row and Gray and Kable will support Wand in the front row. This is easily a balanced pack and every man is fast and a hard worker. Canowindra also has a solid pack, but the Dubbo six should hold their own easily.

Here is the Dubbo side:
Full-back: R. Clymo.
Three-quarters: J. Head, W. Sing, C. Woods, W. Patman.
Five-eighth: E. Bennett.
Half-back: M. Wheeler.
Forwards: F. Gray, J. Wand, R. Kable, J. Frost, A. Reilly, R. Owens.

Canowindra will be represented by:
Full-back: W. Newcombe.
Three-quarters: T. Clyburn, S. Nicholls, A. Clyburn, J. Richie.
Five-eighth: J. Stubbs.
Half-back: E. Grant.
Forwards: T. Lupton, E. Clyburn, B. Cassidy, F. Thurtell, R. Grimshaw, S. Hodge.

Article from: The Dubbo Daily Liberal and Macquarie Advocate, Saturday, July 15, 1939. Republished courtesy of ACM/Dubbo Daily Liberal and Macquarie Advocate..

Passenger Train Next Stop Canowindra

Wikimedia Commons, The Free Media Repository.

RUGBY LEAGUE
Dubbo Determined To Regain J.W. Cup
Season's Record Wellington Match as Preliminary to Canowindra

July 1939

On Sunday week, Dubbo will travel to Canowindra in quest of the Johnnie Walker Cup. Despite recent reverses, the Blue and Whites are confident that this time they will come home with the coveted silverware.

Even allowing for their disappointment at the form shown in some matches, supporters have been too prone to criticise the local team adversely. Dubbo's record this season is far better than some people realise.

After a series of trial matches with other towns to enable all candidates for representative honours to be given a try-out, the first series game of the season was played against Forbes for the Johnnie Walker Cup. Since then, Dubbo has played 11 matches, winning seven and losing four.

LOSING MARGIN SMALL

The losing margin in each case was five points, eight points and five points respectively. There is nothing in this record to discredit the local lads.

In those 11 matches Dubbo has defeated the strongest teams in the Group, including Canowindra, Forbes and Parkes. Each of these teams also has a victory over Dubbo, so the honours are even.

Against Forbes Dubbo lost the first match 2-7 and won the second 13-8. The team defeated Canowindra 12-8 and then went under to the Southerners 7-15. Parkes was defeated 7-4 in the first match and in the second Dubbo went under 2-7.

It is remarkable but true that in each of the games in which Dubbo was defeated, lucky tries by the opposition mainly were responsible.

STARS MISSING

For several weeks the local team has been without the services of such players as Clarrie Friend, Mick Wheeler, Bill Patman, Aub Reilly and Claude Woods. Those who have taken their places are just getting into form.

Next Sunday, as a preliminary to the Johnnie Walker Cup match at Canowindra, Dubbo will meet Wellington at Wellington.

The Blue and Whites are determined to win well and stem the tide of bad luck that has flowed against them. Last season, after a series of reverses, Dubbo finished with splendid victories. Don't be surprised if history repeats itself this year.

Article from: The Dubbo Daily Liberal and Macquarie Advocate, Saturday, July 15, 1939. Republished courtesy of ACM/Dubbo Daily Liberal and Macquarie Advocate.

1948 Dubbo-Warren Johnnie Walker Cup Teams

A "blast from the past", the attached photo shows Dubbo and Warren teams in the 1948 Johnnie Walker Cup. The competition was contested between football teams from across the Central West including:

Wellington, Forbes and Narromine. Note the players' high-top boots, long before Nike or Adidas cut-off football boots.

Courtesy of: Geoff Mann, Sports Journalist, Dubbo.

1953 Dubbo CYMS Wins Johnnie Walker Cup

Dubbo CYMS took the Johnnie Walker Cup from Forbes with a 15 to 3 victory last week and will defend it against Peak Hill on Sunday. This picture shows some of the players around the Cup at training on Wednesday.

Team members:

Back Row: Noel Healey, Terry Carolan, Mick Wilson, Ray Hardie, Don Fraser, John Kempston, Garry Yeo.

Front Row: Terry Peisley, Ray McTiernan, Neville Bowe, Tim Smith and Tony Linnane.

Courtesy of: Blast From the Past, Dubbo CYMS Old Boys.

1897 Inaugural Football Challenge Cup Match

St. Helens and Bartey Cup Final Teams at Wembley Stadium

The 1897 Challenge Cup was the inaugural staging of the Northern Rugby Football Union's Challenge Cup and involved 52 clubs from across England from the 1896–97 Northern Rugby Football Union season.

The tournament was played over six rounds in March and April 1897, culminating in the final which was won by Bartey.

Challenge Cup Competitions spread to Australia and by the early 1920s the prestigious Maher, Jack Hore Gold Memorial and Johnnie Walker Cups were entrenched in Southern and Western NSW.

Source: Wikimedia Commons, The Free Media Repository.

1906 Tichborne Challenge Cup Football Team

1906 team was one of many district teams who challenge each other for the end of season supremacy and Cup.

Back Row: N. Dampsey, Jim Venables, E.B. Davis, Jack Lynch, Ted Gibbons, Ted Bowman, Jack Beckus,

Second Row: Bill Le Lagadec, Tod Pascoe, Bill Bowman, Hughie Leonard, Bill (Cauley) McMillan, J. Clune.

Front Row: Jim Hocking, Archie Carson, Ted Collins.
(Player on extreme right unidentified).

Courtesy of: Ian & Judy Chambers.

Challenge Cups Come To An End As Group Premiership Competitions Take Over

Maher Cup:
The first Maher Cup challenge was on the 17th August, 1921 when Gundagai defeated Tumut (holders) 11/4. Challenges continued with fierce competition throughout the years and finally came to an end on 5th June, 1971 Tumut defeated Young 43/4.

There was much discussion between all the leading clubs at the start of the 1972 season, none of them showing any interest in challenging for the Maher Cup. Group competitions remained and the Maher Cup was retired. As a result, the Cup is now on permanent display at the Tumut R.S.L. Club under the control of the Tumut Old Boys on behalf of Group Nine.

Maher Cup

Jack Hore Gold Cup:
The first Jack Hore Cup challenges started in 1926 when Canowindra played six matches and was successful in all. The rivalry between team challenges was fierce and Cargo an extremely strong competitor. The challenges continued up until 1960, when Canowindra defeated Cumnock in the Eastern Zone Group 11 grand-final at Molong.

To complete the season, Canowindra challenged the holders of the Cup, Cumnock. Under the rules, the holders had the privilege of the home ground and the challengers had to travel. Both teams had suffered injuries in the grand-final match and were short of players. Canowindra's team was going to forfeit as players were not keen to play, but during the week, the news that Cumnock was in trouble was received and it was decided to send a team. Cumnock forfeited at the ground and the Cup was handed on to Canowindra. The Cup is in the care of the Canowindra and District Historical Museum.

Jack Hore Gold Cup

Johnnie Walker Cup:
The Johnnie Walker Challenge Cup was proposed at a meeting in Dubbo on 28 June, 1922 and officially introduced on the 22 July, 1922 when the Cup was presented to Dubbo Rugby League by the Johnnie Walker alcohol company.

Gilgandra became the first challenger and Dubbo won its first eight challenges until a combined Geurie, Wongarbon and Arthurville team upset the holders in August.

The Cup continued until the mid-1980s when interest started to fade. Disappeared in the 90s?

Johnnie Walker Cup

Clayton Cup: Symbol Of Country Rugby League Supremacy

The Clayton Cup is a trophy awarded by the Country Rugby League to the NSW country rugby league team with the best overall record for that particular season. To be eligible, the team must win the highest level of competition in its region. Usually, the winner of the Clayton Cup goes through the season unbeaten.

The Cup was donated by Reub Clayton, an early rugby league administrator in country NSW and was first awarded in 1937 to West Tamworth Lions and continues to this day.

The North Tamworth Bears joined a selective group of country rugby league teams by receiving the Clayton Cup symbol of supremacy in 2019.

The Bears have won the Cup three times in their history: 1951, 2014 and 2019.

Reference to Clayton Cup – Wikipedia: Winning Teams 1937 –2019.

Clayton Cup

1937-1976 Clayton Cup Winners	
1937 West Tamworth (Group 4 Rugby League)	1960 Goulburn Workers (Group 8 Rugby League)
1938 Nimmitabel (Group 16 Rugby League)	1961 Ballina (Group 1 Rugby League)
1939 Wagga Magpies (Group 9 Rugby League)	1962 Warialda (Group 19 Rugby League)
1940 Henty (Group 9 Rugby League)	1963 Tweed Heads Seagulls (Group 18 Rugby League)
1946 Port Kembla (Illawarra Rugby League)	**1964 Oberon (Group 10 Rugby League)**
1947 Bombala (Group 7 Rugby League)	1965 Tullibigeal (Group 17 Rugby League)
1948 Cootamundra (Group 9 Rugby League)	1966 Picton Magpies (Group 6 Rugby League)
1949 Tumut (Group 9 Rugby League)	1967 Casino (Group 1 Rugby League)
1950 Bathurst Railway (Group 10 Rugby League)	1968 Darlington Point (Group 20 Rugby League)
1951 North Tamworth (Group 4 Rugby League)	1969 Tarcutta (Group 13 Rugby League)
1952 Gundagai (Group 9 Rugby League)	**1970 Delegate (Group 16 Rugby League)**
1953 Young (Group 9 Rugby League)	**1971 Cobar (Group 15 Rugby League)**
1954 Orange CYMS (Group 10 Rugby League)	1972 Cobar (Group 15 Rugby League)
1955 Young (Group 9 Rugby League)	1973 Gunnedah (Group 4 Rugby League)
1956 Maitland (Newcastle Rugby League)	1974 Queanbeyan United (Group 8 Rugby League)
1957 Temora (Group 9 Rugby League)	1975 Albury Blues (Group 13 Rugby League)
1958 Coonamble (Group 14 Rugby League)	**1976 Bombala (Group 16 Rugby League)**
1959 Dubbo Macquarie (Group 11 Rugby League)	
Highlighted teams above are pictured on the following pages.	

1938 Nimmitabel Rugby League Team Clayton Cup Winners

Back Row: N. Green, J. Shelley, W. McMahon, F. Parkes, F. Clark, F. Peters, P. Mooney, E. Taylor.

Middle Row: G. Thornton, B. Burke, G. King, A. Payten, M. Freebody, B. Adams.

Front Row: R. Kielty, H. Belichambers, B. Buckley, G. Thiseton, E. James, J. Thornton.

Courtesy of: Group Sixteen Rugby League. Alan Wilton, President.

1947 Bombala Rugby League Team Clayton Cup Winners

Back Row: Ray (AL) Yelds, Billy Reed, (Nobby) Clarke, Charlie Kimber (Coach), Brian Collins, John Cotterill, Keith Jones, Laurie (Tubby) Wilton, Joe Elton.

Front Row: Athol Stewart, Don Stewart, Jock Johnson, Jim (Bandy) Yelds, Roy Smith.

Football jumpers donated by Light Horse Brigade (Yellow on Red).

Courtesy of: Group Sixteen Rugby League. Alan Wilton, President.

1950 Bathurst Railway Rugby League Team Clayton Cup Winners

Group 10 Premiers and Western Challenge Cup Winners:

Back Row: S. Logan (Delegate), W. Ezzy (Ass Secretary), M. Colley, V. Sargent, E. Hailey (Patron), R. Whiley, T. Copeland, J. Kennedy (Trainer).

Middle Row: J. Gunning (Vice President), J. Coleman, K. Tonkin, E. Garlick (Captain-Coach), K. Wright, J. Thompson, J. O'Toole (Secretary).

Front Row: S. Griffin, L. Hadley, M. Logan (Ball Boy), D. Oates, M. Gornall.

Insert: M. Kennedy.

Courtesy of: The Western Advocate.

1954 Orange CYMS Rugby League Team Clayton Cup Winners

Back Row: John Kelly, Jim Thurn, Ted Mitchell, John West, Reg Mitchell, Roy Kerwick, Vic Byrne, Tony Kelly.

Middle Row: Mick Newland (Coach), Lloyd Davidson, Des Crump, John Hennesy (Captain), Rev Noel Grant, Tom Kerwick, Ted Hazzard, Bill Carroll (Manager).

Front Row: Tom Hagar, Peter Cardwell, Terry Ryan (Mascot), Ted Hayden, Luke Commins.

Courtesy of: Group 10, Orange CYMS Rugby League Club.

1957 Temora Rugby League Team Clayton Cup Winners

Back Row: B Roberts, B. Matthews, L. Henman, E. Coleman (President), P. McGrath, L. McMullen, B. Roberts, K. Malby.

Middle Row: J. Stephenson (Selector), E. Curran, J. Kerry, L. Gillard (Captain), D. Winbank, A. Lynch, S. Barrington (Selector).

Front Row: B. Howe (Masseur), J. Broad, R. Allen, John Milton (Mascot), R. Smith, D. McKenzie, F. Meale (Treasurer).

Courtesy of: Brian Hughes & Temora Independent.

1958 Coonamble Rugby League Team Clayton Cup Winners

1958 1st Grade Group 14 Premiers & Clayton Cup Winners

Back Row: Brian Byrnes, Alan Head, G (Pudden) Head, Ron Pellett, Tumbler Edwards, Ray Hyde, Geoff Ryan.

Front Row: Noel Trudgett, Roley Green, Cecil Wright, Joey Evans, Colin Head, Jimmy Slack-Smith.

Courtesy of: Paul Wheelhouse and Roley Green.

1959 Dubbo Macquarie Rugby League Team Clayton Cup Winners

Back Row: T. Rutherford, R. Bartier, D. Teal, R. Light.

Middle Row: C. Rich (Strapper), P. Rawinson, B. Perry, A. Curry, D. Schiemer, L. Delaney (Treasurer).

Front Row: R. Pack (President), R. Ridley, B.Pilon, L. Nosworthy (Captain), D. Moore, J. George, R. Lane (Secretary), K. Jamieson (Mascot).

Courtesy of: Dubbo Macquarie Rugby League Club.

1964 Oberon Rugby League Team Clayton Cup Winners

Back Row: Rolf Trudgett, Gordon Rawlings, John Harvey, Peter McCurtayne, Jock Schrader, Ken Nicholl, Don Elwin, Ron Brown.

Middle Row: Peter Richards, Trevor Grady, Norm Brown, John Rush, Laurie Evans.

Front Row: Bill Fawcett, John Brien, Brian Harvey, Col Elwin.

The all-conquering Oberon Tigers made Group 10 history in 1964 when they not only became the first team to win four consecutive titles, but also claimed the historic Clayton Cup trophy.

They would become the last Group 10 team to date to win the cup.

Courtesy of: The Oberon Review News.

1970 Delegate Rugby League Team Clayton Cup Winners

Back Row: Tom Ventery, Eddie Sellars, Paul Clear (Coach), Kenny Callaghan, Mike Nixen, Arthur (Chicken) Jones.

Front Row: Barry Reed, Johnny Callaghan, Dennis Callaway, Bill Nichol, Max Clear, Mark Reid (Mascot).

Missing: Col Kirby, Toby Black.

Courtesy of: Group Sixteen Rugby League. Alan Wilton, President.

1971 Cobar Rugby League Team Clayton Cup Winners

Back Row: M. Ralph, "Gidgee" Robinson (Strapper), John Josephson, Neil Basedow, Ray Hamilton, Peter Bannister, Tom Knight, Brian Lawrence.

Front Row: Barry Grace, Stan Ralph, Bob Clark, Les Houghton, Jim Ralph, Jim Goonrey, George Greer, Brian Heap.

Courtesy of: John Collins, The Crowing of The Roosters, Bob Clark Collection.

1972 Cobar Rugby League Team Clayton Cup Winners

Back Row: Les Houghton, Harry Marshall, Peter Shanahan, John Josephson, Robert Gordon, Peter Fox, Brian Heap.

Front Row: Peter Bannister, Brian Lawrence (Captain Coach), John Stephens, Bob Clark.

The Cobar "Roosters" were the only Country Rugby League Team to win the Clayton Cup in consecutive years (1971/1972).

A record that has not been broken.

Courtesy of: John Collins, The Crowing of The Roosters.

1976 Bombala Rugby League Team Clayton Cup Winners

Back Row: John Wilton, Reigh Callaway, John Spellman, Terry Perkin, George Ford, Gary Morering, Ross Sturgeon (Treasurer).

Middle Row: Claude Thornell (President), Marty Black, Paul Ryan, Russel Yelds, Anthony Ridgway, John Ingram, Frank Morton (Secretary).

Front Row: Peter Loseph, Tim Stewart, Brian Lawrence (Captain Coach), Neville Brotherton, Colin Ryan, Terry Morering.

Courtesy of: Group Sixteen Rugby League. Alan Wilton, President.

Teams awarded the Clayton Cup within consecutive premierships

There are a number of teams listed below who have won consecutive premierships in Western and Southern Regions of N.S.W. However, winning the Clayton Cup as they say is the icing on the cake.

Oberon has been the most successful Country Rugby League Team creating record consecutive premiership wins and a recipient of the Clayton Cup.

Group 14	Coonamble Bears was awarded the Clayton Cup in 1958 – at the same time winning three consecutive Group 14 premierships (1957-1959).
Group 15	Cobar "Roosters" was awarded the Clayton Cup in two consecutive years 1971 and 1972 and at the same time winning Group 15 premierships.
Group 11	Dubbo Macquarie was awarded the Clayton Cup in 1959. At the same time winning consecutive Group 11 premierships (1959-1961).
Group 9	Temora was awarded the Clayton Cup in 1957. At the same time winning consecutive Group Nine premierships (1957-1959).
Group 10	Orange CYMS was awarded the Clayton Cup in 1954. At the same time winning three consecutive premierships (1952-1954).
Group 10	Bathurst Railway was awarded the Clayton Cup in 1950. At the same time winning three consecutive premierships (1948-1950).
Group 10	Oberon Tigers was awarded the Clayton Cup in 1964. At the same time winning seven consecutive Group 10 premierships (1961-1967) and by far the best record in Country NSW Rugby League.

Scoring match winning try as the final bell sounds

Courtesy of: John Collins, The Crowing of The Roosters, Karen Walsh.

About the Author

Greg Riach was born in Parkes NSW and attended both Parkes primary and high schools.

Although he played rugby league in five sevens and six sevens school teams, as well as in knockout carnivals and intra school matches, rugby league was not to be his sport of choice. All of his friends played hockey and so at the age of sixteen he joined them and continued playing until the age of thirty-one.

Greg played and coached premiership winning teams and coached Western Districts Colts Hockey Team in the Zone Championships held in Parkes, defeating Sydney in the final. He was also the holder of NSW State Hockey Umpires Badge.

Greg's teaching qualifications include Diploma of Education, Bachelor of Education Degree, Diploma HVAC & Refrigeration Engineering. As a teacher he compiled and wrote a number of technical student manuals for trade and diploma courses.

Greg eventually retired from Ultimo TAFE as Head of the Refrigeration and Airconditioning Section in July 2018. Although he has spent almost half of his life in Sydney, he still has solid roots in the country and as was once said, "You can take the boy from the country but you can't take the country from the boy."

A Yarn with Pat Jarvis

Right: Greg chats with Pat Jarvis at the local Glebe Coffee Shop. Pat who is always ready to talk about and advise on Rugby League had a great rugby league career which included representing New South Wales and Australia. He played for St George, St Helens, Eastern Suburbs, Canterbury Bankstown and North Sydney Bears and then later went on to captain-coach Mudgee Rugby League Team.

Pat said he always wanted to play with Billy Smith which he did so in the St Gearge Reserve Grade side.

Pat Jarvis: From Wikipedia, The Free Encyclopedia.

Author Reflection

The objective of compiling this book was to highlight the importance which rugby league played in the Western and South-Western Districts of NSW from 1920-1976. As the years rolled on the game gradually changed from its simple beginnings through to its current form.

Although the game has faded somewhat in the country towns, one can only hope a resurgence is on its way.

I hope you enjoy the journey as much as I have. It has been a wonderful experience moving through the years with the players, teams, referees, spectators and administrators who made the game such a wonderful spectacle in regional NSW.

Greg Riach.

BIBLIOGRAPHY

CYMS Old Boys: "Blast from the Past 1971-1980" (Dubbo, 2018), https://dubbocymsoldboys.com.au/19711980.

Wikipedia: "Country Rugby League", https://en.wikipedia.org/wiki/Country_Rugby_League.

Hughes, Brian and M. V. Sheehan: *The Famous Maher Cup: The Final Years* (J. A. Bradley & Sons, 2010).

Pollock, Neil: The Maher Cup, *Group 9 in the 1920s-1960s* (2015).

Ross, Barry: "John Hobby: A Bush Rugby League Legend" (Men of League, 2017), https://menofleague.com/john-hobby-bush-rugby-league-legend/.

NSW Rugby Football League: *The Rugby League News* (Sydney, 1920-1973), https://catalogue.nla.gov.au/Record/397000. Magazine, various volumes, National Library of Australia collection.

Worboys, Ron: *Jack Hore Memorial Gold Cup: A Brief History* (Canowindra and District Historical Society, Canowindra, 1992).

Further Reading

Collins, John: *The Crowing of The Roosters: The History of Rugby League in Cobar* (Cobar NSW, John Collins, 2017), https://catalogue.nla.gov.au/Record/7540781.

Heads, Ian: *The Night the Music Died: How a Bunch of Bushies Forged Rugby League's Last Great Fairytale* (Concord NSW, Stokehill Press, 2014), https://catalogue.nla.gov.au/Record/6450672.

Ross, Barry: *Underground Secrets to Faster Running* (Lulu.com, 2005).

Ross, Barry: *A Long Time Between Drinks: 1912-2012: Celebrating 100 Years of Corrimal Rugby League Football Club* (Corrimal Rugby League Football Club, Corrimal NSW, 2012), https://catalogue.nla.gov.au/Record/6290457.

Solling, Max: *An Act of Bastardry: Rugby League Axes Its First Club* (Walla Walla Press, Sydney, 2014).

www.ingramcontent.com/pod-product-compliance
Lightning Source LLC
Chambersburg PA
CBHW041710290426
44109CB00028B/2831